T0302311

Inflation, Unemployment and Capital Malformations

The volume deals with the main problems faced by capitalist economies, inflation and unemployment, in a new and original way, and provides the theoretical foundations for quantum macroeconomic analysis. Its aim is to allow English-speaking economists and interested readers to have a direct access to the analysis provided by Schmitt in his 1984 book *Inflation, Chômage et Malformations du Capital*.

Orthodox economics has failed to provide a consistent insight of the pathologies hindering our economies, and both the academic and the economic worlds are much in need of an alternative approach capable of explaining the origins of these pathologies and how they can eventually be disposed of. Schmitt's volume provides a revolutionary explanation of the cause of today's economic disorder as well as an innovative solution allowing for the passage from disorder to order. Neoclassical and Keynesian theories of any type are essentially based on equilibrium analysis and this is why none of them has ever been able to provide a consistent macroeconomic analysis based on macroeconomic foundations. This is what Schmitt's book aims for: developing a new analysis built on identities rather than conditions of equilibrium, in order to explain the objective origins of inflation and unemployment.

In this volume, Schmitt introduces a new, revolutionary analysis centred on the concept of quantum time. The topics analysed by Schmitt cover the entire field of national macroeconomics, from production to capital accumulation, the leading role in this ground-breaking investigation being played by what he calls the theory of emissions. The ensuing macroeconomic theory is built on a set of laws derived from the monetary nature of our economic systems and defines the logical framework of inquiry into modern macroeconomics.

Bernard Schmitt was a full professor of Monetary Macroeconomics at the Universities of Burgundy (Dijon), France and of Fribourg, Switzerland. He was also the co-director of the Laboratory of Research in Monetary economics at the Centre for Banking Studies in Lugano, Switzerland. Among his main publications are: *La formation du pouvoir d'achat, Monnaie, salaires et profits, Macroeconomic Theory, A Fundamental Revision, Théorie unitaire de la monnaie, nationale et internationale, La France souveraine de sa monnaie,*

External Debt Servicing. A Vicious Circle, and a number of contributions to collective books as well as papers published in peer-reviewed journals.

English translation and foreword by

Alvaro Cencini, Università della Svizzera italiana, Switzerland.

Xavier Bradley, Université de Bourgogne, France.

Routledge Frontiers of Political Economy

Capital Theory and Political Economy
Prices, Income Distribution and Stability
Lefteris Tsoulfidis

Value and Unequal Exchange in International Trade
The Geography of Global Capitalist Exploitation
Andrea Ricci

Inflation, Unemployment and Capital Malformations
Bernard Schmitt
Edited and Translated in English by Alvaro Cencini and Xavier Bradley

Democratic Economic Planning
Robin Hahnel

A History of Monetary Diplomacy, 1867 to the Present
The Rise of the Guardian State and Economic Sovereignty in a
Globalizing World
Giulio M. Gallarotti

Markets in their Place
Context, Culture, Finance
*Edited by Russell Prince, Matthew Henry, Carolyn Morris, Aisling Gallagher
and Stephen FitzHerbert*

China's Belt and Road Initiative
The Impact on Sub-regional Southeast Asia
Edited by Christian Ploberger et al

For more information about this series, please visit: https://www.routledge.
com/Routledge-Frontiers-of-Political-Economy/book-series/SE0345

Inflation, Unemployment and Capital Malformations

Bernard Schmitt

**Edited and Translated in English by
Alvaro Cencini and Xavier Bradley**

Routledge
Taylor & Francis Group

LONDON AND NEW YORK

First published 2021
by Routledge
2 Park Square, Milton Park, Abingdon, Oxon OX14 4RN

and by Routledge
52 Vanderbilt Avenue, New York, NY 10017

Routledge is an imprint of the Taylor & Francis Group, an informa business

The volume is the English translation of the book Inflation, chômage et
malformations du capital, published in 1984 by Economica: Paris, and
Castella: Albeuve (CH).

British Library Cataloguing-in-Publication Data
A catalogue record for this book is available from the British Library

Library of Congress Cataloging-in-Publication Data
A catalog record has been requested for this book

ISBN: 978-1-138-36980-1 (hbk)
ISBN: 978-1-032-00703-8 (pbk)
ISBN: 978-0-429-42846-3 (ebk)

Typeset in Times New Roman
by Taylor & Francis Books

Contents

Figures

Acknowledgements

Our warmest thanks go to Catherine Bradley for her linguistic assistance as well as to Banca Stato of Canton Ticino for supporting our project financially.

Foreword

by Alvaro Cencini and Xavier Bradley

First published in French under the title of *Inflation, chômage et malformations du capital*, Schmitt's tenth book is a milestone in his lifelong research on monetary macroeconomics and the founding text of *quantum macroeconomics*. While developing the concepts he had first elaborated in *La formation du pouvoir d'achat* (1960) and in *Monnaie, salaires et profits* (1966), in this long and demanding book he introduces the new, revolutionary analysis centred on the concept of *quantum time*. The topics analysed by Schmitt cover the entire field of national macroeconomics, the leading role in this ground-breaking investigation being played by what he calls the theory of *emissions*. Let us make it clear at once that, although the concepts of emissions, quantum, wave-like and corpuscular are similar to those used in physics, Schmitt's quantum economics is not in the least derived from physics. That analytically independent research projects in different fields may converge and point to similar concepts should not come as a surprise. On the contrary, it should be seen as a sign of a paradigmatic change, of a new phase in the history of human scientific thought.

Like in all of his numerous texts, published and unpublished, Schmitt's analysis is rigorously logical. His arguments unfold in a compelling way, taking the reader on what might at first appear to be a rather too arduous journey into abstraction. Yet, this impression soon fades away if one accepts to be guided by logic and follow Schmitt along his path. Correctly used, abstraction is important because it enables a better understanding of reality, which remains the true object of scientific investigation. Schmitt's analysis is a clear example of how useful abstraction can be for uncovering the logical principles on which macroeconomics rests and the origin of the pathologies affecting our economies at present.

Quantum time

Schmitt presents the concept of quantum time at the beginning of his book, in a general introductory section entitled *The quantum of time*, comprising three chapters devoted to the relationship between production and time, expenditures and time and the concept of emission respectively. In these three initial chapters we come upon the founding principles of Schmitt's macroeconomic analysis, namely those of production, money and emission. The reader finds himself deep at the heart of macroeconomics from the outset, being confronted with the task of determining whether or not production 'takes time', whether or not it can be considered as a continuous or discontinuous function of time. Schmitt's answer to both questions is negative, which makes it immediately clear that the analysis he advocates is in open contrast with commonly held ideas on the subject. The reader is made aware of the fact that the economic analysis of production must not be confused with its analysis in physical terms. Whereas the physical process of transformation of matter or energy is set in chronological time, the economic process of production is instantaneous, and its chronological time-dimension is zero. This is so because, from an economic viewpoint, production is the event that gives matter or energy a new utility form. Conceived by man, the new utility form is entirely non-dimensional; it is not a physical quality added to matter or energy, but the end result of a process through which the project born in man's mind is finally achieved. It is only at the very instant this process is completed that physical output acquires its new utility form. Economic production is concentrated in that instant.

What Schmitt shows is that production is a timeless event regardless of its being considered in real or physical terms. The crucial point here is that economic production is not a transformation. In his imagination man creates, but what he creates can only be a utility form with no proper value or dimension whatsoever. Economic product, the instantaneous result of production, is thus given at one go, at the moment matter or energy acquires this new form. In the absence of money, the economic product thus created is immediately appropriated as a new value-in-use. Production is immediately accompanied by consumption and the economic product created by production is at the same time destroyed, making room for a physical use value.

From an economic viewpoint, production and product define one another, even though the latter is the result of the former. Production is measured by the product and vice versa, which means that the product cannot be determined by the integral of production over time. An instantaneous production is no production at all, and its only meaningful result is a product equal to zero. Any analogy between production and velocity, and between product and distance is groundless, because while an instantaneous velocity is positive, production tends to zero when time tends to zero. As Schmitt shows, equation

$$\text{Product} = \text{production} \cdot \Delta t$$

is therefore true only for $\Delta t = 1$, that is, only if it takes the form of

$$\text{Product} = \text{production} \cdot 1$$

This apparently trivial equation is in reality extremely significant, because it implies the fact that production is not a function of continuous or discontinuous time but relates to a finite and indivisible period of time: a *quantum of time*.

Despite the many useful contributions by philosophers and scientists, we still do not know very much about the nature of time. Our knowledge is almost entirely limited to the way we measure it, and to its relationship with space. Schmitt's concept of quantum time provides a new insight into this fascinating and elusive subject, the idea being that time can be *emitted* in finite lumps called quanta of time. Besides the traditional conception of chronological time and its unidirectional flow, quantum time appears as a new reality associated with production and consumption and allowing for *reversibility* or *retroaction*. At the very instant a new production takes place – that is, matter or energy acquires a new utility form – the period of the continuum during which the physical process of transformation has occurred is instantly covered by a wave-like circular flow and emitted as a whole and indivisible period of time. In other words, the economic product is nothing other than a quantum of time. In the absence of bank money, economic consumption coincides with production both in chronological and in quantum time. It occurs at the same time and, since it refers to the same product, it defines the same quantum of time. Conceptually distinct from physical consumption, economic consumption does not take time; it corresponds to the appropriation of the product by consumers, an event that cannot be distinguished from production were it not for the fact that money separates them chronologically. In this particular case, the introduction of quantum time does not substantially change anything except our intellectual perception of a reality that remains nevertheless the same. Yet, as Schmitt shows in the second chapter of his book, the same relationship between economic production and time applies equally well to monetary expenditures and time.

As with production, expenditures could also be analysed in their relationship to time, without referring to money. However, it is when we consider the role of *monetary expenditures* that analysis provides the elements for a better understanding of our monetary economies of production. Thus, Schmitt concentrates his investigation on monetary expenditures and concludes that 'like production, every expenditure is a wave-like operation the effect of which is to quantize a "piece" of continuous time' (Schmitt 2021: 20). In the same way as production and product are one and the same thing, expenditures and sum spent are the two sides of the same coin. Equation:

$$\text{Sum spent} = \text{expenditure} \cdot \Delta t$$

has only one possible meaning, namely that sum spent and expenditure are necessarily equal for whatever period of time:

$$\text{Sum spent} = \text{expenditure} \cdot 1$$

Like production, an expenditure is an instantaneous event that refers to a finite period of time emitted as a quantum in a wave-like movement at infinite velocity. Contrary to what happens in physics, where velocity has a limit, because physical displacements occur in a pre-existent space, in economics production and expenditures are instantaneous events – their 'velocity' is infinite – defining an instantaneous displacement *in time*.

The first expenditure considered by Schmitt is the one that refers to production: the payment of wages. Since in nearly all our economies wages are paid in money, the payment of wages calls for an explanation of what money is and where it comes from. Concentrating our attention on bank money, we have to establish whether banks can issue money as a positive asset or as a mere spontaneous acknowledgement of debt with no positive value whatsoever. Schmitt, who had already thoroughly investigated this topic in his previous books, starting from the fact that, logically, banks can issue money only as an asset-liability, shows that the emission of money makes sense and has a purpose only if it is associated with production. It is through the payment of wages that money is created, because it is through this payment that the product acquires a numerical form and is literally emitted as a sum of money.

The theory of emissions

The theory of emissions is at the core of Schmitt's analysis. The concept of creation plays a central role, but it would have to be dismissed as metaphysical unless it were accompanied by that of destruction. Hence, production is a creation and at the same time a destruction: the product acquires a new utility form from which it is immediately expropriated as a new value-in-use. Likewise, money is issued as an asset *and* a liability. The payment of wages is no exception; the product is emitted as a sum of money that must immediately be destroyed. But how can we avoid the apparently inevitable conclusion that if creation and destruction are simultaneous the final result can be but zero? Logic is compelling and Schmitt one of its best advocates. His explanation is difficult but rigorous; it is thanks to quantum time that simultaneity can be reconciled with chronological distinction. Created as a sum of money at instant t_0, the product is finally destroyed at a later instant in chronological time, t_1. And yet, creation and destruction are simultaneous in quantum time, because they both define the same quantum of time.

Money is emitted in each single payment, which means that it cannot survive between payments. At the instant of the payment of wages, t_0, money is created-destroyed; likewise, it is created-destroyed at t_1 when the final purchase of the product, economic consumption, occurs. Taken literally, the claim that the product survives as a sum of money between t_0 and t_1 is therefore not correct and must be further investigated. As a matter of fact, the payment of wages implies not only a creation-destruction of money, a necessary consequence of the flow nature of bank money, but also a creation of income. As a result of this payment, wage-earners are credited with a positive amount of income immediately deposited with their banks. This result is *net*, wage-earners being credited-debited in money but only credited in income. Thus, production is a net creation of money-income, the result of the association of physical output with money as a numerical form. It is true that money disappears as soon as wages have been paid; yet an instant is all it takes for a bank deposit to be created in favour of wage-earners. Created at t_0, income is destroyed at t_1, in the final purchase of the product. As any other expenditure, the final purchase of a product is instantaneous and defines the emission of a quantum of time, to wit, of the same quantum of time emitted at t_0, when goods were produced. Separated by a positive interval of chronological time, production and consumption are therefore simultaneous in quantum time; they are the two complementary parts of a single emission, of the creation-destruction of income.

Economics is a science only if it rigorously complies with logic, and according to logic nothing is created out of nothing. It is certain, however, that products are not the result of a mere physical transformation of matter or energy. Production gives a new form to matter or energy, and this form is created by man's inventiveness. The task of economics is to explain how physical output is transformed into a product, how it acquires a non-dimensional form. Schmitt's analysis provides a perfectly articulated explanation founded on the theory of emissions, where any creation, i.e. positive emission, is accompanied by a simultaneous destruction, i.e. negative emission. The difficulty of this analysis lies in explaining how the simultaneity of creation and destruction can produce a positive creation. Schmitt overcomes it by showing that economic production takes place in quantum time, that it is an instantaneous wave-like movement that quantises time. Quantum time allows for production, the positive face of emission and consumption, the negative face of the same emission, to take place at different instants of the continuum while complying with the necessity of their simultaneity. It is in quantum time that simultaneity is preserved, and quantum time is what characterises the specific nature of economic events, from production to consumption. Quantum time is not a useful device introduced into economics to make it sounds 'scientific'; it is a concept deeply rooted into economics, the only one consistent with the fact that production is at once instantaneous and positive, that product and production define one another and are positive only if they refer, instantaneously, to a positive period of time. What is true of production is also true of consumption, an instantaneous event inscribed in quantum time. Finally, production and consumption prove to be the two sides of a single emission, of a creation-destruction. Although separated in chronological time, these two half-emissions coincide in quantum time, consumption being *retroactively* simultaneous with production.

In our advanced economies, the emission of products as quanta of time is mediated by bank money and corresponds to the payment of wages. The utility form expressed numerically in money units and wages becomes the economic definition of the product. In other words, product is time, a quantum of time, and wages are its units of measure. Shall we infer from this that product is transposed from quantum to chronological time in the form of wages? A positive answer to this question would contrast with the principle of double entry, which establishes the necessary equality between credits and debits. Indeed, as soon as income (wages) is formed as a bank deposit and entered on the liabilities side of a bank's balance sheet it is lent, that is, it is entered on the assets side of the ledger. Firms are the initial beneficiaries of the loan of wages. Thus, the income of wage-earners is deposited and lent to firms, which, immediately and implicitly, invest it in the purchase of a stock of goods, namely, the goods produced by wage-earners and financially deposited with the banking system. The initial purchase of produced output transforms it into a stock and the income invested by firms into a capital. It is in the form of capital, more precisely of capital-time, that income is transposed from quantum time into chronological time. As Schmitt tells us, capital is what allows for income, created at t_0, to be finally spent and destroyed at a later instant t_1: capital is what links present with future. At t_1, when income holders purchase the product they had initially deposited in the form of income, capital-time is cancelled and income re-created to be definitively destroyed through its final expenditure.

Capital and the role of banks

As Schmitt's analysis shows, while the intermediation of money is necessary to give goods a numerical expression, without the explicit presence of banks, the financial intermediation of banks is a necessary condition for the existence of capital. Without the financial intermediation of banks, income could not be lent to firms and transformed into capital-time through its initial investment. What is true of capital-time is also true of fixed capital, its advanced form. Indeed, fixed capital is but an avatar of capital-time and neither would exist if banks did not establish a necessary link between savings and investment. The formation of capital-time is the direct result of the initial investment by firms of the income saved by income holders and lent by banks. The formation of fixed capital is less straightforward; it goes through the realization of profit and its investment in the production of capital-goods. This time savings takes the form of profit and its investment is the expenditure of profit in the production of instrumental goods. The theory of capital, therefore, requires the previous elaboration of a theory of profit.

In *Inflation, Unemployment and Capital Malformations* (1984/2021), Schmitt develops further the theory of profit he has worked on since his PhD dissertation. In particular, he shows once more that profit is included in wages, that it is derived from wages, the sole source of macroeconomic income. He then incorporates the theory of profit into his theory of emissions showing that the formation of profit and its expenditure are two half-emissions taking place at different instants of the continuum but coinciding retroactively in quantum time. Profit takes shape in the product market through the sale of consumer (or wage-) goods at a mark-up. This is common knowledge. What is not so well known is that profit cannot logically be spent by firms on the same market. If it could, profit would be spent in the purchase of consumer goods and the whole production would consist of wage-goods only, thus reducing profit to zero. It thus follows that profit must be spent on the labour market, within the payment of wages. Despite its apparent absurdity, this conclusion is the only one in line with a theory capable of explaining both the formation and the spending of profit, its two necessary and complementary aspects. What must be explained, then, is how a profit formed at t_1 can be spent at t_0, where t_0 is an instant preceding t_1 in the flow of time. The answer lies in Schmitt's concept of quantum time and in the retroactivity it involves. Formed in the product market, profit is retroactively spent on the labour market, because the payment of wages and the final expenditure of income are two halves of one and the same emission, and define therefore the same quantum of time. In other words, what happens at t_1 enables us to re-interpret what happened at t_0; the formation of a positive profit at t_1 provides a new piece of information about what was produced at t_0. Namely, it tells us that part of the goods produced at t_0 consisted in wage-goods and part in profit-goods.

Schmitt's 1984 book is analytically subdivided into three parts. In the first part he develops the analysis of the profoundly logical nature of a monetary economy, while in the second he analyses the pathological working of the current economic system; finally, in the third part he introduces the principles of a reform designed to take the system from disorder to order. The first part ends with the theory of profit and the explanation of capital-time; the second starts with the analysis of fixed capital. In fact, in the present system of payments, the investment of profit defines its pathological expenditure in the production of a period following that in which it is formed. It is this overlapping of productions that explains, in Schmitt's 1984 book, the appropriation of fixed capital by what he calls the set of disembodied or depersonalized firms. The expenditure of profit on the labour market is flawless when profit's formation and expenditure pertain to the same production. On the contrary, when profit is spent within the payment of wages of a *new production* its expenditure is the source of a pathology whereby instrumental capital is forever subtracted from the economic ownership of households.

Inflation and unemployment

As the title makes clear, the aim of Schmitt's book is to provide an explanation of inflation and unemployment by relating them to the pathological process of capital accumulation. Neither pathology is clearly defined, or correctly understood, by mainstream economics; their analyses are superficial and far too simple to account for two disequilibria that apparently should reciprocally compensate. The traditional approach to inflation and unemployment is microeconomic and rests on the interplay of supply and demand. Explanation is reduced to the working of a law that, as Schmitt used to tell his students, could well be taught in kindergarten, and nothing is said about the logical possibility of reconciling the disequilibrium between supply and demand with their necessary identity. Contrary to mainstream economics, Schmitt's quantum analysis is macroeconomic. Its aim is to determine the logical laws, of a macroeconomic nature, which define the framework within which economic agents are free to operate, their decisions having no repercussion whatsoever on the laws determined macroeconomically. The distinction between macroeconomics and microeconomics is clear and so is that between their reciprocal laws. Macroeconomics is not the result of the addition or aggregation of microeconomics. Despite what is widely believed and taught, macroeconomics, which concerns the working of the economic system considered as whole, is not the transposition at the global level of what occurs at the disaggregated level. It is the system as a whole that sets the rules of the game; economic agents are free to play as they wish, but their behaviour cannot modify the rules. This is confirmed by the fact that macroeconomic laws are logical *identities*, while the so-called microeconomic laws are mere *conditions of equilibrium*. An identity is an equality that is always necessarily true; a condition of equilibrium is an equation only occasionally and temporarily satisfied. The former is totally independent from human behaviour, the latter depend entirely on it. Inflation and unemployment, which are macroeconomic disorders, must be explained starting from macroeconomic considerations and consistently with the macroeconomic identities characterizing our economic systems.

Inflation is usually defined as a situation in which global demand is constantly greater than global supply. It is explained by referring to all the causes that increase consumers' demand without increasing to the same extent the supply of firms. All these explanations, whether pertaining to the category of supply-side economics or to that of demand-side economics, miss the crucial fact that the only logical relationship between global supply and global demand established by the economic system is that of an identity: $D = S$. As Schmitt's analysis proves, any time a production occurs it creates the amount of income necessary and sufficient for its final purchase. Global demand, measured by the amount of income available in the system, is therefore necessarily equal to global supply, which is nothing other than the product the production of which is at the origin of income. Put simply, it is because Supply and Demand are twin results of the same operation, namely economic production, that they define the two terms of an identity. What has to be explained, therefore, is how D can be greater than S though necessarily equal to it.

The analysis developed by Schmitt in his 1984 book is revolutionary not only because it introduces the concept of quantum time, but also because, according to his theory of emissions, it is based on a more advanced logic than the ordinary, binary one: *quantum logic*. One characteristic of quantum logic is that, as a number of philosophers and mathematicians have done, it rejects the principle of the excluded middle. The case of inflation is an example of quantum logic: analysis shows that D can be both equal and greater than S. What production establishes is the identity of S and D *in income terms.* Let us suppose production to be measured by 100 wage-units. The income thus created being equal to 100 wage-units, the identity $S \equiv D$ follows at once. Yet, if the number of money units were increased from 100 to 110, the initial identity:

$$(1) \quad S(100) \equiv D(100)$$

would take the form

$$(2) \quad S(100) \equiv D(110)$$

Identity (2) means that, although S and D are always equal, the numerical expression of D is greater than that of S. Far from being contradictory, the simultaneous identity and inequality of S and D provides the clearest definition of inflation: a decrease in the purchasing power of each money unit. If, despite its numerical increase, D always holds the same value it is because each unit of money expressing D loses part of its initial purchasing power, that is, part of its content in products.

The challenge lies in explaining how an inflationary increase in money units can occur given that production is always at the origin of a strict identity between S and D. Schmitt shows that it is in the process of fixed capital formation that an additional demand occurs on the labour market, a demand that comes on top of that exerted in the product market, thus creating a nominal gap between S and D. When, as is the case at present, profit of p_0 is invested in the production of another period, p_1, its expenditure on the labour market defines a positive demand for instrumental goods additional to that exerted in the product market by the wages distributed in p_1, which include those paid out of the profit formed in p_0. Defined by Schmitt as *benign*, this inflation has no direct consequences for households, because wage-earners can exchange that part of their wages that has been emptied of its real content, namely the capital goods appropriated by depersonalized firms, against the stock of consumption goods formed in p_0 and corresponding to profit. However, the pathological formation of fixed capital will have a negative impact starting from the subsequent period, p_2, when the use of instrumental capital entails its amortization.

The correct definition of amortization provides another example of the need to reject the principle of the excluded middle. Indeed, amortization is at the same time a re-production and a new production of fixed capital. For part of instrumental capital to be replaced, it is necessary to produce the replacement goods required by amortization, so that it would be a mistake to consider amortization either as a mere re-production, or as a new investment. Both aspects are simultaneously present, and their co-existence is far from contradictory. Having clarified the concept of amortization, Schmitt analyses what happens in the third period and shows that the pathological formation of fixed capital occurring in p_1 has the annoying consequence of causing, in p_2, the formation of an inflationary profit equal to the value of amortization. Starting from p_2, an inflationary gap appears that cannot be neutralized through the purchase of an accumulated stock of consumption goods. While it would be pointless to summarize here Schmitt's analysis of inflation, it might be useful to emphasize the macro-economic nature of his approach. The behaviour of economic agents is altogether irrelevant to his analysis of inflation. Whatever decision they take, it cannot modify the identity of S and D, which is the direct expression of a law applying to the economy as a whole. S = D is the logical starting point of the analysis of inflation and not a point of equilibrium that excludes the presence of inflation. If a nominal difference does emerge between S and D it is not because economic agents have failed to complying with the logical laws of macroeconomics, which they cannot do, but because today's system of payments clashes with these laws.

The case of unemployment provides further proof of the originality of Schmitt's analysis. What has to be shown here is how global supply can be greater than global demand despite their logical identity. Mainstream attempts to do so are naïve and at odds with the principle of double-entry as necessarily applied by banks. In particular, the idea that income holders could cause a deficit in demand by refraining from spending their savings is in open contrast with the fact that banks lend, always and necessarily, the totality of their deposits (whether they are forced to lend part of their deposits to the central bank or not is irrelevant here). In no circumstance can even the smallest fraction of income be removed from the banking system and certainly not through savings. Yet, it is undisputable that involuntary unemployment is a serious disorder affecting our economies and that deflation (D < S) is its main cause. Once more it is thanks to quantum logic that an explanation can be provided of how Supply and Demand can be nominally different, yet necessarily equal.

Schmitt's argument initially refers to a law enunciated by Marx, but not proven, known as the rate of profit's tendency to fall. Schmitt shows that, as capital accumulation and over-accumulation increase, the economy is less and less capable of remunerating the accumulated capital because profit, the source out of which interest is paid to capital, cannot increase more than the amount of wages. This is so because profit is derived from wages: once profit is equal to wages, that is, when the economy produces half to the benefit of wage-earners and half to the benefit of firms, it can no longer increase. This means that, once this limit is reached, capital can no longer increase at the same pace, otherwise profit would be insufficient to remunerate it. From this point onwards, the rate of profit inexorably drops until it reaches the level of the market rate of interest. At that point, deflation becomes its most probable consequence. Two alternatives are available: to reduce investment or to invest part of what was previously invested in the production of capital-goods in the production of consumption-goods. In the first case, global production would immediately decline and unemployment rise; in the second case, employment would initially remain unaffected, but deflation would settle in. The latter is the most interesting case, because it shows how global supply can be nominally increased with respect to global demand. As Schmitt explains, the investment of profit in the production of goods intended for sale in the product market increases S by an amount of goods that have already been purchased, therefore 'demanded', on the labour market. However, while S increases nominally, D remains unchanged, no additional income being formed by the new production of consumer goods financed by profit. The difference between the amount of income available in the system and the value of goods supplied in the product market defines a deflationary gap that inevitably leads to a drop in production and a rise in unemployment.

Schmitt's analysis of inflation and unemployment has the merit, among others, of providing an explanation of their coexistence. Mainstream economics fails to do so; the two disequilibria being of opposite sign, they cancel each other out. To show that in reality they do not one must prove that they may be the twin results of one and the same process. This is what Schmitt is able to do through his analysis of capital accumulation and over-accumulation. Inflation is the first consequence of fixed capital amortization in a system in which capital is appropriated by depersonalized firms. The inflationary profit that takes shape in p_2 is in its turn the cause of deflation when it is invested in the production of consumption-goods. Hence, the same process leading to inflation can also lead to unemployment, two distinct pathologies that coexist in advanced capitalism.

From capitalism to post-capitalism

Besides identifying the logical laws of monetary economies and explaining the emergence of disorders such as inflation and unemployment, Schmitt's macroeconomic analysis provides the principles of a reform that opens the path from disorder to order, from today's pathological capitalism to post-capitalism. What the reader must clearly understand is that this transition concerns the mechanism through which payments are carried out by banks and the way they are entered into their ledgers, and not the transition from a system where capital plays a central role to one without capital. What is wrong is not the existence of fixed capital, an undisputable resource of any economy, regardless of its socio-political structure, but its appropriation by depersonalized firms. In our economies, alienation is a fact, the outcome of a modern form of man's enslavement to pathological capital. Everybody suffers from this state of affairs; all households or income holders are the victims of today's exploitation exerted by capital. The remedy cannot be political (in a socialist economy pathological capital is no less present and harmful than in a liberal economy). In post-capitalism, fixed capital will still be central, but no longer taken from, or denied to, the economic ownership of the undifferentiated set of households. The change needed is of a structural nature and will impose no constraint at all on economic agents' behaviour.

Banks and firms are at the same time economic agents working for their own benefit and monetary and/or financial intermediaries serving the economy as a whole. In their capacity as intermediaries banks and firms play a central role in any monetary economic system, in capitalism as well as in post-capitalism. Banks provide the numerical vehicle needed to carry out payments and the financial intermediation necessary for the existence of capital. Firms collect savings in the form of profit, which they then invest in the production of instrumental goods. What distinguishes capitalism from post-capitalism is that in the latter banks' and firms' intermediation will be carried out in accordance with the true nature of money, income and capital. Today this is not yet the case. Which is why we are all, to a man, expropriated of the ownership of fixed capital to the benefit of depersonalized firms or, to use another metaphor, of the international financial bubble. If we want to escape the consequences of the pathological accumulation and over-accumulation of fixed capital, inflation and involuntary unemployment, we need to devise a mechanism that stops an invested profit remaining available in the financial market. An invested profit is an income fully transformed into capital, that is, an income no longer accessible for financing purchases on any market. In post-capitalism, this will be ensured by the automatic transfer of invested profit to the department of fixed capital of banks. In total, banks will have to introduce a distinction between three departments and enter their payments in these departments according to a mechanism designed to automatically prevent any mix-up between money, income and capital.

Schmitt's reform is clear and straightforward and might seem too simple to the reader used to thinking of economic events as intricate and unstable combinations influenced by conflicting interests of numerous economic agents. There seems to be two alternatives: either to consider inflation and unemployment as the inescapable consequences of a system that can only tend toward (an elusive or precarious) equilibrium , or to consider them as the consequences of a mechanism that can be corrected in order to get rid of them once and for all. If acceptable, the first alternative would imply that the best we can do is to try to control the two disequilibria and learn to live with them. The advantage of this alternative is that the analysis supporting it is *conceptually* elementary and can be mastered without any major effort; the disadvantage is that disorder becomes an integral part of any economic system, an unavoidable state of affairs. The second alternative rests on a far more complex conceptual analysis, much harder to grasp. Once completed, however, the analysis provides the correct understanding of inflation and unemployment and shows what has to be done in order to get rid of them for good. The two anomalies are no longer considered as somehow intrinsic to any economic system, but as the result of a pathology that can be eradicated through a reform of the system of payments. As Schmitt shows in the critical part of his 1984 book (Schmitt 1984), devoted to the analysis of mainstream economics, general equilibrium analysis as well as the neoclassical interpretation of Keynes's theory in terms of equilibrium between S and D are seriously flawed, because of the logical indeterminacy of relative prices. It thus follows that the first alternative must be rejected on theoretical and factual grounds: an economic system based on direct exchange is a logical absurdity and is nowhere to be found in the real world. The attempt to explain our economic systems starting from the direct exchange of real goods fails, and with it the endeavour to develop economics around the concept of equilibrium. Before being exchanged, real goods and services must be produced, and our economies of production are monetary. It is therefore on the concept of money that economic theory must be founded, which implies that economic analysis must switch from conditions of equilibrium to identities, from behavioural adjustments to logical laws deriving from the nature of money, income and capital.

An economic system is man-made, and it is not utopian to believe that man can arrive at a perfect understanding of its logic and laws and of what must be done to respect them. Inflation and unemployment are not natural events embedded in a system that had its origins somewhere in the universe. Likewise, capitalism is not the unavoidable outcome of a process unfathomable to the human mind. The transition from disorder, capitalism, to order, postcapitalism, is within reach. It could be just around the corner, made possible by Schmitt's quantum macroeconomic analysis and the reform it points to. Very soon, inflation and involuntary unemployment will become a thing of the past and a new era of orderly economic expansion will replace the present phase of latent economic depression. Let us not deceive ourselves: Schmitt's reform alone will not be enough to guarantee the move to a better and fairer society, a society that is more equal, ethical, truly democratic and ecological, but it will provide a sound foundation on which to build it.

The reader will probably be very surprised by the structure of this book. It obviously does not follow the academic standards. In its original French version, the book contains (apart from the preface and foreword):

- a general introduction of 42 pages divided into three chapters, one of which has only one page;
- four central parts;
- a general conclusion of 102 pages divided into four chapters;
- a series of ten synopses that, over 133 pages, examine again in details the main concepts;
- a four-page glossary of the key words (for this English version, we have added an index and a bibliography to facilitate the work of the reader).

This extraordinary composition raises the question of such a choice. We must at once dispel an interpretation that might come to the reader's mind: this is not the consequence of negligence. If anything, Bernard Schmitt was very rigorous in his work and he attached great importance to matters of form. The perplexing structure of the book is deliberate because it serves a purpose.

Schmitt knew that, in this book, everything would be new and thought provoking. His objective was therefore to guide the reader through an intellectual journey, to enable the passage to a completely different vision of the working of the economic system. The huge task of revising one's perception of economic phenomena required this unusual route.

The book does not follow a linear development but moves along a spiral of arguments. This uncommon method is justified by the fact that the objective is to identify the deep causes of the dysfunctions affecting capitalist economies. Given that all the remedies emanating from mainstream economic thought have failed to cure unemployment and inflation, the conclusion must be that it is indeed the representation of the economic system that is at fault. Schmitt had therefore to familiarise the reader with a new perception of economic phenomena to guide him to first "see" the roots of the dysfunctions and then to understand what reforms may truly prevent the pathologies from happening over again. The spiral was the adequate form to digest the new vision progressively and understand how the new concepts enabled going deeper and deeper into the study of the economic system. In this respect, when Schmitt goes back to a particular concept, it is in order to dig further into the complexities of the system.

The fascinating aspect of the book is that each time a concept previously introduced is revisited, Schmitt is able to present new arguments without repeating those offered before; but, ever more striking, he is able to do so without ever contradicting himself. Unlike Keynes who, in the *General Theory* (Keynes 1936), had great difficulty maintaining the logical coherence of his arguments along the whole book, Schmitt spirals around the problems with the same analytical tools and is able to enlighten all the facets of the working and dysfunctioning of the capitalist system.

It is true that reading this book requires patience and a lot of attention, but the reward is that even if one has not quite mastered an argument, the subject will be revisited later under a different angle that may provide a new insight. In this respect, the series of ten synopses in the last part of the book provide both a summary and a systematic treatment of the whole analysis.

Let us conclude with a few remarks concerning our English translation. Our main concern was to provide a translation as faithful as possible to Schmitt's original text without making it too literal. Even though Schmitt spoke perfect English, he preferred to write his texts in French, which allowed him to express himself at his best. His linguistic style is outstanding, his wording rigorous, his lexicon rich and appropriate. It is well known that French authors are not afraid of abstraction, and Schmitt is no exception. By choosing to preserve as much as possible the lexical and stylistic peculiarities of Schmitt's book, we accept the risk of imposing an additional effort on the English reader. In a scientific text, logical rigour must prevail, and what we have mainly attempted to do is to preserve this aspect of Schmitt's book.

Foreword by the author

The economy as well as economics are in crisis. The objective of this book is to demonstrate that both crises have a common origin.

Two great theories are confronting each other, Marxism and neo-classical "laissez-faire". It is obvious that, on both sides, the analyses are often "nuanced": we shall stylize them in order to reveal their sharpest meaning.

Marxists prepare the revolution of the economic and social organisation of our countries based on a theory already complete in its main principles; the theoretical revolution would already be achieved; it would only be waiting to be implemented.

Neo-Classics on the contrary think that one needs to allow the free play of the economy's natural "mechanisms", any human intervention would bring more harm than benefits.

In spite of appearances, those two doctrinal positions meet on the essential point: both sides agree that theorists cannot "re-invent" the laws of the economy.

Marxists contend that they can use laws to put an end to the exploitation of man by man. Let it be well understood that the objective is not to alter the law of production; even in a communist society, labour will be the unique source of the product and it will be distinct from labour power; the surplus value will always be equal to the difference between labour and labour power. Therefore, the revolution will not bring a new "production process"; every man at work will go on using up less power than the value of his product; but the new judiciary, moral and sociological laws will prevent Capital from monopolizing the surplus value, which will on the contrary be redistributed. Whether or not money is finally conserved, the distribution of the produced value depends on the will of men, especially of the proletariat. In this sense, the value of the product is a sociological magnitude. It is in the power of man to modify all the value ratios in order to channel the surplus value to whomever he wishes. Undoubtedly the amount of surplus value produced in each period depends on the organisation of society. Production will therefore also be affected by the revolution. But a deeper reality will remain out of reach: the objective distinction between labour and its power, that, at the end of his life, Marx claimed to be his great discovery. Even if society succeeds in altering dramatically the adjustment between the two terms, it will remain that in any period the economy will have at its disposal a surplus value – a new product that it can freely allocate – exactly equal to the difference between the observed amounts of labour and labour power. Thus, at the deeper level, the economy will always be operating under the same law: a man's labour brings about the entire value newly produced and the worker and his family will necessarily absorb it according to the amount of labour power spent. The fundamental law is immutable.

The same permanence of laws is postulated by neo-classical theories. Nobody created the economic laws; the scientist will just confine himself to discovering the "nature of things". It is true that here the self-effacement goes even further; it is not only that laws are what they are, but one has to avoid intervening on two levels where it would be expected that man might react: to modify the social environment in which the laws apply and to redress the consequences deemed to be harmful or unjust. The reason for their "superb indifference" does not originate in a lack of generosity; Neo-Classics on the contrary are searching for the optimum, individual and social. They are convinced that the free play of supply and demand will result in the best possible allocation of natural resources and the full employment of human resources. Any intervention by the legislator will inevitably be "rough", the beautiful layout of economic facts being far too intricate to allow the "surgeon" to operate without causing irreparable damage.

But those two doctrines are suddenly put in doubt. In several domains, like biology, chemistry, botanic, and medicine, science today is able to legislate; it does not just observe the laws: it creates them. Men are expecting the same from economics. The blind working of the laws of production and distribution has become unbearable because it generates inflation and unemployment. Science has henceforth two objects; after having unveiled the internal logic of the positive laws of production and distribution, its final task is to invent a normative, "new logic", whose implementation would enable to avoid the disorder in its two aspects, price increases and growing unemployment.

Quantum macroeconomics is a new method; but it also constitutes a new stage in the development of our science. The crisis in thought will then come to an end. Classical thought constitutes a thesis that logically calls for the antithesis. Production conceived of as a causal process presents a grave defect: it pertains to metaphysics. Man does not create (except in thought and art) and his labour does not produce. The "economic matter" is not any more real than the table is present in the mind of the observer. The decisive progress of neo-classical thought, compared to the Smith-Ricardo-Marx tradition, precisely resides in abandoning value, imagined as a fabric distinct from the matter and the energy of the physical world. However, the anti-thesis, a total rejection of the classical doctrines, is too drastic: the truth is in the union of the opposite teachings.

Quantum analysis enables us to come back to the idea of production, while avoiding giving it a disproportionate meaning. Human labour does not produce any "axiological" matter, but only the increased utility of material objects. The two values identified ever since the beginning of economics, exchange value and value in use, are therefore retained and fundamentally redefined. Only exchange value can be quantified; it is equal to the quantity of money created by human labour. If the economy were not monetary, it would not contain any measurable value and economic facts could not constitute an object of science. But, in our concrete economies, wages are effectively a sum of money created by labour; thus, bank money is not issued by financial institutions but solely issued by the activity of workers in the country: the primary function of (clearing) banks is to "valorise" labour's product by bringing it to life in money. As soon as money income is spent, in the final purchase of produced goods and services, exchange value is replaced by a value in use: the product is then just a useful matter. And the utility of goods is not measurable. If neo-classical theorists have obstinately tried to measure it, this is because, by rejecting production, they were left without any concept of exchange value. As soon as science is again grounded on produced value, it recognizes that goods and services are useful, to house-holds and firms, at the instant they cease to belong to the abstract realm of political economy. Only products can be formally grasped, because useful goods and services are just a catalogue of motley objects. However, products are homogeneous for the reason already mentioned: they all result from human labour and they all belong to the category of "concrete numbers", the monetary wage-units created during the period.

Quantum macroeconomics enables the solution of the second crisis that is actually taking place. As soon as thought becomes positive, it is operational: it gives man the practical command over real operations. Science becomes an awareness and it thus naturally extends into the formulation of norms. Inflation and unemployment are disorders, the "mechanics" of which is now unveiled. The transition from positive analysis to recommendations is thus the smoothest that can be imagined: the same logic applies everywhere. Inflation and unemployment are entirely due to the existence of "empty emissions", part of the wages issued in the period being purely nominal from birth, empty of any product. Once this fact is recognized, the remedy is very clear: the disorder must be prevented, the emissions must be filtered, so that the economy only produces "full" wages. The prescription could only meet one obstacle: an analytical incomprehension.

It is often believed that disorder is willed or maintained by powerful, selfish interests and that the only conceivable solution requires a class struggle. The reality is less bellicose. Empty emissions benefit no one; the economy will be profoundly liberated, across all social classes, when productions only bring real incomes. The difficulty is not to defeat vested interests but, and it may be as daunting, biased ideas. Only those minds ready to welcome a revolution in thought may accept quantum macroeconomics. Actually, the young genera-tions unencumbered by the teachings of a too recent tradition, and more impatient towards the Crisis, are ready to learn and to carry out a wisdom that does not belong to anyone in particular but is the collective product of classical, neo-classical and modern thinkers.

The first part is a brief introduction to quantum time. Production does not belong to continuous time; on the contrary, it is an act that "quantifies" the continuum. The product is therefore itself a quantum. All products are time quanta. The various products are not homogeneous except in reference to time. For products to be economically homogeneous, it is necessary and sufficient that production be a double-effect operation, capable to quantise the *"numéraire"* as well as time. We shall demonstrate then that the product is a two-dimensional space, its time dimension being likened to a quantum or indivisible constant.

As soon as these fundamental analytical difficulties are overcome, the functioning of domestic economies will appear in a new light. In the second part of this work, we shall show then that monetary wages embrace entirely the domestic product. Incomes other than wages are contained within the wage circuit. The "telescopic" integration within wages of interest, rent and dividends is the solution to the difficult problem of the "transformation" and of the "realization", raised for more than two centuries; the solution is at last achievable, thanks to quantum analysis, which rejects the principle of the excluded middle.

Another progress follows. Wages, which encompass the entire domestic product, immediately define capital-time, the unique form of all social capital. No capital could ever come into existence in the economy if wages were not issued in bank money. Even fixed (or instrumental) capital belongs to the category of capital-time.

The third part shows the exact aetiology of inflation and unemployment. All the operations observed on the markets (of producing services, of products and of financial claims) are emissions. However, if all emissions were full emissions, Say's Law would prevent any oversupply crisis; inflation too would be impossible. Empty emissions are the only pathology in the economy. They are caused neither by the activity of banks nor by the behaviour of firms. Quite the contrary, empty emissions are purely the consequence of a mechanism at work. It is clear that we are in the domain of "quantum mechanics". Empty emissions automatically result from the amortizations of the fixed capital accumulated over successive periods. On this crucial point, the demonstration is arduous; but the effort is not lost since it allows economic thought to reach the malady at its core: amortizations generate a dual production, or a capital overaccumulation. Activities of firms are then divided into two sections, the core and the "crown". In the core, all emissions are full emissions; in the "crown", on the contrary, all emissions are empty.

Since the writings of Smith, Ricardo and Marx, economic science has marked a close interest for the division of the domestic economy into two sectors; this research has progressed thanks to the more recent studies by Keynes and Kalecki. It seems that it is now coming to its conclusion. The production of investment-goods is not in itself an activity distinct from the production of consumption-goods. If there were no pathology affecting the economy, investment-goods would just be a category of consumption-goods and there would be no need to divide industrial production into two sections. But, in addition to the capital goods formed by the "productive consumption" of part of the issued wages, goods produced in the empty emissions are also identified; now, the division of the industrial activity into two sections is a logical necessity: in the "crown", workers receive a nullified income. The existence of purely nominal incomes explains the two opposite "disequilibria": global demand is in excess; and, paradoxically, global supply is in excess too, once excess demand feeds, in the "crown", a production of wage goods, or, in the core, loans to households.

The dominant theory is obviously unaware of the aetiology of inflation and unemployment; we shall show briefly the consequent inefficiency of all the remedies commonly advocated. Economists are looking in the direction of behaviour, whereas neither households nor firms can avoid the disequilibria, whatever their actions and decisions, whether previsions are perfect or not. The malady is beyond any conscious action: it results from a blind mechanism that overpowers everybody.

The only remedy is in the division of the banking activity into three "departments". The organisation of the first two departments ensures that no money may be created through a financial intermediation; the third department takes charge of any increase in instrumental capital. Fixated in clearing banks, capital is the property of all the income holders. For the very first time, economics is getting hold of a concept that it used to borrow in vain from legal science; the collective appropriation of the means of production is both an empty concept and an inefficient measure, unless it means reducing the "crown" in favour of the core: formed in the core, instrumental capital is owned by the anonymous set of households. The domestic economy will no longer experience either unemployment or inflation once, in each period, all emissions are full emissions only.

The last part consolidates what has been learned by relating it to the history of economic analysis. For the Classics, exchanges were absolute. According to the Neo-Classics they are relative. However, in reality, all exchanges are absolute. Provided that the mind penetrates economic reality at a deep enough level, it sees everywhere only one type of operation: all economic flows are emissions and all emissions are either creations, destructions or creations-destructions of wages. Even empty emissions are no exception. Relative exchanges are the objects of microeconomics that is thus superseded by macroeconomics.

An extended synopsis will summarize, by way of demonstrations sometimes different, the main laws of quantum macroeconomics.

Bernard Schmitt

General introduction

Quantum time

Any production is carried out in time. A production the duration of which is nil is itself nil. Whatever the action deployed, its result can only be measured if it is applied during a period of time that is itself measurable. Any production observed over an infinitely small amount of time gives an infinitely small product.

Apparently clear, the relation between production and time is in reality subtle and even unsettling. The rigorous reasoning that we are going to follow leads to a conclusion completely unexpected: *production does not take place in continuous time; it is on the contrary defined in an indivisible time.*

Even though the existence of "indivisibilities" has been recognized for a long time, especially in economics, indivisible or quantum time is a discovery that alters the foundations of our science. Up until now theorists were reasoning quite naturally in continuous time, given integrally (the continuous analysis proper) or in a series of successive periods (the discrete or periodical analysis); in both cases, it is supposed that any interval of finite time can be divided indefinitely, until infinitesimal lengths of time. Once the necessary link between production and indivisible time is brought to light, the theory is based on an entirely new foundation that renders obsolete the whole corpus of previous explanations.

Posited in infinitely divisible time, production was a fiction; it only existed in the imagination of scientists, without any relation to the reality of facts. Given this fundamental failure, one better understands the state of current theories, their inability to explain concrete economies, their functioning and their maladies. The analyses are closed on themselves, the first and primordial act of the economy being grasped in a chimera, "continuous" production or, identically, the production continuum. In no place on our planet, is production, even the smallest, placed in continuous time. Theorists describe therefore, at best, the economies of some unknown world where a curious logic would prevail.

After having discovered production in quantum time, we shall observe that expenditures, especially monetary ones, answer the same definition. We shall notice therefore the same gap between the accepted theory and facts. According to common explanations, expenditures are posited or "extended" in continuous time, that is to say in an environment where, in fact, they could not exist. All current theories proposing the "income-expenditure models" that the Anglo-Saxons have showered us with, take expenditures as flows, magnitudes-per-unit-of-time, where time is supposed to be infinitely divisible. This is to say that explanations are based on nothingness, no expenditure being logically able to be posited in continuous time.

The last section of the short introduction to quantum time will show the identity of two operations defined in quantum time. *In economics, any expenditure is a production and any production is an expenditure. The domestic economy is therefore based on one unique operation, defined in the indivisible time: production, or, identically expenditure.*

1 Production and time

Production is an action or a movement. Therefore, it would seem that production is a velocity, the space covered during one unit of time. But then what is the space covered by a production? If we answer that this space is the product, we formulate a proposition that has two opposite aspects:

- if it is true that a production is equal to the product by unit of time;
- it is absurd to consider as a given that the product is a space to be covered by production; this is because the product cannot exist before production.

The only available "tool" to fight and reduce contradictions is the use of logic. We shall try to apply it. We shall be very attentive because it is a difficult question.

We shall first separate production from the movements known to classical mechanics. Production is original, because it is a movement that creates a space "in front of itself", whereas conventional movements are motions in a predefined space. We shall draw from this a fundamental conclusion: negated in the case of conventional movements, the Eleatic paradoxes remain true as soon as the movement, instead of being the motion of an object through a given space, has *to create the space in the motion*. The paradox cannot be resolved in continuous time. Thus, any scientist who would still locate production in a time considered as a continuum would leave political economy under the influence of a fundamental flaw (all the more damaging for no longer hidden); if production is an immobility (let us say it is immobile) through time, it will necessarily be so in space too: under these conditions, any production will be nil in perpetuity. Production is formally possible only if it is a positive motion in time.

Zeno's paradoxes are dissolved as soon as the movement is defined or located in quantum time. We shall therefore show that *production is not a motion through space but a motion through time*; it is precisely because production "quantifies" time that it creates a space, namely the product. A positive movement through time, production is not a motion through a space but on the contrary the creation of a space. We shall induce from this that the product is a "quantized" time. In other words, the product has a known measure, the measure of the production's length of time. It is clear that this measure varies with products and does not confer them any homogeneity. It is true that time is objective and that its measure prevails on everyone. Thus, a product that is identified to the quantum defined by one day of labour has the same time-dimension for every observer, the duration of one calendar day being the same for everybody. However, another product that has the same time-dimension bears no objective relation with the first, especially since the two productions may come from two different people. Consequently, the products do not belong to any common measuring space. To create that space, another operation is therefore necessary. Economics gave a name, a long time ago, to this common measure of different products: it is the *numéraire*.

In the concrete domestic economy, *the product is formed in quantized time and simultaneously in* numéraire. *Thus, the product is a time-space and a number-space.* Although the product is a two-dimensional space, these two are (non-simultaneous) alternatives: one of them, indifferently, is therefore a simple factor of proportionality, a constant which can be logically reduced to the number 1 in the series of natural numbers. Once the analysis has reached this result, it will have arrived at the fundamental conclusion, according to which production is defined in time considered as the set of whole numbers. It will be possible to reduce the product of any individual to a time-dimension equal to the indivisible number 1, only the *numéraire*-dimension will differentiate the various products in their common measuring space.

The theory will then be able to carry on with the study of monetary expenditures. Production brings about the *numéraire*-product because money is introduced into the production process. If money were not present within the act of production, the product would only be a time-space, and the domestic economy would produce only disparate and incommensurable goods. Money is the sine qua non condition for the existence of the *numéraire*. The *numéraire*-product is the product in money, the money-product.

I. Production is a motion that confirms the Eleactic paradoxes; any production is an "immobile motion" in continuous time

We may start treating this subject from its easiest angle. The fact that the individual or national production is necessarily nil in continuous time cannot escape anyone's attention, provided this fact is given its most simple mathematical expression: if production were taking place in the continuum, the annulment of production-time would imply the annulment of production itself.

In a second phase, it is easy to show that production is an original movement, distinct from all types of motions known to classical mechanics: production is not a motion within its product, or along its product; it creates it.

It will then be interesting to go back to Zeno's paradoxes, the current relevance of which is acknowledged by logicians. Any movement in a pre-determined space avoids the paradoxes; how could the movement not take place given that it runs in a space already "laid out"? The real difficulty is far more profound: the arrow would not move and the hare would not catch up with the tortoise if those moving bodies had to produce the space right before them. But, precisely, production is a movement of that type: it creates the product, it does not run through the product. The thought process is therefore caught between the two terms of an alternative:

- the moving "spot" follows a predetermined space and is immobile in time because it only follows time in its flow;
- the moving "spot" creates a space; in this case, it is inconceivable that it should be immobile in time.

In other words, motions in a space are necessarily nil in time; on the other hand, only positive movements in time can logically create a space. Economics will only start to apprehend production once it conceives it as a positive movement *in time*.

We shall show that production is a movement in time in that it quantifies continuous time.

Production is necessarily nil in continuous time

The most fundamental problems only enter the realm of conscience once it has become possible to solve them. If they were to surface before, they would halt the progress of science. That is why production is a movement the originality of which has never been discovered; without further inquiry, economists have equated it to a velocity. Is it not intuitively the case that the mathematical value of the product depends on two factors, the measure of production and the time of its application? If twice the amount of production is applied three times as much, is it not obvious that the product is multiplied by six? This is expressed with the following equation:

$$Product = production \cdot time$$

Whatever the (positive) measure of the production under scrutiny, the product is zero if that production is applied during a zero length of time. The nullity of the product results from the time-factor, which is nil, and not from production itself, "instantly" positive. This is because, if production were zero at each instant, the product could never be positive. The analogy with the motions of classical mechanics is striking: the speed of the moving body being known at each instant in time, the whole move is the product of the speed by the time of duration of the movement. It is clear that a constantly zero speed would not allow any movement, whatever the duration of that zero speed.

But *this analogy is* erroneous; it is completely so; classical mechanics does not give us even a proximate solution to our specific problem. We shall be persuaded of that by the distinction of two cases.

Case 1. Production is constantly positive during a finite time interval, as small as we wish.
Case 2. Production is constantly zero during a finite time interval, as small as we wish.

It is clear that case 2 gives us the result of classical mechanics: the product is constantly zero during the observed time interval. But case 1, the only interesting case, can only result in an infinite product in a finite interval, whereas the product of a finite speed by a finite time only gives a finite movement. We shall ascertain easily that the divergence comes from the fact that production is nullified at the same time as the product is, whereas speed is not nullified when the time of application tends towards zero.

To simplify the reasoning, lets us assume that production is not just constantly positive in the interval of time under consideration, but is also constant. We shall soon see that this assumption is in reality a logical requirement, because constancy does not have the same meaning depending on whether it is a production or a velocity in the realm of classical mechanics.

At first view, constancy of production must be represented as follows.

Blaise Pascal once said that we must reason correctly on incorrect graphs. We have therefore divided the rectangle in its two equal parts. In A and in B, production is the same. Production in period *pa* is equal to production in period *pb*. We deduce that the product of period (*pa* + *pb*) is twice as large as the product of period *pa*. This implies tautologically that production of period (*pa* + *pb*) is twice as large as production of period *pa*. This result is absurd since production is constant over the whole period under consideration, (*pa* + *pb*). Thus, in mechanics we would not say that the constant speed of the moving body is twice as high in the entire period as in its half *pa* or *pb*. The absurdity becomes more and more patent as the period is further subdivided.

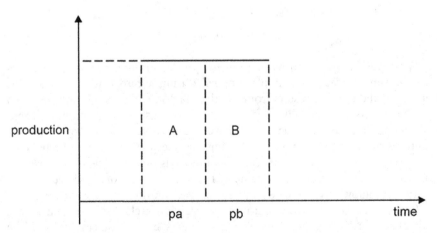

Figure 1.1 Production as a constant function of time

Assume n the number of equal divisions. We face the following contradiction:

- in each division, production is equal to the production of the whole period (since production is constant);
- in the whole period, production is equal to n times the production of each division.

Finally, if we assume that n tends towards an infinitely high number, the production of the period tends also towards an infinitely high number although it is, by assumption, constantly equal to a finite given number. The reason for the contradiction is quite clear: the product of any period is equal to the production of this period, whereas in mechanics the displacement of a moving body is not equal to its speed during the interval of time under consideration.

The divergence is equally striking when we divide (instead of multiplying) the production by n. When n becomes very high, each elementary period becomes very small; at the limit, it is close to zero; production is then also almost zero: it follows that in an infinitely small period, production is infinitely small. The "instantaneous" production is zero. But, if production is zero at each instant of period $(pa + pb)$, how could it be constantly positive in that time interval? In classical mechanics, the nullity of instantaneous movements does not imply the nullity of instantaneous speeds.

The correct representation of production in relation to time is therefore completely different. This is so because the constancy of production must be understood as its *unicity* in the period: production is constant in any period because only one production – only one act of production – is taking place there. Unlike velocity, which "adheres" to the continuum, production is a *leap*: it relates all at once to the whole period. Production is therefore represented by a point (on the vertical axis) corresponding to a segment (on the time axis).

However, the point-segment correspondence might still be avoided. And it would be really desirable that it should, because it precludes the use of the mathematical tools that are needed by theorists, differential equations and difference equations. If it were indeed necessary that a whole period of time (therefore an infinity of "time points") should elapse to define one single numerical value (a unique point) on the vertical axis, production could not be "formalized", which would exclude the primary economic operation from the field of magnitudes open to scientific investigation.

Two methods have to be explored in order to reduce the correspondence between production and time to a point-to-point relation.

First attempt. A certain length of time must probably elapse before it might be possible to define a first production. During that preparative stage, production is zero, but it suddenly becomes positive. As soon as it has become positive, production follows the principle of inertia: it stays at the level it has reached, unless an "external shock" induces another leap, positive or negative. The result is shown in the well-known *staircase* representation.

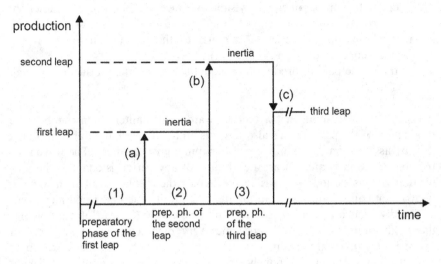

Figure 1.2 The staircase representation of production as a function of time

No production exists yet in the preparatory stage of the first leap. The principle that no production is instantly formed is therefore complied with; it is necessary that a measure of finite time elapses (interval 1) before the first positive production can appear, in leap *a*. As soon as production has suddenly changed from zero to *a*, it is maintained at this level by sheer inertia until the advent of the second leap, prepared during period 2; from now on, inertia maintains production at the level *a + b* until the advent of the third leap, prepared in period 3; the new level of production is then equal to *a + b - c*.

The method that we have just followed has the great advantage, as mentioned earlier, of maintaining production in the field of assessable objects. If production were a movement with a zero inertia, no production could be "tracked" through time and the consequence would be that production, individual and national, could not be conceived of as being a function of time whereas no instantaneous production exists in real economies.

However, there is no doubt that under closer scrutiny the method followed above is completely unsatisfactory: it is illogical. Consider for example the production in period 2; it is constantly equal to the numerical value *a*, given by the first leap. We can therefore reason within period 2 exactly as we have in continuous time. In truth, time is indeed a continuum in period 2. The contradiction detected previously is asserted again under two aspects. The period is divisible as soon as it carries over, by inertia, the result of the previous leap; it is indivisible only with regard to the preparatory stage of the second leap; but any division of period 2 will find the production at its level *a*: it follows that the production of the whole period is any multiple of production *a*. The second aspect of the contradiction is equally absurd: if we divide period 2 in an infinity of infinitesimal periods, production is roughly equal to zero in each division, whereas at the same time its value is constantly equal to *a*.

The "leap functions" are ill-fitted to production, the study of which must follow another path, hitherto unknown. The inertia of production through time is absolutely nil; this is precisely what distinguishes it radically from the velocities of classical mechanics. A velocity is an inertia through time because successive instantaneous speeds do not add up; production is a non-inertia in time because the productions of the successive periods do add up, whatever the length of the periods under consideration: the production of *n* periods is *n* times the average production of one period. It is obvious that the speed of the moving body during 60 minutes is not equal to 60 times its average speed during one minute. Two important consequences are induced. Like leap *a*, leap *b* is a primal leap: in a general way, any production is a brand-new leap, from zero, any previous numerical value being deleted at the very instant it appears; this is required by non-inertia. On the other hand, even if it is indisputable that production is a movement through time, it cannot be followed up in time: it is not carried over by the flow of time. Thus, as soon as the analysis follows the usual paths, it searches into time to find production where it cannot be and it concludes, wrongly of course, that if the movement does not take place in time, it cannot be a flow (in relation to time), even though production is undoubtedly that in reality. In truth, we have to ensure that we satisfy both aspects of any scientific approach: it must conform to facts and logic. And any production conceived of as an inertia through time is a "formal monstrosity".

Before taking the right path, let us briefly reject the second method which might be expected to still save traditional analysis.

Second attempt. It is agreed now that production is a unique numerical value for the whole period of reference that has been chosen. If we retain a finite period, it is clear that production is represented by a point in relation to a segment. But is not the point-segment relation a consequence of arbitrarily choosing a finite period? One might as well speak about the constant speed of a moving body in a measurable time interval, even a lengthy one. If the arrow moves at a constant speed for a whole hour, its speed is a "one-time" phenomenon (it takes a unique numerical value) even though it is related to a segment in time. To transform the point-segment correspondence, one only needs to shorten the period of reference until it is reduced to an instant or a point. This might also be the case, one might think, for production. It is obvious that, if the period is chosen to ensure that it is represented by a segment on the horizontal axis, the corresponding production, assumed to be constant during the period, is given by a point on the vertical axis. However, it would be sufficient to reduce the period until it is transformed into a one-time magnitude so that it faces the constant production, which is a one-time magnitude as well. Mathematics might then be applied because it is no longer asked to "treat" the relation (necessarily indeterminate in its field) between the infinitely large number of points constituting the segment of time and the unique point of production.

But a close examination of the alleged analogy holds a great surprise; in fact, we meet again the original definition of constancy with regard to production: the moving body has a constant speed if its speed is the same in every point of the time under consideration; on the contrary, production has a constant numerical value in the period because it is a non-repetitive (during the period), *unique action*. The speed repeats itself at every instant; production only exists in the space of one instant, even though it is related to the whole period. The distinction between the two cases, which could not be more marked, appears more clearly in the attempt to reduce the period of reference until it is a "point in time". If production were an action continuously present within the period, it would exist at every one of those instant, like velocity; but in fact, *the production of one instant can only be positive if it is immediately related to the whole period*; in other words, the production of one instant of continuous time is logically zero.

Instantaneous speed relates to one instant and not to the whole period during which it is applied; instantaneous production would necessarily be zero under those conditions. It follows that the segment of reference cannot be reduced indefinitely: without keeping an elementary period (the shortest we might choose) that would still be finite (measured by means of "standard" mathematics), we condemn ourselves to grasp only productions of a zero amount. The analysis of positive productions presupposes a series of elementary periods, none of which is reduced to the dimension of infinitesimal numbers. This is how the idea of *quantum time* prevails. One is allowed to choose any length of time, long or short; even more, the choice is totally indifferent because the productions of successive periods add up to each other. But, as soon as the elementary period is chosen, only *one* corresponding act of production can be detected: any production is instantaneous or a one-time event, the efficiency of which extends at once to the whole period. The conclusion is therefore inevitable, even if it means discarding mathematics, because of its inability to grasp the object of research: production is not just a unique numerical value but an action which is a unique event during the whole period under consideration.

We have to accept it; production is a quantum phenomenon, fundamentally distinct from all the magnitudes known to classical mechanics: although situated in time, production is not a function of time, because, devoid of any inertia through time, it is an action that disappears at the precise moment of its appearance, its attachment to the totality of the quantum of time being defined instantly.

All the errors of logic generally committed with regard to production come from a confusion that we had announced. It is agreed that production is a movement through time. Hence, it is naturally conceived of as a movement carried by the time-continuum, a movement in space. The error is a fundamental one for a reason that becomes obvious as soon as it is stated:

movements in any space "reinvent" that already given space; production, on the contrary, *creates a space*, the product-space being not the "environment" in which production is defined, but the result itself of production.

Production is an original movement, distinct from any movement known to classical mechanics

However, between production and its product, there is a relation that is *independent from time*. Let us, first of all, give two tautological examples of this relation. If production is zero, the product cannot be anything else but zero; the converse is also true. On the other hand, if a positive production is multiplied by a positive number, the product is multiplied by the same number: thus, if production is doubled, the product is doubled; again, the converse is also true. Those two propositions are not fulfilled in the case of the speed of an object in movement through a given space: if the move is zero, it is not certain that the speed is also zero; it suffices that the duration of the movement be zero. Identically, the multiplication of the speed does not give any result if it is not applied in time. Unlike velocity, production is in a relation of equivalence with the product, that is totally *independent from time*.

$$(2) \quad production = a \cdot product$$

If we assume $a = 1$, we just mean that production and product are two magnitudes specified in the same measuring scale. As there is no reason to change the scale when we consider production instead of the product, the second relation can be simplified.

$$(2) \quad production = product$$

Production is the operation and the product is the result; measured in the same unit and in the same scale, both magnitudes are necessarily equal to each other, one and the same measure being applied indifferently to both.

Classical mechanics only accepts equation *1*. But relation of equivalence *2*, which is the reason for production's originality, necessitates another definition of the *integral* of the movement through time. Because the product is instantly equal to production (this equivalence being independent from time), whatever the chosen (finite) period of reference, *the integral of the movement through time is equal to the instantaneous movement*. If we persist in speaking of integrals in this situation, we must say "quantum integral", the mathematical product of the movement and its time of application being equal to the movement itself.

The time has come to rehabilitate the Eleatic paradoxes: any analysis that situates production in continuous time gives itself a production that is "immobile through time" and, as soon as production only follows time, this leads to a result which is, in all certainty, zero at all times.

If, as assumed by the accepted theory, production is a movement situated in the time-continuum, it confirms Zeno of Elea's paradoxes: standing immobile in time, production constantly results in a zero product

Let us consider time as viewed by classical physics; it is defined by the uniform shift of a "point of time". Let us borrow the definition offered by Isaac Barrow (1630–77), the immediate predecessor of Isaac Newton as "Lucasian Professor of Mathematics" at the University of Cambridge.

> Time is made up either of the simple addition of rising moments, or of the continual flux of one moment. A line, being the trace of a point moving forward, may be conceived as the trace of a moment continually flowing. Time can thus be represented by a uniform right line. Divisibility is always possible, infinitely or indefinitely. Instants are infinitely small parts of time in which infinitely small spaces are moved through.
>
> (Baron 1969: 240)

Thus conceived, time defines the continuum.

But it is important to note that the science of production – political economy – is itself based on continuous time. It would be utterly ineffective to *start* from quantum time; production could no longer be defined, because quantum time is its result. The granular nature of time is the result and not the precondition of the operation. In physics also, time would be a quantum if it were about the creation of a space and not just to move an object through an already given space.

In mechanics, the velocity of the moving body is defined in an already existing space, inside which the move takes place. Let us continue the analysis of Barrow.

> Any degree of velocity can be generated starting from rest, or the lowest degree of velocity, by increase, or continual flowing, in the same manner as a line may be produced by the apposition of points or by motion, or time by the succession of instants. Velocities can, accordingly, be represented by straight lines at right angles to the line representing time; the space enclosed represents the aggregate distance covered during the motion.
>
> (ibid.: 240)

Thus, the moving body moves through a space that it "reproduces". It is precisely because the path already exists, before being covered, that Zeno's paradoxes do not preclude expressing velocity as a function of time and, therefore, calculating the integral movement by the method of the "infinitesimal". The problem would be far more daunting if the arrow had to create the space "in front of itself". Even the analytical works of Karl Weierstrass (1815–1897) would then be ineffectual. Since it does not quantify time, the arrow is only moving through space: it is immobile through time. More exactly it is "*chrono stationary"*. Time flows and the arrow moves on carried by that flow, at the same "speed" as that flow; it follows exactly *Barrow's point*, the continuous flow of which defines the time-continuum. The brilliant intuition of the Greek thinker keeps therefore all its paradoxical force: the moving body is *immobile through time.*

But the immobility or zero action (in time) could not create any object, any space; immobile in time, the arrow does not create any space: it does not move through space either, unless it was already existing and was already measured, independently from the movement of the arrow. If the space covered had to be created in the movement itself, Zeno's arrow, carried by the time continuum, would never reach its target, even though the sum of the terms of a geometrical series might converge in spite of the infinitely great number of its terms. The mathematical aspect of the problem is banal in the end. Immobile in time, the arrow can only mean a space determined in a completely different way, entirely unknow yet.

In economics, space does not exist before the movement (production). It is indeed legitimate to view the product as a space. But precisely, the product does not exist before production, its only source. Therefore, the paradox finds here its full application in physics, when the problem to be solved is not simply one of ballistics but concerns the origin of the n-dimensional space that defines the universe. *If production were just adhering to the time continuum, it would be a non-action through time and, therefore, would create a strictly zero space or product. The product is a space that has time quantized by production as one of its dimensions.*

The dominant theory gives a circular definition of production

In the dominant economic theory, a magnitude is said to have a dimension in time if it is the product of time by a primary magnitude that is itself posited on a "time-point", Barrow's point. We can use again the image of velocity in mechanics. The distance travelled has a dimension in time because it is the product of a velocity (the primary magnitude) by its time of application. If the instantaneous velocity is calculated at the limit, by the distance travelled during an infinitely short time, the circularity of the reasoning reflects the fact, already stated, that the space travelled is predefined. Thus, the magnitudes are "dimensioned" in time because they adhere to the flow of time. Time is the factor by which the primary magnitudes are multiplied, the time-dimension of which is zero. The result of the multiplication is only the cumulative repetition (even if n times, where n is an infinitely high number) of the primary magnitude, devoid of any definition in time.

Production quantizes time

The logical analysis of production dictates another teaching. Production quantizes time; that is to say, *it grasps at once a portion of continuous time*: the first result of production is therefore the definition of a quantum of time. The product is not posited in time; it *is* itself a piece of time. We see therefore that the primordial dimension of the product, which is a space, is quantized time. *Considering a product posited in time instead of the product that has time as its "fabric", the ready-made theories only hold a lifeless object, an empty concept.*

In fact, the theorist is confronted to a dilemma. If he defines production as a function of its supposed "factors" (labour, capital, land), he is unable to place the productive activity in time. The "production functions" are built and analysed without any regard to time. But, inversely, if the theorist decides to study production in terms of time, he is no longer able to relate it to its supposed factors. In both cases, failure is certain. How could the factors produce outside of time? The production functions are exercises in elementary mathematics elaborated in the closed field of mind games. If a factor effectively starts to produce, this will necessarily take place in time and, being unaware of it, the analysis lets its object slip away at the very moment it was becoming a reality.

On the other hand, if production is at once set in time, it defines a magnitude that is only measurable by the product, like the velocity of a mobile is only measurable by the distance covered. The circle is a vicious one; since it does not pre-exist production, the product can only be measured by production; but how then could production be measured in products?

The product is a quantum of time

"Quantum analysis" solves the dilemma. Production is the primary act; it is production that measures the product. *The product is nothing else than a quantum of time and its measure is that of the quantized time.* On the other hand, the definition of the "factors of production" is no longer left to the imagination of the scientist. Logically, it is only the action quantizing time that is able to produce. We still have to discover what this action is: it is exclusively a "projection" or an "emission" from *man*.

Production quantizes continuous time because it is the completion of a (human) project

The demonstration is relatively easy because it appeals to intuition. Let us start from time, the continuous flow of which is represented by the x axis. It is certain that every production has a precise origin on this axis. Let us assume that a production started at instant t_0 is completed at instant t_n (also perfectly determined). The analysis above has established that production is zero within the interval (t_0, t_n).

Whatever the division of the interval, production is zero inside this division; even more, production is zero in the sum of the divisions: it is positive only over the *whole* period. Thus, a half-completed product is "neither made nor to be made", as the French would say (*"ni fait ni à faire"*). If production were extended in the continuum, the product would be formed slowly and smoothly; we might then speak about a fraction of the product, as if it were the finished product, divided by a number. Half a wheel would be a wheel divided by the number 2. In reality, it is absolutely clear that half a wheel is only a half-wheel from the point of view of the completed wheel; if production is ended at the stage of half the wheel, then it is *totally ineffective*: the wheel does not half-exist, it does not exist at all. The same "totalizing" effect can be observed for services: a traveller to New York would not be half-satisfied if the plane were to transport him just from Paris to Shannon. It is useless to multiply examples: any production started at instant t_0 and completed at instant t_n is formed in one single movement at t_n, the period is continuously covered only during the preparatory phase, a "work in progress".

In truth, current theories admit that a production has to be prepared, in order to appear in a leap. Yet, the leap is taken into account by the leap functions already mentioned. One imagines that, once executed, the leap leaves a trace in continuous time. The following leap would then be based on the trace left by the preceding leap. We have shown that this is not at all the case. A first journey from Paris to New York does not provide a new basis to start a (second) journey; similarly, the first production of a tangible object does not shift durably the product to a positive level: any new production has to start from zero. All this would be obvious if abandoning the leap functions did not lead the analysis to an entirely new conception of the production–time relation. Since the "first" leap does not leave any trace in chronological time, the "second" leap is as much a *first* as the preceding leap. The representation of production in time is therefore similar to an electrocardiogram. But two fundamental differences increase considerably the conceptual difficulty:

- each heartbeat takes time (it is located in the continuum), whereas production, taken at its end-point, is instantaneous at t_n;
- each beat extends only over the fraction of chronological time taken by the beat, whereas production, which "occupies" only instant t_n, extends over the whole period (t_0, t_n).

The case of production requires an upgrading of the "analytical tools": the time-quantum must be added to the time-continuum. As mentioned before, the question is not to abandon time conceived as the set of real numbers. *Any production is completed at an instant in continuous time. But production is a non-zero movement in time; and it is in that respect that it quantizes time.*

This is the moment now to offer the clear explanation of the "quantization" of continuous time.

Let us consider the x axis, constituted by the continuous movement of the "Barrow point". At instant t_0 where our production starts, it rests on time, that it follows "pointwise" until instant t_1. During this whole "journey", production is a movement belonging to classical mechanics, a chrono stationary movement. It is precisely because the movement adheres passively to the flow of time that it does not create a space. But nothing is lost yet because it is acknowledged that no product will appear inside the period (t_0, t_n). We must therefore focus on production at instant t_n, the instant of its completion. Witnessing the completion of production, instant t_n is when the totality of production can be seen because production only exists once completed. In order to embrace the reality in its two inseparable aspects, production is extending from t_0 to t_n while only coming into existence at instant t_n, the analysis has to equip itself with a movement that is original but already known to physics: the *wave-like* or *undulatory* motion. A wave is a back-and-forth movement. But, only an instantaneous back-and-forth movement can reflect the dual reality of production:

- production extends from t_0 to t_n; it has therefore to "travel" over this length of time;
- production is uniquely situated at instant t_n; it has therefore to be at t_n even while traveling from t_0 to t_n;
- the only solution – but it is entirely satisfactory – is to acknowledge the undulatory nature of production: at instant t_n, production is a wave, a motion through time, observed from t_n to t_0 and identically from t_0 to t_n.

Production is a wave-like motion

The fact that the undulatory movement through time defines firstly the journey from t_n to t_0 enables to ignore the common sense argument that no movement can "straddle" time in the direction of its flow, by moving faster than Barrow's point. Instant t_n being subsequent to instant t_0, it is true that it would be contradictory to give ourselves the instantaneous journey from t_0 to t_n, because t_0 would then be in t_n. The incoherence is lifted once the journey is first covered in the opposite direction. Being cast from t_n to t_0, the wave keeps open the gap between the two points in time; even the complementary journey, from t_0 to t_n, no longer implies the concurrence of the two instants, since the wave-like movement only happens after the passing of time (t_0, t_n).

The undulatory nature of production also corresponds to intuitive thinking. If a production only exists once completed, whilst requiring a steady effort over time or over a period, this is because it is the matching between a project and its achievement; thus, it is only the "mechanistic" conception of production that is rejected: if production were coming from a machine or from the land as well as from human beings, it could only occur in continuous time and the product would be a "space" going back to the origin of the universe. Production would be a vain word, an empty concept. The economy produces because this is where human beings accomplish their "material projects".

Labour quantizes times. Production does not quantize the time of labour

Any human production (a redundant expression) is the emission of a wave, the instantaneous journey and in both opposite directions of the time "consumed" by production, by the worker's activity, in all the industries of the domestic economy. We see that the Classics were not so far from the truth when they considered the product as a coagulated time. Their theory would have even been perfect if they had simply said that human labour brings about a product identical to a coagulated time or a quantized time. However, the evolution of science followed an intermediary stage, the result of production viewed as a coagulated time of labour. It is clear today that *labour quantifies time and that labour is not itself quantized or coagulated.*

This error has a grave consequence; labour being fictitiously projected in its result, one naturally imagines that the product has a labour-dimension whereas it only has a time-dimension. This explains that science, from Ricardo to Marx, ended in a blind alley: assumed to be present inside the product, labour was to provide the common measure, beyond the diversity of goods. In fact, no labour is incorporated into the goods and therefore products stay different. It would be naïve to believe that the production of one same person brings two identical products provided they result from an equal time of production. *A fortiori*, the products of different persons are incommensurable, without any solution being offered by the comparison of their quantized times. If product i and product j are equal quantized times, logic does not allow to elide time, in order to conclude that the products are equal or interchangeable. In other words, *the quantization of time is not a measuring operation: it brings the product not its measure.* The products can only be measured if they are brought into a relation of equivalence with numbers.

After the Classics, science has rightly taken an interest in the *numéraire* theory. If, in addition to its time-dimension, the product does not acquire a *numéraire*-dimension or a number-dimension, it will not be brought into any space of measure. Domestic production is a measurable or "quantifiable" movement because it both quantizes time and numbers.

II. In concrete economies, the domestic product is formed in quantized time and simultaneously in *numéraire*

The product can be defined independently from time, in a pure numéraire

As above, let us represent production on the vertical axis and time (in its flow) on the horizontal axis. We know that the correspondence between production and time is a point-segment relation. However, where is the point for a given period? We cannot tell, unless production is, on the y axis, carried on a measuring scale. We have to "calibrate" the axis. Only the *numéraire* can achieve this.

The product has two dimensions if, and only if, production is itself a dual undulatory movement. We have not represented the waves through time but only the waves that quantize the *numéraire*: for example, wave i creates the *numéraire*-dimension, $P1 = a$, of the product from period 1. We then arrive

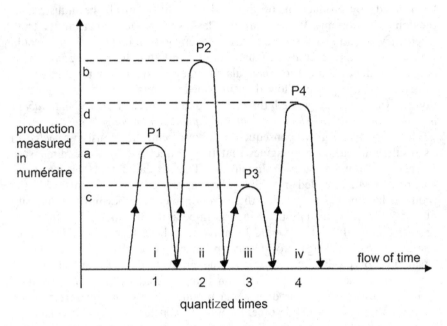

Figure 1.3 The relation between production and quantized time

at an interesting conclusion. The wave that travels through time is not yet completed at the moment of completion of the wave covering the *numéraire*: the two quanta are therefore the transformation of one into the other. We can thus express the product of each period only in *numéraire*, the time-dimension being reduced to a factor of proportionality equal to the number 1. We can achieve this very simply: by dividing continuous time in a series of equal quanta. This results at once in two equations:

production of period q · duration of period q = production of period q;

product of period q = *numéraire*-dimension of the product of period q.

The conclusion that we have reached requires a formulation that brings in full light the opposition of the theories:

- classical mechanics likens time to the set of real numbers;
- production theory likens time to the set of positive and whole numbers.

The first question that comes to the mind is obvious: what is the nature of the *numéraire*? We shall answer this very briefly, because the *numéraire* is identified to money, which is the very object of this work.

III. Production brings the *numéraire*-product because money is introduced in the production process

The numéraire-*product is the result of a "salaried production"*

One reflexion will be enough here. Let us suppose that the isolated worker contemplates creating a two-dimensional product; he will not succeed: the *numéraire*-dimension will necessarily be missing and the product will only be some quantized time. The product can only be formed as a number if it is changed into a number. And it is inconceivable that man, if he keeps away from any exchange, will succeed in transforming his product into a *numéraire*: he will always just obtain some pure quantized time. The *numéraire*-dimension of the product can only appear if the act of production is, as we have shown, a doubly undulatory operation; in other words, to obtain a *numéraire*-product, the worker has to produce "twice at one go", first for the firm (where the product is deposited in its time-dimension), then for himself (under the form of the product in its number-dimension). Hence, *only the wage-regime enables the formation of the product (individual and national) in its* numéraire-*dimension.*

2 Expenditures and time

IV. Like production, expenditures (in particular monetary expenditures) are defined in quantum time

We shall establish without much difficulty that all expenditures are related to time in the same way as we have just identified for production. This conclusion does not depend on the nature of the economic expenditure. However, we shall concentrate on monetary expenditures, because, both in writings and in facts, they occupy the prominent place.

Instead of directly examining expenditures in time, it is probably more informative to start from the explanations given by established scientists. If we choose Paul Samuelson's writings, it is not because his position would be an odd one in this matter; on the contrary, it reflects so beautifully the main thought that one would need to search among the most recent essays of some particularly worried theorists, to find elements of a timid divergence from the body of doctrine of which Samuelson is an authorised representative. The step-by-step presentation and the concomitant dispelling of the error will lead us logically to the exact definition: like production, every expenditure is a wave-like operation, the effect of which is to quantize a "piece" of continuous time.

An expenditure is not a flow in continuous time

If we proceed by elimination (from what was achieved before the discovery of time quanta), nothing can be reproached to this author: being certainly not a stock, an expenditure is, like an income, "a rate, a flow of dollars" (Samuelson 1966–77: I, 162). Apparently innocuous, this definition has weighty consequences, even in the realm of economic policy.

Let us represent an expenditure "as a function of time", like the one that can be found page 1156 of the second volume of the *Collected Scientific Papers*.

Straight line *i* is the representation of the (constant) expenditure in the period; straight line *j* enables to define the rectangle that gives the integral of the expenditure, the product of the flow by time, i.e. the amount spent. The

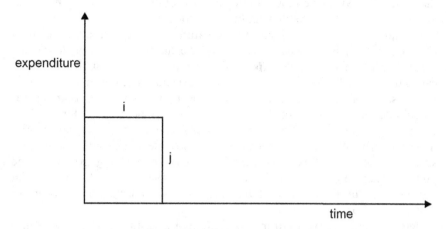

Figure 2.1 Expenditure as a function of time

error is clear and is stated very simply: logically, the integral of the expenditure in the period is given linearly by the measure of straight line *j*.

The mistake is so obvious that one hesitates to attribute it to Samuelson. However, the author's further reasoning dispels the qualm.

The succession of expenditures does not define a flow in continuous time

On this point, the error appears in many papers. Concatenated in time, expenditures constitute a flow; "one impulse [expenditure] follows another in a continuing steady stream" (ibid.: II, 1163). Let us consider only one other quotation that has the added merit of introducing the problem of the Keynesian multiplier, presented in such a way that we shall be able shortly to verify beyond any doubt the depth of Samuelson's mistake.

> Two alternative definitions of the multiplier are met with in dynamic sequence analysis. The first measures the multiplier by the increased level of income finally reached as the result of *a continual stream* of a unit of expenditure, repeated in every period. The second, which may be called the cumulated multiplier, is measured by summing throughout all time the increments in income resulting from a unit, non-repeated, impulse of expenditure.
>
> (ibid.: II, 1191)

Even though extraordinarily amazed by this, our mind is asked to accept two mutually exclusive formulations: one single expenditure is already a flow and the series of concatenated expenditures would be a flow as well. A flow is movement, a stream; it is therefore really difficult to conceive of a movement that is itself moving, the movement being then both the shifting of the object and the object shifted, the flow and the flow of the flow.

It is quite certain that to conceive the nature of an expenditure is no small task for anyone. But in the quoted texts, the naiveté is without doubt disproportionate. If one single expenditure is already a flow, it forms a concatenation in itself, not together with *other* expenditures. On the other hand, if, in a series of expenditures, each element is a "non-flow", an instantaneous magnitude, the succession of the expenditures over time does not form a flow. Even in the dictionary, a flow is a continuous movement; one cannot build a flow from elements, none of which defines a movement. We may conceive of a succession of elementary movements, with each one taking over from the previous one; we would then obtain one single movement, made up of partial movements. But a succession of zero movements defines a single movement that can only be zero.

Before examining the third mistake, one that is so fundamental that it has undermined the whole corpus of post-Keynesian macroeconomic theory, in the "income-expenditure" models, let us summarize the first two by contrasting them briefly with the corresponding truths.

An isolated expenditure is not a flow. If an expenditure were a flow, it would be a continuous movement and, more precisely, an uninterrupted movement in an interval of continuous time (or of the continuum). Let I be this interval. Our reasoning elaborated for production may be applied here. If the expenditure is, for example, constantly of 100 fr. in time I, it is of 100 fr. in each part of this period of time: the total expenditure of the period is therefore indeterminate; it is as large as we wish, because, to increase it, we only need to multiply the number of elementary periods included in I. It is clear that the assumed expenditure is of 100 fr. for *the indivisible whole* of period I. But it can be induced that the expenditure is a *unique* event, even though it relates to a whole period; it is a magnitude instantly related to a positive length of time. This is to say that the expenditure is not a continuous movement; it is a "one-time" event, of no duration. In truth, an expenditure is a wave-like motion that covers instantaneously, and in both opposite directions, the related period. Therefore, *the payment of a monthly income is an expenditure that, if carried out at the end of the month, is a movement the efficiency of which takes effect immediately at the beginning of the month, to go forward in time until the moment of the payment.* In no circumstances could a wage be paid continuously; it is necessarily paid all at once.

A series of expenditures is not a flow. One might try to avoid the absurdity of a "flow of flow" by using the idea of relays mentioned above. A first expenditure would be maintained during a limited period; then a second expenditure would take over; and so on. But one quickly sees that this way of proceeding is not viable; if the first expenditure dies out, the second one could not extend it unless it started from zero (everything would have to start all over again); and if the first expenditure is maintained, the second one is added up, it is not extending it either. Thus, logic allows *a priori* only two solutions:

- the expenditure is a movement with limited inertia over time; in this case, the "second" expenditure starts from the *tabula rasa*;
- the expenditure is a movement that is maintained over time; the "second" expenditure (and all the others) is therefore added up to the first instead of extending it. This demonstrates that the series of expenditures cannot in any way constitute a flow. Indeed, any expenditure is a movement the inertia of which is so limited that it is extinguished at the very moment it is carried out. *All* expenditures are therefore *primary* expenditures; none is just the continuation over time of a previous expenditure.

We observe that the two mistakes come from the fact that Samuelson confers on expenditures a positive inertia over time. It is obvious that the complete absence of inertia is extremely puzzling to the mind, because this forbids the determination of expenditures in relation to each other.

The third mistake, by far the worst, is in a way the product of the two preceding ones. The inertia (illegitimately) conferred on expenditures is taken as the starting point of a dynamic explanation of the formation of expenditures in the domestic economy.

The chain of expenditures over time does not constitute a dynamic

The quotation above (Samuelson 1966–77, II, 1191) is enough, unless reinforced by the elementary graphs of II, 1156. The author develops the famous theory of the Keynesian multiplier, and nowhere else is that theory as much out in the open. Let us give the highest possible value to the multiplier, which is the case when the inertia over time of each expenditure is unlimited. Even in this case where it should be continuously increasing with the passing of time, the multiplier is just a coefficient that will blandly be constantly equal to 1.

Let us consider the "cumulated multiplier", "measured by summing throughout all time the increments in income resulting from a unit, non-repeated, impulse of expenditure" (ibid.: II, 1191). Let us represent the accumulation over time of the successive expenditures (as in II, 1956, figure c).

If logic were complied with, both in the text and in the representation, the expenditure of period 2 would be added up to the expenditure of period 1; there would be no reason for stopping: all the expenditures would be cumulative over time, so that in period n the sum of the cumulated expenditures since the beginning would be equal to n times the initial expenditure.

But the idea of a cumulative effect from one expenditure over time (or in a dynamic process) is totally absurd in any event, whether or not expenditures have an inertia over time. If the inertia were zero, every expenditure would be a movement that would cease at the very moment of its production: expenditures *2, 3, 4*, etc., would not even exist. But because expenditures, by assumption, have a perfect inertia over time, expenditure *2* is only the continuation of expenditure *1*: the expenditures of p_1 and p_2 constitute in fact

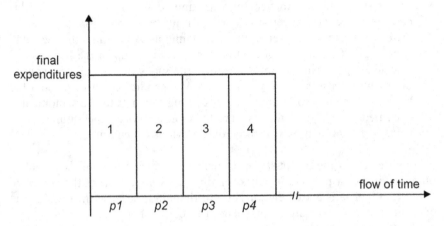

Figure 2.2 The "cumulated multiplier"

only one expenditure. For the same reason, expenditures *3, 4* etc., are all coming from the first expenditure, which is like a spacecraft on its orbit (moving indefinitely, if frictionless). The only possible defence would be to say that expenditure *2* is new; but then the inertia over time of expenditure *1* would be limited to period *1* and we would abandon the assumption of a unique, "never repeated", expenditure to consider the case of the "continuous flow of a unique expenditure, repeated in every period". Let us therefore consider this case.

There is no need to draw another diagram. Let us just reason a little bit. If the expenditure in period *1* had a (perfect) inertia within the limits of this period, we could divide p_1 in any number of subperiods, *1', 2', 3', 4'*, etc., so that the "*continuous* flow of a unique expenditure, repeated in each period" would be given *inside the "unique" period* p_1. Only one reason prevents us from proceeding in such a way: it is that expenditure *1* is referred to in period *1* as an indivisible period. But then we have to accept the consequence: any expenditure specified in *some* period will be referred to that *entire* period. Thus, no expenditure observed during period *2* can come from period *1*, or else it would be referred to period (*1 + 2*) and to its *division 1*. We can induce that any expenditure from period *2* is new, not just in that period but also at "all times". The "multiplier by the increased level of income finally reached as the result of *a continual stream*" is therefore a great absurdity.

Suppose we were talking to a representative of the exact sciences to ask him to follow that strange logic. All monetary expenditures are instantaneous events (the time to transmit the information between the impulsion given by one of the parties and its reception by the other party is purely "technological"); credit and debit are necessarily instantaneous; the expended amount, the result of the operation, also comes about in an instant, no positive expenditure being the payment of an amount of zero; but, be attentive, in spite of the instantaneous nature of the expenditure and of its result, it is placed right from the beginning in continuous time, where it will therefore persist until an undetermined date. The "duration" of the expenditure, its extent over time, is an important fact, because an economy that prompts new expenditures in the period under consideration will not start them from zero but, quite the contrary, will base the new expenditures on the previous ones, as far as these are persisting, exactly like a new boost given to a spacecraft will act on its given trajectory in order to modify it.

An example will enable the ideas to be set on a firm ground. Let us assume that the sum of all the expenditures carried out during the previous periods will determine in the current period a persisting total expenditure of x francs; the amount of new expenditures of y francs (carried out during the current period) adds up then to the expenditures of x francs coming from the past, so that the expenditures observed during the current period will amount to ($x + y$) francs. Let us be well understood: we are not saying that an economy that spent a sum of x fr. and then spent y fr. has spent ($x + y$) in total; economics is far more serious than that. It has made a truly great discovery: the act of spending takes place in time so that the expenditures from the past extend their effect into the present to add up to the amount formed by the new expenditures. The leakages (in the sense of Keynes's theory of the multiplier) are zero when the effect of all expenditures is extended indefinitely. Under those conditions, period 2 will experience the effect of period 1 expenditure in addition to the effect of its own expenditures. The two expenditures, y fr. and x fr., are actions of period 2 even though the x francs measure an action that originated in a previous period. In the case of zero leakages, an economy that casts an expenditure of x francs in each period will find itself with an expenditure of x francs in the first period, of $2 (x)$ in the second one, of $n (x)$ in the nth period. Thus, even though the expenditures decided in each period are only of x francs, expenditures increase and multiply with the passing of time, so that in each period, in addition to the expenditures that it decides to cast, the economy experiences expenditures that are mechanically imposed by the sole effect of the previous impulses; from the second period on, the economy spends (in spite of itself) twice x francs, although it only decides to spend x francs in the period.

Our scholar from the "hard" sciences will turn away, amused and slightly worried. This is because the deep illogical character of the whole "discourse on the multiplier" is really pathetic. How could an expenditure, decided by people in period 1, "force" the hand of people in period 2? The amount spent – result of the operation – may persist; but (and we should say that this is obvious) the expenditure, the act of spending, is not self-renewed: in contradistinction with their result, expenditures of period 1 cannot be imported into period 2, where the only expenditures that can take place are those decided within this period.

The *dynamics of expenditures* is an absurdity, the word is not too strong. By what sort of wonder could the agents revive into period 2 the expenditure they cast during period 1? If they cast a new expenditure, it will be new indeed: it is not at all the duplication or the "persistence" of a previous expenditure. In other words, in any period, any expenditure is a "live" action of the period and not the lifeless continuation of previous actions.

The incorrect view of the "dynamics of expenditures" comes from the fact that any expenditure is both instantaneous and nonetheless set in a positive length of time

Theorists have started from the fact that monetary expenditures have a time dimension; they are not "Poisson events". We are indeed considering the time dimension of the expenditure operations themselves and not just of their results. That dimension is undeniably positive. Up to this point nothing is wrong. But how can a time dimension be given to instantaneous operations? Only one example came to the mind: the "instantaneous" velocity in classical mechanics. Expenditures were therefore deemed, without any thorough examination, similar to a movement taking place passively during a certain length of time. Now the error is complete. Two fundamental differences come to the fore as soon as we put things in perspective:

- no mechanical movement taking place in time has an immediate effect; whereas, at the very moment of a credit meeting the corresponding debit, the expenditure is completed;
- any expenditure that would have a certain depth in continuous time, even the smallest conceivable, would give rise to an infinitely large result (an infinite sum spent); but, the multiplication of a finite mechanical movement by a finite length of time produces a finite result.

The correct solution is given by "quantum analysis", that we have already presented in relation to the operation of production. All expenditures are instantly related to their period of reference, which is therefore a *quantum of time*, an indivisible whole. In all rigour, if we do want to represent (domestic) expenditures on two axes, we need to indicate the passing of time (therefore the continuum) on one of them and the *numéraire* on the other. Monetary expenditures are measured in *numéraire* (and not initially in money). For each period taken from the continuum, we find one and only one expenditure (the sum of all instantaneous expenditures related to the period). As in the case of production, we can transform the quantum of time into a unitary quantum, equal to 1. To this effect, we only need to divide the continuum in equal slices; the expenditures are then compared to each other according to their *numéraire* dimension. Finally, no expenditure defined in a quantum of time can in the least be facing another quantum of time. It is therefore logically and mathematically impossible to "determine" successive expenditures, one in relation to the others: in this sense, any expenditure is "alone in the wide world". The theorist must therefore invent an entirely new method of inquiry and turn away from "calculus".

To study the relation between expenditures and time, we cannot use differential equations nor finite-difference equations

In his ambitious article "Some notions on Causality and Teleology in Economics" (ibid.: III, 428–72), Samuelson studies the comparative application of differential calculus and differential equations to economic magnitudes.

> Does reality dictate that true causal analysis should be thrown into the form of 'cause now creating effect later', requiring us to use a difference-equation formulation? Or, since time intervals can be cut down as much as we like, does reality call for a differential-equation formulation? [...]. In economics, I believe Richard M. Goodwin has argued that events take place in finite time and our observations come in discrete intervals, and that therefore in principle a difference-equation formulation is optimal. Against this, economists such as R.F. Harrod have asserted the equally one-sided view that derivative flows are somehow more fundamental than lagged differences. Most modern physics involves use of Newtonian derivatives and partial derivatives. At least one physicist, perhaps influenced by the conceptual importance of the quantum theory, has proposed that all physics be recast in terms of finite differences; and my old teacher, E.B. Wilson, the last student of Willard Gibbs and himself a distinguished mathematical physicist and statistician, once told me that Gibbs mentioned, in his last years, an attempt to express as much as possible in terms of finite differences. In a sense, the quarrel is an empty one, involving unimportant semantic distinctions. In a sense, the answer can be arbitrary, depending upon the convenience of the investigator.
>
> (ibid.: III, 439)

It is completely true that the real problem is not to choose between those two mathematical methods which, in the days of Newton and Leibniz, were already very close to each other. The option to take is far more fundamental: we must reject both methods *at the same time*, since economic reality is beyond the reach of those two. This is so because production and expenditures are not just dated events, appearing inside intervals of discreet and finite time; a much bigger intellectual effort is required to grasp them: these events are original compared to all the magnitudes that can be treated by the equations of the first or the second type. Production and expenditures are *movements in time*, whereas physics, even quantum physics *as viewed by Samuelson*, only deals with movements within a predefined space. Far from being movements in an already existing space, expenditures do create a space: they are undulatory movements the *speed of which is infinite in time*.

The consecutive analyses of production and expenditures have shown the very great analogy between these two events. Before proclaiming their *identity* in the last section, let us once again describe the operation of the "quantization" of continuous time.

A new formulation of the quantization of continuous time

At the beginning, the time continuum, the continuous movement of Barrow's point, is given. It is true therefore that initially "the intervals of time can be divided at will". However, stopping at this observation prevents us from grasping these essential events that production and expenditure are and, instead of using mathematics applied to economics, as believed, we have the use of mathematics for an outer space economy where expenditures and production would be movements endowed with a positive inertia over time. This logic "from another world" is very strange because it implies that expenditure and production are movements in the space of the sum spent, or in the space of the created product. On our planet, production and expenditure are not movements in any space since the *product-space* and the *number-space* are created by these events. Production and expenditure are absolutely not movements through space but exclusively movements through time: the time dimension of these events is precisely defined by the wave that quantizes an interval of the continuum, by going through it in an instant, going and coming back at one go.

To go back to our example, the payment of a monthly salary grasps the calendar month as one *indivisible* whole, the monetary expenditure (the formation of wages) being instantly effective over the whole period of the relevant month.

In the next chapter, we shall just sketch the identity of the two events, every production being an expenditure and every expenditure being a production. This question goes beyond this brief introduction since quantum macroeconomics has no other object than the study of productions-expenditures.

3   Production and expenditure constitute one unique event: the emission

In the body of this work, it will be revealed that the fundamental illogicality on which traditional macroeconomics is based, and which makes it unable to grasp production and expenditures, comes from the absence of negative numbers of which the analysis has no knowledge. Of course, economists do know about subtractions, the imputation of negative numbers on positive numbers. But they don't know about the imputation of negative numbers on the number zero. With apparent common sense, these theorists refuse to "cut into" the number zero. However, if the economy were actually functioning without ever creating any negative number, production and expenditures could never appear in it, unless of course in the fictitious representations of the "incomes-expenditures" models.

Once negative numbers are introduced, we understand at once how the scientific determination of events remains possible even though they don't have any consistence in the continuum: absolute determination "replaces" relative determinations. Up until now theorists were considering a world where nothing is created and nothing is lost; under those conditions, the events could only remain completely indeterminate unless they were related to each other in the continuum: in what other environment could they be grasped in a mutual determination? Thus, the position of an object moving in a space can only be identified in relation to its (immediate) nearest position. In economics, events do not share any neighbouring relations. They can nevertheless be perfectly determined, because of the simultaneous creation of equal positive and negative magnitudes. *Any production and (identically) any expenditure is an emission, creation-destruction of the same object, the product and the sum spent.* Every expenditure creates a product and every production is an expenditure. The theory of emissions embraces the whole field of macroeconomics.

Part I

The functioning of the domestic economy: from wages to capital

In the history of economic thought, emission occupies an important place, at least since David Ricardo's theory. However, it is generally believed that the emission of money is strictly a banking operation and, even more restrictively, that it only concerns central bank money since clearing banks do not issue any money. In reality, they do, in the same capacity as the Central Bank, the "Issuing Institute". Moreover, we must abandon the naïve idea according to which money is issued by banks: *human labour only is an emission*. Even in the current state of our economies, experiencing inflation and unemployment, every monetary emission, without any exception, brings about a money which "body" has one origin only: human labour.

In common language, one speaks of the purchasing power of money; in more scientific terms, real money is being contrasted to nominal money. At the same time, the purchasing power of nominal money, in other words real money, is identified with the product (in goods and services) that human labour is periodically depositing in money.

The theory draws from this a great simplicity. We shall show that *every (monetary) payment is an emission of wages.*

At first sight, this judgment is too narrow since money is used in all markets and not just in the payment of wages. As soon as the analysis reaches a deeper level, it brings together events that seemed unrelated. In the products market, wages are issued negatively: the selling of goods is a monetary operation *identical*, but for the sign, to the payment of wages. The operations observed in the financial market then also belong logically to the unique category; there, wages are spent both positively and negatively: they are preserved through a *transfer*. Again, the payment technique is that of an emission and, more precisely, the emission of wages.

Let us repeat it, every payment carried out in the economy in any bank money is either a creation of wages, a destruction of wages, or a creation-destruction of wages. The day this fact is understood, macroeconomic theory will have acquired a new power, entirely focused on one operation, its only fundamental object.

A doubt comes at once to the mind: wages are not the only category of income. Are not the formation and spending of profit, rent and interest emissions too? But these incomes are not wages. Apparently, the theory of emissions would have to be generalized to all categories of income. To remain at this level, would indicate a high degree of candour. Emission is not an empty word, but a very precise operation the action of which is, as we have demonstrated, to *quantize the continuum*.

It is difficult to attain this result; but as soon as the analysis reaches this depth, it will no longer doubt the unicity of the operation anymore. Taken lightly, production can be identified to all sorts of actions: even the wind is a factor of production. But, taken seriously, production is a solemn operation: in the dictionary it means a creation. And one cannot really see clearly how the wind might create anything. Human labour can do it and, apart from theology, human beings are the only beings able to create, to "create-destroy".

From that, one necessarily induces that wages are the only objects being produced, in the exact sense of the word, the only incomes that are created in the whole economy.

But then, what should we do about profit, rent and interest? We shall provide the exact solution: for the first time in the history of economics, the analysis is able to overcome the principle of the excluded middle. We shall demonstrate that the creation-destruction of non-wage incomes is incorporated in the creation-destruction of wages. Any scientist knows that surplus-profit has never been explained, i.e. never been integrated in the general theory of economic events. In classical analysis, profit cannot be "realized", because it can only be formed through the expenditures of wages. In neo-classical analysis, profit cannot coexist with general equilibrium, where profits and losses are nil by definition. The theory of emissions signals the third stage, where profits are at last perceived as they are in reality: *denatured wages*.

We shall verify that any non-wage income has its unique source in the (direct and indirect) wage bill periodically formed by domestic production. It is not in vain that Keynes proposed to use the wage-unit as the measure of all economic magnitudes. Even in an economy in crisis, we shall observe the existence of only one initial or original category of income from which all others are derived: wages.

In this first part of our work, we shall study the functioning of the domestic economy, without considering its disorders. However, we shall go up to the threshold of the analysis of the dysfunction because we shall explain the transformation of profit into capital. In this area, which is of course at the heart of our field, "quantum analysis" brings simplicity again, the only one able to give knowledge a degree of insight high enough to master its object.

Any capital belongs to one category only, that of savings or *capital-time*. The brilliant intuitions of Ricardo will then be confirmed. The fusion into one unique category of the different types of capital formed in the domestic economy results in another synthesis, the one John Hicks called for: real capital (or material capital) and financial capital are one and the same reality.

4 From production to consumption: the creation and destruction of wages

The introduction has shown that the act of production cannot be situated in the time-continuum. Production only exists in the operation of the "quantization" of time and of the *numéraire*.

Now, the analysis may progress by an important step: positive production is only one aspect of the movement that, as we have briefly announced, implies logically and in the same thrust the opposite operation, negative production, consumption.

Any act of production is a production-consumption, a wave. The same operation creates and destroys the product, or the "space" defined by the quantized time and, identically, the quantized *numéraire*. To mark clearly the undulatory character of production, we shall call it emission (V).

Then we shall rapidly lead our reflexion through its natural stages, following the historical evolution of the phenomenon of production.

Initially, production is purely real. Money is excluded when the labourer produces for himself, in appropriating his own product. Real production has all the characteristics of an emission. This is the reason why productions-emissions still correspond in their most modern appearance to the definition of purely real emissions. We know however that in the absence of money the *numéraire*-dimension cannot be given to the product, which has then only the time-dimension, unable to provide a unit of measure common to the various products (VI).

It is well known that bank emissions do not constitute the first apparition of money by far. However, it is usually thought that for centuries money was initially material, therefore distinct from modern currencies. This is not the case. Well before the generalization of the wage-regime, therefore well before industrial revolutions, money was already commonly exchanged against the product of labour: the first monetary wages appeared in the products market and not in the producing services market.

It is worth pausing a while on the proposition we have just stated. When we observe economic events with the "eye" instead of using the mind, we conclude without hesitation that the exchange of a good against money is an operation between two goods, even if one of those goods is the result of current production. If the analysis is based on this starting point, it can only miss the specificity of money. How can we be surprised then by the radical incapacity of theories to integrate money in the world of real magnitudes? Reality is far subtler. The exchange of money is ambiguous. If the good sold is a new product, logic cannot *a priori* rule out the possibility of a completely different interpretation of the exchange: instead of being carried out between a real good and a monetary good, it could be that the exchange takes place between the real form of the new product and its monetary form; in that case, the operation does not imply, in spite of appearances, two distinct goods, *but the same good under its two forms*.

As one might suspect, it is the subtle interpretation that will be confirmed; money can be introduced or "integrated" only because goods are products and because producers are changing them into other products: these therefore go through the money form, the undifferentiated form of all products. In those conditions, if we add money to the n produced goods available on the markets, money is not an additional good but the general equivalent of the n real goods. Thus, it is not necessary to have the wage-regime in order to have money. Monetary exchanges have existed since the beginning of societies; but ever since the start, centuries before the birth of enterprises could be talked of, money was distinguished from real goods, precisely because it was, as today, their nominal form, their mould. And throughout history, one operation only has been able to cast real goods into money: production. It is therefore simplistic to represent the exchange between money and real goods as an event defined in the products market, even if the products are only actually sold in this market: the operation goes back to the act of production, where it defines the conversion of real goods into their monetary form.

To simplify let us base the analysis on the wage-regime in the strict sense. Material in appearance, gold currency or silver currency is in reality issued in a circular flow, the wage circuit. Here again, laziness of mind would talk of movements of gold or silver between firms and workers. True enough a movement in both directions would be taken into account; but, precisely, this would overlook that the two flows are connected and constitute a single one. The analysis is starting to grasp its object as soon as it acknowledges the unity of the flow, to define it as Adam Smith did: it is a "turning wheel", the "great wheel of circulation". From then on, the "spatial" movement is only the surface of the event, which in reality is expressed by the emission of a wave, a back-and-forth movement in one thrust. *Workers do not obtain money distinct from the product but as the nominal form of their product*: therefore, gold and silver are implicated in the operation only as far as they are themselves part of the product; and, even then, they define the real product and not its nominal form. In no way will any part of the monetary gold or silver pass into the new product. The introduction of the so-called material money in the act of production is fundamentally identical to the "circulation" of any kind of money, even completely dematerialized (like bank money): it leads to the bi-partitioning of the real emission, human labour. Being a complete monetary emission, the payment of wages is a half real-emission.

Through the intermediary of a firm, a worker issues his product "on himself", but he obtains it firstly in the monetary mould. The material substance of money recedes to make way for the new product, which alone defines the "purchasing power" of wages. In conjunction, the spending of wages is a half real emission, even though it is a complete monetary emission. The two half real emissions form a unit; they are complementary. We shall discover therefore that the spending of wages quantizes a time interval and a *numéraire* exactly identical to the time interval and to the *numéraire* already quantized by the payment of wages. The identity of the two half operations means their *simultaneity* – subsequent to the payment of wages (in the producing services market), the spending of wages (in the products market) – is logically subjected to the *law of retroactivity*, to take effect at the very same moment of the initial payment of workers (VII).

The rigorous observer sees therefore that money finds its fundamental explanation and its complete form even before the intervention of banks. Banks would never have been able to start issuing if, at all times, human labour had not already defined a complete emission. This proposition is all the more powerful that the converse is obviously not true; real emissions are autonomous: they do not presuppose the existence of monetary emissions (except, as we know, in relation with the measure of the product). In perfect accordance with logic, the historical evolution happened over four (partially overlapping) stages:

- emissions were initially exclusively real emissions; it was the age of the labouring man, consuming his own product with his family and inside the "clan";
- then money was introduced by men, in the exact measure as they were giving away their product against the product of someone else's labour; at this stage, money is indifferently material money or bank money (as it was later to be) because the *materiality* of money stays outside of the transaction;
- then firms were created to organize human labour and its division; again, the payment of wages is identically the same whether it is carried out in material money or in bank money;
- finally banks have monopolized monetary emissions; now, any intervention of money in the act of production is carried out in bank money, a perfectly dematerialized money; useless in the operations where it was like suspended, since it was not involved in them, the materiality of money has finally disappeared and money has become what it always was, and finds its "body" in the new product; any previous matter was cast in the "monetary circulation" fictitiously, by the effect of a wrong reasoning.

The result is that the emission of bank money is the union of two stages: as a pure number or *numéraire*, money is actually created by banks; as a

product, or real money, it is solely issued by firms and, even more fundamentally, by the paid workers (VIII).

It will not be difficult to apply to bank money the analysis of the wage
circuit already developed in the study of the emission of the so-called
material money. Any emission of bank money is a half real emission and a
complete nominal emission: the rule is the same for any money. It is so also
in its second aspect: any monetary emission is a *nominal* circuit completed
at once. Finally, the union of the two half real emissions closes the circuit
of *real* money; the "body" of bank money, that is, the product, is created
and destroyed in the same operation, a complete real emission. The spending of wages taking place retroactively at the moment of their formation,
the circuit of real money is instantaneous, like the circuit of nominal
money (IX).

The explanation of the wage circuit will be concluded by a very simple representation, that of a sphere. The unique power of creation that banks have is to
empower themselves *ex nihilo* with an amount of money equal to zero, the
"zero sphere". That is already a lot because the zero sphere is the foundation
of nominal emissions. The emission of nominal money from the zero sphere
results in two nominal monies of an equal amount but of opposite sign: the
positive money and the negative money. But, since the emission of nominal
money merges with the half emission of real money (payment of wages), the
zero sphere is transformed into a representation of *real* money; the negative
money contains the product not yet sold, therefore the positive money is not
the simple measure of the domestic product but its definition. The monetary
income, of economic agents and of the nation, is the income *in money* and not
the measure of income in physical goods.

The distinction is quite clear. In a metre of fabric, the metre is the measure of the fabric; in one franc of product, on the contrary, the franc is the
product itself, the product "in the money" and not simply the monetary
measure of the product. We shall study carefully this radical distinction; it is
all the more useful because, in the public opinion that resonates even inside
the scientific community, monetary income is often considered as a claim to
real goods. In reality, money is the definition of the product: it is the milk
not the bottle.

To be convinced visually, we only need to split the zero sphere in two half-
spheres. Because of the production-emission, the two half-spheres undergo
opposite deformations; let us start with the "slices": the surface of one of
them is *carved out* (formation of the negative money); the surface of the
other one is *bulged* (formation of the positive money). At this stage, it would
suffice to join together the two halves to obtain again the unchanged zero
sphere. But the explanation has not reached its term yet. We still have to
take into account the product in physical goods and services. At the precise
moment the negative money appears, it receives the product, which fills up
the cavity. Finally, an even slice faces a bulging slice. The two half-spheres
can no longer be assembled without the complete sphere having a *positive*

outgrowth, the only tangible manifestation (and the only presence) of the domestic product.

Cast into wages, money is the unique domestic product: literally, all the sectors of activity in the economy have produced the same "item", units of money and nothing else. Production will arrive at the diversity of physical products only at a later stage, when monetary income will cease to exist. We shall have no difficulty to show that the spending of income is a destruction of money and that, initially replaced by nominal income, the product will eventually go back to its place, through the destruction of money. Strictly speaking, however, the product disappears *at the same time*, because it does not exist anymore except under the identity of useful and consumable goods, the "values in use" (X).

V. Production is a wave-like operation, an emission

In the introduction, we observed that production comes into being at the moment of its completion; before that it is nothing but a "work in progress"; then, at its exact conclusion in chronological time (the continuum), it is suddenly all done, an individual whole.

Production is a movement in time

We have already drawn attention, in order to criticise it, to the idea one is tempted to adopt that production is a "leap function". It is true that, nil until its achievement, production is completed at once, in one leap. However, we know that the leap function is only confirmed if the magnitude, once formed, is placed in time to be maintained there unchanged until the advent of a new leap that would increase or reduce it. Precisely, we know that this condition is not satisfied; production is an original phenomenon, because it is devoid of any inertia through time: it is by nature unable to maintain itself in any length of time, as short as it may be.

As a flow, no production has any future: it is entirely turned towards the past, which it travels back (up to its starting point) to come again instantly to its point of achievement.

This being a key element, we have to repeat it although it is already well established. It is absolutely impossible that production (the operation) should be a movement that, after its completion, is laid out in time. The reason is certain: as soon as production is ended in t_n, it is a movement in time defined by the instantaneous travel, "against time", of the interval separating instant t_n from instant t_0 of the beginning of the project. Instead of being chrono stationary, like the movements known up until now, production embraces at once the chronological time elapsed since it started. Since production goes back in time, it is obvious that it is not deposited on one point of time (Barrow's point) that it would follow in its flow towards the future; production is only a movement towards the past.

Production is a dual flow in continuous time, positive and negative

Defining the quantization of time (t_n, t_0), production cannot stop at instant t_0, because it is completed at the later instant t_n. We meet again the proposition formulated in the introduction: as a wave-like movement, production quantizes time (t_n, t_0) and simultaneously the opposite time (t_0, t_n). The production of individuals, firms and society as a whole, is a simple wave through time and this is why it cannot be carried or transported by the flow of time. Being a movement towards the past, production is identically a strict return to the present ("contemporaneous" to its completion).

If production, as a flow, is only brought about in an instant, is it not possible nevertheless to conceive the existence of its *result*, the product, during a positive, more or less lengthy period of time? Production cannot run in the flow of time, this is absolutely certain; but could the product follow the chronological flow, to disappear only on the day more or less distant when economic agents consume it *proprio sensu*? Is not the product like this table or any other object of the physical world, able to follow the flow of time to be found again in the same state (or slightly affected by "entropy" – but then nevertheless preserved in another state) at a certain date in the future?

Like production, the product has a strictly instantaneous existence

We have no difficulty imagining the product as a matter that, experience teaches us, has an (unlimited) duration. However, we must avoid confusing human production with the creation of the Universe. Let us not forget the truism according to which man cannot produce any physical matter. In reality, the product of man is not a matter at all. We even know what it is: quantized time (and *numéraire*). Being wave-like, production is a creation-destruction; that is to say that quantized time, i.e. the product, does not, by a single instant, survive production, which, in all certainty, is instantaneous. *Any product (in goods and services) disappears at the very instant it comes about.*

If a doubt persists, it is because modern man has no longer the experience of a directly real product; money is interposed. However, it is evident that the monetary product, income, is located in time, even if it disappears in the final purchase of products (a disappearance that will have to be established against the deeply rooted belief that income spending by some forms the income of others).

What then is the method to be used if we want to move from opinion to knowledge? We must study real production in the case of workers appropriating their own product. We shall demonstrate that the appropriation of the product is precisely its destruction as a product and its denaturation into a "utility" or "value in use". On this basis, we shall then show that the interposition of money does not modify the conclusion: even a monetary product will cease to exist at the precise moment it is formed.

VI. The direct appropriation of his own product by the worker

It is easier to understand the act of production if we analyse it until we isolate the elements that are integrated in a single whole.

Production is not material

To produce is firstly to conceive future results from existing raw materials. A production is first a *projection*.

However, in its final state, transformed with more or less success depending on the project, there is no doubt that matter remains itself; it is preserved in the process. In other words, production is not an enrichment of matter. Let us point out rather that some part of the treated matter is lost, in that it will not be found in the finished good.

It would be a mistake to view production as an addition of matter and the product as an "added matter". It would be as mistaken to talk of "added value". The mistake would be all the more serious that, money being left aside by assumption, value could only be defined "in" the good, like an axiological quality added on to the physical properties of the object. It is clear though that economic goods do not receive a second nature from their production; they do not contain an atom that is not material. The idea of the intrinsic value is a great naivety of the mind. No more than the gross product, is the finished product endowed with an "economic mass"; its mass was and is purely physical.

If the representation of an intrinsic value has prevailed among scientists from the beginning of our discipline, it is because production is not at all yet defined by stating the equality of the objects as "inputs" and "outputs" of the process; why launch a movement which *raison d'être* would be purely and simply to return (and with even a loss) the initial matter?

The reflection must therefore keep at a distance from two opposite mistakes: in fact, production does not bring any new mass; however, the produced good is, in a fundamental sense, distinct from the initial object.

The distinction cannot relate but to the form; the finished good does not have the same form as the raw material: production is precisely the transformation of matter. From this proposition, though obvious, the conclusion mentioned is strictly induced; the product disappears – as a product – at the moment production is completed: the product is finished at the precise moment it comes into existence.

To produce is to introduce matter into a utility-form

The projection may be viewed as the movement that introduces matter into an imaginary mould: gross matter is progressively poured in. The imprint of an imaginary form is given in one go to the object, when the mould is "filled up". We face again the quantum nature of the event, production being nothing more than the completion of a project, that is the sudden meeting, after a more or less long preparation, of matter and its imaginary form. At completion of the movement, the form is no longer imagined; it is the "negative" of a real object, the moulded matter, the instantaneous product.

The "value" of the product is its form

If its value is the definition of a product, it must be conceived of as a simple form. We are now far away from intrinsic value. An economic value is not a specific mass but the utility-form of a material mass. The economic value is not found in the object but, so to speak, *around* it.

Thus, we can conclude that the value or identically the product exists only if two conditions are satisfied:

- physical matter is poured into the projected form (the utility-form);
- physical matter is defined at the immediate contact with the utility-form.

However, the second condition is only satisfied at the very instant production is completed.

The destruction of the product at the instant of its formation is thus confirmed

As soon as it is filled up, the mould dissolves because imagination is replaced by reality. It would be funny to view the mould like an eggshell still stuck to a chick. As soon as the product is completed, it is consumed; language is revealing.

To sum up, it is important to distance one's thought from the two preconceptions according to which economic value is either an axiological matter or the "material form" of a physical matter. In reality, value is just the immaterial or imaginary form of physical matter. It is still true of course that, moulded into this form, matter has a new utility or an increased utility; but utility is a relation between object and human being, not a property, even formal, of the object.

The utility-form is not a "substance": it is immaterial

It is not surprising that the value-form was viewed by nineteenth-century economists as if it were a wrapping having a certain substance; otherwise they would not have been able to grasp it, even in thought. But, the value-form does not exist, except as a "utility-form". This verdict is trivial and we must strictly abide by it: matter "emerges" from production with a new utility, but without any fabric that would now clothe it.

An isolated worker completes his project slowly; as soon as it is done, the product is defined by the coinciding of imagination and reality, and disappears at once, the object deposited in time being a useful matter but just a matter and not a matter associated to an economic form. Even isolated, any human production (or any human labour) is a wave-like movement, creation-destruction of the product conceived at the instant of its completion.

Therefore, in spite of appearances, consumption is not an operation distinct from production. If, even in the common view, production precedes consumption, this is because consumption is considered essentially in its biological or technological meaning, the good being subjected to a "digestion", a deterioration and wear that may take a considerable time. It is perfectly true that an apple is eaten after, and sometimes well after, being picked. But, in itself, an apple is not a product, except for the Physiocrats. A wild apple is consumed in the same way as a cultivated fruit. Consumption is an economic concept only if it is related to a product: the destruction of the product-apple and not the digestion of the fruit-apple defines the consumption of the apple, in the exact economic meaning of its "negative production".

It is certain that any persisting doubt is lifted when the mind reaches a clear definition of the *product*. It is neither matter nor materialized labour: it is a quantum of time. In the same way as production is the action of covering instantly and in a "loop" the time of preparation of the product, the latter is created and destroyed by the same wave. This does not mean that the product is defined in a contradictory manner. It does exist in an instant, the matter moving at once to a higher degree of utility, the increase being only measured, in the absence of a *numéraire*, tautologically by the duration of the quantized time.

Let us remark right now that the introduction of the *numéraire* and the money-*numéraire* will not alter the conclusion; even numbers cannot constitute a cloth for the matter: the *numéraire*-form (or the money-form) will be the temporary definition of the product and not its lasting wrapping.

The instantaneity of the unique operation of production-consumption is verified in all conceivable cases, in particular in the wage-regime, even if remunerations are paid in a "material" money.

VII. The payment of wages in a so-called material (non-bank) money is a wave-like operation, as the spending of wages instantly prolongs their formation

As announced before, we are founding the analysis on the wage-regime in a restricted sense, in the way it has spread through industrial revolutions, by the separation between firms and workers.

The payment of wages is not a displacement of money

If induction were a direct reading of facts, whereas it is actually a reading of "theorized" facts, one observation would prevail at once: the injection of money into the payment of wages is an operation of pure conservation, the same money units being found intact in the hands of workers. Money is represented as a body or a matter moving through a (Euclidian) space; the distance between firms and workers is covered by the mobile (the species), which does not incur any "deformation" in this operation, which is purely its transportation.

In reality, a thoughtful theorist is stopped at once in his tracks. The exchange of money against labour has to be explained; it is not enough to just postulate it. It is true that this exchange is observed, who would deny it? But precisely, it has to be understood, to be grasped intellectually; otherwise, a nominal wage will remain a raw fact instead of becoming an experimental reality. If we merely say that a mass (material money) is exchanged against an activity (human labour), we amplify the problem instead of solving it. And it would be completely incongruous to rely on an alleged experience; no observer has ever witnessed an exchange between mass and activity, except in a mediocre mental representation, entirely fabricated. Any valid experimentation is the implementation of a theoretical question, an inquiry. Facts do not speak for themselves.

Wages are not the result of a money expenditure: they are the product of a labour expenditure

The method to follow is dictated by the strict logic of the emission. A worker issues the real product and his wages are the result of the emission. It is obvious that wages are substituted by the real product, the payment being in money and not in kind; nonetheless, wages are the product of the worker. Thus, the idea of the transportation of money in a predetermined space will disappear at once. Wages do not originate from an expenditure by firms but solely from labour, the expenditure, the effort, of wage-earners. Labour is an expenditure and it is the only expenditure that brings about income. This means that the emission of wages is based on the real emission: the worker issues his own product; but, instead of receiving it directly in kind, he obtains it *initially* in money.

Wages are taken from a zero mass, only the spending of wages – not their formation – is an exchange between money and product.

The formation of wages is an absolute exchange, the exchange of the product against itself

In modern studies, the exchange money-product is considered as a reciprocal relation; if money buys products, in the same movement products buy money; the purchase of money by products is actually stated in numerous articles and books. However, this is not a semantic issue but a fundamental problem. Depending on the answer, either we build the relative exchanges theory or, on the contrary, the absolute exchanges theory.

As we have just seen, facts settle the issue provided we ask them an intelligent question. It is not true that the formation of wages is an exchange of money against a product, because the product exists at the "exit" of the exchange and not at all at its "entry". Coming to life immediately in money, the product cannot be exchanged against money, except in the operation of the payment of wages: *the destruction of wages is a purchase, but the creation of wages, far from being a purchase, generates the incomes that will be cast in the purchases*. In the real world, we observe therefore two expenditures of opposite signs: the formation of wages (the first expenditure) is the absolute exchange, the *conversion*, of the real product into a monetary product; the expenditure of wages is the second absolute exchange, the monetary product being changed into the real product. *Money and product do not coexist either in the first expenditure or in the second*. If the product is a mass (it would be better to say that it is a space), we never observe the existence of the two masses face to face; on the contrary, the same mass is initially monetary (and in this, it is not real, it is not so "physically"), then real (which means that it is no longer monetary).

The emission of wages transforms the number-money into the product-money

The inductive truth complies with the theory of emission. Cast in the payment of wages, money is still a pure number; it becomes a *product-money* in the paid wages. If firms use a material money to pay wages, appearances will be deceptive: the monetary gold and silver used to pay the new productions have long ceased to exist as products; they were so only at the instant of the completion of their own production. From then on, material money is a "value in use". However, cast in the circuit, money is useful only as a number, a written number carried by any kind of matter, for example one same metal, which ensures the homogeneity of the concrete numbers cast by the various firms. In all rigour, money comes therefore to life at the precise instant it is formed in wages; before that, it is a collection of concrete and homogenous numbers.

Let us conclude this brief analysis of the so-called material money. The payment of wages defines a *real* emission because wages are identified with the product that they replace. More precisely, the formation of wages is a half real emission; the complementary half emission will come by the spending of wages. But what is the interval of time quantized by the expenditure of wages? It is defined by the "production time" of the real goods that wages replace. This results in a proposition that we shall analyse more in detail when dealing with bank money: defining the same movement of quantization of chronological time, the two half emissions are simultaneous, because the second one takes effect retroactively at the precise moment of the formation of the real product or, identically, of the payment of monetary wages.

But let us start by introducing bank money.

VIII. Being merged with the emission of wages and more deeply with the emission of the product, the emission of bank money starts from a pure collection of homogenous numbers or units of nominal money

Money creations are not primitively the act of banks, because any payment of wages, in any money, is a money creation. Just like the emission of wages is the form of the real emission, it is right to say that money is present in the wave-like movement defined by every act of production, including the case of the activity of an isolated worker, which is, in the past or today, outside the wage-regime in the strict sense. A worker who sells his product neither in the producing services market nor in the products market is nevertheless an issuer; however, the emission of the product is in itself a monetary phenomenon. Banks arise therefore in a world where emissions are already numerous since any productive activity – any human labour – is a perfect emission. The idea according to which money can logically be created only by banks, any non-bank money being subjected to the law of conservation – nothing is created and nothing is lost – a completely false idea, derives its apparent legitimacy from a bad conception of bank money.

In fact, money issued by banks is only the faithful image of the money created in the economy, outside of banks. The only important difference, between these currencies, concerns capital, financial and real, which, as we shall see, cannot be net for the whole society, unless it is formed in bank money. An economy devoid of bank money could not accumulate for itself any capital, unless it were a capital both positive and negative, a pure relation between lenders and borrowers. It is still premature to talk about capital. However, as far as money and monetary incomes are concerned, bank emissions are only the "resumption" of real emissions, defined by all the acts of production, i.e. the labour expended in all sectors of the economy.

Let us explain the emission from a *deposit bank*. In all logic, we must first demonstrate that the bank has pre-existing money; otherwise, it could not act. But presupposed money should in no way be confused with the money issued, because the emission would be given in a *petitio principii* or in a vicious circle. The money that the bank must have at its disposal from the beginning is a collection of units of account. However, the paralogism is not avoided; this is because a concrete unit of account, capable of becoming a money, is already so, especially because in reality no separation between the two aspects of money, unit of payment and unit of account, can be observed. Only one way out is left open: we must establish that the bank can freely create, ex nihilo, a zero money. Based on the zero money, reasoning will lead to positive money.

The emission of bank money is first of all the emission of a word or a promise by the banks

It is quite remarkable that, to succeed in its project, the bank only needs to be endowed with one, single initial power, the ability to speak. The bank speaks;

it utters, *emits*, a word. Let us notice carefully that the francs are first issued in words, which is logically possible even before the francs exist: they are *promised*. It is true that we must proceed by following strictly the inner balance of the argument; it would be wrong to attribute a cause or an object to the indebtedness of the bank. It is in fact a *spontaneous* indebtedness; if it were not, it would lose any explanatory power, because the bank would then be submitted to the obligation of payment and it could not, in the same operation, get both into debt and pay. But how can we integrate the necessary spontaneity of the operation into the very foundation of the analysis? This is very simple. *It is imperative to assume that (in the emission) the bank does not purchase and does not give anything to its client.* Not only is this condition far from being artificial but it is satisfied daily in all the banking operations of *intermediation*. We shall soon see that *all* banking operations are intermediations.

We can now move a step further. The bank tells its client "I owe you x francs" and it adds "you owe me x francs": the "reciprocal debt" is the definition of the spontaneity of the operation.

We have already reached the last step. To ensure that the circle defined by the emission of the "word from the bank" does not turn into a short-circuit, it is necessary and sufficient that the exchange of promises (about the same object) involves *the payment of a third party*, credited by the bank's client.

The analysis of the bank emission is completed; if it seems unfinished, the reason resides in a well-known fact: bank money is only finalized in its symbiosis with real money issued by the economy in the production operations. If we separate intellectually what is unified in reality, we perceive bank money as a simple promise, positive for the "payee" and negative for the "payer".

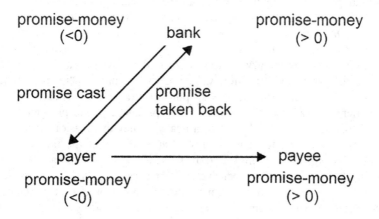

Figure 4.1 The bank emission

In the way we have presented it, the bank emission is indeed a wave-like movement since, in the same operation, the same promise is cast to the "payer" and taken back. (Let us get rid of a mistake that might come up; it might seem that the client of the bank has to give back the promise only *later*; but if it were so this would have an unacceptable logical consequence: the bank would have had actually paid whereas it only has promised to do so. The correct analysis is circular: the promise that is cast is only the promise that is taken back; the two promises exist one for the other and each one of them would fall through if the other one was not present simultaneously). This perfect emission leaves the following marks: a positive amount of promise-money for the payee; the same, but negative, amount for the payer.

At the end of the introduction, we emphasized the importance of negative numbers in economics. Here we meet them for the first time in the emission of money. It is worth pausing and reflecting on this, even briefly, the more so because negative numbers always seem a bit strange. The promise addressed to the payee is instantly taken back from the payer. However, it is obvious that the promise is actually taken from an amount of zero since the payer never had it before (it is formed immediately on the third party). The rest is only a question of simple deduction: a positive promise-money taken from a zero amount results in a negative promise-money.

Tautologically, the amount of promise-money issued is both positive and negative in the deposit bank, where we can check that the operation complies with the principles of any emission, the creation and the destruction in the same action of the same object.

The only remaining difficulty concerns the *fiduciary* nature of the money thus created; it is a *promise*. But logic is more demanding; we have to explain the actual payment, which prevents us from limiting ourselves to the promised payment. Precisely, *bank money cannot exist by itself; it only takes effect when merging with real money in the operations of production.*

In the analysis of the emission of wages in material money, we have observed that no (monetary) matter is moved in the operation as workers receive their own product in money. This is to say that the "intrinsic matter" of non-banking money is so to speak "put into brackets"; it is used neither in the payment of wages nor in the following purchase of the product through the expenditure of wages. The use of a heavy money in emissions-productions is therefore a pure waste. It is on this precise point that the intervention of banks is efficient: since money is only present in the remunerations already carried out, it is uselessly expensive to cast a precious value in use in the payments, i.e. the emissions that form and destroy income; it is sufficient and far cheaper to cast in the emissions a pure promise of money, since the money formed in wages is solely created by workers (Wr) in an operation of the set Wr onto the set Wr.

Accordingly, we understand easily the transformation of promise-money into actual money itself.

Transformation of the promise of money into actual money

The bank promise is distinct from money for a precise reason; as a promise, money is not yet a good. That is to say, in itself the promise is not a real object, it is the promise of an object: the promise is a purely nominal magnitude. Only one event must happen in order for the promise to become money: it must be "filled in" with a real object. *The injection of a material object into the bank promise is precisely observed in the emission of the product by workers.* Having the identity of a worker, the payee receives from firms the product in the form of a bank promise. It follows that the promise is no longer a nominal magnitude but a real object, the product contained in the form issued by banks.

Let us go back briefly to the demonstration that we have just given because it brings some important knowledge: banks cannot, by themselves alone, create money. We knew it already regarding real money, the unique source of which is human labour. Banks do produce real money to the extent of the workers they employ. We must therefore respect the elementary distinction between banks as firms and banks as issuers. The cost of the emission in human labour is not just negligible; it is absolutely nil. The reason is that the emission has the consequence of establishing a lender-borrower relationship: the cost of the operation is therefore entirely borne by the financial market. Being a zero-cost operation, the emission brings also a zero *real* money.

Now we can generalize the conclusion to *nominal* money. It would seem that banks create the nominal money transformed into real money by firms (including marginally the banks). In reality, even nominal money is created by firms, meaning by the workers they employ. The evidence is in the generation of money from the promises of money. Banks are perfectly able, like any person, to produce words; on the other hand, unlike "ordinary" people, they can set in motion the circuit of promises through the triangle of which they are the summit, the others being the client and his correspondent. In so doing, banks raise, face to face, an amount of positive promise-money at the credited agent and an amount of negative one at the debited agent. Money is not yet born (the *logic* of the events is not completed even though the *chronology* is). And the distinction real-nominal is not yet applied, because nominal money is a money and not a promise: by issuing their promises, banks do not give birth to any money, even a nominal one.

We have to conclude that the two monies are not just born at the same time but also from one single action: the labour of human beings. As soon as the physical product is deposited into the negative promise-money formed in the firm, money is fully constituted; it is no longer a promise. At the moment the bank promise finds its object in the (new) product, it is replaced by money proper. The mutation of promises into money is the result of labour, it is not at all the consequence of the bank emission.

The money issued in production is a nominal and real magnitude; nominal money is a pure form; real money is the product contained inside the form

The relation money-product may be expressed in terms of form and content. Bank money is a pure form born from the bank emission merged with the real emission that, alone, brings the product contained within this form. *Form and content are given at one go* – it is therefore inconceivable that the form should stay empty during a certain length of time -, the conjoint emission of bank money (the "mould" of the product) and real money (the product instantly deposited in the mould). Finally, any money created by banks is in reality issued in the operations of production, so that the body of any bank money – that is to say any bank money as far as it is accounted for in the assets of any agent – is exclusively caused by the real emissions, which, as a whole, define the national product.

The very common belief that banks are able to add assets (monetary ones, of course) to the assets created by production is illogical. Only one way is left open in this respect: it is logically possible that the monetary forms are created additively. Let us be precise about what is the exact issue here, one that we shall meet again when studying inflation. Before carrying out a somewhat deeper examination, we could think that the monetary assets and the real assets exist separately from each other. Under these conditions, we could conceive of the autonomous creation of monetary assets that would go on looking for real assets (on the goods and securities markets), in the hope of carrying out exchanges with them. If the available real assets were not in sufficient number, we might imagine that the "unsatisfied" monetary assets could stimulate domestic production; the increased employment would bring new real assets able to enter into a partnership with the hitherto frustrated monetary assets. Such ideas have been around for more than two centuries and had already been vigorously opposed by David Ricardo in his severe criticism of Jeremy Bentham's theory. Today this question has been settled. Whoever has knowledge of the theory of emissions knows that monetary and real assets are always born in a perfect merger; no monetary asset can ever chase or seek a real asset. Each unit of bank money is immediately born with its body, only the origin of the form (a nominal magnitude created by banks and production) and the product (a real magnitude born solely from production) are partially disjointed. The two emissions, nominal and real, are nevertheless perfectly homogeneous, because right from the beginning they constitute one single emission; money is born instantly with its body, the domestic product, the result of the real emission.

The union of the product-content with the money-form defines income, the existence of which is positive over time

The intercession of money in the act of production, whether the monetary units are of a banking or a material nature, results in the formation of an income that is set in time. It is of the highest interest to note, at every useful opportunity, that political economy would not be concerned with income, its formation and its distribution, if these magnitudes could not be grasped *in time*. However, without money, income has only an instantaneous and shapeless existence. Money is therefore the central object, the heart of our discipline. Monetary incomes, and them alone, are deposited in the continuum, where they can be observed in order for them to be "formalized".

Nevertheless, the law always applies: any income, even a monetary one, only exists in the space of an instant. In conclusion of the brief examination of material money we have announced, in relation with bank money, the definitive dispelling of this apparent dilemma.

IX. A monetary income is set in a positive length of time even though it obeys the fundamental law ruling over any income: it only "lasts" during an instant

In the absence of money, income is purely instantaneous

Let us go back only briefly to the purely real income created in an economy where money would be present neither in the producing services market nor on the goods and securities market. In this case, the product is a one-dimensional space, because the monetary dimension is lacking. We have then the tautological equivalence between production and product; each particular production quantizes a time that is specific to it. Since the operation of production is a wave – a movement from the present to the past and back to the present – it is logically unable to cast its result in chronological time. We induce from this that the product, or identically income, does have a unique instantaneous existence, if money is set aside.

Intuition, by the way, corroborates this conclusion since the product is essentially a suspended value in use and that state cannot be granted to it except in very special conditions; any appropriated product is already a constituted and efficient value in use, a utility; in order to grasp an object that is on the point of becoming a value in use, but is a product, the analysis must be held in very narrow limits: the product is formed at once at the end of a production process and an instant later it is already a pure value in use. We understand therefore that the product gets its specific identity as a "value in exchange" at the precise moment when the production process is completed.

Money, especially bank money, brings on the second dimension of the product.

Money, especially bank money, confers a positive duration to income

This is so because monetary wages have the product (of workers) as a "body". Wages are altogether real products and money or *numéraire*. As a real product, wages have the dimension of the time quantized by production; as money, wages are a collection of concrete numbers. It is essential not to lose sight of the fact that the two dimensions are united to define the product in money; it is indeed one same and unique space with two equivalent dimensions. Thus, as soon as the money cast in the final purchases stops being a product-money to become a pure number-money, the product in money itself ceases to exist, as one of its dimensions (and let us repeat it, they are both necessary) has been dropped.

The question to be solved is then clearly formulated. When does money cease to identify with the product? Even though the answer is formally the same for any money, bank species provide an easier solution, because bank money disappears purely and simply as soon as it ceases to coincide with the product. Material money remains after its expenditure in the final purchases; in this regard, one might therefore think *a priori* that the preservation of money corresponds to an equal preservation of the product. We know well that, in reality, it is as matter and not as money that material money survives after its expenditure. However, the distinction requires a certain intellectual discipline. On the side of bank money, the reasoning is much easier; there is no question of the monetary matter surviving money, which is no longer material at any stage. The only problem is therefore to assign money the date of its "death". As soon as it is known that money dies at a precise instant, it will be obvious that at this instant money ceases to identify with the product (even if the product, *stricto sensu*, must disappear simultaneously).

The solution that comes first to the mind is that of the "deposit" in time of the product-money or of monetary income. It is inconceivable that money should not be deposited in time, for the simple reason that it is inconceivable that it should not be deposited in the (issuing) bank during a perceivable and measurable duration. At the instant of its birth, income is deposited on a "point of time", the Barrow point, that it follows in its flow, until the moment wages are spent. Not only does this first-hand analysis seem plausible but bank money offers a very beautiful confirmation. Indeed, if wages were spent and destroyed at the instant of their formation, the bank emission would not be a wave but a vicious circle: workers would be credited and debited of the same amount and in the same movement. The payment of wages can be associated to the real emission only *if the credited amount is net among workers' assets*. The debit of workers in the accounts of the bank can only take place later.

However, the final word has not yet been said. We are no longer clueless about how it all ends up. But let us sum up our findings because they are in fundamental opposition to the dominant teaching. It is important to distinguish two types of durations.

1   The duration of a created income: it is clear that this duration is variable depending on the income, of the various economic agents and even of one given agent; it is measured by the persistence of the claim of workers on banks.

2   The duration of the formation of a given income: here it is the length of time that elapses between the moment when production starts and the moment it is completed.

Unlike durations of type 1, which depend on how the agents freely behave, durations of type 2 are standardized by the rhythm or the frequency of the payment of wages. If wages are always paid at the end of the current month, all the periods of production are calendar months, the production of any worker being started at the beginning of the month and completed at the end, even if the purely physical product is to be available on the market only much later (like the very first work to build an atomic pile). In fact, the first results of "long term" labour are bought right at the moment of their completion at the end of each month, the final purchases being then, as we shall soon confirm, carried out through the intermediation of the financial market.

However, it is the durations of type 1 that is involved in the specific problem we are dealing with at the moment. Income holders keep it for a more or less long time: they save it instead of consuming it immediately. This time the duration is totally independent of the production time, as the income of one month may be saved for any length of time, at the choice of its holder. All this is obvious. The problem only becomes interesting when one analyses the time-dimension of the final purchase, whatever the date of this event. The mistake that presents itself with strength is already well known; one does not doubt, initially, that unlike the expenditures forming income, consumption expenditures or income-destroying expenditures are "Poisson events", because, apparently, they only take place in a zero-length of time, in an instant.

One can only discern the mistake if one agrees to inquire into the nature of the final purchase: income expenditure is an *emission*, exactly like income formation. One is then very close to the correct analysis, according to which the payment of wages *breaks the real emission into two half-emissions*, the second being precisely defined by the income expenditure. One can induce that, whatever the date it takes place, the final purchase relates to the period of production, the same one that already defines the initial emission, the payment of wages. Duration 1 is therefore replaced by duration 2, which is the time-dimension of both the positive emission of wages and their negative emission, the selling of the product.

Now the conclusion is at hand. We meet again the analysis of the introduction: the two quantized times, one by the payment of wages and the other by their expenditure, are superimposed; it necessarily ensues that monetary income will have not existed beyond the instant of its creation. Even though workers are debited "later", their debtor payment is efficient because it takes effect from their initial creditor payment. The debtor recording "goes back" in time until it coincides with the corresponding creditor recording. Thus, the two true statements are both preserved; the expenditure of income is *at first posterior*; however, *it takes effect retroactively*, so that, in the last analysis, it is immediate. Through the superimposition of the second half-emission on the first one, the claim acquired by workers on banks finds its objective counterpart, right at the start, in the cancellation of this claim, following the sale of the product: nothing could show more clearly the true role of banks; they cast a real money, the product in its monetary form, on the persons who thus receive right from the start their own product, even if it is true that they end up converting the monetary product, in order to obtain the (same) product in kind.

To conclude the analysis of the formation-expenditure of wages, we propose a simple graph, where it appears clearly and to the naked eye, so to speak, that the social product is really and uniquely a sum of money.

X. Domestic production represented by the "zero-sphere": the product is deposited in time only under the identity of bank money

We have acknowledged the existence of "zero-money" as the foundation of money creation by banks. Considered in their creative function, banks have at their disposal, at any time, a "sum" of zero units of money. The reason is that, let us repeat it, money comes into existence from a simple promise. Banks are therefore naturally able to create a sum of money of zero; and this is enough because any positive money originates from the zero money.

The initial endowment of banks is the zero money

Let us offer again the rigorous demonstration of the ability of banks to create a zero money. It is agreed that the creation of the zero money is not carried out during a "first stage", chronologically distinct from the creation of positive money. What has to be demonstrated is something completely different: within the emission of positive money, the part played by the activity of banks ends at a zero money that they are able to generate *ex nihilo*, whereas the positive money comes from domestic production only. Without any doubt, banks are able to cast their "promises"; this is the first point. However, in the circuit of bank emission, the promises are formed both negatively and positively, depending on the role under consideration. Right from their formation, the promises are transformed into money, *proprio sensu*, by the product being incorporated in them. In the result thus obtained, the perfectly constituted money is absolutely nil within the bank as well as in the economy: everywhere, it is both positive and negative for the same amount. Nevertheless, money is present in its whole desired dimension because the transactions on all markets can, from now on, be carried out in money. Banks create freely a zero amount of money because they create freely the bank promises that are automatically transformed into (a zero) money.

Let us represent the zero money by the "zero-sphere" that we shall divide at once into its two halves.

Graphic representation of the positive units of money issued from the zero money

Our objective is to shape the surface of the section of each half-sphere in order to show exactly the result of domestic production. Each half-sphere held by firms is hollowed out; a (spherical) hole is cut out by an amount equal to the x units paid in wages.

The half-sphere held by workers is dome-shaped; the (spherical) dome that appears there is the amount, equal to x units of money, of direct and indirect (social benefits) salaries created in the period.

We can use this representation right now to confirm the precise role of banks in the creation of money. In any case, the real product does not come from deposit banks, which are considered here only as issuing entities and not as firms. The important question is the following: are banks able to create *net* monetary assets? The answer can be seen directly in the two half-spheres. Monetary creation generates the two opposite changes in shape, the cavity and the bump. We only need to reassemble the sphere, to see that *after* the creation of money and *before* the payment of wages, the amount of money created is nil because the zero-sphere is strictly preserved in its original state.

Even if it is true that, at the moment it is issued, bank money is at once an asset, this does not result from the activity of banks. The little positive half-sphere (wage-incomes) and the little negative half-sphere (the debts incurred correlatively by firms) fit together perfectly when we reassemble the two half-spheres. And, let us repeat it, this reunion of the two half-spheres is given before the payment of the income arising out of production and paid in bank money. Even though income is still fully present, the monetary assets constitute a zero sum for the community as a whole since the zero-sphere does not show any positive "bulge".

Money is an asset because it absorbs, in the strongest possible sense, it "imbibes" the real product of the nation. Let us indeed bring in the real product of wage-earners. It comes into being in the negative money created in the firm. We can infer that all the hollow parts are filled up at once and that the shape of the half-sphere held by all firms eventually stays the same. The absorption of the physical product fills up the cavity and the half-sphere is unmodified, without any reshaping.

 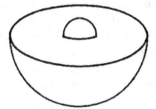

Figure 4.2 The two half-spheres of monetary creation

Let us stay for a while in this place that we have just browsed; it is probably the right time to dispel the "thickest" confusion affecting and clouding economics. Academics are no better accustomed than the general public to figure out flows; by far, they prefer to process tangible data. When they consider studying money in this way, especially in its relationship with real goods, they imagine the coexistence, side by side, of goods from the two categories.

With this starting point, the whole deduction is predetermined, whatever the degree of sophistication it may reach in the mathematical or "literary" development. Everything is lost right from the beginning. Being exchanged (in the mind) against the product in goods and services, money must lend itself to the construction of a series of relations of equivalence, the terms of which are nominal magnitudes on the one hand and real magnitudes on the other hand. One must therefore say that this particular amount of money is worth that particular real good, the latter being apprehended in its physical dimensions.

However, this value relationship has no reality in the world we live in: money and goods do not entertain any relation of any sort (except the philosophical relation of identity) since they constitute a unique reality, one sole magnitude which property is precisely to be composed of the two, nominal and real, aspects. Before casting the (new) product into the monetary cavity, we can see clearly, with this very simple representation, that money does not exist yet as a positive magnitude; it is therefore too early to intend comparing it to any kind of physical object. And the comparison cannot either succeed later, when real goods are already cast into the monetary cavities; because the two terms then constitute only one entity.

We understand that money is never the measure of real goods, unless it is the tautological measure of the real goods already transformed into money: in "counting" the units of money – the number of money units created in the payment of wages – it is the product that is counted since it comes into being in the monetary shape. Money never measures a real good as distinct from or separated from money: in the end, money is counted, that is all. All the theories that aspire to compare wages to the product of wage-earners are looking at a problem that is fundamentally incorrect, non-existent. Monetary wages *are* the real product.

We can clearly see the naivety of comparing the "performances" if we ask the following question: how can we be sure that the product of workers will find enough room in the monetary cavities? Conversely, is it not possible that the product might be bigger than the cavities and, therefore, that it may "overflow"? These two opposite worries are as futile as each other; the reason is that money and the product are comparable dimensions (belonging to the same measurement space) only when they are united as one single, same reality: it is therefore unthinkable that the product could either be bigger or smaller than the negative money created in the payment of wage-earners. This allows us to go back to developing the main explanation, in order to finalize the demonstration that *the unique product of the domestic economy is, in every period, a sum of money.*

If we intend, on the contrary, to list the goods and services produced, we just make a list and nothing more; it is logically impossible to sum up or aggregate the various physical products, because they are only heterogeneous and dissimilar "values in use". Science, which only deals with what is "quantifiable", embraces the product in its perfect uniformity, as it solely exists in the monetary cavities. After that, it is too late.

Facing the half-sphere in F (the set of firms), which cavities are immediately filled up by the product of wage-earners, the positive money will remain: during the whole time when physical product is kept deposited within negative money, wage-earners hold the zero half-sphere to which has been added the bulge of positive money, equal to the x units of wages that have been issued.

The following experience is extremely instructive. We reconstitute again the zero sphere by fitting together the two half-spheres and we observe that it is the whole sphere that is subjected to a bulge or an increment, the addition of the x amount of positive money (see Figure 4.3).

Melted into the monetary cavities, the physical product disappears in-there without any trace; the unique reality of domestic production – but it is indeed a perfectly tangible reality – is the increment of the whole zero-sphere: all the workers of the country produce only one "item", units of money.

As simple as it may be, the representation of the zero-sphere is the visible evidence of the error of the four common conceptions of money, already considerably weakened by their incoherent cohabitation in people's and pseudo-scientific mind.

The four fundamental errors of the common conceptions of money

First erroneous notion: money is just the measure of the product

It would therefore not belong itself to the category of products. In 3kg of nails, we don't have nails and in addition kilograms, because the measure of the nails does not belong to the category of the nails: it is not a nail. The case

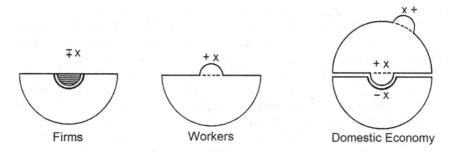

Figure 4.3 Production as a net increase in income

being considered the same, it would be said that in 3 francs of nails we don't have both the nails and the francs, the latter being only the instrument of the (economic) measure of the nails. But the parallel is spurious, because, in a monetary economy, no physical product is a value in use before being bought.

During the first phase of its existence, the physical product is replaced by the money born from its cost of production. Therefore, together with the other goods, the nails are first "lodged within the money", in the negative money the creation of which defines production. The creation of x units of money, the social cost of the production, is both positive and negative. In the negative money is found the whole product, including the nails; conversely, the x units of positive money are the only value in use created by the economy since the physical goods still have a zero value in use, being "sucked" into the negative money. The expenditure of the x francs, including the 3 francs to buy the nails, leads to the second phase of the existence of the physical goods which are at last positive values in use. Dislodged from the negative money by the purchase, the product is a value in use replacing money, which is at once obliterated, since the x units of positive money collide with the x units of negative money. The zero-sphere is simply reconstituted in its initial state: it has lost its positive bulge. Expelled from the zero-sphere, the physical goods have fallen into the "consumption sphere".

Therefore, during all their existence, the three francs are not the simple measure of the nails but are indeed their *alter ego*. In the first phase, the nails are formed in money, and in the second phase, the three francs are transformed into nails. It is true indeed that the *francs* do not *prolong* the nails. Nevertheless, the francs are not the simple measuring device of the nails: they *identify* with the nails until the moment the francs give way to the "nails in nails", whereas they were in francs up to then.

Second erroneous notion: money is the counterpart of the product

Money belongs to the category of products, but it would be an earlier product (on a first scale) facing the current products (placed on the second scale of the two-arms balance). The error comes to the fore with a very simple observation. If money were an earlier good given for a current good, the payment of wages would be a purchase in the same way as the expenditure of wages.

However, in the payment of wages, firms could purchase the new product only if it were formed first in the hands of workers; we have remarked already that this is not the case: the product forms directly in the firm. A more sophisticated argument may be given in the same direction. If all the monetary payments were purchases, banks could not create any money and purchases would all be eradicated, at least the purchases carried out in bank money, which however, as we know, do exist.

The creation of money can be positive only if it *brings on income*; it would not be enough that it would carry it. If the operation were done in the conservation of income, the negative money would be immediately filled in by the positive money and the physical product could never "enter" the money; under these conditions, any creation of money would be nil. Only the introduction of the product into money enables the separate existence of positive and of negative bank money. Once the two monies are cohabitating right from the beginning, they will fight against each other and will at once cancel each other out. In factual reality, money is not the counterpart or the counter value of the new product but its very definition. The physical product being first forced into the negative money, positive money is not its representation but its "presentation": monetary wages are the only presence of the product in the whole country.

Third erroneous notion: money is a claim to the product

This error is not as deep as the previous ones; in a sense, money is indeed a right to collect the product. However, it is a very peculiar right, unknown in any other area. Usually, a claim on an object supposes the positive existence of this object; otherwise, the right or claim is itself nil, at least in its effect. In the present case, the object is totally annulled in the negative money; but the right is nevertheless positive, even in its effect.

Therefore, the positive money is not a claim to the product; it is the product itself. Let us repeat it tirelessly, society produces money and it produces nothing else, until money disappears; then it will be said that society produces physical goods and services and nothing else. It will never be the case that society produces both physical goods and, conversely, units of monetary income.

The notion that money is a claim to the product is nearly correct for another reason. When we study the theory of capital, we shall see that financial capital is a money born from the destruction of an income through saving. In this sense, money is a claim to an income. The essential criticism remains: money is never a claim to the product. Money is a claim to the product only as far as it is a claim to a (future) income, therefore a claim to a future money.

Fourth erroneous notion: money is a nominal magnitude, facing real magnitudes

This error is known under the name of nominalism or numeralism. Money would simply be a name or a number that would have an autonomous existence, detached from the thing designated or from the object counted. Money would be in search of the product that it would only meet in the exchanges. The naivety of separating nominal from real becomes conspicuous with the consequent impossibility to bring them together.

Kept at a distance from each other, the name and the product are condemned to stay apart, each in its realm, without any practical or intellectual operation capable of casting money onto the product nor the product onto money: this is *dichotomy* in its most perfect state. In actual fact, money is indeed a nominal magnitude but, this is now well established, it is from its inception associated to the product, indissolubly, like the form to its content. Nominal wages are identified to the real product because the physical product is one with the negative money. The analysis does not apply to two distinct objects, but to one unique object the presence of which is duplicated; the product materializes first in money – it thus fills in the monetary cavities and gives rise to the positive bulge of the zero-sphere – and a second time in kind – the physical product being detached from money as soon as the zero-sphere loses its increment.

No error is perfect; therefore, each of the four errors gives way to a grain of truth. Let us spell out the four "grains".

MONEY IS THE MEASURE OF THE PRODUCT

If the product were not the integration of a + and a – within the zero-sphere – it would not be measurable. The negative quantity appears in the banking emission. It immediately gets as a counterpart, and therefore as a counter value, the totality of the physical goods and services produced by wage-earners.

The relation of equivalence is certain: wage-earners receive their own product under the species of the positive money created in the bank emission, a money that is identical (but for the sign) to the correlative negative money. We can induce that the negative money and the corresponding physical product neutralize each other; they are born additive to each other (resulting from the same emission, therefore being homogeneous) and their sum is nil. The relation of equivalence, which defines the measure, has, for its two terms, two purely physical magnitudes: on one side the number-money and on the other side the matter-product. Nothing could bring closer those two magnitudes if they were not born in the same measurement space: but human labour is the only origin for both of them since the negative number-money can only be generated by the intervention of money within the real emission.

In his controversy with Henri Poincaré, Léon Walras intuited the original nature of measurement in economics. Usually, we do not measure with numbers but with dimensions that are "counted" in numbers (x units of length, mass, volume, etc.); but *the products do not have any economic dimension, except for the quantized time and numéraire.*

Thus, the number is itself a dimension of the object and it is no longer just the numbering of a dimension of the object. The monetary emission changes the product into a number, the sum of the money units (each elementary unit being the "concrete" number 1) formed in wages. This sum is equivalent to the product, not that the product and the sum of wages would have a common dimension, but, more intimately, because these two magnitudes *are* a unique dimension, the quantized *numéraire*. The relation of equivalence is here the strongest that can be conceived of, it is *an identity*.

Nominal wages are the domestic product's identity; they are therefore equal or equivalent to the product because they are equal or equivalent to themselves.

MONEY IS THE COUNTERPART OF THE PRODUCT

This is true, not in the simultaneity, but through time. Money is not additional to the product; it is therefore really this product under the form of an equivalent. Nevertheless, money is not in "parallel" with the product; in this instance, the equivalent replaces the product, it does not coexist with it. As long as the zero-sphere remains endowed with an increment, money exists alone, the physical product being an integral part of the zero-sphere. Money is nevertheless the counterpart of the product, in a new sense: it suffices that money disappears for the product to appear.

MONEY IS A CLAIM TO THE PRODUCT

It is perfectly true that money is an asset in that it "specifies" the physical product; it is not an asset in itself. However, one must again acknowledge the extreme originality of money, which is distinguished from any other economic magnitude. In general, a claim refers to an object that is distinct from the claim, a property title is not the property itself. However, money, a claim to a product, *is a product*. The object of the monetary claim is money. Income-money is the claim to the product enclosed in the negative money. The separation or split between the monetary claim and its object happens only at the instant when the claim is "exercised" and destroyed: then the object comes out of the claim to live separately from it, as a value in use.

The increment of the zero-sphere is the claim to the physical product included in the sphere; it is only through the destruction of the claim (the annulment of the increment) that its object becomes instantly positive; it comes out of the monetary sphere: it is as if the house only comes into existence at the instant it is exchanged against the title to the house; but we must still add that the analogy is validated only if the house stops existing the following instant.

MONEY IS A NOMINAL MAGNITUDE

It is true that even the so-called material money is immaterial. The only matter of money is the physical product that is embodied within it. However, deprived of a body, money would not exist. It follows that, if money is a nominal magnitude, it is so only because it is identically a real magnitude, that is, money in its body (the product), or, without it, a zero money. Nominal money and real money coexist within the same object. It would therefore be vain to claim to be able to organize exchanges between nominal magnitudes and real magnitudes.

The only exchanges that exist in reality are the emissions: the physical product, cast into the negative money, is, by birth, changed into money;

then the expenditure of the positive money changes income into a physical product. The first exchange is a creation, the second one is a destruction. They are nevertheless exchanges because, taken at the instant of the first emission, the physical product becomes a monetary product; and in the second emission, the monetary product becomes instantly a physical product; the conversions are carried out "inside" the creation and the destruction, where we observe the real-to-nominal mutation then the nominal-to-real mutation.

As soon as we bring together in one set the four truths included in the listed errors, we obtain the quantum theory of production; money inserts itself within the real emission, effecting thereby its bipartition: the first half-emission generates money in place of the real product, kept in waiting; the second half-emission destroys money and replaces it by the real product, which appears therefore for the first time and definitively in the realm of values in use.

The strongest teaching of the theory of emissions is also the strangest: wages (W) are the unique category of the domestic income (Y).

Monetary wages (W) encompass the totality of domestic income (Y)

$$(1) \quad Y = W$$

In current parlance, one would say that definition (1) is not credible. But a scientist does not judge according to credibility; his criterion is truth. Money would not be present anywhere in the economy if it did not appear already in the very first operation, that is production. And the integration of money in the process of production is a rigorous law that no one can break or even modify or "soften".

The monetary economy is the image of the economy of exchange or of barter, money being unable in any case to alter the relation of exchange, both terms being logically *real*. Acknowledging the existence of monetary transactions that would not be pure real transactions, between goods and goods, or from product to product, does not reveal an observing mind but, less grandly, introduces error and arbitrariness in operations the true nature of which is of great purity and simplicity.

It is true that the monetary economy seems less perfect than the barter economy, which could not be threatened by any disorder. Is it not obvious then that money disturbs the beautiful order of the transactions? Ideally, money would never force itself as a final object, limiting itself on the contrary to comply entirely with the exchange between goods. However, the world does not live in perfection. And how could we avoid giving credence to the hypothesis of money *interference*? As soon as the exchange is broken, should not the mind go all the way to the introduction of another category of exchange, where money would be one of the terms instead of being only its medium?

The correct conclusion is much more satisfactory for the mind. In any conceivable case, money, especially bank money, is injected into the domestic economy only through the channel of the emissions. Moreover, any monetary emission is strictly identical to a real half-emission. There is no example whereby money would not be created within the concrete economy by the emission of wages, an emission which, as we have seen, is positive (in the producing services market), negative (in the products market) and both positive and negative (in the financial market). Any other representation would come from a wild imagination.

The "half-knowledge" stops at money viewed as a final object of transactions. We thus find that a real good is exchanged against money.

This exchange, which would be a particular case of (the) relative exchanges of the type is introduced in the theory of production by means of two successive monetary transactions,

First exchanged against money (A), the product is finally found again in the opposite exchange (B).

Under these conditions, why would exchange (B) be perfectly superimposed on exchange (A)? This question opens the way to numerous deductions and hypotheses. The law of the integration of money in the real exchanges being thus left to the discretion of "scientists", one is free to detect on the markets the formation and expenditure of all sorts of incomes, wages being only one type of income amongst many others.

Who would complain against the extreme simplicity of the true theory? Through his work in all the sectors of activity, man is the only issuer of the domestic product. If money mediates – as is indeed the case in the wage-regime – it is issued by one single operation, human labour. It is therefore "definitively

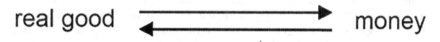

Figure 4.4 The exchange between good and money

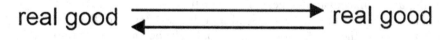

Figure 4.5 The exchange between two goods

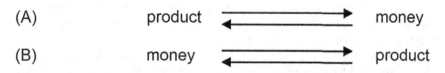

Figure 4.6 The intermediation of money

true" that wages are the unique category of the nation's income. Whether or not the economy experiences disorder, whether or not it is in equilibrium, it only comprises *wages*.

But then how can we explain the presence of non-wage incomes, profit, rent and interest?

XI. Non-wage incomes are created and destroyed within the movement that creates and destroys wages: the circuit of non-wage incomes is incorporated in the circuit of wages

The theory of emissions is the only one capable of explaining the existence of non-wage incomes

Let us point out at once that the explanation of the formation and expenditure of non-wage incomes can only be given by way of the theory of emissions. Up to now, theorists have succeeded in formalizing the working of an economy that comprises only the income of factors or of producing services: surpluses – meaning incomes that do not correspond, for their holders, to any cost of production – were analytically impossible to grasp. In Keynes's *Treatise on Money* (Keynes 1930), surplus-profit is still excluded from the category of (the) incomes forming the domestic income.

Today, thanks to quantum analysis, income can be conceived of in its complete reality: wages are the only incomes defined by a net and final cost (the cost of production of goods and services); labour only is "costly" and (monetary) wages are the exact measure of the labour spent; all the other incomes are derived from wages: they originate from them. The mass of wages is the "profit fund".

The formation of non-wage incomes in the expenditure of wages is an operation that declares itself firstly in the products market, by a (positive) difference between price and cost of production of "wage-goods"; but the same operation – that of the formation of non-wage incomes – is simultaneously present in the producing services market, non-wage-goods being retroactively taken from workers right from the emission of wages.

Let us examine again the general explanation.

The product of the nation is issued in a unique operation, that extends to the totality of the goods and services produced: the emission of (monetary) wages. But the emission of wages identifies perfectly with the real emission. Money is simply interposed in the act of the real production and the interposition of money is defined by the payment of wages. Thus, the creation-destruction of wages is an operation strictly identical to the real emission: the two operations constitute only one by merging together: the emission of wages merges with the real emission.

That is to say that every income comes to life under the identity of a wage, direct and social (child benefits, health benefits, company contributions to their employees' pensions, unemployment benefits etc.). It is therefore logically impossible to find any income in the community that might not be initially defined in wages.

To write the domestic income in the equation:

$$Y = Wages + Other\ incomes$$

is a fault against logic because any monetary emission is the substitution *ab initio* of nominal wages to real wages. Only the payment of human labour can bring about an income. Even the other incomes therefore can only be created within wages.

Thus, the analysis faces a major difficulty. Undoubtedly the social product is divided into wages and other incomes lumped together in the comprehensive category of profits.

$$(1)\quad Y = Wages + Profits$$

As wages extend to the totality of domestic income, profits can only be nil; conversely, if profits are positive, wages do not contain the whole domestic product. The contradiction is blatant. The theory of emissions, and that theory alone, succeeds in dispelling it. Equation (1) is correct if we connect it to equation (2) and if we hold both relations at the same time.

$$(2)\quad Y = Wages$$

Indeed, the two equations are not on the same plane. Equation (2) is the definition of the *formation* of incomes. *Every* income, wage or non-wage, belongs, at birth, to the category of wages. Equation (1) defines the *expenditure* or the destruction of incomes.

Other people than wage-earners contribute to purchasing domestic output.

Formation of Income:

$$Y = W$$

Expenditure of Income:

$$Y = W' + Pr$$

The whole problem of profits is summed up in the relation between magnitudes W and W'.

We shall present the analysis of this relation in three propositions that, in spite of appearances, will prove perfectly compatible with each other.

- Wages W' are smaller than wages W and the difference (W – W') is a transfer in the products market.
- Wages W' are smaller than wages W but the difference is a transfer (equal to W – W') in the producing services market.

- Finally, the positive difference between W and W' subsides entirely in the production of non-wage-goods. Once this resorption is completed, we obtain the identity W = W'. However, in spite of the identity between W and W', profits, that are not wages, are positive.

In the end, the study of profit is an application of the theory of emissions: we shall observe that the theorem according to which W' is both smaller than W and equal to W invalidates (through quantum analysis) the principle of the excluded middle.

Profits are initially transfer incomes obtained in the products market

Spent in the products market, wages W are destroyed only as far as W'; the difference (W – W') defines profits, the transfer incomes.

Right from the start, it is essential that the mental eye should embrace the two worlds at the same time, the positive money *and the negative money* created in the emission of wages. If the amount of wages (formed in workers' assets or elsewhere) issued in the period is W, we observe, facing these positive wages, an exact equal amount of negative wages, –W. It is true that negative wages do not appear as a net amount; the reason is that the physical product is lodged there-in and fills them up without any excess or shortage. Nevertheless, two strictly equal wages are facing each other, W and –W.

However, the logic of the emission does not at all require that wage-earners should be the only agents in the economy to cast positive wages onto negative wages; this task may be shared between workers and other people, provided one can explain the transfer of part of wages to the benefit of these people. Thus, let W' be the total cost of production, measured in the emission of wages, of the product obtained by wage-earners when they spend the entire amount of W.

It is clear that expenditure W causes the meeting of positive money +W with negative money –W'. Since positive money is destroyed only in the clash with negative money, it follows that only part W' of W is obliterated in the meeting of +W and –W'. We can induce from this the proof we were looking for; wage-earners spend W and, in so doing, destroy W'; the difference *is no longer a wage but is still an income* (a positive money deposited in time), a profit in the broad sense. Profit is then equal to W –W'.

Let us give a stylized, numerical example. In the production of the period, the economy generates 100 units of wages. Suppose the totality of wages is spent to buy goods and services the production of which is defined by the emission of 80 units of wages. Under these conditions, the 100 units of spent wages clash with 80 units of negative money and are immediately destroyed for that amount. The remainder, 20 units of money, survives in the hands of the new beneficiaries: 20 units of wages are transferred from wage-earners to the holders of all kinds of profits. In their turn, profits are finally spent. As it is logical to anticipate the same difference between "price" and "value" on non-wage-goods as on wage-goods, the expenditure of 20 units of profits will meet initially only 16 units of negative money; a second profit, of 4 units of money, is formed. However, the first profit (equal to 20 units of money) is taken from wages; the second profit (equal to 4 units of money) is on the contrary taken from the first profit. We see then that the expenditure of profits does not eventually generate any transfer income; any profit that is spent is entirely destroyed at 100% because any profit that survives the spending of profits is again spent as a profit. We have therefore the following chain of operations.

Cast in the expenditures in the products market, the sum of wages forms a profit that is eventually destroyed in this same market. The destruction of wages is their conversion in wage-goods; similarly, destroyed monetary profits are converted in non-wage-goods, their final form.

Why is it necessary to continue the analysis? This is because, at all times, theorists have been aware that a positive difference between the sum of prices and the sum of values of the goods and services bought in the markets must be explained, not just in its amount, but more deeply in its principle. Quantum analysis enables the brightest light to be cast on this problem.

On the one hand, we have the simultaneous creation of positive and negative wages ($+W$, $-W$) and on the other hand the simultaneous destruction of these wages. One cannot conceive of any operation that might define the total expenditure of W and nevertheless the only partial destruction of W, up to W'. If W is spent, it is that all of W is destroyed and not only its part W'. Any other conclusion violates the theory of emissions. Briefly, there could exist no monetary expenditure that would not bring the same arithmetical (or absolute) result in each of the two worlds, that of positive magnitudes and that of negative magnitudes. If expenditure W is completed for the amount W in the realm of positive magnitudes, it is inconceivable that the operation would only extend to the amount W' in the realm of negative magnitudes. In the explanation that we have offered, the transfer ($W - W'$) is an expenditure but – and this is where the formal error lies – the transfer is neither a creation-emission nor a destruction-emission: undoubtedly a profit is created in this operation but this is done from wages already existing, which is logically impossible.

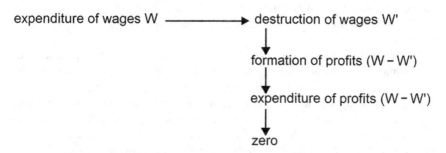

Figure 4.7 The formation and expenditure of profit

Let us formulate the theoretical quandary in the language of the old theories. Money has a determined value; it is confronted with real goods that also have a very definite value. The source of both values is in the production (for the Classics) or in the exchanges concluded within general equilibrium (for the Neo-Classics). In both cases, it would be illogical to accept the existence of non-zero differences between prices and values. Indeed, for the Classics, prices are given in the exchanges in the products market; however, in this market, goods confronted with each other are already defined in value (from the factors of production market); the exchange is not concluded simply between physical goods but between their values; it follows that prices are only the (nominal) expressions of (real) values: any non-zero difference between price and value would be absurd because it would mean that the agents would give a value to obtain an unequal value. In neo-classical theory, the conclusion is equally strong; exchanges are simultaneously determined on both markets; it follows that price and value are the different names of one and the same magnitude: again, one cannot see how prices could be greater than values.

The new analysis therefore does not reveal the problem; but, for the first time, it gives the solution. Indeed, neither in the classical theory, nor in the neo-classical theory does the logical equality of prices and values allow the formation of incomes in the products market: quite the contrary, the logical equality of prices and values is formally opposed to the emergence of incomes in the goods market, by the positive differences that would appear between prices and values. However, in reality, there is nevertheless a whole category of incomes that emerges from the sale of produced goods. The theory is therefore both logical and adequate to facts only if it succeeds in explaining the formation, in the products market, of positive incomes of transfer (dividends, interests, rents), without the difference between prices and values, the source of the transfers, being in opposition with the law of the logical equality between prices and values.

The problem seems without any solution since it has all the appearance of a pure contradiction in terms. However, the solution does exist: it belongs to the analysis of emissions. Up to now, we have demonstrated the formation of (non-wage) incomes in the expenditure of wages. We still have to prove that the positive difference between prices and values involved in the formation of non-wage incomes eventually subsides, while allowing for the existence of incomes of transfer.

The transfer of wages in the products market is the correct explanation of the formation of profit. The resolution is found in the now well-known fact of the contraction in a single movement of the operations concluded in both markets. Any operation observed in the products market is retroactively effective in the producing services market. We know well that it is necessarily so because final purchases define the second real half-emission, correlative to the first real half-emission given in the payment of wages. After the retroaction, the transfer of part of the wages has already been carried out in the producing services market. Under these conditions, the transfer is logically unimpeachable, because it no longer involves any difference between prices and values.

The transfer of wages in the products market is finally resolved in a transfer in the producing services market

Let us offer two proofs of the identity price-value in the presence of non-zero profits, one synthetical and the other analytical.

Synthetical proof of the identity price-value in the presence of zero, negative, or positive (this latter case being obviously the most frequent) profits.

The argument is based on the unicity of the emission underlying the two monetary emissions; therefore, it is based eventually on the unicity of those two emissions themselves. The formation and the expenditure of wages define the same wave-like movement. We have established above that the second half-emission, subsequent in chronological time, coincides exactly with the first one in quantum time. More precisely, the two half-emissions, formation and final expenditure of wages, are movements that quantize the same piece of continuous time. That is to say, let us repeat it, that the expenditure of wages takes effect retroactively at the instant of their formation: incomes have only an instantaneous life.

From here, it is easy to figure out the distinction of the cases, depending on whether the domestic economy includes or not non-wage incomes. Let us visualize by arrows the flows of formation and expenditure of wages.

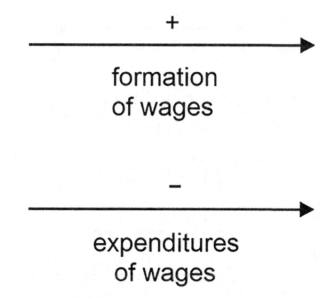

Figure 4.8 Formation and expenditure of wages as disjoint events

Because of the retroaction, the two arrows coincide (see Figure 4.9).

We see at once that any division of the negative arrow defines an identical division of the positive arrow: if a part of wages is transferred in the products market, an equal part of wages is transferred in the producing services market (see Figure 4.10).

Twenty units of wages are formed in profits in the negative flow (expenditure of wages); we induce that 20 units of wages are spent in profits in the positive flow (formation of wages).

Any difference between price and value would be the sign of a different distribution of the two flows between wages and profits. Since the two flows are in fact "pressed" one onto the other, the formation of wages is subdivided in exact accordance to the expenditure of wages.

There remains only a problem of interpretation. Any magnitude carried by one arrow corresponds to the same magnitude on the other arrow, except for the sign. The negative arrow shows that out of the expenditure of 100 units of wages, 20 units define a formation of profits. The meaning of the positive arrow ensues: of the formation of 100 units of wages, 20 units define a profit expenditure.

Let us generalize. Assume that x is the wages issued in the period and y the wages transformed into profits. The partition of the product is easily understandable on the side of the wage expenditure: of the purchases equal to x, workers obtain $(x - y)$. If the explanation were to stop here, the price of wage-goods would be equal to x for a lower value of y. But the movement is only considered at half-way; we must complete it with the payment of wages. Thus, workers obtain their wages from two sources; for $(x - y)$ wages are paid from

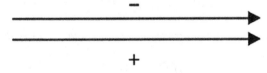

formation-expenditure of wages

Figure 4.9 The formation-expenditure of wages

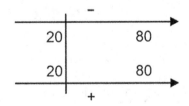

division of the product into wages and profits

Figure 4.10 The division of the product in wages and profit

zero profits and for the complementary part, *y*, wages come from the profits *y*, the expenditure of which is already present in the producing services market, due to the retroaction of the reflux on the flux.

Let us now reason in the unity of the flux-reflux.

- In the payment of wages, firms spend *y* units of profit and obtain *y* units of products.
- In their expenditures, workers apparently cast *x* units of wages. But it would be a mistake to end here, because the total available income is only of *x* units of wages. Since *y* units of profit are spent in the payment of wages, workers who spend *x* units of money only spend $(x - y)$ units of wages. The discrepancy defines the transfer, observed identically in the two markets, of *y* units of wages in profits. In simple terms, we shall say that the *x* units of money obtained by workers (in direct and indirect wages) contain $(x - y)$ units of wages in the case where a share *y* of wages *x* is formed in profits. With a bit more sophistication, we realize that the difference between the units of money and the units of wages formed to the benefit of workers recedes as soon as the merging of the flux and of the reflux is perfectly grasped. We must avoid thinking in a chronological perspective. Workers do not receive *x* units of money but only $(x - y)$ units because *y* units are taken and transferred to firms in the *two* markets; thus, workers receive $(x - y)$ units of money positively and *y* units both positively and negatively: in the end, monetary wages are of $(x - y)$ units only.
- To conclude, the price of non-wage-goods, obtained by the expenditure of profits, is *y*; the price of non-wage-goods is $(x - y)$: the corresponding values are strictly equal, *y* and $(x - y)$. The products are sold at their exact value; nevertheless, profits (*y*) are taken from wages (*x*).

Let us sum up briefly the method we have followed, in order to emphasize that we must first reason chronologically, then in simultaneity: the flux creating wages precedes the reflux; but eventually, the reflux of wages in the final purchases takes place *at the same moment as the flux*.

1 The reflux is posterior to the flux. It is essential to keep the time interval (defined in the continuum) between the creation of wages and their expenditure. At first, firms issue x units of wages; it is formally impossible that this emission should contain any amount of profit: the x units of wages are created for the benefit of workers only. This result cannot be altered by taking into account any anticipation.

   It is possible that firms anticipate making y units of profit on the sale of their current product. However, we would commit a fault against logic if we were to infer that firms could, especially thanks to bank credits, spend their profits in the producing services market – in order to have the non-wage-goods produced – before the sale of products had effectively brought to them monetary profits y. The reasoning would be caught in a vicious circle.

In reality, whether anticipated or not, profits can come to life only from created wages: profits (y) are taken from wages (x). Profits cannot be generated – even in advance – by reducing the emission of wages. It is therefore certain that workers obtain first, in direct and indirect wages, the totality of the new social product. Profits are zero at first, even in the case where expectations allow to conclude without any great risk of error that, in the domestic product equal to x units of wages, the amount of profit will be eventually equal to a (positive) part y of x. The initial nullity of profits simply means that the production of non-wage-goods brings on wages.

2   Whether or not profits (y) are anticipated by firms, the domestic product of the period is entirely issued under the form of the "wage bill" (x). Now, let us suppose that profits have been perfectly anticipated, the error of prevision being nil (neither positive nor negative). In this case, part y of wages is, right from the start, issued for the production of non-wage-goods.

Let us understand well that, even in the production of non-wage-goods, domestic income is entirely issued in wages. The production of wage-goods brings on wages equal to (x - y) units; the production of the other goods creates wages equal to y units; the total production of the period is defined by the x units of income born for the benefit of workers only.

Expectations being assumed exact, workers spend x units of wages for the purchase of the totality of the wage-goods newly produced. If they allocated to this purchase a lower amount, anticipated profits would be higher than actual profits; the difference might reach the sum of y, which would be confirmed if the expenditure of wages for the purchase of wage-goods would only amount eventually to (x - y) units.

We thereby understand perfectly that the realization of profits depends entirely on the amount of wages spent for the purchase of wage-goods: for profits to be positive, the selling price of wage-goods must be higher than their cost of production (measured in wage-units). Wage-goods being sold for x units of wages, whereas their production has cost only (x - y) units of wages, we see that the anticipations of profits are correct: profits are therefore not at all generated by anticipation; quite the contrary, determined freely by the agents, the purchases on the goods market will confirm or infirm them.

In the present case, we have supposed that the sale of wage-goods brings effectively x units of wages to firms, whereas the production of these goods has cost them only (x - y) units of wages. A profit can only be generated in the products market, in the positive difference between the price and the cost of production of wage-goods. The reader will notice that if the expectations were not correct, any error would be perfectly mendable:

- thus, if wage-goods were sold for an amount of wages lower than x units, part of the non-wage-goods already produced would lack financing; the deficit would be necessarily compensated by borrowing, for the benefit of firms, the part corresponding to the wages earned in the production of non-wage-goods;

- conversely, if wage-goods were eventually sold for an amount higher than x units of wages, part of the wage-goods produced during the period could not be sold in the expenditure of new wages; two equal sums would be formed facing each other, an unexpected monetary profit and a stock of wage-goods not (yet) sold; in this case, the final profit is at the level of realized profits: it is higher than y insofar as the complete expenditure of current wages leaves within firms a stock of wage-goods produced during the period; the unexpected monetary profits will be spent in the purchase of the product of a subsequent period, the production of non-wage-goods reaching thereby the level of actual profits, whereas it was initially only equal to the amount of anticipated monetary profits.

As the anticipation of profits has no bearing on their realization, let us maintain the assumption that expectations will be eventually confirmed. Under those conditions, production of non-wage-goods, decided "ex ante", is equal to the demand for these goods, as expressed in the products market. Tautologically, the production of wage-goods is, in the same period, equal to the amount of final purchases of wage-goods.

It is essential to understand that the two final demands, relative to the goods of the two categories (wage and non-wage) are mixed together in the expenditure of wages x issued in the total production of the period. The break-down of expenditure x between the two categories of goods is entirely carried out through the formation of monetary profits: a final demand of non-wage-goods emerges if and only if the amount of wages used to purchase wage-goods exceeds the sum of wages created in the production of these goods; the excess being equal to y, the expenditure of x units of wages is divided into two branches: for (x - y), expenditure x is a final purchase of wage-goods, and for y, expenditure x is a final purchase of non-wage-goods. Expectations being assumed correct, the monetary expenditures of the two categories meet exactly the real goods of these two categories, (x - y) for (x - y) and y for y.

3   A positive difference between prices and values is therefore observed in chronological time: however, this difference, equal to y, is formed only on wage-goods, the total selling price of which is x for a cost of production of (x - y). Non-wage-goods are purchased for a final expenditure equal to y, the exact amount of their cost of production.

4   The positive difference between price and value disappears even for wage-goods. This is so because the emission of (x - y) units of wages in the production of wage-goods is the expenditure of a zero profit, whereas the emission of the y units of wages in the production of non-wage-goods is the anticipated expenditure of the y units of profit that will be formed in

the products market. Dividend goods are acquired at once by firms (on behalf of non-wage income holders); as soon as wages y are paid, the corresponding goods become the property of the holders of interests, rents and dividends, because profits (y) are already spent in the emission of the y part of wages x.

5   Finally and even though it is a necessary stage both in reasoning and in the chronological order of concrete events, the formation of any difference between price and value cancels out in the logical reinterpretation of the emission of wages: the positive difference between wage-goods' price and cost confirms, measure for measure, the production of non-wage-goods; any difference between price and value being now cancelled out, the production of non-wage-goods signifies the expenditure and the destruction of monetary profits in the very operation of the payment of the corresponding wages. We shall come back to this whole question, because its importance is capital.

Before moving on to the second proof of the price-value identity, it is worth examining (quickly) the case where monetary profit would be *negative*. Let us recall the two arrows representing the positive flux (creation of wages) and the negative reflux (expenditure of wages): the two flows being superimposed on each other, any division of one is the equal division of the other. The sum of profits, y, is therefore a part of x. If y is positive, the part of wage-goods is reduced by the same amount. If y is zero, wage-goods cover the whole product of the period. However, it would seem that one cannot find in x any part y that would be negative. This is indeed impossible if y means the amount of profits of firms, taken as a whole. To obtain negative profits, these must be defined on certain firms in relation to others. A firm obtains a positive profit if it sells goods to wage-earners at a price higher than their cost of production. Symmetrically, the profit of a firm is negative as far as it sells wage-goods at a price lower than their cost of production. However, the (negative) difference between price and value defines tautologically an income that is used to purchase wage-goods produced by other firms.

We can see therefore that any negative profit defines an equal positive profit, even though the converse is obviously not true. The conclusion is then that only positive profits are interesting when we consider the firms as a whole facing workers also taken as a whole.

Let us consider now the analytical proof of the price-value equality.

Analytical proof of the price-value equality *in the presence of zero or positive profits*

The foundation of the new approach is always the same: the formation and expenditure of wages belong to a unique movement, the production conceived of as a to-and-fro operation, i.e. as a wave.

Any production, even that of a sole worker, is a wave-like process. We might therefore build the theory of circuits (the identity of the "tos" and "fros" or of values and prices) on every particular operation of every sole worker. However, it is not necessary to break down the domestic economy at this point; it is sufficient to stop at the level of firms. The circuit is defined on each firm and for each production, the latter defined by the measure of quantized time and *numéraire*. If wages are paid monthly, it will be the monthly production of each firm.

Each firm issues its own money

The emission of wages by firm q is a double operation, the creation and the destruction of wages Wq; however, the double operation being unique, only one money is present in the wave, the money issued in wages Wq; let us call it Mq. It is logically certain that, in the sale of its product, firm q absorbs and destroys money Mq and no other money. Again, it is important to overcome false appearances. It is a truism that Fq sells its product to any income holder; thus Fq finds in its receipts any kind of money, Mn; this a flat tautology (see Figure 4.11).

But it goes without saying that a truism cannot go against a truth. Even though Mn is not "immediately" the money issued by Fq, we have "mediately" the identity

$$Mn = Mq$$

Once again, to deny the identity of Mn and Mq would mean the dissociation of the two fluxes, the union of which defines the production of Fq. The only solution left – but it is fully satisfactory – is to conclude that, through "general or generalized exchange" in the products market (anybody buying anything), Mq is changed or converted into Mn. And it is not at all difficult to explain the conversion or the mutation of Mq into Mn.

Let us consider the simplest of examples with the domestic economy comprising only two firms.

Firm *1* creates money $M1$, which, let us assume, is spent by workers Wr1 entirely on the purchase of the goods produced in $F2$. Let us apply the theory of emissions. It introduces the following constraint: a money $M'2$ is taken out of $M2$ so that we obtain $M'2 = M1$.

However, the theory of emissions is even more demanding. Not only is money $M'2$ equal to money $M1$, but it is *identical* to it; it is its transformation or conversion. The reason is that money $M1$ enters the negative money

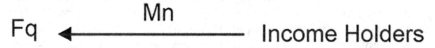

Figure 4.11 The sale of the product to income holders

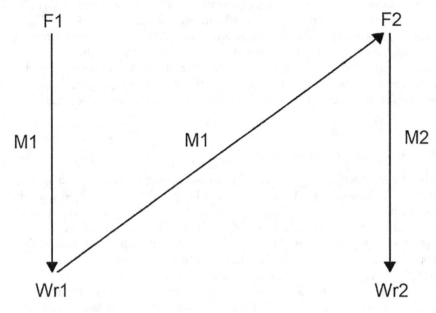

Figure 4.12 A two firms' economy

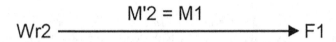

Figure 4.13 The replacement of *M2* by *M1*

created by *F2* in the emission of wages *M2*. It follows that money *M1* dislodges part of positive money *M2*, that it replaces in negative money *M2*. The
substitution being carried out in the negative money, it takes place similarly
in the positive monies: in its expenditure on the product of *F2*, *M1* has
become the part of *M2* equal to *M1* (*M1* is now only the measure of a fraction of *M2*). We arrive therefore conversely at the conclusion that it is handy
to formulate with the well-known clause: it is as if workers Wr1 were buying
the product of *F1* to exchange it, at the market price, against the equal part
M'2 of the product of *F2*.

The circuit, or the identity flux-reflux, is defined autonomously on each
firm, *M1* for *M1*, *M2* for *M2*, and so on if the economy comprises other
firms. The outcome is a surprising but indubitable piece of information: the
profit of any firm is a part of the income produced by this same firm. No firm
can find a profit in the product of another firm.

Every profit made by *Fq* is a part of the income created by *Fq*. This is so
because *every firm sells its product only to its own workers*.

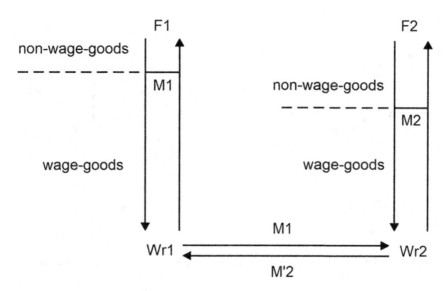

Figure 4.14 The identity of each firm's fluxes and refluxes

It may be useful to go back for a while to the proposition that we have just underlined, because it seems to diverge from common sense. The careful reader knows though that the necessarily "internal" character of purchases results logically from the wave-like nature of production. And common sense is not shocked since internal purchases are based on general exchange (the definition of which, let us repeat it, is that anybody buys anything at any sum of (available) money to anybody), any income holder buying freely the "items" of his choice, on any market, goods or securities. The only difficulty is to conceive of the simultaneity of all the operations: thus, in the previous example, Wr1 buys for *M1* the product of *F1* in the very same movement that sees the exchange of this product – which is therefore never deposited in the assets of Wr1 – at an equal price, against a product of *F2*.

Since any firm *Fq* only finds, in the sale of its product, the money that it has created, the proposition underlined above is well established. It is formally impossible that *Fq* should make a profit, but in its own product. In other words, only workers Wr*q* produce the profits of *Fq*. The formation of the profit of any firm is a special case of the emission of wages by that firm.

The analysis of flux-reflux *Mq* of the money issued by *Fq* reveals the existence of flows *M'q* and *M''q*.

The distinction of *M'q* and of *M''q* within *Mq* does not initially cause any difficulty since the two divisions comply with the definition of production: *M'q* and *M''q* are the creations-destructions of wages. The only problem is in the "quantification" of *M''q*. What is the part of the creation of wages and

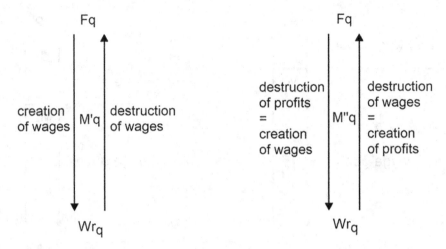

Figure 4.15 The flows of the creation-destruction of wages and of the creation-destruction
of profit

identically of their destruction that defines the destruction-creation of profits? Thus reduced to its true dimension, the problem is a minor one: $M'q$ is the part of the product of Fq the price of which is equal to wages Mq. As for $M''q$, it is tautologically the complementary part of $M'q$ in Mq. We arrive thus very naturally at the heart of the "mystery" of profit. The formation of profit is an expenditure of wages; the expenditure of profit is a formation of wages; thus, the destruction-creation of profit is a movement already included in the creation-destruction of wages, even though no profit is identified to wages.

The analysis of profit therefore shows that prices are not higher than values.

The price of wage-goods is higher than their value only because it includes the price of non-wage-goods

It is clear that workers Wrq pay both wage-goods ($M'q$) and non-wage-goods ($M''q$), even though they only obtain wage-goods. The formation of profits is therefore in compliance with the equivalence of values and prices; how could it be otherwise since this equivalence is the expression of the flux-reflux identity, the very definition of every production? No discrepancy between price and value is eventually logically conceivable. The apparent discrepancy ($Mq - M'q$), is the cost of production or the value of non-wage-goods, so that price Mq less the corresponding value is identical to zero.

Let us conclude this brief study of profit by a rather "dramatic" formulation.

Wages cover the whole product; profits are a part of the product; however, a profit is not a wage; the emissions (of wages) are therefore a refutation of the principle of the excluded middle

Since Adam Smith's writings, an interesting problem has been raised, that of the equivalence between income and product. In the "rude state of society", wages cover the product, no more no less. As soon as other incomes appear, due to the appropriation of land and to the accumulation of financial and instrumental capital, it is difficult to maintain the theory within the constraint, albeit necessary, of the equality, in the same units of measure, of the sum of incomes and of the sum of products. Any positive or negative discrepancy is the sign of an analytical error, therefore of the imperfection of the theoretical apparatus.

In this respect, let us consider three hypotheses on which to work.

1   A profit (by that we mean everywhere to be the comprehensive category of the non-wage incomes) is an income that does not correspond to any additional product. The economy produces only in the emission of wages; a profit is therefore "an income without a product".
2   The profits of each firm correspond to a specific product of the other firms. Thus, the economy produces non-wage-goods in addition to wage-goods, but no firm produces internally the (non-wage) goods corresponding to its own profits.
3   Finally, each firm, making a profit, spends it necessarily (according to the constraints of logic) to buy or finance an equivalent part of its own product. It is agreed that the "internal" exchange is carried out through "general exchange".

It is easily demonstrated that only hypothesis 3 is compatible with the complete clearing of the domestic product. In the two other hypotheses, the equality of the sum of incomes and of the sum of products cannot be guaranteed.

Only hypothesis 3 complies with the equality of income and product.

The proof is obvious for hypothesis 1. Any wage corresponds to an equivalent product; any profit corresponds by hypothesis to a zero product. It follows at once that income exceeds the product. It is certain that reality is not respected, except for the part of profits that is inflationary. Any non-inflationary profit remains unexplained. Another formulation of the same deficiency emphasizes the formation of (non-inflationary) profit. This category of income remains necessarily empty because the sale of the product – wage-goods or, identically, the goods corresponding to the wages issued – can only trigger the reflux of the income created, that is, the sum of wage incomes, and nothing more.

The rejection of hypothesis 2 requires a little longer reflexion; let us do so by using a quantified example. The economy comprises two firms that issue wages according to the following graphs.

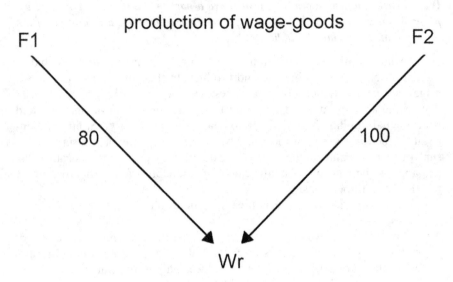

Figure 4.16 The production of wage-goods

Measuring in wage-unit, Firm 1 makes a profit of 20 units and Firm 2 a profit of 50 units.

On the graph, in accordance with hypothesis 2, firm 1 produces the dividend goods for firm 2 and conversely. We can now put our finger on the

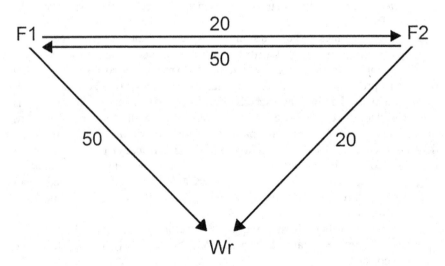

Figure 4.17 The production of non-wage goods

purely logical difficulty to which hypothesis 2 inevitably leads. Firm 1 sells its wage-goods for 80 + 20 units of measure; otherwise, it would not make a profit (= 20). But the sale by *F1* of the non-wage-goods produced for *F2* can only bring an additional profit, which, if the same proportion is applied, is equal to ¼ of 50 units. Similarly, on the sale of the non-wage-goods that it produces for *F1*, firm 2 makes an additional profit of ½ of 20 units.

The additional profits reproduce the difficulty encountered under hypothesis 1; the domestic product is "over-sold", which means that the profits derived from the sale of non-wage-goods cannot be realized.

Only hypothesis 3 allows the conciliation of two requirements: non-wage-goods are equivalent to realized profits (20 in monetary profits and 20 in non-wage-goods for *F1*, and 50 for 50 in *F2*) and the production of non-wage-goods brings no (additional) profit.

Let us follow hypothesis 3 in the rectified graphs (see Figure 4.18).

This time, each enterprise produces its own non-wage-goods. We see with satisfaction that the "imputation" problem, well-known to theorists, is solved at last. Firm 1 sells its wage-goods for 100 units of measure and thus makes the profit allowing it to produce 20 units of non-wage-goods; for its part, *F2* sells its wage-goods for 150 units of measure and realizes thereby the exact financing of the production of its non-wage-goods.

The 250 units of "measure" constituting the receipts of firms are nothing other than the wages issued in the total production; the expenditure of those wages forms a total profit of 20 + 50 units, the exact value of the non-wage-goods produced during the period.

The real problem of imputation is entirely solved: social product and domestic income coincide perfectly. However, two false problems still subsist; and false problems are often more challenging than real ones.

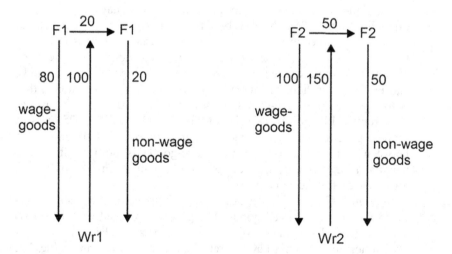

Figure 4.18 The production of wage- and non-wage goods by each firm

(A)   It is possible that non-wage-goods are not finally appropriated by firms but by their beneficiaries, for example their shareholders. In this case, it is logical to suppose that, like wage-goods, non-wage-goods should be sold at a price higher than their cost of production.

(B)   Whoever should be the final owner of non-wage-goods – the firm *stricto sensu* or its beneficiaries – it is highly probable that non-wage-goods are going into the general exchange: before reaching their final holders, they are sold and other goods are bought in their place. Again, we have to take into account the fact that the price of the goods is higher than their value.

However, whether it is A or B, *prices would be greater than values only in an incomplete reasoning*; the sum of the discrepancies is necessarily nil on each firm (*lato sensu*, that is including the holders of the incomes produced in the firm).

(A)   Firm 1 sells its non-wage-goods to its shareholders, for example; the price obtained is 25 units of measure; however, the additional profit (= 5 units) is both positive and negative; the dividend holders lose it in their expenditures and earn it in their receipts; identically, the firm earns it in its sales and loses it in the distribution of dividends. *Only profits earned in the sale of wage-goods are net.*

(B)   We still have to examine the release in the general exchange of the non-wage-goods held by the firm *lato sensu*. Let us take arbitrarily the example of Firm 2 this time. It has at its disposal non-wage-goods equal to 50 units of measure. It casts these goods into general exchange and therefore sells them for 75 units of money. However, let us recall that the generalization of exchange is an operation that follows the rule of the circuits; the supplement of receipts implies an equal supplement of expenditures: the +25 only exists because it is linked to a –25, expenditure or additional injection of F2 into general exchange. Let us use again the "as if" reasoning; the owners of non-wage-goods buy them for 50 units of money, then they exchange them against other goods, chosen freely; exchange is agreed at a price of 75 units of money; that is to say that non-wage-goods are sold for 75 units of money and at once replaced by goods the price of which is identically of 75 units of money; general exchange being completed, we see that the difference between price and value of non-wage-goods is both positive and negative in the same transaction: sold for 75 units of money, the goods are replaced for the same price.

The only effect that is not necessarily nil concerns the costs of production of the exchanged goods. The goods purchased and the goods sold in general exchange do not have necessarily the same cost of production: they do not have therefore necessarily the same value. Let us be very clear on this subject: in the receipt-expenditure of the 75 units of money, the holders of non-wage-goods sell a product of a value of 50 to receive a product of a greater, smaller or equal value: the three possibilities are offered by logic. However, in all three cases, the good purchased is substituted to the good produced and, so to speak, embraces its cost of production. Finally, the goods are always bought exactly at their cost of production – or at their value.

Let us conclude by drawing the consequence of the fact that only hypothesis 3 is confirmed.

By dictating hypothesis 3, *logic invalidates the principle of the excluded middle.*

Let us consider the firms as a whole (*F*) and the sum of wages issued in the production of wage-goods (*W1*), *W2* being the sum of wages issued in the production of dividend goods (see Figure 4.19).

At first, it is essential to fight against a vicious circle. To succeed in producing dividend goods, it is not enough that *F* should cast *W1* + *W2*, in order to retrieve this sum in the sale of wage-goods only. In that case, profit would be self-financed, which is absurd. In reality, profit *W2* only exists if it is realized by the deconstructed firms (the parts of the whole *F*), each one capturing a fraction of the wages issued by the others. The game is not a zero-sum since wages are captured on the sale of wage-goods exclusively and captured wages are fully returned in the production of dividend goods.

In a word, the production of dividend goods is not the cause of profit but its effect.

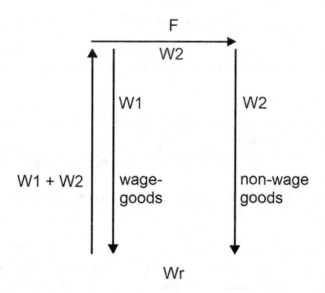

Figure 4.19 The expenditure of wages and the purchase of non-wage goods

We see very well that the global economy has only wages, $W1 + W2$, as incomes. However, no profit is a wage. Positive profits (Pr), equal to (and not identical to) $W2$ are nevertheless available in the economy. The principle of the excluded middle is broken for the reason given above, the expenditure and the formation of wages include the formation and the expenditure of profits.

There is a positive profit, even though all the incomes formed are wages, and all the incomes spent are wages.

We can now put an end to the analysis of profit by going back to the distinction of wages W and W'.

Formation of income:

$$W$$

Expenditure of income:

$$W' + Pr$$

For any non-quantum theory, profit bites on wages; in other words, if W' were equal to W, profits would be nil. The theory of emissions brings a surprising teaching, in two parts:

- W' is logically equal to W;
- nevertheless, there are positive profits.

Indeed, we have:

$$(1) \quad W = W1 + W2,$$

The sum of wages being equal to the wages issued in the two productions, those of wage-goods and those of non-wage-goods; and

$$(2) \quad W' = W1 + W2,$$

the sum of the wages spent being logically equal to the wages earned in the two productions; and finally:

$$(3) \quad W = W - W' = 0 \ for \ Pr > 0.$$

Profit (Pr) is equal to W2. However, all wages are strictly zero profits. The equation:

$$Pr = W2$$

has a meaning that can only be grasped in the theory of emissions. Let us repeat the formula, because it is essential: the formation of profit is an expenditure of wages; the expenditure of profit is a formation of wages. *The circuit of profits* (their formation-expenditure) *is therefore embedded in the circuit of wages*, of which it is a nested category.

By the expenditure of *W2*, workers form a profit, the expenditure of which is the formation of *W2*.

Let us represent the two half-emissions by two half-circles.

Half-circle *a* corresponds to the formation of wages, half-circle *b* to the expenditure of wages. Profit *a'* is formed in half-circle *b*: expenditure *a'*, the destruction of wages, is a creation of profit. For the destruction of profit *b'*, one has to refer to half-circle *a*: expenditure b', creation of wages, is a destruction of profit. The circular flow of profit (*a'*, *b'*) is indeed included in the circuit of wages (*a*, *b*) even though it is defined solely by the flows of creation and destruction of wages.

Invested profit is the definition of fixed capital. However, fixed capital is a particular case of capital-time, which is constituted of saved-up wages.

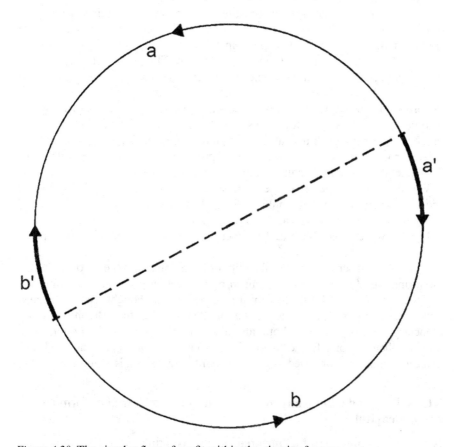

Figure 4.20 The circular flow of profit within the circuit of wages

5 Capital

One may imagine a society where there would be no capital. In the public opinion, machines are viewed as capital. This is not quite correct. It is true that, in our economies, machines constitute capital, but they are not so due to the fact that they are machines. We shall show that the first capital, the "mother-type" of all other forms of capital is simply the time that separates current income from its future expenditure. Even capital in its most "solid" aspect, fixed or instrumental capital, is logically reducible to capital-time. But it is not at all logically necessary that machines should derive from a capital-time. Thus, a society deprived of capital could be equipped with machines, even sophisticated ones, instruments available to human labour. In fact, purely instrumental capital belongs to the prehistory of capital, which takes its modern meaning by the transformation of income: any capital in the proper sense is both monetary and real. If a "capital" is purely real, it belongs to the category of pianos; instruments do not all have the same purpose; they serve to consume or to produce; nevertheless, any instrument is a value in use, even if it is used in the process of production.

We shall briefly describe the functioning of production-emission in an economy where no capital would be formed (XII).

Then we shall introduce capital-time (XIII).

Finally, we shall establish that fixed capital is formally reducible to capital-time (XIV).

In a brief post-scriptum, we shall verify that the "quantum theory of capital" – the formation of capital being explained by production-emission – accomplishes the synthesis awaited by the two historical schools of thought, capital being a "fund" for one group of theorists and a "matter" for the other. Resulting from a monetary emission, capital is both, and in an organic whole, a claim on a future product (therefore on a future "matter") and a claim on banks (a "fund"). Theory joins with reality as conceived of by accountants: any capital is a sum of money.

XII. When production-emission is closed onto itself without forming any net capital

Is money cast in wages of a "material" or of a banking nature? The monetary emission is identical in both cases. The expenditure of wages takes effect retroactively at the instant of the payment of wages, and the real product exists under the form of an income only in the space of an instant.

At first, the theory of capital examines wages in relation with duration, between the instant of their creation and the chronologically posterior instant of their expenditure. In the interval, are not wages "awaiting" and, in this case, are they not already a capital?

A positive answer would be erroneous. It is agreed, indeed, that wages are the definition of the product. In all rigour, it is therefore incorrect that wage-earners are waiting for the product or, identically, that the product is await-ing in firms. The theory of production-emission lifts any dichotomy between wages and product, which is already fully in the hands of wage-earners even before the expenditure of wages, a simple conversion of the product-in-money into a product-outside-money.

The correct analysis leads to the existence of two incomes and, from that fact, to the absence of any capital: wages earned and not yet spent define the income present in chronological time, under the form of the product in money; as soon as wages are spent, and at this precise instant only, the product exists under the form of the product in kind. At no time is income replaced by capital.

Capital is a lent income

The formation of capital depends on a specific operation easy to discover: *the loan.* Suppose indeed that part of the wages are lent by their holders. Then, a third market is added on; up till now, the emission concerned only the pro-ducing services market and the products market; now, the financial market intervenes.

It is important to note that the perfection of the emission is not affected by the intrusion of the third market. This is because any financial operation originates from an income, the result of the first half-emission, and finds its purpose in the expenditure of the borrowed income, thus in the second half-emission. The effect of the loan is simply to transfer an income so that the creation of income, carried out on one person, ends in the destruction of income on *another person.* If we leave aside the identification of the agents to focus only on the domestic economy, it is clear that the loan is a zero-sum operation, the financial capital of the lender is exactly compensated by the negative financial capital formed in the borrower's assets. From the point of view of society, no income is transformed into capital, the income of lenders being simply captured and spent by borrowers.

In spite of the introduction of the financial market, the economy is func-tioning without any net capital, even if an instrumental "capital", which might be assumed to be of an advanced technology, is available. At this point of the analysis, not only is there no capital in the proper sense in the economy but, *a fortiori,* its production mode is far from corresponding to what is meant by capitalism.

We shall not find capitalism until the second part of this book. However, capital is at hand, first under the form of pure capital-time, then under the form of fixed capital, a more sophisticated form of capital-time.

XIII. Capital-time

The equality of loans and debts is a tautology; and no force can break tautologies; it seems therefore that it should be formally impossible to define an operation that brings in a positive financial capital without creating a negative financial capital in the same movement and in the same measure. If this impossibility were to be confirmed, society would only ever have at its disposal a zero sum of (financial) capital.

There is a net financial capital in society

A rigorous inductive reasoning establishes, against all expectations, the effective existence of a net financial capital relatively to society as a whole. This does not mean obviously that the tautology breaks down; in reality, the equality of loans and debts is a false tautology because there are loans, of a considerable amount and continuously renewed, *to which correspond only zero or cancelled debts.* We shall find therefore, facing each other, positive loans and zero debts; we observe then the existence of a net loan and thus of a positive (financial) capital in the global economy.

We shall offer the proof by stages.

The emission of wages is not a credit operation; it is incorrect to assimilate bank money to credit or to credit money. If we wish nevertheless to talk about credit in relation to the emission of wages, we have to specify that it is a very original credit, a *quantum credit*, a creation and not a transmission of money.

In an economy comprising a financial market to which banks are associated, bank money is at once transformed into the object of an *ordinary credit*.

Obtained by the automatic transformation of a quantum credit, an ordinary credit is a relation between persons and objects and not a relation between lenders and borrowers. The persons credited are lenders indeed; but nobody is correlatively debited: the credits define thus a financial and *real* capital, net for the whole social body.

Global capital is a bridge that the whole society casts between present and future. Capital-time is diminished in each (banking) operation that brings forth a borrower facing lenders. In their function as financial intermediaries, banks bite into capital-time by making future incomes current. Any future income that becomes current is a destroyed capital. The last stage is perhaps the richest in lessons. *Capital can only come to life in bank accounts. Any economy deprived of banks would be logically devoid of any capital.*

Let us consider again these different points.

Production-emission is not a credit operation

Since David Ricardo, theorists have been trying to demonstrate the mutual independence of the two banking operations, money creation and financial intermediation. Quantum analysis substantiates the Ricardian theory, which is consistent both with common sense and formal logic. To create is not to transmit, to transmit is not to create.

What is the initial operation? Undoubtedly, it is production, the emission of wages. Incomes are created; then they can be transmitted.

The confusion between money creation and financial intermediation is not an objective one; it resides in the mind and comes from the fact that emissions are naïvely assimilated to a transportation in a (Euclidian) space. Coming from banks, money is pictured as a vehicle moving between the Bank Building and the house of the person credited. Since, according to this image, money exists at the very source of money, it can be set off by the credit channel. However, everything collapses at the first serious reflexion: money is created positively in (new) wages only.

No money is therefore transported in the emission; in particular, no money is lent in the production-emission.

Nevertheless, could we not conceive of the emission of bank money as a credit operation concluded between banks and firms? The creation of money would be the opening of a credit, the counterpart of which would be differed until the repayment.

This interpretation of the facts does not pass examination. Banks cannot be the first transmitters of money since each unit of money comes to life downstream from banks. If money is transmitted, it can be so initially only by its first holders: workers.

Put shortly, a money that does not yet exist cannot be the object of any credit.

The theory of emissions provides the clear solution. Quantum credit is a creation; only ordinary credits are transmissions. However, the distinction of the two credits raises no difficulty.

- We know that quantum credit creates two equal monies face to face, one positive and the other negative.
- Ordinary credit transmits the positive money (created in quantum credits).

Any payment on one of the three markets defines a quantum credit: income is created in the producing services market, destroyed in the products market and (possibly) transmitted in the financial market. Thus, an ordinary credit is carried out by way of a quantum credit; the lender pays the borrower: as in any payment, the payment of the borrower by the lender (the seller of financial claims) is a creation-destruction of money, an emission, a quantum credit. The transaction in the financial market is an ordinary credit for the simple reason that the lender loses a positive money to the benefit of the borrower:

he transmits it to him. Once again, the transmission does not take place in the quantum credit, which has the sole effect of creating the two monies, the positive and the negative ones; in the quantum credit, the positive money literally comes from a zero money, whereas in the ordinary credit the positive money of the borrower comes from the positive money of the lender.

To sum up, semantics allows credit to be called the operation of money creation. But logic imposes imperatively that this very peculiar credit should comply with the following rules.

1   No (positive) money is cast in this credit because money is the result and not the input of the operation.
2   No (positive) interval is implicated by the operation since the creating bank is immediately paid: it receives at once a negative money and an equal positive money.
3   Finally, in its movement (in opposition to its result), the operation does not come at all into contact with the financial market.

We have called quantum credits the credits satisfying these three criteria. If money emission is a credit operation, it is indeed a quantum credit. Only ordinary credits give substance to the financial market.

In an economy equipped with a financial market, the emission of bank money immediately deposits its result on this market

We address here the fundamental principle of the theory of capital. As soon as it is created, an income is deposited in continuous time; but it could not exist (or subsist) in bank money, except under the form of a capital. Let us prove it briefly but rigorously.

An income has a purely instantaneous existence. It is not necessary to go back to this first proposition, which is only the application of the fusion of the two half-emissions into one operation. The operations in the products market constitute a unit with the (preceding) operations in the producing services market: the union being (retroactively) realized, it does appear indeed that the income will have only existed at the instant of its creation.

The purely instantaneous existence of an income is true even in chronological time. We could easily give credence to a false reasoning. Income would exist in continuous time until its annulment in the final purchases; without doubt the annulment of income is retroactive; but it still has to take place; until the final purchases, income is thus deposited in the continuum. In truth, this argument is exact in any economy where money is not bank money. But everything is different as soon as the emission of wages is an operation taken up by banks. Indeed, banks are financial intermediaries. Even if it is true that the creation of income is not a credit operation, since the new income results from human labour and not from the banks, income is lent right from the moment it is formed. The creation of income is not an operation of credit, but the income created is at once the object of a credit operation. As soon as it is created, income is lent by its holders until it is "withdrawn". That is to say income is instantly transformed into *savings*, or identically, into *capital*.

Traditional theory also recognizes that income is lent from its birth until its withdrawal by the lenders. The accepted theories go even further: they consider the action of income creation as an operation of credit. We know that this is going too far. The operation of income creation is not an ordinary credit. The fact remains in all theories that an income created at instant *t* becomes right from instant *t* the object of a loan, when this income is created by banks.

At the instant of its creation, every income is lent by its holders to the bank that issued it. Clarity requires here that we should respect the distinction of the two operations:

- income is formed in a quantum credit; it is therefore defined by a positive money for its holders and an equal negative money formed in the firm;
- the income created is instantly lent to the bank; it is thus the object of an ordinary credit; in the hands of its holder, income is transformed into a (financial) capital; correlatively, firms "lose" the negative money formed in the income emission; it is indeed identical to say that the holders lose the income, the positive money, and to say that firms lose the corresponding negative money. *The two monies are replaced by* financial claims. Any income holder is instantly transformed into a purchaser of financial claims; symmetrically, firms are instantly transformed into sellers of financial claims: they owe the bank, which has taken up for them the operation of the payment of wages, the income created.

After the (instantaneous) transformation of income into capital, the bank no longer has either the positive or the negative money born in the emission; *it is now only a financial intermediary: it has a claim on firms and it faces income holders who, now, have a claim on it.* Let us understand well that if income has not been created in an intermediation (but by labour), it is nevertheless at once the object of a perfect intermediation: the holders of wage and non-wage incomes lend these, without any delay, to the bank that, for its part, lends them at once to firms. Firms will owe the bank the incomes lent to them as long as they are not spent (by their holders). Incomes not (yet) spent are therefore no longer incomes: they are capital under the form of a claim or of a security on the bank. Symmetrically, firms no longer hold the negative money because they have contracted a debt towards the bank. The bank is therefore finally defined as a pure financial intermediary: in the same operation – the reinterpretation of income emission – the bank borrows the income (from its holders) and lends it (to firms). Let us repeat it tirelessly; the "reinterpretation" does not replace the fundamental interpretation of the emission: if income were not first created before being transmitted, it could not be transmitted since it would not exist. But as soon as income is effectively born, it can be transmitted. It is so at once, at its very birth, since the bank receives in deposit the income newly created and lends it in the same movement to the firms that have issued the wages.

As soon as we grasp the instantaneous transformation of quantum credit into an ordinary credit, we understand – for the first time – the nature of capital.

Any bank money newly formed is instantly transformed into capital net for the whole society

Let us recall that the demonstration aims at identifying loans to which correspond only zero borrowings. This is the only way (financial) capital can avoid cancellation. However, there is only one operation fulfilling this criterion: it is the transformation of income creation, quantum credit, into an ordinary credit.

As we have just established, the emission of wages having immediately deposited its object in the financial market, the product will have remained in the negative money only for an instant. As no expenditure of wages (or of derived incomes) is yet positive – income cannot be spent, in chronological time, in the very operation that forms it – we see that the product dislodged from the negative money (that no longer exist) stays in the producing firm, where it defines a stock.

Given this, one must answer the following question. Are the goods in stock an increase in the wealth of firms or on the contrary in that of income holders? The answer is imposed by logic.

- Firms "earn" the stocks in the operation where they lose the negative money created in the emission of wages.
- Income holders earn a claim on the bank in the operation that transforms their income into a capital.
- It follows that the "gain" of firms is nil, whereas the gain of income holders is net. Indeed, firms lose the negative money because they replace it by an equal debt of positive money: they owe the bank the money that the bank owes income holders. The goods in stock are therefore the (economic) property of income holders.

Let us summarize the operation. An income comes to life in a quantum credit. At this stage, the firm holds a negative money and the product "within" this money; correlatively, income holders possess the positive money, the product in money. However, quantum credit is at once transformed into an ordinary credit: the income is deposited in a bank. Income is therefore formed into capital in the assets of its holders; symmetrically, the firm loses the negative money and the product "within" that money, to the benefit of income holders; indeed, the firm "owes" the stocks to the bank, that "owes" them to the income depositors.

The emission transformed into an ordinary credit brings face to face the products in stock (in the firm) and (in the hands of the holders of wage and non-wage incomes) the right to collect these stocks. Income is at once destroyed to be replaced by a net capital – both financial (the claim on the deposited income) and real (the stocks) – the claim of income holders being a real one and not a personal one. Only the stocks correspond to the claim of savers, firms being only the "geographical" location where products are deposited like in a baggage room.

That the capital-stock should be net for the whole society is proved also by the fact that the sale of the stocks reproduces a previous income instead of involving a new income.

Any (financial and identically real) capital is a bridge between the present and the future; the goods in stock define this bridge in the eyes of the whole society

If Peter borrows from Paul, he will pay what he owes out of his future income; in this way the bridge is built: Paul's current income is lent, and Peter's future income is given as a counterpart. However, the bridge is laid only in front of Paul, because Paul's capital is negative for Peter and society will only find a zero sum there.

The goods in stock define a completely different bridge between current income and future income because, this time, it is thrown in front of the whole society. As savers withdraw the funds constituted in the transformation of quantum credits into ordinary credits, firms sell their stocks: savers therefore do not draw on the new income; they simply activate the previous income, frozen in the stocks.

The diminution of the stocks may be caused by banks themselves.

By lending income holders' savings, banks speed up the clearing of stocks; in so doing, they work to reduce and even annul the social capital-time

Let us present the bank's activity in its logical division (see Figure 5.1).

The first operation (1) is the emission of income transformed into an ordinary credit. Income holders (Wr) are the depositors of the created income, equal to x. Deposited income is lent by the second department (II) to the first (I). Finally, the income is lent to firms (F) for which the bank has issued wages x.

In the second operation (2), the bank lends to some agent, X, the income deposited by its holders. Insofar as its holders collect the deposited income themselves, X coincides with Wr.

The income collected by X is spent to the benefit of Y. Step by step, income reaches the firms; let us assume that Y is the final holder of the lent income: the expenditure of Y on F defines the clearing of the stocks. On balance, we observe that, stocks being cleared, society no longer has any capital(-time) available. The positive capital of Wr (insofar as it does not coincide with X) is compensated by the negative capital of the borrower, X.

Deposit Bank

	department of emission (I)				department of intermediation (II)			
	assets		liabilities		assets		liabilities	
(1)	F	x	II	x	I	x	Wr	x
(2)					X	x	Y	x
(3)					Y	x	F	x
balance	F	0	II	0	X	x	Wr	x

Figure 5.1 Banks' lending of income holders' savings

Thus, let us assume that the holders of wage and non-wage incomes have not spent them (entirely) in the products market; the remainder is lent by the bank to X. The expenditure of the income derived from the financial market accompanies the expenditure of the income in the products market, and the totality of the stocks is cleared. Together, agent Y and income holders cast *x* units of money in the final purchases in the products market, the exact sum of income created in the period. In "recycling" savings, the bank thus contributes to a fast clearing of current product. It is precisely because the existence of the bank emission is the *sine qua non* condition for the constitution of a net capital in the whole society that banks are able, in their intermediation activity, to reduce and finally cancel the capital born from the transformation of current income.

An economy without banks would be devoid of any net capital

Net capital and *a fortiori* capitalism find their conditions of existence in the existence of the banking system. Indeed, only the interposition of banks between firms and workers allows financial and real capital to evade the tautology of loans and debts equality. It is all the easier to demonstrate it since the tautology seems to rule and that, in the absence of any bank, it is far more surprising to see it challenged than confirmed.

It is true, however, that firms and workers do not need banks at all to carry out perfect emissions. The physical product is deposited in the "material" money that is negative in the firm. But, precisely, it is inconceivable that the product should come out of the negative non-bank money to form stocks; if the product breaks loose, it is definitively acquired by households. This is so for an obvious reason: if an operation of ordinary credit gets hold of part of the income created in the emission, in the absence of bank intermediation it can only be a contract agreed between the holder of a saved income and a borrower, i.e. a symmetrical operation, the sum of which is nil in the whole social body. If a bank were interposed, the emission of wages would be submitted to reinterpretation, the quantum loan being automatically, and on the spot, transformed into an ordinary loan.

If banks are set aside, the emission no longer involves a third party; it follows that the payment of wages is no longer a loan, even a quantum one, but a payment operation pure and simple. If a loan were nevertheless to intervene, it would only take place in a distinct operation, secondary and subsequent, income holders buying financial claims in the financial market in exchange for part of their earnings. Then, the seller and the purchaser of the financial claims correspond to each other and financial capital is both positive and negative for the same amount: it is nil in the whole society. Stocks themselves could not take shape because it is only one of two things: either products are sold and reach their final recipients, or they are awaiting and therefore remain within the negative money, thus under the form of income and not under the form of (stock-) capital.

We have just established that the emission of bank money is the sole source of financial and real capital in the global economy. The proof is reinforced by a nearly obvious consideration; as soon as wages are paid, firms get indebted to banks (in conformity with the reinterpretation of the emission): they sell financial claims to banks. However, it can be demonstrated without any difficulty that these financial claims are not a net indebtedness but are perfectly compensated debts.

If the sale of financial claims were effective or net, firms would derive from them a positive income that would finance their purchases. The reality of the operation is very different: born from the emission of wages, the indebtedness of firms is not the source of a purchase but only the financing of stock.

It would be absolutely specious to claim that the goods in stock are bought by firms, because they hold them only for their final sale to households. Indebtedness and stocks are therefore the two opposite results of the same operation, the transformation of the emission of wages into an ordinary credit. The two opposite effects compensate each other; the sold financial claims define a debt, a liability; the corresponding stocks are an equal asset; the asset and the liability born from the single operation compensate each other perfectly: the real owners of the stock are the holders of the positive financial claims (the financial bonds bought from the banks), i.e. the savers. We verify again that the positive financial claims are net whereas the negative financial claims are compensated (by the stock).

The truth according to which any net capital-time in the global economy is formed in bank money is of primary significance. It means that the "heart of capitalism" is to be found in banks. Because, as we are going to see now, fixed capital is only a particular case, a sophisticated form of capital-time.

XIV. Fixed capital, a sophisticated form of capital-time

It is conventional to say that the increase in fixed capital, i.e. net investment, has two distinct sources, profit (or self-financing) and borrowing in the financial market. We are going to show first that the two sources actually coincide: in both cases, it is the expenditure of profit by firms on their own behalf that defines investment.

The analysis of fixed capital is therefore logically situated in the continuation of the analysis of profit.

If we consider the operation of investment retrospectively, we see that monetary profit is first a form of *savings*: in its first state, a capital-good is constituted of *stocked wage-goods* facing monetary savings. Thus, at birth, fixed capital, which takes the form of saved wage-goods, is purely a *capital-time*.

Then, we have to explain the expenditure of monetary profit, its conversion into physical goods. In this respect, we shall examine again the formal rule governing the expenditure of any profit, to the benefit of firms or to the benefit of the non-wage-incomes holders. Whatever their destination, profits are always spent in the producing services market, since it is only wages that may be spent in the products market.

The conclusion is then getting closer. The conversion of monetary profits into investment-goods supposes not just that profits should be spent in the producing services market – which is true for any profit expenditure – but again that profits should be spent into a new production, posterior to the production of the wages from where monetary profit comes (by derivation).

Investment appears finally in its completeness: it is the conversion of a stock of wage-goods into a "stock" of capital-goods or instrumental capital. It will be confirmed therefore that fixed capital is a transformation or an "avatar" of a pure capital-time.

Every investment originates from a firm's profit

The proof can be given very quickly. If the funds are borrowed, it means that the profit of the firm is advanced. Thus, an investment is the expenditure of a current (already realized) profit or the expenditure of an actualized profit (that will be realized and that is already available now, because it is exchanged against the already realized income of the lender). In conclusion, an investment is always the expenditure of a firm's profit.

The unicity of the financing of net investments is confirmed by the fact that any money spent for this purpose corresponds to an equivalent stock of wage-goods.

Any money cast in investments corresponds, measure for measure, to wage-goods stocked in firms

Assume the amount of issued wages is 100 francs and 20 francs is the profit formed in the production of the period. Thus, for an expenditure of 100 francs on the goods market, workers obtain the new product for up to 80 units of measure. Being captured wages, monetary profits define the "forced" savings of workers: the lost (captured) wages are necessarily lacking for the sale of (wage-) goods. It is tautologically identical to say that 20 units of wages are formed in profits and that a measure of 20 units of wage-goods is not collected or purchased by wage-earners.

The formation of the monetary profit defines an equal "non-clearing" of wage-goods.

However, the monetary profit has yet to be spent.

The expenditure of monetary profit is an operation defined in the producing services market

Let us follow the previous example. If firms, as a whole, distribute the profit as non-wage incomes, we have the situation represented as follows (see Figure 5.2).

The argument is already well known; it suffices to recall it: the 25 units of money defining the formation and expenditure of non-wage incomes contain only the 20 units of wages captured in the sale of wage-goods. The expenditure of the redistributed profits is thus used up in the formation of the wages of workers producing the non-wage-goods.

We observe that, in the case of graph (1), profit is spent in the financing of the wages owed for the production of non-wage-goods. Even though profit is thus spent in the producing services market, its expenditure is identically present in the products market in the same period, 100 units of wages being cast into the purchase of the wage-goods currently produced, for a value (or a measure) of 80 units of wages.

The redistributed profit is thus spent on both markets in the same period. Due to the with-profit sale realized by firms, workers receive for the production of the period only 80 out of the 100 units of wages, the difference being the financing, operated retroactively from the emission of wages of the period, of the production of non-wage-goods.

The invested profit answers the same logical constraint; it is spent in the producing services market, in the emission of wages. However, the constraint is even more rigid: the investment of profit implies a new emission of wages.

The investment of monetary profit is operated in a new production

In the case under scrutiny, where firms spend the monetary profit on their own behalf, another scheme will apply (see Figure 5.3).

It is essential to understand the necessity of the distinction of two periods: one, p_1, when the monetary profit is formed and the other, p_2, when it is spent and converted into investment-goods. It would be illogical to confuse the two periods. As soon as non-wage income holders are no longer concerned, the set of firms is alone with itself. It results that if the profit expenditure were maintained face to face with the very same product, the sale of which has

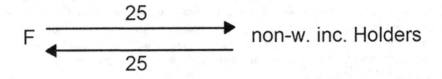

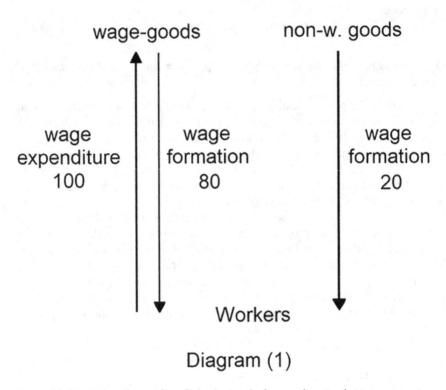

Diagram (1)

Figure 5.2 The expenditure of profit in the producing services market

formed the profit, the formation-expenditure of profit would constitute a vicious circle.

Even though graph (3) still carries the distinction of the products, wage-goods are sold with-profit for the reason that capital-goods are not sold at all: profit is nullified by the clearing deficit and, consequently, investment is also nil (see Figure 5.4).

We easily see the origin of the disappointment: non-wage incomes being, by hypothesis, withdrawn from the circuit of profits, it is logically necessary to remedy, through the distinction between periods, the now missing distinction between persons (firms and income holders). The expenditure of monetary profits by *F* to the benefit of *F* is an operation that avoids circularity, provided

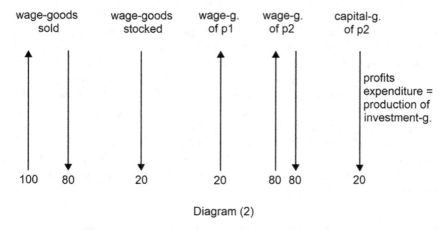

Diagram (2)

Figure 5.3 The expenditure of profit by firms on their own behalf

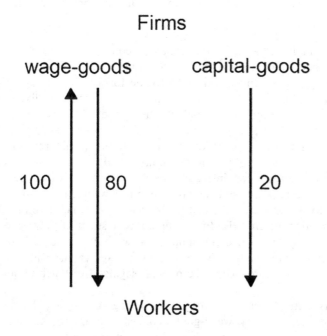

Diagram (3)

Figure 5.4 The cancellation of profit

the monetary profit formed in the sale of the product of one period is spent in the production of another period. Therefore, it is truly graph (2) that gives the correct image of reality. For the sake of simplicity, we suppose that the production of period 2 does not bring any profit. Profit realized in the sale of the product of period 1 is spent in the emission of wages of period 2: in p_2, 20 units of wages are effectively taken from the pre-existing monetary profit. Capital-goods, formed in p_2, are bought by firms (as a whole) in the producing services market, by the expenditure of the previous profits, entirely dissolved into wages of the current period (period 2).

The required demonstration is therefore completed. Capital-goods, or investment-goods, are not the primitive form of fixed capital but its secondary form, obtained by the "productive consumption" of the wage-goods saved in the formation of monetary profit.

Fixed capital is the definitive form of the wage-goods saved because of the formation of monetary profits: fixed capital is a transformation of pure capital-time

Let us consider the formation-expenditure of profits in the case of investment.

- The formation of a profit determines the equivalent creation of a stock of wage-goods. This stock is the first definition of *fixed* capital. Indeed, fixed capital goes back in its existence to the formation of monetary profit, of which it is only an "avatar". The first "content" of fixed capital is therefore a collection of stocked wage-goods, in other words a pure capital-time.
- The expenditure of profit defines the internal transformation of fixed capital, the content of which, first constituted in wage-goods, is changed into capital-goods or instrumental capital. After the expenditure of profit, fixed capital is still capital-time, but now time is definitively "moulded into the product", the instrumental form of which allows it to evade consumption indefinitely. Fixed capital is a stock of wage-goods transformed – by productive consumption – so that its sale to households is postponed from one day to the next: every fixed capital will be consumed tomorrow, in accordance to the popular saying "free lunch tomorrow".

Whereas untransformed (simply saved) wage-goods will be sold some, more or less distant, day, wage-goods converted into fixed capital are *fixed savings*, the dissolving of which is forever postponed, from one day to another. Nevertheless, it is time, and nothing else, that is fixed in the instrumental capital.

The theory of capital that we have just offered in its broad lines answers the need for a synthesis formulated by John Hicks: any capital is both a fund (or savings) and a matter (or a stock).

XV. The approach of capital by the quantum analysis of income results in the synthesis between financial capital and real capital

> If it is capital in the volume sense that is being measured, capital is physical goods; but in the value sense capital is not physical goods. It is a sum of values which may conveniently be described as a Fund. A Fund that may be embodied in physical goods in different ways. There are these two senses of Real Capital which need to be distinguished.
>
> I do of course borrow the term Fund from the history, and to the history I now turn. I am going to maintain that the distinction is quite ancient; it divides economists, ancient and modern, into two camps. There are some for whom Real Capital is a Fund – I shall call them Fundists; and there are some for whom it consists of physical goods. It is tempting to call the latter Realists; but since one wants to emphasize that both concepts are real, this is not satisfactory. I shall venture in this paper to call them Materialists. (Materialists, I mean in the sense of Dr. Johnson's refutation of Berkeley's idealism – ...)
>
> (Hicks 1977: 152)

The opposition of theorists in two schools is the sure sign of a division of truth into two "half-truths" or, identically, into two "half-errors". More fundamentally, the two camps are found to be at fault as soon as capital is grasped in its two aspects simultaneously, which is necessary, the truncated reality being entirely conceived outside of the real world. However, if it is true that, as for any scientific progress, quantum analysis of income formation requires considerable attention, the reward is commensurate with the effort, particularly in the essential area of the conception of capital and capitalism.

Today, economics can be operational because the foundations of the unitary theory of capital have been laid down. We shall show that the dysfunction of the domestic economy is entirely caused by the rule of Capital. The aetiology being found, the cure follows, so that economics becomes what it has never ceased to be teleologically, i.e. political economy.

Before starting the study of the Crisis, let us sum up in a few lines the unitary conception of capital, a magnitude both material and financial.

In its origin, every capital is a wage

We shall reason of course on bank money. The product of the period appears entirely in the emission of wages. Banks being present in the financial market, income is instantly destroyed and wages (together with non-wage incomes, known retroactively) are transformed into capital. The physical product is first deposited in the negative money; this is the phase when the income exists, during which the positive money (units of wages) is the very definition of the product. Quantum credit being instantly transformed into an ordinary credit, the physical product is at once dislodged from the negative money, disintegrated in the collision with the positive money: income ceases to exist and a capital replaces it at once in a strict equivalence. Income is replaced by a monetary capital (to say financial capital is a redundancy), an equal right to the future income that will form effectively in any "withdrawal" carried out by the holders of wages, rent, interest and dividends, on the banks on which they have a claim. At each withdrawal, saved income is reproduced, and the physical product follows once again the law of the emission: it becomes again an income, i.e. a product within the negative money, to be withdrawn in the same movement, this time definitively, since it is denatured into a simple value in use at the disposal of households.

When it first appears, any capital is a patrimonial value formed to the benefit of income holders, not in firms

Capital is initially a "suspended" income, the future income of the holders. Any current income that is found again at a future instant exists during the interval under another identity, precisely that of a *capital*. We understand therefore that any capital has its primary origin in the instantaneous transformation of newly issued wages. No holder has the time to spend his income at the instant of its formation; any holder saves therefore his income until the time (of his own choosing) of spending it in the products market. Savings are not an income but a capital.

Saved wages are a dual reality, a product stocked in a firm and a claim on this product in the assets of income holders

The two aspects of "Real Capital" mentioned by Hicks are thus created in the same flow, the automatic and instantaneous transformation of quantum credit. The claim of income holders on banks is the sole exact measure of the physical product constituted in material capital (the stocks) and held in firms. The synthesis is perfect. The product was born in money; if it exists now in kind, this is because it is duplicated: on one side we find the claim (savings), and on the other the object of the claim (the stock).

Neither the claim (the financial capital) nor its object (the material capital) may be conceived one without the other. For the claim, it is a truism; a claim without any object being null and void. For the object, its conjunction with the claim is no less necessary since the product – even though it is in kind (and not in money) from now on – is not yet sold to households.

A part of saved income is formed into firms' capital

It is certain that all savings finally spent in the products market are an annulled capital: the product is withdrawn from the stocks; correlatively, the claims of households on banks are destroyed.

The only type of capital that can subsist results therefore from the transfer of part of wages to the benefit of firms. We have demonstrated that this transfer is a flow simultaneously present in the markets for products and for producing services.

Right from its formation, any profit is a capital. Being a *financial* magnitude, profit is a claim on banks; being a material magnitude, profit is a real claim. Stocked wage-goods face monetary profits, for the exact measure in which wage incomes are transferred to firms.

A part of capital-profit is finally destroyed in the withdrawal of the corresponding stocks

This is clear; any profit distributed in non-wage incomes is destroyed under its double aspect: households consume (destruction of the financial capital) and in doing so withdraw an equal amount of stocks.

The complementary part of capital-profit, invested profit, is fixed; incorporated into matter, financial savings remain there permanently

Profit is invested in a univocal operation, the payment of new wages from previous wages captured by firms.

From there, it is clear that investment-goods are the new, definitive, form of the wage-goods initially stocked by the saving of income holders. The production of the new period, which engenders capital-goods, dislodges wage-goods and replaces them at once, in the unchanged "stock", by instrumental capital. Finally, tools, machines and equipment are wage-goods the saving of which is irrevocable since they indefinitely avoid being consumed by households.

The one-to-one relation of financial capital and material capital is again fully satisfied. We do verify therefore the coexistence of savings (financial capital, equal to the wages captured and invested) and of the "stock" (material capital, product in kind of the emission of wages fed by profits). To take Hicks' expression, financial capital is "embodied" into investment-goods.

Part II

The dysfunction of the domestic economy: from capital to capitalism

The study of the dysfunction of the domestic economy is entirely renewed by the theory of emissions. For the first time we can seriously hope to get an inside understanding of the disorder and resolve it by the newly discovered remedies.

Inflation is today recognized as the essential "disequilibrium" of our economies. Even unemployment is considered a consequence of inflation.

Theorists agree to define inflation as the positive difference between money and product, nominal magnitudes outweighing the corresponding real magnitudes. The difficulty then is only beginning. It consists in locating the discrepancy; does it appear between the masses or, radically, in the very operations giving rise to money and real goods?

The theory of emissions settles this prejudicial issue and puts the problem at its true level. When the masses, money and product, are already formed, they are in all cases – whether inflation is nil or positive – defined in their perfect union, no money being able to contain a smaller amount of product.

6 The quantitative theory and the quantum theory of inflation

The quantitative theory of money, which, it is true, has formulations scattered all through the history of economic thought, to the point that in no time did it exist as a completed body of explanation, is thereby undermined. If at any instant the country owns x units of real money, it possesses exactly x units of products in money, the precise measure of the real goods that would be found in the expenditure of the x units of money. The idea that money exists on one side, "without any product", and that the product is elsewhere, "without any money", comes from a great naïvety. In truth, money is, at all times, the form of the real goods not yet sold to households, like the bottle is the form of the liquid or the gas it contains.

XVI. Any money is instantly filled up with an equivalent product

There cannot be anywhere even one unit of money empty of product, because the form-money is born immediately "full of product". The proof is that any money (even a "material" one) is created both positive and negative; however, the two monies are held at a distance one from the other only by the product integrated in the negative money. As soon as the mind annuls the product in money, it would contradict itself if it were not annulling money as well, positive money replacing at once the product within negative money.

The monetary theory adequate to the facts is the quantum theory and not the quantitative theory. It can be demonstrated again in another way.

Money and product are not two distinct masses

Let us suppose that we are persisting with the idea according to which the correspondence between money and product is a relation between two positive masses. According to this theory, the relation is given in the exchanges. Indeed, if the positive, nominal and real masses do coexist, we cannot see how they could meet or cross, except in purchases. Thus, let us enumerate all the instants when exchanges are observed; let us call them instants t. At any instant t a relation exists between a quantifiable mass of money and a product determined in its physical dimensions. There is no correspondence between money and products at the instants that do not belong to the *t* series, since any exchange is carried out at an instant *t*. We deduce from this the refutation of the quantitative theory, at the successive instants *t* and within their intervals.

- At instants *t*, money takes the measure of the product. How could it be "too big" for the product, since the two masses measure each other only when exchanged? For a discrepancy to take shape, two distinct operations would be needed: one that would render the two masses commensurable, and the other that would cause, within the same measuring space thus created, the increase of money compared to the product. The exchange being the unique operation available to the quantitative theory, it can therefore at best create the commensurability of money and the product and not, in addition, the expansion of money relatively to the product. To require both the measure and the excess on that measure – the discrepancy relatively to the initial measure – is to ask the impossible, namely that the same operation, the exchange, should give two distinct measures of the product in money, a weak measure (defining the common measuring space of the product and of money), and a strong (inflationist) measure.
- In the intervals between instants *t*, money and the product remain, by hypothesis, in two worlds completely foreign to each other; not only could inflation not be determined in these conditions but, being a relation between money and the product, it is obliterated at any instant not belonging to the t series.

In quantitative theory, inflation is simply the (unexplained) increase of prices

It is true though that inflation may be grasped by the quantitative theory because it appears in the simple comparison of the monetary prices of a basket of goods at two distinct periods. If the price of the basket is 110 fr. today for 100 fr. a year ago, inflation is said to reach an annual rate of 10%. The phenomenon is just described; hence, we cannot reject this "definition" of inflation, which does not bring any explanation. In all rigour, far from being solved, the problem is not even formulated. Is inflation a disorder and, if it is, is it a disease affecting money or a deficiency of the production system?

Confronted with these elementary questions, quantitative theory reveals its inadequacy. It claims to detect through exchanges the reason for the increase in the general price level, the price of the basket. However, concerning the relation money-product, exchanges in the real goods market are just a web of tautologies, from which no knowledge can be drawn, either on the state of money or on the evolution of the production power of the domestic economy.

Science would be placed at the starting point of the right track only if exchanges in the products market formed a continuity in time, so that the relation between money and the product could be followed dynamically. Since no exchange allows itself to be "smoothed" through time, successive exchanges are like islets in an emptiness of exchanges, so that the theory cannot succeed in establishing the slightest link between today's and yesterday's transactions. We know that today's prices are higher but we do not know why at all.

The analysis could grasp the two prices together only if they were two successive states of the same magnitude; however, no price (in the sense of the exchange) is moving through time; every price exists at one instant, where it disappears. It follows that today's price is a magnitude not only different but distinct from yesterday's price, another magnitude, without any parentage link with the first one. Any supporter of quantitative theory has therefore to reply to the ordinary enquiring man that not only does economic science not know why prices are higher, but also, in all logic, it does not know why today's prices and yesterday's prices belong to one same measurement space.

Unable to find the link, the scholar is none the wiser than the layman.

It seems that a way out may still be open: the use of expectations.

The explanation of a price increase by the expectation of the increase is circular

Prices increase because agents expect them to do so.

In view of such a hypothesis, it is important to maintain clarity. If expectations have an effect, it can only be through influencing the evolution of prices; in no case can they create this evolution from scratch.

If prices were linked together through time, it is conceivable that by affecting the behaviour of agents, expectations would cause the variation of prices; but, insofar as the analysis is unable to establish a link between successive prices, it is in vain that it has recourse to expectations, no inexistent movement being able to be either slowed down or accelerated by behaviours.

The enquiry arrives at the same conclusion by a slightly more abstract way. Even expectations cannot go through the transaction-less periods: they exert their effect – provided it is not entirely imaginary – on the transactions when they are carried out. Agents are buying now because they anticipate the price increase. However, whatever their power, expectations affect the link between money and the product and not both masses separately.

Neither available money, nor the volume of products on sale depend today on the prices expected today; at most, we may count on expectations to contribute casting money onto the product with more or less ardour. Since the quantitative theory is unable to grasp the interaction between money and product, except in actual exchanges, the links that might be influenced by expectations have strictly no consistency.

Briefly, within the quantitative theory, expectations are an acceleration defined in relation to a non-existing speed. Taken only in the products market, prices do not move through time (their speed is zero); expectations speed up or slow down the evolution of prices, a movement the existence of which is not only left unexplained but, even more, is formally denied.

XVII. The theory of emissions is the only one able to explain inflation

The theory of emissions introduces a new dimension that is needed to position the problem of inflation. It is true in any theory that the link from mass to mass, between money and product, can only be grasped at the very moment it is formed; it is also certain that this link only exists during the time of exchange, i.e. within the limits of an instant. However, even though it complies with the two constraints, the quantum theory brings the distinction of the operations and of their results. Exchange is no longer conceived of as the relation between masses but as the operation of which the masses are the result or the effect. Product and money result from the emission. Even though it exists only during an instant, the relation between money and product exists therefore in a dual way: firstly, in the *operation*, which is identically the emission of money and of the product; secondly in the *result* of the operation, the monetary income and conjointly the physical product. However, if in the result of the exchange (the emission) we can only read the tautology of the identity of money and product, the preliminary examination of the operation itself enables one to arrive at the "theorising" of inflation, because emissions are full or empty.

- Full emissions create the measurement space of money and product.
- Empty emissions do not modify that space, but they introduce in it a "product-less money".
- Hence, the same total operation, the sum of the emissions observed during the period, explains both the constitution of the measurement space and, within this space, the discrepancy between nominal magnitudes and real magnitudes, any empty emission being an addition to the monetary income facing a constant real income.

The quantitative theory of money is, as we saw, unable to conceive inflation; it can only receive its description passively, as given in the evolution of an index, the price of a goods basket.

The quantum theory of money grasps inflation, which is now a concept and no longer a gross fact. It is even easy to represent the new conception, with the help of the "zero-sphere" and of its positive bulge, the domestic income.

Representation of inflation by the distinction in the production sphere of a "core" and a "crown"

Embedded in the negative money, the physical product is absorbed and annulled; its only reality is in the correlative positive money, the definition of the product (in money) and not just a measure of the physical product.

Money issued in wages is the measure of the product because it *is* the product. The two masses do not therefore face each other; at the instant it gives birth to it, the monetary emission changes the product into money, like a larvae into a butterfly. No more than the butterfly would look at the larvae, that no longer exists, does money look at the product, the existence of which is still annulled inside the negative money.

It is legitimate to represent the product inside wages, the positive money being the simple form or the mould of the product-content. Any emission of wages, direct or not, is the creation of an inhabited or full money, since the physical product is somehow the lodger of nominal wages. The correspondence is perfectly defined, since wages incorporate the product of remunerated workers.

Now, the representation of inflation is greatly facilitated (see Figure 6.1).

With the help of two concentric spheres, projected on a plane, we perceive well the analytical progress of the theory of emissions in relation to the quantitative theory. The observation of facts begins now at the level of the operations creative of the two masses, product and money; up until now, the only retained operation, "relative" exchange, concerned the two masses already constituted.

A new confrontation between quantitativism and "quantism"

Quantitativism relies on the relation of goods between themselves; exchange, conceived as a link between the various goods, cannot rule the creation of the two terms of exchange. If goods do not pre-exist, it will not be possible to grasp them in a network of exchanges.

General equilibrium provides no information on the formation of the exchanged goods. This fact is often expressed by referring to the law of conservation; transactions on the goods and securities market conserve the exchanged goods, nothing being created or destroyed in the process.

Emissions of the period

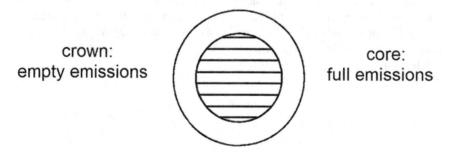

crown:
empty emissions

core:
full emissions

Figure 6.1 The representation of inflation

But the consequence of this inertia is severe: given that money intervenes in the field of explanations only at the moment of its exchange with real goods, it admits for each situation of general equilibrium (highly theoretical, by the way) only *one* relation with the set of products and financial claims; the fundamental criticism is thus confirmed; money cannot ever be compared to itself – neither at a given moment, nor through time – a comparison that would yet be of the most basic necessity since the theory aims at examining the "health" of the monetary economy.

Everything changes as soon as the analysis is able to turn to the operations instead of just looking at their results. The theory of emissions does not express itself *after* that product and money have already been formed. Its object is on the contrary the study of creations. Immediately, the research is revitalized because the emissions belong to two categories:

- full emissions deposit the product into the money (the two masses being from then on coextensive, merged one into the other);
- empty emissions create a "product-less money".

In each period of production, corresponding to the frequency of the wage emissions, it is therefore possible to compare money to itself.

The "crown" represents the emission of a supernumerary, inflationist, money, whereas, in the core, any money is accompanied by its equivalent-product. (Notice that we are using the words "crown" and core both for the emissions and their results.)

In all periods, it is now possible to determine the inflationary gap.

Even more, we can follow over time, through successive productions, the effect of empty emissions on the evolution of the prices of the products deposited, by each new emission, in the wages (of the core).

The aetiology of inflation is thus known. However, unemployment has the same origin. We shall verify this.

Then we shall examine the remedies usually offered: neither inflation nor unemployment are efficiently tackled since the origin of the disease is not well known.

Finally, we shall present the true solution, that follows the high Ricardian tradition. The reform of bank accounting will ensure the appropriation of the means of production by households as an anonymous whole. Thus, the economy will no longer experience any empty emission. The disease will be eradicated.

7   Inflation and unemployment have the same aetiology: empty emissions

According to the dichotomic conception of money, inflation and unemployment are either "real phenomena" or "monetary phenomena", one could almost say at the choice of theorists. One speaks of structure and conjuncture, defective information and errors of anticipation, bad coordination between decision centres, irrational behaviour of income holders, economic policy influenced by national interest at the expense of the "overall balance", as they say nowadays. Balance of payments and budget deficits are also incriminated. In no way is this an exhaustive enumeration and its items could not either constitute the components of a meaningful theory: they are rather the reflection of "moods" and constitute easy weapons in the hands of party men.

The discovery of the quantum nature of every act of production within the nation brings much more than hope: it logically leads to the solution, the unravelling of inflation and unemployment. Keynes was absolutely right; the economic problems do not deserve to monopolize the concern of human beings; more noble questions, cultural, religious, artistic and even metaphysical are overshadowed; it is high time to bring them back to the fore.

The Crisis has one, single "cause": empty emissions.

Already in the positive economy (hence stricken by disorder) every unit of money is a product and every product (not yet cleared) is in the money: the dichotomy between the nominal and the real is a pure chimera. The only disorder is in the immediate clearing, at the expense of domestic income, of part of the product.

An emission is empty precisely in that it casts a product into money but only to dislodge it at once, in the same movement. The proper order requires that each product "inserted" in money should stay there until the income thus created is spent.

We shall outline the theory of empty emissions in six considerations.

If banks cast in ordinary credits money they do not have – and we shall see that this is logically possible – they issue money empty of any product. We shall demonstrate however that the empty emissions of this first type can almost never happen and moreover that their effect is not cumulative over time.

Net investment is the first serious case of an empty emission. However, money issued in the investment of profit finally finds a "body" in the wage-goods saved during the formation of the monetary profit.

Nonetheless, the empty emission defined by a net investment has far-reaching consequences; this capital will escape the reach of income holders and this "dispossession" will explain the malignant emissions.

Indeed, since fixed capital is withdrawn from income holders, its amortization causes the "dual" production of profit-goods.

The amortization of fixed capital engenders an empty money which, in advanced capitalism, is finally equal to a third of the total industrial production.

Empty wages have no purchasing power. We thus demonstrate the coexistence of two opposite discrepancies that, in their factual conjunction, can only be explained by the theory of emissions:

- global demand is larger than global supply by the whole amount of empty emissions (the inflationary gap);
- global demand may however be insufficient; it is so insofar as empty emissions produce wage-goods; in this case, demand – which is yet nominally larger than supply – is unable to absorb the totality of the products on sale (the deflationary gap).

8 The two benign cases of empty emissions or of inflation

XVIII. First benign case of empty emissions: banks lend more money than they borrow

A whole study should deal with the movements of money, coming in and going out of banks. Let us focus on the basics.

The two functions of deposit banks

Banks issue money. However, they also have another function; they receive and bring to the financial market a part of the income issued.

In its money-creation function, the banking system (deposit banks linked together through the Central Bank) is in a monopolistic position. But, concerning financial intermediation, banks are competing with other institutions, like savings banks, insurance companies, investment banks and investment companies.

The logic of the distinction is very clear. Taken in their creative function, banks are "entry points"; in this, they are neither buyers nor sellers, even in the financial market. When banks, on the contrary, are only transmitting a money already issued, they sell financial claims (to borrow money), and they buy financial claims (in order to lend the borrowed money).

Simply for convenience, let us distinguish in each bank: bank I and bank II. Bank I creates and destroys domestic money periodically in all the operations of payment and expenditure of wages (operations repeated n times in the intermediary transactions). Bank II is present, with the other financial institutions, in the financial market, where it brings together savers and final borrowers.

If bank I and bank II were distinct establishments, the analysis would be greatly simplified and, more importantly, no empty emission could come from banking activities. However, we have to accept reality in all its complexity; in fact, every deposit bank is, in its unity, both a bank I and a bank II. The confusion of the functions in one institution does not mean their confusion in one operation. It is fortunate that, on the contrary, the purity of the operations is maintained most of the time, and thus that the same bank creates without transmitting and, on the other hand, transmits without creating, as required by logic. Reality being neither totally imperfect nor perfect, a bank may happen to be not just both a bank I and a bank II, but to be so in one and the same operation, which is logically wrong.

Sometimes banks create in a financial operation

Let us represent the anomaly in "T-accounts" as in Figure 8.1.

First of all, bank I issues the income (its negative form) of the period; it thus creates x units of negative money in the firms and x units of positive money in the assets of workers and, more generally, of households. This is operation *1*.

Operation *2* traces the automatic transformation of the x units of created income in x units of savings or monetary capital.

Let us recall that this mutation is immediate: it means that at the instant of its formation, every unit of income is saved, i.e. lent in the financial market. It is necessarily so, since money is of a banking nature. Income holders acquire, at the instant they are paid, a claim on bank II. A relation is thus created between bank II and bank I. Bank II receives income x in deposit; it is precisely this deposit that defines income x transformed into savings; correlatively, bank II is released from its liability towards households; now, it owes x francs to bank II.

The anomaly arises in operation *3*. Bank II, which has at its disposal all the savings x, lends an amount y greater than x. If the loan were at most equal to

The Unique Establishment
(The Same Deposit Bank)

	bank I				bank II		
	assets		liabilities		assets		liabilities
1	F x	Wr	x				
2		Wr	$-x$				
2		bank II	$+x$	bank I	x	Wr	x
3		F	$+x$	borrowers	y	F	y
3		bank II	$-x$			F	$-x$
3						bank I	$+x$
4 (balance)	0		0	borrowers	y	Wr	x
						F	$y-x$

Figure 8.1 Lending through money creation

x, everything would be "normal". However, if bank II were not the same person or the same establishment as bank I, but an autonomous institution, the function of which would be of pure financial intermediation, it could not lend a sum greater than x; it would be like the most beautiful girl in the world who can only give what she has.

The problem arises only from the conjunction of bank I and bank II in the same institution: factual reality imposes this "complexity", because every deposit bank is both a creator of money and a broker of savings. It may happen therefore, in the current state of this world, that bank II lends effectively a sum y on the basis of a sum x received in deposits, although y *is* greater than x.

The bank lends y to some agents; let us remark however that the loan carried out by bank II is posterior to the formation of deposits x; it is therefore possible and even probable that the holders of savings x withdraw some of it for themselves. In the sum y of the money that "leaves" bank II, we must take into account the withdrawals by savers: y is therefore the sum of withdrawals and loans. Since y is by hypothesis greater than x, the difference, $(y - x)$, is created by bank II.

Let us repeat the list of events. Bank II has received x units of money in deposits; but it lends (or gives back) y units of money, where y is greater than x. This is logically possible since the only rule is the equality of the sums indicated on the assets side and on the liabilities side of the bank. Every sum created as a supernumerary $(y - x)$ is indicated on the assets side, where it designates the debt of the borrowers, and on the liabilities side, where it represents the deposit of the agents paid by the borrowers.

Operation *3* can be simplified. Let us assume that the sum of the withdrawn savings is nil and that borrowers cast sum y in the payment of firms. Finally, borrowers owe y to bank II, which owes y to the economy, of which x is owed to savers (Wr) and $(y - x)$ to firms as a whole (which owed x and have received y).

The anomaly is in the fact that the sum lent (y) by the financial intermediary is greater than the totality of available income (x). We see that the sum of $(y - x)$ francs *is created in an empty emission*, households carrying, after the operations in the financial market, y units of money onto x units of product only. Firms sell the current product against the sum of available income, a sum that, from x units initially, is brought up to y units by bank II.

Operation *3* is possible for the amount of y, therefore above x, because the equivalence of assets and liabilities is complied with in the bank for the sum of $(y - x)$ as well as for the sum of x. Up to x francs, bank II lends its assets, its claims on bank I; beyond that, bank II creates new deposits for the whole amount of money lent without being borrowed; instead of feeding the loan, deposit $(y - x)$ to the benefit of F, is its consequence.

In the balance of operations *1, 2, 3*, we find that bank I has annulled all its entries, whereas bank II only retains Wr in its liabilities for x (provided Wr has not borrowed anything and does not coincide in any way with the bor-rowers) and F for $(y - x)$; the corresponding assets are the debt of borrowers.

The confusion between monetary and financial operations is possible because they are carried out by the same banking establishments

It is obvious that the empty emission would not happen if the same person were not uniting banks I and II. It is precisely because the same deposit bank is a point of emission and a financial intermediary that the confusion of the operations can happen: the sum $(y - x)$ is created *ex nihilo*; it is created by a savings bank (bank II) that lends more money (y units) than it has borrowed (x units).

No non-bank financial intermediary can lend what it does not have; a bank can do so; it only needs to create by lending. We might even say that in the current state of accounting regulations, the bank is not aware of bank II mixing up into the functions of bank I; being joined in the same accounts, the operations of creation and intermediation coexist, so much so that the bank never knows the amount of deposits it has at its disposal to feed its loans in the financial market.

Thus uncovered, the situation seems so fraught with dangers that one is all set to blame the faulty functioning of banks for most, if not all, the empty emissions afflicting the economy. This judgment would be far too severe. In reality, taking into account three factors results in reversing the verdict: the share of the empty emissions due to the activity of banks is practically negligible.

The interference of monetary operations in financial operations is a benign disorder

Let us give just three reasons in a cursory form.

1   Insofar as the creation of money is based on a product, money is unable to leak out of the circuit of its issuing bank, except in compensated operations, as the bank is becoming a creditor and a debtor of other banks for the same amount. Indeed, the clearing of the product draws back to the bank the very same money it had created.

2   As soon as the creation of money exceeds production, the bank incurs the probability of losing the excess in favour of other banks. This probability on the totality of the excess becomes a certainty on its part: a share, as small as it might be, of the money created in excess will be found in other banks. It follows that any creation of money in an operation of inter-mediation (therefore a faulty creation) ends up in the indebtedness of the issuing bank. Subjected to the "golden rule" of the balance of its accounts, the bank will make sure it avoids opening its circuit: it acts, experimentally, in its daily operations, in order to always maintain a

closed circuit. The daily adjustments, negative and positive, maintain the sum of the creations of money at the level logically allowed. In the end, all bank emissions are full.

3   *The third argument is by far the most important.* Any operation of ordinary credit is a zero-sum operation through time. Thus, in each period, the amount of loans in excess is diminished by the settlement of the excess loans reaching maturity. In other words, the empty emissions due to the activity of banks *are not cumulative over time.* If, in the past, important leaks had happened in the circuit of a bank, which is already very unlikely, these leaks, even totally renewed in the period under scrutiny, would not have any effect because they would be compensated by the consequences of the previous leaks. The empty emissions originating from banks would only be threatening if the excessive creations of money (carried out in the intermediations) were following a continuous growth. The observation of reality reveals a completely different behaviour: forewarned, by the induced indebtedness, of their possible past mistakes, banks would redress them instead of aggravating them.

To conclude, empty emissions would have no significant impact if they were exclusively caused by the imperfection of the accounting rules imposed on banks. It is true that, in its current state, double entry accounting is not sufficiently compartmented in banks, to allow the visualization of the assured analytical distinction of operations whether they create or transmit money. But the ensuing confusion brings its own remedies and we have to look elsewhere for the true origin of empty emissions.

XIX. Second benign case of empty emissions: net investment

We are now starting the study of the "heart of capitalism".

In order to ensure a successful start to the analysis of the pathology, for it exists not only in ideologies but also in facts, where it takes, in the eyes of everyone, the form of an increase in prices and of a persistent high level of unemployment, it is useful to sum up the mechanism of net investment, logically reducible to the formation of a capital-time.

Nothing enables yet to conclude in the existence of an anomaly or a disorder. However, the deepening of the analysis reveals the double nature of net investment; it introduces empty emissions into the working of the domestic economy.

The double nature of net investment

A *reminder of the "first nature" of net investment*: it is the formation of a capital-time.

The accumulation of simple capital-time – due to the saving of wages not transformed into profits – is a (positive, negative or zero) operation that is situated inside each period of production, between the boundaries defined by two successive emissions of wages. That is to say, the operation under consideration involves only one period at a time. If income holders accumulate part of their current earnings, they accumulate a capital-time; the accumulation is net for the whole society, provided that current saving outweighs current "dissaving".

Net investment is a little more complicated accumulation of capital-time. This time, the reasoning has to be logically carried over two distinct periods: profit is formed from wages of one period, and it is spent in the emission of the wages of another period. It is indeed inconceivable that, taken from wages of one period, profit should be invested in the wages of the same period. We know already well the reasons for this impossibility. But because we are facing a really strange fact, we must not fear repeating ourselves too much.

In period p, 100 units of wages are produced by the domestic economy. Of those 100 units, we assume that 20 units are formed into profits. Henceforth, we conclude in the existence of a "theoretical fork".

- If the 20 units of wages earned in profits feed dividends (or any other non-wage income), formed outside of firms, the corresponding real goods – dividend-goods – are the fifth part of the product of period p. Indeed, firms are finally confronted with the existence of 100 units of wages, of which 20 units are distributed, for a real product itself incorporated into the 100 units of money. The expenditure of wages, 80 units on one side and 20 units on the other, defines the clearing of the product of period p, to the set of holders of wage and non-wage incomes.

- Everything is profoundly different if, instead of being distributed, the 20 units of wages earned in profits feed net investments, i.e. expenditures to the benefit of firms. (let us note once again that the analysis of this new situation is unchanged in the case where wages earned in profits come from the financial market; the bonds bought by workers "advance" the profits of firms). This time, the expenditure is a very peculiar movement, in which the set of firms (F) is both the origin and the end. Any net investment is an expenditure of F on F. Let us suppose that, failing to realize the originality of the new situation, a theorist would maintain the preceding conclusion, by positioning the investment in the same period the wages captured in profits were formed. This scholar will soon realize that he is heading the wrong way, because the sum of profits can only be zero in those conditions. The production of period p brings 100 units of wages; if the investment of 20 units of profits means the purchase of part of the product of period p, we see that the sum of the sales of this product is equal to its total cost of production (in wage-units). It follows indeed that profit is nil. If, in reality, the invested profit is obviously positive, it is that reality complies with logic: firms invest their profits of period p into the production of a later period.

Being a surplus, the profit of one period can only be invested into a *sub-sequent* production.

The terms of the "theoretical fork" can therefore be reformulated in the following way.

- *Distributed* profits are incomes formed and spent into the production of the same period.
- *Invested* profits are formed in the production of one period and spent into the production of another period.

In both cases, production is equal to 100 units of wages per period. When profit is distributed, the real profit of period p is the (hashed) part of the product of p. Consequently, production of the subsequent period, $p+$, does

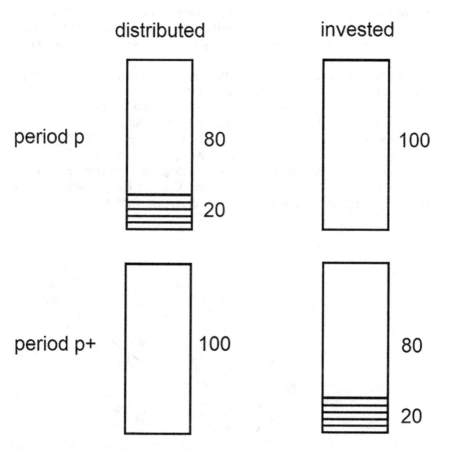

Figure 8.2 The expenditure of distributed and invested profits

not include, in the payment of wages, any expenditure of the earlier profit. If profit is invested, it is on the contrary the payment of wages of period p that is free from any expenditure of the profit of p: the 20 units of profit are now the (hashed) part of the 100 units of wages spent in $p+$.

(A small difficulty still stands; the products of p and of $p+$ are of course interchangeable; it is therefore possible that firms may choose the investment-goods (the increase of their instrumental capital) in the product of p; none-theless, even then, investment-goods are bought by the expenditure of profits in the emission of wages of $p+$: the capital formed in $p+$ is just exchanged "in advance" and at market prices against an equivalent product of period p).

The opposition between the cases is complete; *distributed* profit is retro-actively spent at the formation of wages earned as profits; meanwhile, *invested* profit defines an irreversible capital-time; facing the invested profit, 20 units of the product of period p are saved forcefully.

Firms making the profit are F'; we observe the correlative formation in F'' of savings in wage-goods, equal to 20 units. Equivalent to the wages captured in invested profits, the saving of wage-goods is a definitive capital-time, the production of period $p+$ (up to 20 units) being not the annulation of these savings, but only the conversion of its object; wage-goods are replaced inside savings by a fixed capital.

In its 'first nature', obviously harmless, net investment is therefore only a more complex form of capital-time accumulation.

The "second nature" of net investment: it is an empty emission.

This is where the demonstration starts to be a bit difficult.

As long as the theorist has, before his eyes, only wages and distributed prof-its, he can only have knowledge, in the producing services market, of operations of one unique type, every emission of wages being, on these conditions, a zero purchase in the products market. The expenditure in the producing services market of distributed profits is taken from the products market.

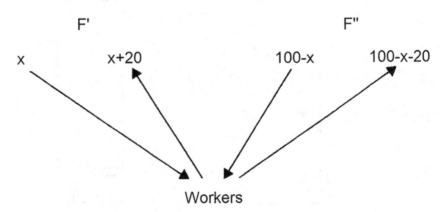

Figure 8.3 Profit and savings

Let us specify clearly the elements of the "experiment" that we have to undertake. We are not considering the retroaction of the expenditure of wages on the operation of their formation, because the retroactivity of the destruction of wages is foreign to our current discussion. If we nevertheless introduce a retroaction, it concerns only the part of the wages captured into profits: as soon as profit is taken into account, we cannot, indeed, ignore the wages spent and destroyed by its formation. We find therefore in all cases – even for distributed profits – that the formation of profits defines a purchase right from the emission of wages, a purchase in the products market.

However, and this is the essential point, if the formation of profit introduces positive purchases in the payment of wages, the final expenditure of wages is *reduced accordingly*. The wages spent in the producing services market will no longer be spent in the products market. The enunciated theorem is thus demonstrated in its validity range. No emission of wages defines an additional purchase in the products market.

Let consider again the often-used example.

The hashed parts are, for *a*, the expenditure of profits included in the creation of wages and, for *b*, the creation of profits included in the expenditure of wages. After *compensation*, we observe that wages are formed in a movement free of any destruction of income and, symmetrically, that wages are spent in a movement devoid of any creation of income.

We meet again the lesson, the validity range of which is thereby circumscribed, according to which the formation and the expenditure of profits are a circuit within the wage circuit.

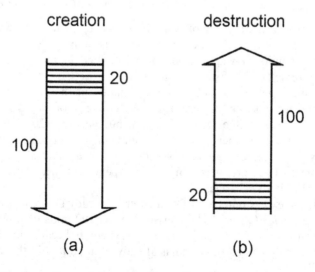

Figure 8.4 The formation and the expenditure of profit

Thus, after the emission of 100 units of wages, 100 units of income are available in the products market; conversely, after the expenditure of this income, we observe that the final purchases in the products market are reduced to the sum of 100 units of wages. The formation and expenditure of distributed profit add absolutely nothing to the sum of the expenditures observed in the products market.

The reader senses *a contrario* to what conclusion the analysis will very soon lead him: the investment of profit is an *additional* purchase in the products market.

The proof is rigorous. It comprises two parts.

1. Allocated to investment, profits have the power to buy labour

Neither wages nor distributed profits will give their holders the means of exploiting to their benefit, the labour of others. Agents have only the possibility of collecting the product, i.e. the goods the production of which has already taken place and given rise to wages and other incomes.

However, profit is invested in a completely original operation; it buys labour; it is the remuneration of the latter. This time, labour itself is a commodity; it is bought by the transformation of profits into new wages: if, over 100 units of wages issued in period $p+$, 20 units are so from the profits formed on the previous product, by investing profits, firms buy a fraction of the labour of period $p+$, exactly the fifth part of the working population in $p+$ (measured in wage-units). In its investment, profit is a purchasing power on human labour.

Let now consider the second part.

2. The purchase of labour is identically the purchase of the product of labour

Indeed, by buying the activity of workers, for up to 20 units of wages, firms buy in the same movement the product of this activity, real goods for an amount of 20 units of wages. The goods acquired in the purchase of the activity of workers define fixed capital.

By bringing together the information included in the two parts, we find what we had to look for. In period $p+$, the emission of wages is 100 units, whereas the sum of the corresponding final purchases is 120 units of wages. Income holders have at their disposal 100 units of wages (partially distributed in interests, rents and dividends); for their part, firms have already spent 20 units of wages in the products market, an expenditure included in the emission of the 100 units of wages.

Where is the excess purchase? The answer is already given; it is in the *payment of wages out of profits*. The emission of the 100 units of wages in $p+$ is full only up to 80 units; for the remainder, it is *empty* because the product of the fifth part of employed workers has already been bought in the emission of wages itself.

The holders of the 100 units of income created (and deposited in time) in $p+$ have the power to buy only 80 units of the product of $p+$; the difference is the fixed capital accumulated by firms. We observe indeed that in the 100 units of wages issued, 20 units are empty (of any product).

In other words, even though 100 units of wages have been issued, the product of $p+$ is only deposited in 80 units of wages, the difference being the immediate increase of fixed capital accumulated by firms.

The emission of wages is *full* when the formation of wages does not coincide with the expenditure of profit. The emission of wages, on the contrary, is *empty* as far as it identifies itself with the expenditure of profit, a condition that is fulfilled in the investment of profit.

Let us carefully note that the empty emission is not the remuneration of a pseudo-labour. The activity of period $p+$ produces a measure of 100 new goods, of which workers only receive 80 units in their wages of 100 money units. Capital-goods are deposited neither in the money wages nor in time; they are, on the contrary, directly appropriated by firms.

We still have to prove the benign character of the empty emission when it is defined by net investment.

Net investment is a benign empty emission, because the wages lost are compensated

The production of period p engenders a profit; the production of period $p+$ invests it. We see therefore that the effect produced on wages is compensated.

The wages issued in $p+$ do not contain the capital-goods produced there. However, wage-earners paid in $p+$ grab the wage-goods saved on the product of p, when profit is formed. Finally, the wages issued in $p+$ correspond to 100 units of products, 100 units of wage-goods, of which 20 units come from the previous production (p).

It is still true that the production of $p+$ includes an empty emission, but it is harmless since the capital-goods instantly withdrawn from the real wages (100 units of wages only retaining 80 units of purchasing power) are exactly compensated by the wage-goods saved.

Even though investment is a harmless empty emission, it prepares the malignant emissions, that exist only because of the amortization of fixed capital.

XX. Benign in itself, the empty emission defined by net investment has grave consequences; it results in the "expropriation" of the holders of income (including profit): fixed capital eludes them

If the production of capital-goods were a full emission, excess demand due to investment would be nil. But, in reality, excess demand is positive, as we have established. One might be tempted to reduce it by feeding it with the wage-goods initially saved. But the method would be incorrect because a part of the wage-goods would then be bought twice, once already in the formation of profits (the act of saving being a purchase), then in their investment. As soon as duplications are avoided, it does emerge that investment defines a positive and irreducible excess demand. What is exactly is its meaning?

The meaning of net investment as an empty emission: income holders lose the economic ownership of the means of production

We can easily discover it by starting from the opposite situation, where investment would define no excess demand.

Imaginary situation. The whole product of period p (100 units) is bought by income holders, who save 20 units on it. Real savings are used as a "wage fund"; consumption of real savings results in a production (in $p+$) of capital-goods. In the end, domestic income is entirely consumed, $Y = C$, because the category of consumption includes investment, a productive consumption. Over the two periods (p and $p+$), 200 units of products are consumed, of which 20 productively, i.e. for the production of instrumental capital.

Real situation. Right from the start, the divergence shows up. Insofar as wages are transformed into profits, they elude income holders. Hence, two possibilities emerge. If profits are redistributed, income holders recoup their loss, the reduced wages being compensated by dividends. When profits are invested, the dispossession of income holders, on the contrary, is *definitive* (see Figure 8.5).

Teleologically, everything is completed right from the formation of profits, provided they are invested. The empty emission goes back to the formation of profits. In period p, workers who have obtained 100 have actually only obtained 80 because, retroactively, it is true that they have not obtained the 20 units of wages denatured into profits. The empty emission observed in $p+$ in the expenditure of profits, in their investment, is just the (non-cumulative) repetition of the initial empty emission, which happened in p (see Figure 8.6).

Even though the emission of wages is the formation-expenditure of 100 units of money, *only 80 units of real goods are "transported" to income holders by the monetary flow.* Workers obtain a *full* money (=80) and an *empty* money (=20). The result is that the consumption category no longer clears entirely the domestic income since consumption of 100 units of wages only defines a real flow of 80 units. Investment is *additive*; $R = C + I = 100 + 20$. One may notice the confirmation of the fact that investment is an empty emission since the total product of the period is measured by 100 and not by 120 units of wages.

The empty emission constituted by *net investment has thus a univocal meaning.* Total product is measured in the 100 units of full wages first created by domestic production. Invested profit being equal to 20 units of money, firms collect immediately (at the instant of the payment of wages) a measure of 20 units of real goods. This collecting leaves intact *monetary* wages; it only reduces the product within monetary wages. The product collected from within money is withdrawn from households, *to be definitively appropriated by a "non-person", the disembodied set of the country's firms.*

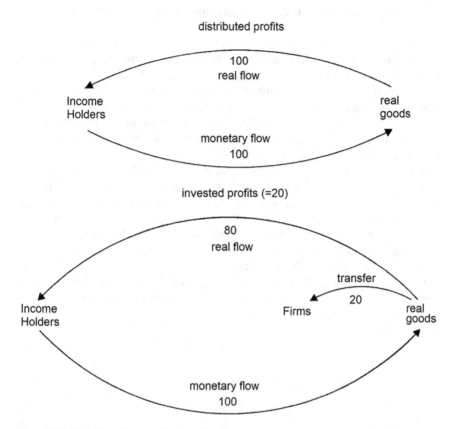

Figure 8.5 Distributed versus invested profits

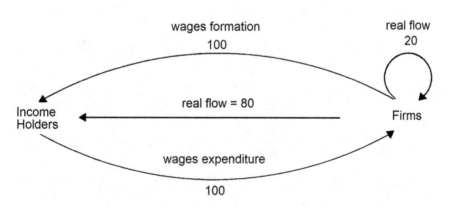

Figure 8.6 Net investment as appropriated by firms

Insofar as it is lost by income holders, the product feeds the *Minotaur*, i.e. Capital.

Let us summarize. If fixed capital were appropriated by the anonymous set of households, it would not originate from an empty emission and, above all, it would not cause any either. Since, in the actual functioning of our societies, fixed capital results from an empty emission, its formation creates an otherwise unknown category, that of the set of firms as *"non-persons"*.

Let us clearly understand that if profits did not exist, or if the investment of profits did not define an empty emission, firms would be persons indeed: they would be identified with their shareholders.

The category of *"non-persons"* is introduced by a *pathology,* net investment being a false emission. The notion of an expropriation of income holders or, identically, of the private appropriation of the means of production, thus takes its true, *economic*, meaning; lacking the new analytical tool, i.e. the theory of emissions, theorists had undoubtedly the intuition of the dysfunction, but they could only formulate it in its *legal* terms. The solution is not at all the same on both sides. We shall come back to that.

But, right now, it is clear that its efficiency will be nil if it is situated at the level of ownership rights. As long as the empty emissions continue, the economy will have to live with its pathologies.

9 It is precisely because fixed capital is the property of a non-person (the disembodied set of firms), that its amortization causes the malignant emissions

XXI. The additivity of consumption and investment

At first sight, the difference in the written formulae seems banal, depending on whether the domestic income is given only in consumption or in the addition of consumption and investment.

$$(1) \quad Y = C$$

$$(2) \quad Y = C + I$$

We know that in the history of economic thought, even recent history, many authors have preferred the first formula, since only the consumption goods are completed; investment-goods are integrated in the preparation of true goods during the phase of their elaboration. This intuition is today confirmed by the logic of emissions.

Definition 2 is not a simple variant of definition *1*. The nominal or monetary expression of domestic income is not the same on both sides.

$$(1) \quad Y = C = 100$$

$$(2) \quad Y = C + I = 120$$

Again, a superficial observation leads into error. It would be naïve to think that investment expenditures are a real addition to consumption. In fact, measured in wage-units, the total product is invariant, so that we have to write the following equation.

$$(2) \quad Y = C + I = 120 \text{ in money}$$

$$= 100 \text{ in wage-units}$$

Investment is a purely nominal addition

Investment is additive to consumption for the only reason that empty emissions are additive to full emissions.

Order would require therefore that investment should be a "nested category" of consumption, in the same way that profits are a nested category of wages.

The dysfunction being set in reality, it is true that its gravity seems doubtful, since it does not matter much that instrumental capital should be the property of anonymous incomes holders rather than of Capital; anyway, the instruments of production cannot function if held by households.

Even the disparity of nominal magnitudes (120) and real magnitudes (100) does not seem threatening, the excess demand only meaning eventually the already-known additional movement: the absorption by Capital of the invested profits of 20.

But the disorder is going to take its true dimension – plain to see with inflation and unemployment – in the next stage, the amortization of fixed capital.

XXII. The amortization of fixed capital

Historical outline of the issue

Since Quesnay and Smith, theorists have sensed the very great importance of the amortization of capital inside the production mode. We also know that Marx gave a great deal of attention to the amortization of constant capital, c, to which he devoted endless developments, electing it as the essential explaining factor for the value of the product in each period. Finally, in chapter 6 of the *General Theory* (Keynes 1936), the object of which is nothing other than the definition of domestic income, Keynes introduces the concept of "user cost", the interpretation of which still attracts a great deal of interest, while at the same time raising huge problems.

In what follows, we shall try to keep in line with high tradition. The great authors were not mistaken. Just as capital is at the heart of capitalism, the amortization of capital, especially with regard to its fixed part, is at the heart of capital. The theory of emissions brings, in this respect, both confirmation and clarification.

The origin of the dysfunction is situated in the investment of profits

Let us proceed with all the rigour required with such a difficult subject area.

It is crucial to start from a law of logic, largely established in the previous developments, requiring that any non-distributed profit should be spent in the producing services market, differently from wage and non-wage incomes that, from the hands of their holders, can only flow towards the products market.

In other words, the firm that holds (non-distributed) profits is not an ordinary income holder but this "non-person" that we have mentioned.

If invested, profits are necessarily spent in the producing services market, where they buy labour, they are dissolved in the remuneration of the workers employed in producing the goods into which monetary profits will be converted (which allows, of course, the free permutation of capital-goods, at market prices, in the general exchange).

We shall proceed forward in the following way. We shall first find again the law just recalled, in order that it should be "alive" in our mind. Then we shall build the circuit of the creation and destruction of wages, account being taken of the amortization of fixed capital. We shall induce the division of the industrial economy into two sections, one that produces wage-goods in the full emissions, and the other *profit-goods stricto sensu*, in the empty emissions.

Reiteration. The expenditure of profits is logically an operation in the products market for any distributed profit and, on the contrary, an operation in the producing services market for any invested profit

The strongest proof is simply based on the identity of the person who spends the profit.

For any *distributed* profit, the formation of the profit is an expenditure "extended" by firms. Under these conditions the profit is, in the hands of its holders, a positive money generated by the formation of an equal negative money in the firms; it is precisely the negative money thus formed which annuls the profit in the firm, in order to distribute it. From then on, the expenditure of the transferred profit is, as for any income, the meeting of two monies, positive and negative. The expenditure of interests, dividends and rents dislodges the corresponding real product that leaves money at the moment the latter is destroyed.

For *non-distributed* profit, the analysis cannot be the same. This time, the question is logically more complex, since firms as a whole (*F*) are both the "issuer" and the "receiver" of the profit expenditure. The expenditure of *F* on *F* has to be explained while avoiding of course a contradiction in terms.

The solution does exist but it is unique: it is necessary and sufficient that the profit expenditure should be a purchase of labour. Still it has to be pointed out that the expenditure in the producing services market, thus financed by profits, is net. We finally arrive at a criterion really accessible.

1   In the case of distributed profits, the sum of the expenditures in the products market is equal to the sum of the corresponding expenditures in the producing services market.
2   In the case of invested profits, the sum of the expenditures in the products market is greater (by the amount of the investment) than the sum of the corresponding expenditures in the producing services market.

The formulation of the criterion is thus the following. The expenditure of non-distributed profits is an *excess* demand; the expenditure of distributed profits is a demand *included* in the expenditure of wages.

Now, we can develop the analysis, provided we take the resolution to maintain it, at all times, in line with compelling logic: any invested profit is taken in an expenditure of *F* on *F*, and any expenditure of *F* on *F* is an excess demand in the products market, carried out through the mediation of the expenditures in the producing services market.

Thus equipped, we can address the problem of constructing the circuit in the case of fixed capital amortization.

XXIII. The circuit of wages in the case of fixed capital amortization

Amortization is a complex operation because investment-goods do not belong to households

Let *a* be the amount of wages issued in the period to produce amortization-goods. Let us first establish the circuit as if amortization-goods were wage-goods in the strict sense. Wages *a* (partially distributed in non-wage incomes) would then be spent for the purchase of the amortization-goods. It would be a "Smithian" circuit.

It is true that, even with this simple solution, wages earned in the production of amortization-goods are spent for the purchase of wage-goods (produced with the help of amortized fixed capital). The purchase of amortization-goods is therefore indirect: the gross profit earned in the sale of wage-goods enables firms to buy the amortization-goods.

Why is the domestic economy not functioning according to this model?

The reason is that fixed capital is not the economic property of households. Let us recall that net investment is an empty emission, the effect of which is to dispossess the set of income holders of the property of capital. The amortization of fixed capital would follow Smith's logic only if capital were fixed in the assets of households (while of course being located in firms, to be used as means of production).

A faithful observation of facts dictates therefore another explanation. Earned in the production of amortization-goods, wages *a* cannot be spent by their holders to buy those goods, because households cannot unite the amortization-goods with the fixed capital they do not own.

It is clear, however, that the circuit of the income created by the production of amortization-goods is as "perfect" as the other monetary circuits.

The enquiry has therefore to be pursued in order to detect the exact channel by which income *a* flows back eventually in the purchase of amortization-goods.

The amortization of fixed capital postulates the transformation into financial claims of the corresponding part of households' income

An interesting idea comes to the mind; income holders cannot buy directly the amortization-goods since fixed capital does not belong to them. But would not the obstacle be lifted if amortization-goods were to reach them eventually under the form of financial claims?

It does seem so. But before confirming this, let us briefly recall the only case we know up to now, that of workers being paid in claims and not in money.

It is net investment. Paid by means of profits, workers obtain an empty income and, in compensation, a claim on the wage-goods saved by the previous seizure of wages into profits.

However, if workers were similarly obtaining claims on the amortization-goods, it would be logical to say that they would be their owners' right from the beginning. The exchange of financial claims against goods would not raise any difficulty. Logically unable to bring their income unto amortization-goods (since, once again, they are not the owners of fixed capital), income holders would be able to buy the amortization-goods by the simple conversion of their claims on these goods.

The only difficulty is then in the initial explanation: are workers, i.e. the producers of the investment-goods, effectively receiving wages that, instead of being income, are finally claims on amortization-goods?

Let us consider the production (of the period), divided in a and a', a being the product in amortization-goods and a' the rest of the product, measured in wage-units. Let us proceed by "stages" of reasoning. Once the enquiry is completed, it will be possible to contract the different stages in building one single circuit, the circuit of wages in the period under consideration.

In a first stage, it is certain that wages a are an income like wages a'. Indeed, the current production of the amortization-goods is not financed by a "wage fund" or by wages previously captured into profits.

At a second stage (of reflexion), it comes into view that income a does not flow back for the purchase of the amortization-goods; it cannot do so: this is understood. Strict logic imposes therefore the following piece of information: the expenditure of income a creates a monetary profit on the firms that sell product a'. Products the (wage) cost of which is equal to a' are exchanged against income $a + a'$.

The third stage is a direct consequence of the second one. The whole theory of profit tells us that profits a made in the sale of product a' cause a partition of this product: for part a of a', workers produce for the benefit of firms, only the complementary part, $a' - a$, defines their real wages.

We are now very close to the conclusion.

Wages a bite into wages a'. If product a were not in amortization-goods, the workers employed to produce a' would receive real wages equal to a'. Given that product a is defined in amortization-goods, producers of a' receive monetary wages equal to a' but real wages equal to $(a' - a)$ only.

The reduction of the wages issued in the production of a' is inevitable because, when they spend their incomes, workers employed in the production of amortization-goods have to compete with workers producing other goods. Once again, income of a total amount of $(a' + a)$ units of wages is spent in the final purchase of product a': it follows necessarily that the producers of a' do not receive the totality of their product in wages but only its part $(a' - a)$.

Let us gather the elements of the explanation that we already have with us. Wages *a* are initially an income. Then they are spent, in competition with wages *a'*, for the purchase of product *a'*. Hence, wages *a* appear under a new identity within the income earned in the production of goods *a'*.

Let us show with two very simple comparative graphs the production of *a'*, before and after taking into consideration the production of amortization-goods. Graph (2) is not definitive because it is formally impossible for a reflux of (*a* + *a'*) to correspond to a flux equal to *a*. The correct solution is to withdraw *a* on both sides (see Figure 9.1).

The interpretation of graph 3 is obvious: income holders spend *a'* to buy (*a'* - *a*). It is still true that, in addition to amortization-goods, the economy produces *a'* and not (*a'* - *a*). The difference, equal to *a*, is a purchase of goods in the producing services market: it defines the expenditure, of *F* on F, of profit *a* in the emission of part *a* of wages *a'*. Indeed, profit *a* is not distributed; if it were, amortization-goods could not be paid (see Figure 9.2).

Undoubtedly, the main difficulty of comprehension is represented by graph *4*. However, the theory is univocal. As soon as a wage already constituted is cast into a (new) emission of wages, the payment is a flux identically present on the two markets: expenditure *a* of graph *4* is both and in the same movement an emission of wages and a purchase in the products market. The analysis of net investments has prepared us well: insofar as firms cast wages in the payment of wages, as in graph *4*, they buy directly the product of wage-earners. Thus, the emission of part *a* of wages *a'* implies a purchase by firms of part *a* of product *a'*.

Since workers who produce *a'* lose immediately (in the very payment of their remunerations) part *a* of their product, wages *a'* are empty up to *a*. The emission of wages *a'* is full for (*a'* - *a*) and empty for a measure of *a*.

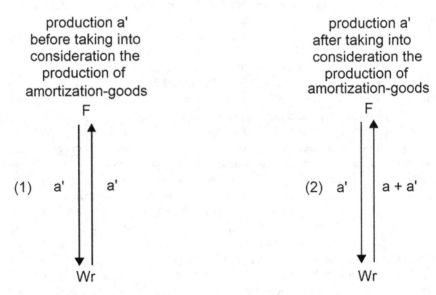

production a'
before taking into
consideration the
production of
amortization-goods

F

(1)   a'   a'

Wr

production a'
after taking into
consideration the
production of
amortization-goods

F

(2)   a'   a + a'

Wr

Figure 9.1 The expenditure of wages earned in the production of amortization goods

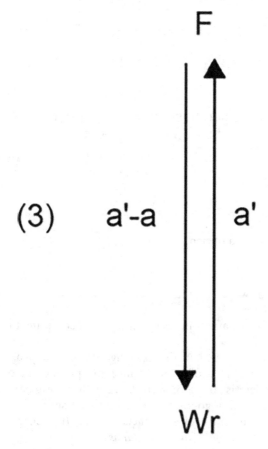

Figure 9.2 The impact of the expenditure of wages earned in the production of amortization goods

We can now bring together the various "stages" of the explanation

In itself, the production of amortization-goods brings an income like the production of any other goods. However, the income issued in the production of amortization-goods, *a*, is (necessarily) spent for the purchase of the other goods, *a'*. It is inevitable that the production of *a'* should be affected: part (*a'* - *a*) of product *a'* is sold against part (*a'* - *a*) of the wages issued in the production of *a'* and, in addition, against the totality of income *a* issued in the production of amortization-goods.

The profit thus made by firms is entirely due to the carrying over on product *a'* of the wages earned in the production of amortization-goods. The profit is the part *a* of product *a'*.

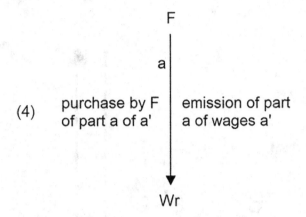

Figure 9.3 The emission of empty wages

Thus, part *a* of wages *a'* is not an income: workers receive it directly *under the form of a claim.*

The object of this claim is perfectly known: it is constituted by amortization-goods, *a.*

Everything is completed in the exchange of the claim against its object: households spend part *a* of *a'* to finance the production of amortization-goods. The problem is solved in accordance with its original position; unable to buy the amortization-goods by spending their income, households obtain them first under the form of a financial capital (the claims): *they pay the amortization-goods by spending these claims.*

Presentation of the global circuit

Let us represent the whole circuit of the production of amortization-goods (*a*) and of the other goods (*a'*) as in Figure 9.4. The flows that are of particular interest to us are the following:

I: emission of wages in the production of amortization-goods.
II: expenditure of the wages issued in the production of amortization-goods; this expenditure is observed on product a', more precisely on its part (a' - a).
II': monetary profit born from the expenditure of the wages earned in the production of the amortization-goods.
II": conversion into product of the monetary profit born from the expenditure of wages formed in the production of amortization-goods.
III"': payment of amortization-goods by households.

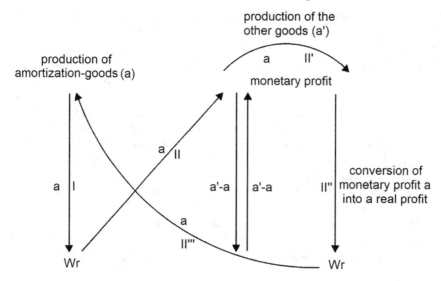

Figure 9.4 The global circuit of the third period

Expenditure (II) of income *a* forms monetary profit (II'); entirely due to the production of amortization-goods, profit (II') is converted into product in expenditure (II"): thus, in expenditure (II"), workers obtain a wage empty of any product, the real profit being immediately appropriated by firms. The wage empty of any product has a clear definition: it is a claim on the capitalized goods. In this instance, capitalised goods are nothing else than the amortization-goods. The circuit ends in expenditure (II'"), the exchange of the amortization-goods in claims against these same goods in kind.

Flow (II") is the "image" of flow (I); this is why we call it *dual production*. The production of amortization-goods has for its logical consequence the production, in the same period and for the same amount, of profit-goods. Let us recall that profit-goods *stricto sensu* are the product of an empty emission (malignant, we shall imply). Expenditure (II") is an empty emission.

The two sectors of the domestic economy

Profit-goods *stricto sensu* are produced in the empty emissions; the industrial economy is therefore divided into two sections.

The *section of full emissions* comprises the production of wage-goods and the production of amortization-goods. The *section of empty emissions* produces profit-goods in the strict sense, by means of a financing that comes automatically from the production of amortization-goods.

The dual character of the production of profit-goods comes to the fore in a synthetic way as soon as the observation takes as its starting point the initial appropriation of investment-goods by firms. If, at the moment of its formation, each

"slice" of fixed capital were the *economic* appropriation by the set of income holders, the amortization of fixed capital would be reducible to indirect purchases, like
the fabric bought with the purchase of a suit: amortization-goods would be brought
to households in the same way as the initial capital. In reality, we know that firms,
considered as a whole, constitute a barrier; investment-goods being held in firms,
amortization-goods will be so as well; in order to bring them nevertheless to
households – since it is the latter indeed who pay for them eventually – the movement of the production of amortization-goods has to be duplicated (see Figure 9.5).

Movement *2* is the induction of movement *1*, amortization-goods being
dislodged, to join the assets of the households, by the profit-goods added on
to capital (initially equal to X). Amortization-goods are paid and, in this
sense, appropriated by households, whereas capital is nevertheless still equal
to X in the firms: profit-goods are the net increase of capital.

The conclusion is that the amortization of fixed capital is not a simple
reproduction of capital, as it would be in the absence of any pathology, but
that it generates a surplus equal to amortization, profit-goods being added on
to capital, $X + a$.

If the amortization of fixed capital were a simple movement (but with the
appropriation of capital by firms being maintained), capital X would be intact
after amortization and its part a would be passed on to households. The
"capitalists" would then be the set of firms for value $(X - a)$ and income
holders for a. In reality, however, the fixed capital transferred to income holders
is in the same movement replaced by profit-goods. By the sole effect of amortization, capital increases therefore by $+a$ for income holders and by zero (and
not by $-a$) for firms: in total, it does indeed increase from X to $(X + a)$.

No empty emission happens in the conservation of fixed capital, when it
goes from X to $(X - a)$, then from $(X - a)$ to X. Similarly, no empty emission is
observed in the production of wage-goods. But the emission of profit-goods,
dual production of amortization-goods, is irremediably empty. It is fitting to
say *irremediably*, because, unlike the empty emission defined by net investment,
the empty emission induced by the production of amortization-goods results in
a money the emptiness of which is not compensated at all; this time, no savings
of wage-goods are waiting to fill in the emptiness. Workers employed to produce profit-goods receive a wage that is definitively empty, the spending of
which can bring strictly nothing to income holders, whoever they are.

In the example of the production of the period divided into:

a, production of amortization-goods;
$(a - a')$, production of wage-goods; and
a, dual production of profit-goods,

wages a earned in production a' have already been used and they are "worn
out" and destroyed at the moment workers obtain them.

Only the first two wages, a and $(a - a')$, contain a product, the sum of
amortization-goods and of wage-goods. Not only is the third wage (equal to

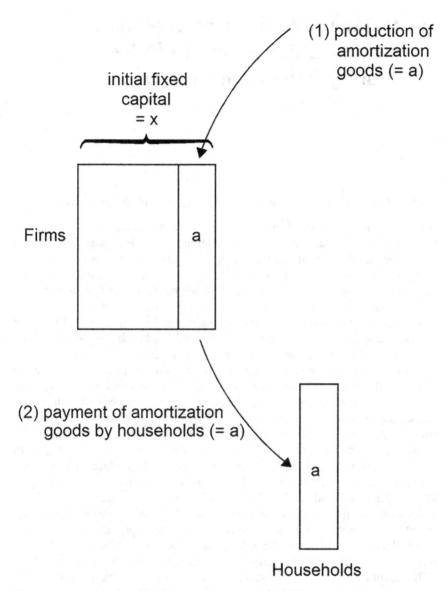

Figure 9.5 The production and the payment of amortization goods

a) empty of any new product, but it is also empty of any previous product (in wage-goods); it only enables income holders to pay the amortization-goods. To the extent of dual production, workers do not produce for income holders; they do not produce for persons: *they are enslaved to Capital.*

10 In the most advanced capitalism, a third of the industries in the country issue empty wages

XXIV. The chain of flows in the case of fixed capital amortization

Any instrumental capital is submitted to its own rhythm of amortization, because of its wear and tear and its technological obsolescence. Thus, a capital of 100 fr., the amortization annuity of which is 50 fr., induces as much empty emissions as a capital of 1000 fr. that is amortizing to the tune of 5% per year. The important factor is therefore the rotation speed of capital.

Let us suppose that the average speed (weighted in wage-units) is of a complete amortization cycle in ten periods, distributed linearly through time. In a far-back period, p, society has acquired an initial fixed capital equal to the hundredth part of the wages issued (in the period) by industrial firms. Again, for simplicity of presentation, let us suppose an equal amount of wages issued in each period. From period $p+1$, we observe that one thousandth of the working population (in the industry, we shall imply) works in each period for the amortization of the first fixed capital, an activity that induces, as we have demonstrated, an equal amount of empty emissions, in the dual production of the production of amortization-goods. In every period $p_q > p$, the thousandth part of labour is employed in the section of empty emissions, to produce profit-goods.

Let us consider now period p_0, defined in such a way that the capital progressively accumulated reaches the value of 10/3 x units of wages, given that x is the amount of wages issued in each period. We easily prove that in a positive state (and not in a normative one) of the mode of production, the capital accumulated up until p_0 can be amortized in the course of time; on the contrary, any additional slice of capital, brought on in the periods $p > p_0$, logically escapes the *pathological* process of amortization. The reason for this discrimination is very clear: it is impossible that more than a third of the population could be employed in each period to produce amortization-goods.

The production of amortization-goods is financed by the "seizure" of the wages issued in the production of profit-goods

Indeed, any production of amortization-goods is twice repeated during the period. Let us demonstrate it.

Dual production is the purchase of profit-goods by the expenditure of the wages earned in the production of amortization-goods, a production that is thus repeated a first time.

The demonstration of the *"second duplication"* is subtler.

Let us recall that the productive activity of the period is divided between a and a', a being the production of amortization-goods and a' the production of all the other goods. The carrying over of income a onto the product of a' is the operation that transforms part a of production a' into a dual production. If income a were not – as it necessarily is – cast into the final purchases of product a', all of a' would be constituted of wage-goods (or, identically, of wage and non-wage goods, to the benefit of the set of income holders). The set of households loses part a of a' for the only reason that the wages issued in the production of amortization-goods are spent in the final purchases of product a'.

We can logically induce that the expenditure of the income earned in the production of amortization-goods is a final purchase of wage-goods, for an amount equal to a: it is this same purchase, and this one only, that forms the monetary profit caused by the production of amortization-goods. Dual production is the consequence of this first purchase of wage-goods, equal to a. However, this first purchase of wage-goods is effectively a duplication of the income earned in the production of amortization-goods.

Let us sum up the chain of flows. The production of amortization-goods creates income a, which defines identically a final purchase of wage-goods. This final purchase generates a monetary profit, the expenditure of which defines the final purchase of profit-goods. There is indeed a *triplication* of the production of amortization-goods, which is repeated a first time in the production of wage-goods and a second time in the production of profit-goods.

We draw from this an important piece of information: in the industries of the country, the production of amortization-goods cannot logically employ more than a third of the working population. Any reasoning that would go beyond this limit would be erroneous.

But what does happen if, in reality, the sum of amortizations has a value higher than a third of the product of the whole set of industries? The simple answer is to say that the excess amortization reduces net investment: it is financed, not by dual production, but by wages, captured exactly as in the case of net investments. The distinction between investment and amortization is lifted – and amortization can be a "Smithian" phenomenon again – as soon as the production of amortization-goods employs more than a third of the working population in the industries of the country. Capital can no longer impute the payment of amortization-goods on households; that is to say, the amortization-goods *in excess* blend with wage-goods.

In the economies of advanced capitalism, a third of the working population in the industry produces for overaccumulation

It is interesting to note that period p_0 is reached sooner or later by every market economy. The famous expression "Spätkapitalismus" is perfectly applicable to every national economy that is on the verge of reaching period p_0 or has already reached it. From p_0 on, we may represent the production of each period by the concentric spheres mentioned above, the small sphere (equal to two thirds of the large one) is filled with the totality of the new products available on the market, wage-goods and amortization-goods, whereas the large sphere includes in addition a totally empty money, the result of the emission of profit-goods, dual production.

The perennial coexistence of the two spheres generates the economic Crisis: inflation and unemployment.

XXV. Malignant empty emissions are the profound explanation of inflation and unemployment

Caused by the amortization of fixed capital, empty emissions are cumulative over time

The disorder is pernicious above all because the empty emissions caused by the amortization of fixed capital are cumulative over time.

We know, *a contrario*, that any empty emission caused by the interference of the creative function of banks in their intermediation activity is not cumulative through time because it logically calls for the opposite disequilibrium, any operation of excessive credit being followed, at term, by the destruction of a money taken from current income. The money created in excess exerts a "demand without supply" in the products market; inversely, the reflux of the excess money creates on this same market a "supply without demand". Thus, the initial disequilibrium cannot spread over time.

It is true too that no empty emission defined by a dual production (of profit-goods) is repeated over time; only a new amortization will induce a new empty emission.

However, we have here to maintain the cumulative effect over time, in the precise sense that malignant empty emissions define an excess demand that is not matched by any excess supply, present or future.

As soon as the economy reaches p_0, it maintains for all the following periods a third of the population in activity in the section producing profit-goods. The same "inertia" is observed for any other (lower) proportion of the production of profit-goods in the total production. The general rule is the following: between the two limits 0% and two thirds of the population employed in the section of profit-goods, once reached, any proportion will be maintained over time (except for "external shocks", of which we shall consider the possibility later).

It is this repetitive character of empty emissions that removes any innocuity. Inflation and unemployment are caused by the cumulative effect or the inertia of malignant emissions over time.

We propose to demonstrate briefly that inflation is a dual phenomenon, because if at its origin it is always defined in production and therefore in quantum time, it is also present in continuous time.

Concerning unemployment, the theory of empty emissions is the only one able to explain it. The paradox will be lifted: even though unemployment is defined by a shortage of demand, it entirely results from the persisting existence of a positive excess demand. It is difficult to conceive of the existence of two opposite discrepancies in the same economy and in the same period. However, unemployment is always due to clearing deficits created by excess demands.

XXVI. Inflation in quantum time

Let us use again the convenient vocabulary of the "core" (full emissions) and the "crown" (empty emissions).

The sum of wages issued during a particular period is $x + y$. All the wages are spent in the purchase of the product of the core. Under these conditions, the excess demand is directly visible.

In period q, the economy has produced goods for an amount of $x + y$ wage-units and it has sold the same goods for an amount of $x + 2y$ wage-units: the excess demand is equal to y wage-units.

All theories define inflation as an excess demand. Demand is "swollen", "inflated" compared to supply. However, the theory of emissions brings two important pieces of information.

- The "general price level" in the core is not defined by the method of indices, which can never be rigorous, but directly by the sum of the emissions observed in the final market of the goods produced in the core. $x + y$ is the exact result we are looking for, whatever the internal distribution of this sum, over the different physical goods composing the product of the core.

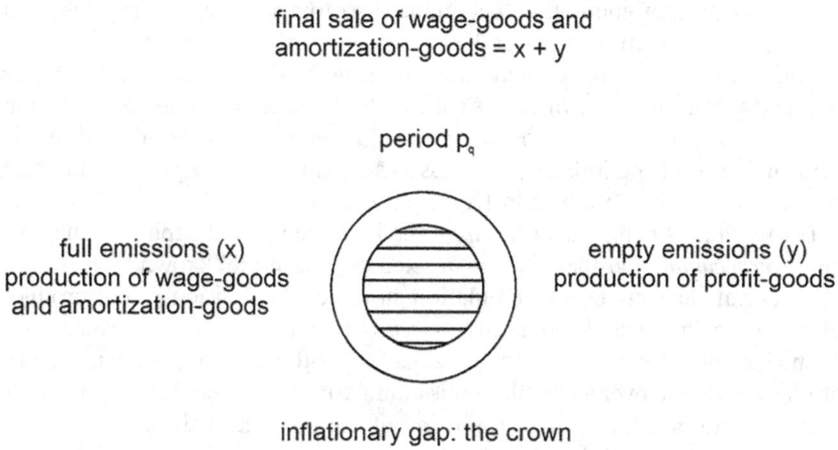

final sale of wage-goods and
amortization-goods = x + y

period p$_q$

full emissions (x)
production of wage-goods
and amortization-goods

empty emissions (y)
production of profit-goods

inflationary gap: the crown

Figure 10.1 Full and empty emissions

- Excess demand does not result in an increase of the general price level from one period to another, but in an increase within the same particular period; the price of the product of the core is $x + y$ in p_q, whereas it is only x in the same period if excess demand is left aside.

The question is not a semantic one since the given definition is always the same: the inflationary gap is the difference between Demand and Supply.

From this definition, the analyses are diverging because they are logical on one side and erroneous on the other. The global demand for the product of p_q cannot be compared to the global supply of the product of another period. To situate the inflationary gap in dynamics is therefore a formal error. The general price level of the product of the core does not increase over time; it increases within the same period of production, due to taking into account the excess demand.

Inflation, the source of which is always in the malignant emissions – therefore in quantum time – generates movements in continuous time, that is inside the core itself.

XXVII. Inflation in continuous time

When we study the consequence of empty emission (y) on the product of full emission (x), the logical distinction between the effect of the empty emission on the totality of the product of the core and, on the other hand, its effect inside the core prevails. Inflation in quantum time brings about the first effect. Now, let us turn towards the second one: what is happening in the core, due to the presence, period after period, of the weighty "crown"?

1. *First effect of inflation in continuous time.* If Capital did not directly employ workers, as it does, in the profit-goods section, the core would extend to the total industrial production and it could logically include wage-goods only, amortization-goods thus belonging also to that category. In these conditions, the production of capital-goods would not be necessary nil. At any rate, the emissions of the core are able to bring some new fixed capital, by the productive consumption of new savings. However, in addition to the formations of fixed capital in the core, we find net investments formed in the "crown". In each period, empty emissions produce fixed capital in the exact measure where they produce instrumental capital.

Let us call, as before, *accumulation* the increase in fixed capital in the core, and *overaccumulation* the increase in fixed capital in the "crown".

It is clear that any overaccumulation supposes the division of the products of the core into wage-goods *stricto sensu* and dividend-goods since, even formed in the "crown", fixed capital calls for dividends, if only under the form of interests. Since overaccumulation is cumulative over time, profits have to be formed to an ever-increasing proportion of the product of the core.

However, any breakdown of product x into wages and profits, defines the increase of the selling price of wage-goods *stricto sensu*, the expenditure of wage incomes having to finance both the production of wage-goods and the production of dividend-goods.

If the increase in the price of wage-goods shows up in statistics, it is because the productivity of instrumental capital is more than neutralized by the increase in the drain of profits on wages. The price of individual goods should decrease; if prices increase within the core, it is that, in spite of the accumulation and overaccumulation of a more and more technologically sophisticated capital, each individual item in the basket has to bear an increasing load of profit-dividends. As soon as inflation thus shows up in continuous time, as the price inside the basket increases over time, it is certain that the effect of overaccumulation has become globally negative.

2. *Second effect of inflation in continuous time.* We are dealing here with the too famous alleged "spiral" of wages and prices. The theory of emissions breaks this false symmetry, and finally gives a true vision of reality: *the price increase comes first*, because it is not the wage increase but the existence of empty emissions that causes it. If labour unions demand wage increases, it is in order to fight, with their limited means, against the entrenched stranglehold of Capital. We even know very accurately nowadays the *modus operandi* of the periodical increase of the general level of wages.

Monetary wages are, we know it well, the definition of domestic income; that is to say, the wage-unit is the unit of measure, the standard of all economic magnitudes, including capital. The general increase of wages is the division of the standard by a scalar (>1). However, if this division affects nominally the new incomes that, multiplied by the scalar, stay equal to themselves, it could not react on the incomes from where the previous accumulations and overaccumulations have come. The scalar *divides* the sum of available capital, in its two aspects (financial and real): capital, a claim on banks, defined in supposedly constant wage-units, is reduced by the increase in the general level of wages. If wages were suddenly multiplied by 2, the available capital in the same period would be abruptly divided by 2. And the reduction in capital implies a proportional reduction in empty emissions.

Consider a numerical example. In the period, wages are increased by a third. Let us suppose that before the sudden increase of wages, the share of empty emissions was a third of total production. The standard of measure is divided by 4:3. It results that the sum of empty emissions changes from a third to 25% of total production: they now employ only a quarter of the working population in the industries of the country. *The increase in wages is the expansion of the core at the expense of the "crown".*

Income holders, all classes together, fight against Capital

Economic life, wrongly called class struggle, since in reality it is the struggle of all the holders of income (including dividend-profits) against Capital, takes the form of a series of pulses. The "crown", repeatedly reduced by wage increases, is reconstituted not less repeatedly, until the abutment imposed by logic, namely the empty emissions maintained in the limit of a third of the industrial production of the country. By the same token, another fundamental point, still mysterious up until now, is being explained.

The amplitude of the pulses is self-perpetuated: the more a country fights against Capital by means of wage increases, and the more it has to keep doing it, as Capital is constantly and automatically asserting again its rights. If a domestic economy is suffering today from a "high rate of inflation", it is by way of inheritance, constant inflation being propagated over time, by the effect of the ever-renewed pulses.

But the other illness is even more worrying, this is when Capital evicts man from his work.

11 The malignant emissions and unemployment

How can science explain that the economy is suffering from both inflation and unemployment? If quantitativism were adequate to facts, there would be an equilibrium, located at point zero of the meeting of excess Demand (inflation) and insufficient Demand (unemployment and deflation). The reality is far more complex; we observe the existence of "stagflation", the coexistence of stagnation and even of unemployment and inflation. A curve, much talked about, traces the conciliation of the two pathologies. But the explanation was lacking. The theory of emissions provides it with all the clarity required.

XXVIII. The theory of emissions provides the profound explanation of "stagflation"

The analysis of the symbiosis of the two opposite disorders takes its decisive start in the acknowledgment of the exact character of the excess demand that defines inflation; it is distinct from any demand hitherto known because it is situated in quantum time.

Inflation in stagflation

Being an empty emission, excess demand is necessary for the clearing of profit-goods. In other words, if demand were not in excess, profit-goods would not be paid; firms could not clear the wage-goods: profit-goods would define the global amount of sales deficit.

From the outset, we are far from the usual representation. Indeed, if demand is in excess, it is because it is higher that the corresponding supply. It seems therefore that the cancellation of excess demand should leave sufficient income to purchase the total product. This is not at all the case. The correct reasoning is based on the terms of the following alternatives:

- either the considered emissions are full, and any excess (positive or negative) in demand over supply is inconceivable;

- or the analysis concerns the empty emissions; in that case, excess demand is not a surplus or an overflow, because it is the only demand that can face profit-goods.

The amount of empty emissions being y, the demand for the total product is x (the measure of wage-goods) + $2y$; equal to y, the excess demand is the purchase of profit-goods at their cost of production; if that demand were lacking, the expenditure in the products market would only be of x wage-units, a sum that would only just suffice for the payment of wage-goods (including amortization-goods): profit-goods would not find any buyers. The disappearance, at one go, of *twice y*, is due to the fact that y units of wages are spent in the two markets.

In its only acceptable logical sense, excess demand is simply the demand sufficient to clear profit-goods. Nowhere in the economy, on any product, is excess Demand defining a (nominal) surpassing of Supply.

If the question is so difficult, it is because it clashes with our usual ways of thinking. Once again, we have to reject the principle of the excluded middle. It is not true that the non-negative gap between Demand and Supply is either positive or zero: excess demand is both a positive gap and a zero gap.

1   Excess demand is a *positive gap* between Demand and Supply. To be convinced of this, it suffices to mention the example. The total product is measured by $x + y$ units of wages; the same product is cleared in final purchases, the exact sum of which is $x + 2y$ units of wages.

2   Excess demand is a *zero gap* between Demand and Supply. The example is conclusive. In the core, the product is measured by x units of money. It is purchased by $x + y$ units of money. However, the y units of wages spent additionally in the core are the financing of profit-goods, the product of the "crown". Relatively to the product of the core, the final expenditure is therefore x units of wages only, the exact amount of supply. Regarding the product of the "crown", it is bought in the producing services market, by the expenditure of the y units of wages captured in the core. There again, the expenditure of wages corresponds exactly to the supply of product, y for y.

Once this first step has been taken – the excess demand emerging as being just sufficient to clear the product – the analysis reaches at last, subjected to an additional little progress, the solution of the problem of unemployment.

Deflation (unemployment) in stagnation

What is the exact nature of the goods produced in the "crown"? They are, tautologically, profit-goods. But it is not at all certain that the empty emissions should produce capital-goods, or instrumental capital. It is conceivable that the "form" profit-goods should be (in total or in part) filled with goods intended for households. Let us explain ourselves.

The core produces wage incomes and non-wage incomes, dividend-profits. However, the share of the dividends reaches its limit when it extends in any period to half the product of the core. Indeed, if workers produce only wage-goods on even days, they provide themselves with the "wage fund" enabling them to produce only dividend-goods on odd days. Once dividends extend every day to half the products of the core, it is therefore impossible to increase them, whatever the needs for remuneration related to the continued over-accumulation of capital. When dividend profits can no longer increase in front of the persistent increase of capital, firms have only the choice between two decisions: to curb the "crown" or to maintain it but in having it produce wage-goods.

We show that both cases, *a* and *b*, give exactly the same results.

a. For want of finding a sufficient remuneration for the totality of the new capital, firms renounce partially to produce it and thus restrict domestic production, in maintaining employment at the level of $x + y'$ (instead of $x + y$) units of wages. The unemployment that sets in extends then to workers the remuneration of whom would have been of y'' units of money in the period. Only one question remains: the inflationist profits are of y; they are invested up to y'; what happens to profits y''? It is certain that they are spent; this is required by the law of the circuit; if profits y'' were not spent, they would not exist, which would be a contradiction in terms. However, the answer is not to be eluded.

The possibilities are even diverse. Let us indicate only one, the plausibility of which is striking: profit y'' is lent to the set of income holders. Capital y'' thus finds its remuneration by taking it from the income of households: the financial market provides the additional income that the products market can

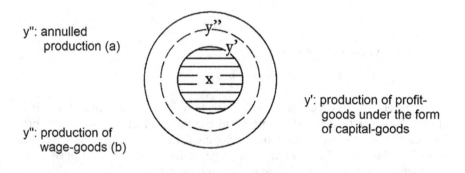

y": annulled
   production (a)

y": production of
   wage-goods (b)

y': production of profit-
   goods under the form
   of capital-goods

production of each period

Figure 11.1 The production of profit-goods under the form of capital-goods and wage-goods

no longer generate. Under these conditions, expenditure y'' carried out by the borrowers, adding up in the products market to expenditures $(x + y')$, really confirms the formation of an inflationist profit y. It is particularly interesting to note that the repeated expenditure, in the financial market and to the benefit of income holders, of a fraction of the inflationist profit, creates an increasing indebtedness of households. In each period, profit y'', recycled in the financial market, is consumed with income x, only profit y' remaining to finance the production of profit-goods. Unemployment persists at the level of the y'' units of wages withdrawn from production.

b. It is perfectly conceivable that firms should take another route. It is agreed that they cannot invest profit y'', for lack of a sufficient return. We conclude that profit y'' can indeed take one of the two distinct forms: profit is transformed into fixed capital, *or simply into capital-time*; it is not therefore necessary, at first view, that firms should reduce the activity in the country, as profit y'' can be invested in the production of wage-goods. However, it is "on appeal" that the judgement becomes conclusive. Any production of wage-goods in the "crown" (or in the empty emissions) *digs a positive gap between Supply and Demand*.

The expenditure of $x + y$ units of wages in the core releases the inflationist profit (y), necessary and sufficient to finance the production of the "crown". If profit-goods are not offered in the products market (being insufficiently "welded" to the pre-existing fixed capital), Demand is not affected by any insufficiency. But for the whole measure of (y'') where inflationist profits are spent for the production of wage-goods, those goods are cast onto the market in front of a *zero* purchasing power. The vice is patent; produced by the expenditure of inflationist profits y'', wage-goods must be sold a second time, that is, in the products market, after having been sold in the producing services market. The domestic economy provides purchasing power y'' *once and not twice*.

Sum of available income in the products market:

$$x + y$$

Sum of supplies in the products market:

$$x + y + y''$$

In the end, firms do not have the choice, hard experience demonstrates it to them. Whether they invest profits y'' in the financial market or in the production of wage-goods, domestic employment in the industries is only validated in the limit of $x + y'$ units of wages: part y'' of the inflationist profit gives the measure of the unavoidable unemployment.

Part III

The remedies usually proposed, their inefficiency evaluated in the light of the theory of emissions

The crisis is not a fatality. If the remedy is lacking, the reason is only because of the imperfection of the diagnosis. The prevalent view in economics is still based on three fundamental conceptions:

- money circulates in the economy;
- global supply and demand are independent from each other;
- inflation and unemployment find their origin in the behaviour of economic agents.

Each of these preconceptions leads to the formulation of false remedies, the inefficiency of which is obvious in the recent evolution of our societies.

12 Money does not circulate in the economy

XXIX. It is naïve to try to influence the "real variables" by manipulating the "monetary" variables

Money is supposed to circulate in the body of society like blood in a living body. An anaemic economy could therefore be invigorated by an injection of (new) money or by activating the money already in existence. This is day-dreaming. In reality, no money circulates between agents. Each creation of money creates a space; it follows that money does not travel through a space.

Any monetary movement is the creation or the destruction of a real product. The distinction between real and monetary variables is therefore pure imagination. Thus, any monetary movement superimposed on the natural flows of the economy, by political decision, is logically redundant. Conversely, a policy of credit crunch holds back the clearing of goods, without acting on inflation.

Finally, an interest or "price-of-money" policy can only affect the income already formed because it influences the distribution of available income between consumption and saving. In no case can the increase nor the reduction of interest have an influence on the level of domestic employment.

No money circulates between the agents; to activate monetary flows is therefore devoid of any meaning and thus of any effect on real flows

One imagines money traveling between agents A and B. As a counterpart, real goods would travel from B to A. If real flows are insufficient in numbers and in volume, it would suffice to act on monetary flows. Any increase in monetary movements would cause an equal increase in real movements.

The "cross-moves" between the goods of the two worlds, nominal and real, constitute the basic postulate of the accepted monetary theory. It really is a postulate and not an experimental reality. Much more, experience and induction disprove the postulate of the opposite flows, monetary and real. There is not, in the concrete economy, a single case of a flow of money, or correlatively, of a product.

"Exchanged" against money, the new product is in fact changed into money, since workers are not paid in kind. As a result, the purely physical product is brought to life in the firm, whereas workers receive the same product, in money. No product has moved. Clearing is the opposite operation, the destruction of the product in the money, at the exact place where it is located, and its conversion in a purely physical product, instantly denatured into a "value in use".

But is not the physical product moving in this latter operation? The answer is negative. The physical product is born from the operation of the payment of wages; from the start, it is organically associated with money. It would therefore be wrong to picture the physical product outside money, at least, as long as the holders detain wage and non-wage incomes. The purely physical product does not belong to anyone yet: it belongs to money. That is to say that even the purely physical product does not move in its clearing; dislodged from its monetary mould, it emerges for the first time to the eyes of all in the hands of households; it does not come from firms, which had only obtained it annulled within the negative money.

Since the product is not moving, is money moving? It is admitted today by everybody that money is "initially" created. By excessive zeal, it is often said that money is created *ex nihilo*. If by this it were meant that a positive sum of money is brought out of a zero sum of money, science would be confused with magic. The creation of money does exist; it belongs therefore to the domain of logic; however, the only non-magical explanation is the following: every creation of money is a dual operation, two equal sums of money – one positive and the other negative – being brought about at a distance from each other.

Thus, the principle of non-contradiction is complied with; after a monetary creation, the existing sum of money is always nil. The transmission of money is the reduction (potentially until annulment) of an existing money. The creation of money is based, on the contrary, on a zero amount of money. The passage from zero to a positive number has therefore to be explained. There is no field of science where a positive number could be extracted from number zero, except by the simultaneous extraction of an equal negative number. If the + were given without the –, number zero would be posited as equal to a positive number.

It is clear, under these conditions, that every operation of money creation is a rigorously zero motion; neither positive nor negative money pre-exist the experiment: they emerge at the exact place where they are deposited. In other words, the creation of money is a positive operation only because, by nature, it is associated with a real production; it is only its *object* that renders money positive. The flow in money creation is identified with the flow in product creation; it does not therefore transport any money. It would even be insufficient to say that money moves at an infinite speed. It is true that the operation is instantaneous, but it does not transport (instantly) money from one place to another. The "quantum leap" is not a money leap but a leap in money creation.

Any (bank) money cast in a payment is newly created

Granted, no money is transported in the money creation. However, are there not, in the various markets, monetary flows or expenditures that are not creations of money? If it were the case, one might still conclude that, except for money creations, money expenditures are positive flows.

On reflexion, money expenditures all belong to one single, identical category, which is far more satisfactory for the mind.

Suppose that money should first be created on A; how could A transmit it to B? Firstly, money has to be taken from A. But two solutions seem possible *a priori*; either money is taken away from A or it is destroyed on A. But, how could money be taken away from A? It could only be so by the operation debiting A. Immediately the idea of the transportation fades away. If A is debited, and equal credit has to be introduced simultaneously, precisely the crediting of B. The transmission of money is therefore a credit-debit, exactly like the initial creation of money.

It is not conceivable that the payment operation of B by A should be done (or effected) before it includes both the debit of A and the credit of B. The simultaneity of the opposite operations, the two aspects of the same transaction, definitively condemns the idea of the flow of money through a space. If money reaches B at the precise moment it leaves A, the distance (A, B) does not define any space but a point. Conversely, if the two agents are not identical, it is because money is not moving between them; or else, once again, it could not reach B at the instant it leaves A. Ultimately, A can pay B only if money is destroyed on A.

The simple transmission of money does indeed belong to the category of money creations; destroyed on A, money is in the same movement created on B.

The initial creation deposits x units of money in the assets of A (provided, of course, an equal negative money is created for the "payer" that we do not represent here). Money can be transmitted to B only through a new creation of money.

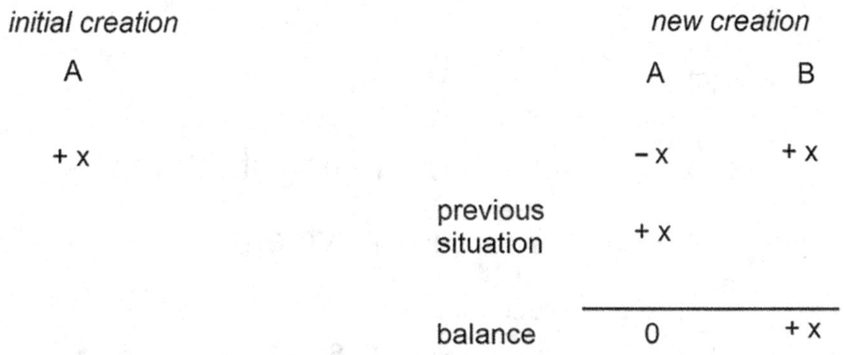

initial creation			new creation	
A			A	B
+ x			− x	+ x
		previous situation	+ x	
		balance	0	+ x

Figure 12.1 The transmission of money

Any expenditure, observed in one of the three markets, is a credit-debit, a creation-destruction, an emission. Money is created in an emission; it is destroyed in an emission; it is transmitted in an emission.

If we are willing to leave aside the crude representations of the circulation of money, where the material media of money (cheque, bill, metal minted in coins, bank note, credit card) are confused with money itself, we see that any monetary flow observed in the economy generates the same absolute amount: positively for the "payee" and negatively for the "payer". It must therefore be well understood that the reduction of a positive amount of money on one agent is never obtained by a subtraction. All the debits are additions of a negative money. The three following cases cover all the possibilities (see Figure 12.2).

Here the payment is a positive production, an emission of wages on B, A being a firm.

One might think that the initial creation of money, from a zero income, is a distinct operation – it would be more fundamental in a sense – from the other money creations, the purpose of which is to bring or destroy a pre-existing positive money (an income). This is not correct. On the side of money, all the creations are identical. The distinction only exists on the side of the product that is brought about in an initial creation whereas it is transported and destroyed in the subsequent money creations (see Figure 12.3).

Households have just transmitted (part of) their income to borrower C (see Figure 12.4).

Households destroy their income in the purchase or clearing of the physical product.

The other possibilities are all reducible to the three-part graph above. We can mention intermediary purchases that are creations and destructions of money included in the creation-destruction of wages, this emission being repeated n times. On the other hand, it is possible (and even probable in a positive economy) that firms pay wages from a position of credit in the bank; they have equity funds.

case 1

A	B	
0	0	initial situation
–	+	payment
–	+	result

Figure 12.2 The emission of wages

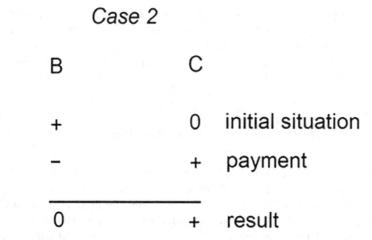

Figure 12.3 The transfer of income

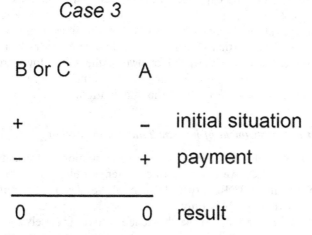

Figure 12.4 The destruction of income

The graph of case *1* does apply nevertheless; it would be illogical indeed to impute the payment of wages on the equity funds, which are of a "circulatory" nature. In any event, the emission of wages is a creation of a new income. Finally, we know that the creation and destruction of non-wage (but formed in the core) monetary incomes define a circuit incorporated into the circuit of wages.

XXX. Monetary flows are real flows

The "anatomical" study of monetary magnitudes and of real magnitudes shows that all monetary flows are identically real flows. The payment of wages is the real flow of the creation of a product. The expenditure of wages is the real flow of the consumption or of destruction of a product. Finally, the formation of savings is the real flow of the transmission of a product, from lender to borrower. This is why it is illusory to expect any result from a monetary policy. The only purely nominal flows are the pathological empty emissions. The unique, logically valid, objective of the policy is therefore to prevent empty emissions.

The futility of any policy aiming at injecting an "exogenous" money in the economy

We understand now the futility of the policies that claim to fight against economic depression by means of an exogeneous creation of money, for example through fiscal policy. At all times, the available money supply is the definition of the product to be cleared. Any money artificially added on is just a redistribution of the same product that, in a sense, is covered with a new clothing, too large for it. The clothing never calls for the body, every new product being born clothed with money in the payment of workers.

Instead of exerting the expected effect on future productions, any "injection" of money has the sole effect of relocating the product, already given, into an inflated money supply. The source of the illusion is now perfectly obvious: it was believed that real flows were the counterpart of money flows; in reality, money is where the product dwells; the same flows are therefore both real and monetary, and the famous dichotomy between nominal and real magnitudes is only a figment of the imagination.

Money is a pure instrument of intermediation in the exchanges

Another naïvety that has currency in the public opinion concerns the velocity of money. If species were circulating faster, would not commerce and industry be stimulated? Reality is less simple. Since it does not circulate, money has no velocity. It is only the delay separating the creation and the destruction of income that can be shortened. This is precisely the role of the financial market.

But the idea itself is wrong, due to the confusion between monetary flows and fluid mechanics; the shortening of the delays does not "stimulate" money against the product; it only affects the product itself, the consumption of which is accelerated. It is a very ill-formed thought that concludes in this way: if products are cleared faster, firms will be able to clear (and therefore manufacture) more products. The global clearing deficit (compared to full employment production) does not result from the laziness of money – any idle money being activated by the financial intermediaries – but, much more profoundly, from its endogenous insufficiency, since the malignant empty emissions destroy incomes without attracting the corresponding product into the assets of households.

For a long time, theorists have admitted the neutrality of money on principle. Defined as an exchange catalyst, money is not a final good.

Even in the model most remote from the theory of emissions, Walrasian general equilibrium, money (identified with the *numéraire*) is the instrument that has the function of breaking exchange into two half-operations. The only complete operation extends from one real good to another real good, money being only interposed.

Hence, quantum theory receives its best confirmation. To state it, it suffices to avoid the fundamental paralogism inherent to the analysis of relative exchanges, when money is present. Exchanges from one real good to another real good raise a formal problem that is without any solution. Money is an intermediary object provided that no exchange ends with money, which would be the case if all sales were *immediately* "followed" by a purchase. This is obviously not what happens in the concrete economy. However, as soon as the purchase is deferred, money becomes temporarily a final good. The theory is therefore incoherent because it defines the same object as a final good and as a catalyst.

The initial position is nevertheless profoundly correct; the use of money divides effectively the exchange into two half-transactions. It is exchange, and not money, that is ill-defined. Money is present in the operation of production and not, as was thought, in relative exchanges. The presence of money within production or emission breaks the operation into two half-emissions.

Now, logic is complied with. Even though the second half-emission (the clearing of the product) is carried out in chronological time after the first one (formation of the product), it coincides with it in quantum time. As a result, the definition is henceforth univocal: at no point in time does money belong to the category of real goods. Any observer able to understand this will no longer doubt the perfect neutrality of money.

Exchanges are absolute; they extend to the physical product through money; being only the form of the physical product, money cannot in any way – even in a pathological situation – either increase or reduce it.

Even in the economy in crisis, money is perfectly neutral. It is the mode of production that is not so, because it generates empty emissions.

The true remedy is not to be found either in the manipulation of interest rates.

XXXI. Interest rates policy is inefficient regarding unemployment

On this problem, incredibly muddled by the so-called Keynesian theories, economists will only find clarity again through the theory of emissions.

The determination of interest does not precede production

In the beginning, there is production. And it is useless to go back to the creation of the world. In each period, the world is restarted again. To require firms to take into account the cost of money in order to determine what level of employment to offer is faultily presupposing interest, which would then intervene before the creation of all the economic magnitudes, since they all proceed from production.

Any interest that precedes current production is, in reality, a magnitude determined after a *previous* production; current interest can only be determined after the new production. It is not difficult to discover the source of the error. It is thought that wages are paid through dipping into an accumulated capital. If it were true, interest would be indeed, like the capital involved, a pre-existing magnitude.

In fact, however, no capital is cast into the payment of wages. Even the profits spent into malignant emissions constitute a capital (the overaccumulation) in the current period. When firms cast their equity funds into the remuneration of labour, the situation is no different from what it would have been if those wages had been paid "*ex nihilo*". In both cases, the new incomes carry an interest because they are transformed into new savings, the capital-time defined by the current product waiting for its sale.

Let us sum up the positive theory

- When firms pay wages by means of "bank advances", the operation is firstly purely a monetary one; it becomes financial by the projection, automatic and immediate, of income in the financial market. Workers are the lenders and firms are the first borrowers. The subsequent operations in the financial market "carry" incomes (through quantum leaps of creation-destruction of money) to the final holders who buy the product. All the operations in the financial market co-determine interest. In conclusion, interest only intervenes in the financial market and it has no effect on the other two markets. No monetary authority could therefore logically commit itself to increase the level of domestic employment by means of a reduction in the rates of interest.
- When firms pay wages from their equity funds, nothing changes fundamentally. Interest due to savers is now taken from the people who, in the banking system, owe the money included in the circulating fund of firms. But the determination of interest answers the same rules as the preceding case. It is only the transformation of new income into new savings that enables the determination of the rates of interest applicable during the period under consideration.

The idea according to which interest enters in the determination of domestic employment is entirely based on a gravely defective conception, where income is viewed as a fluid coming from capital. In fact, the sequence goes in one direction only. Income leads to capital and no capital generates any new profit: even interest is a part of profit, which is a "telescopic" part of wages. Only human labour is a creator of income. If the economy experiences the burden of unemployment, the cause is not to be found in the (doubtful, by the way, given monetary erosion) fact that interests are high.

It is true that investment is sensitive to the rate of interest

It is certain that investment is not insensitive to interest rates. When the rates are too high, financial capital runs away from the sphere of production to take refuge in the financial market, where it can feed, as we have noticed, consumption loans.

However, it is essential to identify carefully the point in debate. Interest rates are too high, granted; but in relation to what magnitude? The determining magnitude is well known to academics, who call it return on capital or capital productivity, or again, in projections, the efficiency of capital. Whatever the name, the magnitude of reference is the remuneration of capital, taken from the profit formed inside the core.

This is where the drama builds up: on one side, interest is determined in the financial market, where the potential incursion of the capital coming from the "crown" has the effect of reducing, and not increasing, the rates; on the other side, the profit coming from the core is delivered to the increasing layers of over-accumulated capital, because of empty emissions.

No harmonization is possible under these conditions, the link between financial interest (Böhm-Bawerk's "Leihzins") and the remuneration of capital (the "Urzins") being broken by the pathology of malignant emissions.

Consequently, it is more correct to say that the rates of profit are too low and that they go on decreasing, rather than attributing the discrepancy between the rates of profit and the rate of interest to a dysfunction (of what sort?) of the financial markets.

But if we persist in believing that investment decreases because of high interests, consumption increases *pari passu*, the incomes left over by investment being, by definition, equally left over by saving: global demand and supply are two equivalent magnitudes. The theories of the investment multiplier are just tales for the "kindergarten".

Precisely, the policy measures advocated in the world today to fight inflation and unemployment are undermined by another vice, as fundamental as the dichotomic separation of real and monetary magnitudes: the alleged dichotomy between global demand and supply.

13 Far from being independent from each other, global supply and demand are logically merged into one unique magnitude; only confusion in the mind can separate them

XXXII. Macroeconomics is not based on microeconomics

All economic laws would be given at the level of "microscopic" magnitudes, to be aggregated afterwards. Global analysis would be nothing other than the science of the aggregates. According to this vision, the key market, in which the magnitudes are determined, is the market of real goods, the products market extended by the financial market.

In truth, the existence of the producing services market is not at all ignored. But, it is admitted that no constraint will be exerted from the producing services market in the products market. It is rather believed that the magnitudes determined in the products market are communicated by propagation (at most, instantaneously) to the producing services market: thus, receipts of the sale of real goods are distributed between the services of labour, capital and land. If the stated laws allow for a perfect distribution of a product already known (because of the equalisation of supplies and demands in the markets of real goods), "without profit nor loss", theorists are deeply satisfied.

It does not come to their mind to start the analysis with production. In effect, either production is not an exchange and therefore cannot be "formalized", which expels it out of the realm of economic science; or production is an exchange but it is then a particular case of exchange in the products market, as the new product can be grasped only in the transformation of a previous product. The economy of production is then only an example of the economy of exchange.

Indeed, the pure economy of exchange is conceived of as the field where the "Marshallian forces" of supply and demand would confront each other, movements that, by definition, belong to two categories, not just distinct but opposed to each other. In its foundations, economics is thus limited to the study of the formation of prices by the reduction of excess demands and supplies, item by item and in the network of simultaneous exchanges or, at an advanced stage (not yet reached), to the study of the dynamic evolution of excess demands and supplies: the passage from one general equilibrium to another.

In macroeconomics, production is primordial

The theory of emissions is, from the outset, far more realistic. It starts from production. The products market is subordinate. Any good coming into the products market is deposited from the producing services market. Even more, no product disappears from the market of real goods to come back later. The withdrawal is definitive. This means that production is never the transformation of a previous product into a new product. Even the "recycling" of a product (a bottle, a newspaper) is an entirely new production, a new labour, an initial emission.

However, even though production does not change the previous product, it is a perfectly constituted exchange because it changes the current product into money. If money were not to intervene, production would indeed elude any analysis. Economics has for its first object the study of money. It is thanks to money that the product does exist; the proposition must be understood in its literal sense: if the product were not changed into money, it would not be deposited in continuous time. The result is that no good could, as a product, be present on the markets to be exchanged (to be bought).

In order to keep the analysis in accordance with the complexity of real life, we must therefore enunciate two apparently contradictory laws that are already well known.

1   The producing services market casts real goods and services onto the products market; as soon as they are removed from this market, goods are destroyed as products; they are now only values in use, more or less durable, at the service of the "well-being" of households.
2   In the products market, prices of real goods and services are redefined; any product arrives "with a price" (equal to its cost of production), but it does not necessarily keep it; prices can be modified to be decreased (the sum of the discrepancies being then logically zero), but they are mostly modified to be increased; the price rise in the products market is net and it is the only source of non-wage incomes.

The double insufficiency of general equilibrium analysis

The analysis using general equilibrium is therefore doubly insufficient. It does not take into account the retroaction of the purchases of products on the purchases of producing services. Furthermore, it explains the formation of prices starting with costs of production still at zero. If the costs are eventually positive, they are so as a consequence of the formation of prices (on the goods market); in reality, costs do not result from transactions in the products market which are, on the contrary "based" on costs. The price of the set of goods is pre-determined in the operation, new in each period, by which the producing services market cast these goods onto the goods market: prices can only be modified within this set.

We can induce that the theoretical approaches through "Walrasians and non-Walrasians equilibria" are affected by the same myopia. They do not take into account the fact that, within the set of real goods present in the market, the reduction of excess demands, positive or negative, is based on costs of production *already given with a rigorous and definitive accuracy.*

The price of the set of real goods is not therefore the addition or aggregation of the prices determined by supplies and demands. The global price is obtained directly (the whole before its disaggregated parts which are not additive, because they include transfers or double uses) by the emission of wages, the source of all the goods present on the markets.

Neo-classical theories give priority to the products market

In the study of inflation and unemployment, it is out of question to blame theorists of the main school of thought for having chosen the products market instead of the organic union of the two markets. The deepest mistakes are unconscious. It is in full ignorance of the facts that Neo-Classics, Post-Keynesians, Friedmanians and Reaganians look for the interactions between money and product on the sole market of real goods and securities. Nobody decides to reject the constraint exerted on this market by the emission of wages; the predominance of the producing services market is not denied: it does not even belong to the field of hypotheses to be examined, since it has not been detected. And it is good that it is so, because it is far easier to obtain acceptance of a data enrichment, even a fundamental one; to convince of an omission rather than of a necessary action.

In reality, any purchase is both an exchange and a production

Let us resume the presentation of the correct theory. To grasp at the same time the two worlds, constituted of real magnitudes and nominal magnitudes, it is ineffective to confine the reflexion within the boundaries of the purchases in the products market; the only method that is suited to the project is based on the couple formation/expenditure of income, united by the most intimate possible relation, an identity. The emission of wages being the half-emission of the real product, the expenditure of wages is called for by their formation with an irresistible force, uniting the two halves into a unique operation. It is therefore not conceivable that the income created and the income spent should not be strictly equal, for the product of each period. If discrepancies nevertheless appear, they do so in full compliance with the identity of global supply (creation of wages) and global demand (destruction of wages).

The only intelligent – non-contradictory – way to define the crisis is in the denunciation of empty emissions, the only operations allowing to reconcile logically the identity of Supply and Demand with the two opposite but simultaneously possible discrepancies: inflation (excess of global demand) and unemployment (excess of global supply).

Instead of looking into that direction – and how could they have done so since no one had opened this way? – academics got lost in running after two fantasies, a Supply independent from Demand and a Demand independent from Supply, as if the relation between the protons and the electrons could be modified at the whim of the experimenter, in compliance with the nature of the given chemical body. Even in economics, alchemical manipulations are bound to fail.

XXXIII. The myth of a supply independent from demand ("supply-side economics")

The idea has the merit of simplicity. The economy must produce more; to this effect, the costs of production must be contained by all available means: to curb the increase of nominal wages, of fiscal and social contributions imposed on firms, of research expenses and cultural investments.

The criticism is of course less easy than these naïveties but it is based on laws that, to be perceived, require a certain intellectual concentration

The wage costs measure the product and not the share of wage-earners in the national product

1   Domestic production experiences only one net cost (all the other costs being transfers): the payment of wages.
2   Whatever the amount of wages issued in the economy, they are strictly equal to the totality of the domestic product. It is therefore formally impossible to lessen the wage costs by the general reduction of nominal wages.

Let us look at these two points.

Wages are the sole cost of global production

If the links between money and real goods resulted from relative exchanges, costs would be reducible to simple prices; in the exchange between tomatoes and pears, no cost is defined except semantically, as the pears have a cost in tomatoes and conversely. Cost is then the name of price. However, in our concrete economies, the cost has an effective existence that cannot be reduced to a price.

The distinction between money and real goods operates the distinction: money is the cost of real goods, which are not the cost of money.

If we legitimately keep talking of prices as magnitudes determined in the products market (precisely in their discrepancies relatively to costs), it would be incoherent to assimilate costs to prices, because, in the products market, the exchange of money against real goods is identically the exchange of real goods against money.

Clarity requires the distinction between two operations.

The first is the *creation of income*. The second is the *expenditure of income*. But the expenditure of income can be understood in two ways. If it is analysed only in the product market, without any regard to relating the measure of the spent income to the measure of the income initially created, we obtain prices and not costs, except in the purely "semantical" sense that we have mentioned, cost being the name for price. For the cost to be its own self, it must be grasped in the first operation, the creation of income, or identically in the second, the destruction of income.

Scientific language should refrain from talking indifferently of prices and costs. The cost of domestic output is the number of money units issued in the process of production. Prices are a more comprehensive reality because, as we have noticed a few times, on average each product is sold on the market at a price higher than its cost of production; otherwise, wage income would not be partially redistributed in profits, rents, interests and dividends. It is quite true – we have said so in the first part of this work – that prices are eventually reducible to costs (or to "values"); but the coincidence is obtained by the partition of the purchasing price into two channels: the financing of the production of the goods acquired by the buyer and, in addition, the financing of the production of non-wage-goods.

In its exact scientific sense, the cost is given in the emission of wages. In this regard, the decisive progress is, in a sense, negative: it must be understood that wages, the definition of the cost of production, have themselves an absolutely zero cost. The difficulty of understanding comes from the fact that the exchange of wages against the product is absolute. Workers do not give the product against "something else"; they give the product in kind against the same product, in money.

The key experiment, the only one capable of opening the eyes of analysts, is the following. Assume that the units of money do not yet exist – thus they are nothing – but are on the verge of being created; they are so in the emission of wages: wages and money come to life together. This is the proof that wages, the cost of the product, have themselves a zero cost: wages are not paid with a pre-existing good, a pre-existing money, but in the emission of money.

As soon as theorists have thus discovered an utterly unexpected category of costs – the costs in a money that comes to life only in the payment of those costs – they know that they must carefully distinguish them from the other costs, those known for a long time and the object of which is a pre-existing money and which, in the last analysis, are only prices.

The costs defined in a non-pre-existing money, are those defined by the payment of wages, the source of all income in the economy.

The costs defined in a pre-existing money are only prices; they are paid from an income already created.

The proof that was searched for is thus reached. Only wage costs are net for the whole society, (because they give birth to income), any other cost being a simple price (because it is the expenditure of a pre-existing income).

We can now turn to the study of the second proposition.

It is formally impossible to ease wage costs by the reduction of nominal wages

A parable might be used. Society includes one single firm, employing one single worker. How can we extend the working day from six hours to eight hours? Is not the remedy that of reducing wages? One may imagine, for example, that an employee might be incited to lengthen his working day, in order to maintain his income, when he now earns in eight hours the wages previously earned in six hours; on its side, the firm will agree to give this additional employment since the cost of production per unit of time is eased in the same proportion.

Is it not true that society is affected by unemployment because the wage level is increasing too fast? Would it not be more reasonable to slow down the increase in remunerations in order for more workers to get employment?

This vision of reality is childish. Let us consider again the allegory. Whatever the variation imparted to the amount of wages of our unique worker, his hourly wages are constant. Whether the firm pays one franc or one million francs per hour of labour, it pays the same sum. And the worker receives invariably the same salary. The reason for this stability of real wages in face of even the "wildest" variation in nominal wages comes simply from the fact that the *product is unchanged, whether it is cast in a large or a small sum of money*: the higher the monetary wages, the more income holders must spend to obtain the product in kind. Wages do not cost the entrepreneur anything and they bring to the worker only his own (hourly) product, which is rigorously unchanged in both cases, whether its "monetary expression" is one franc or one million francs.

Francs really exist – they have a body (the product) – in the wages already paid: francs do not exist facing wages yet to be paid. Even loaded with social contributions, wages are issued in an operation that brings to firms as a whole as much as it costs them; the impact is rigorously nil since the issued income is identically flowing back through its expenditure in the products market. Even if all the wages (direct and indirect) were reduced by half, the whole of the population of wage-earners would receive as before the totality of the social product.

The illusion of "supply-siders"

The profound illusion of "supply-siders" comes from a considerably impoverished vision of reality; they live in a world where nothing is created and nothing is lost, as the product never comes to life and never disappears; any payment of wages is therefore the transfer, in favour of workers, of a pre-existing product: the more products firms "send", the less is left to them. If the crisis is ongoing, it is because firms are deprived; let us agree to take progressively less product from them (by moderating the nominal wage increase) and the result will be beneficial to everybody, because it will restore full employment of men and machines.

The illusion is maintained by what is known as the paradox of composition. It is perfectly true that the identity of the flux and the reflux, or of the creation and the destruction of wages, concerns the set of firms only. Each particular firm incurs a risk, that of being able to get from its final sales only part of the wages that it has distributed. Thus, for each firm, wages have a weight that they lose to firms taken as a whole.

Any paradox is dissipated by a deepening of the analysis. Even for one particular firm E_q the emission of wages has a zero cost, provided the wages issued by E_q flow back on the product of E_q. If E_q goes beyond its ability to create, by issuing wages that, in general exchange, are partially flown back in the purchase of the product of other firms, the workers of E_q find in their wages an "overpayment". In the wages issued by all the firms, only "overpayments" define positive costs. But it is clear that the sum of "overpayments" is necessarily zero in the whole of society. The existence of discrepancies only means that certain firms are enriching others; taken all together, firms are neither enriched nor impoverished by the emission of wages.

It is important to identify the illness at its root. Unemployment is in no way due to the nominal amount of wages nor to the increase in social contributions that bite into a product already given. It is precisely because the persistence of under-employment reduces domestic output that the contributions of firms are increased: this aggravation is the consequence and not the cause of unemployment.

The alleged independence of Supply in relation to Demand encourages a calculating mentality. The alleged independence of Demand in relation to Supply appeals more to generosity. But logic has no time for feelings.

XXXIV. The myth of a demand being independent from supply ("demand-side economics")

A thinker foreign to our science would find suspicious this opposition of schools. If the same reality may be approached from its two opposite sides, is it not that it unites them in one same whole? Is it not forbidden then to separate them?

We find indeed among Demand theorists, the same degree of naivety as among their opponents.

The increase in nominal incomes has no (beneficial) effect on employment

By symmetry, the essential idea would be to increase income to fight against unemployment. It is out of the question, in this respect, to increase the indistinct money supply or to increase its velocity, but more nominal incomes must be distributed, whatever the effect of this measure on money. The justification of this opposite "income policy" is obvious. If the fully employed economy cannot buy the whole of its product, it is because income holders do not have enough purchasing power. Provided they are given the complement, goods will be sold off and firms will be able to hire the unemployed. This amounts to "build cities in the country-side".

The mistake has two components depending on whether the advocated income increase is partial or global.

The increase in the wages of one part of the working population

At the risk of seeming "hard of heart", let logic, which is the same for everyone, speak freely.

It is one of two things.

1   Workers whose wages have increased (for example, unskilled workers) keep buying, in general exchange, thus through whatever goods (of their choice), their own product. In more academic terms, the circuit is spontaneously closed despite the selective increase of wages. In this case, the increment of wages is entirely absorbed by the purchase of the same goods, the wage-goods produced by workers whose monetary incomes are increased. The circuit closes on higher wages as it closed on previous wages. This does not imply that the wages increment does not bring anything to its beneficiaries, let it be clearly understood. In "exchange value" everything is like before. But the workers involved are favoured in that they receive now more "values in use"; for them this is what matters.

However, the objective is not reached; let us not lose sight of it: the aim is to reduce unemployment. In this respect, the situation is not at all improved. The increase in wages would release a surplus of purchasing power, which might then influence the result of a production additionally launched, only if the product of the (relatively favoured) workers would not absorb in its sale the totality of the income created, its increment not excepted. But this is not the case since the circuit closes spontaneously. It is the very hypothesis. All the wages are destroyed in the sale of the product of wage-earners, even in the firm that has granted the increase in remunerations. Despite its increase, no fraction of income is therefore left available on the market, where it could give rise to a supplement of production.

The conclusion is as negative in the second case.

2   The increment of wages is missing for the clearing of the goods produced by the workers involved. It is not difficult to evaluate the consequence. First, the profit of firms that bear the payment of the increment is eroded. More precisely, a clearing deficit emerges. It is logically inevitable since, by assumption, the circuit is no longer closing spontaneously. This means that the purchasing power additionally created is destroyed within the

clearing deficit. There is not an ounce left for the goods the production of which was expected to be stimulated.

Let us turn now to the study of a general increase (in the same period) of monetary income.

The increase in an equal proportion of the wages of all the workers

More success might be expected here, because it is undeniable that the increment is absolute this time: it affects all the workers. The effect of this measure cannot therefore be dissipated within the whole set by favouring one group against another.

However, it remains that the objective is not attained; it even stays as remote as before. A progress would have been achieved only if income were not forming a unique mass, including the increments. Perhaps it is thought that the supplementary incomes constitute a "pocket" ready to be emptied on the product of a supplementary activity, whereas, up to the previous amount, wages are spent to buy current output. Why is reality not obediently following this plan? It is because the purchasing power of money is not like the attraction of one body to another. Money is the mould of the product. If everywhere the product of the period is cast into a larger mould (wages being all increased in the same proportion), more money then will have to be spent to buy the same product. Again, the already existing product entirely absorbs the increase in income and expectations are frustrated: the supplementary income does not operate any "remote" effect on the productions not yet engaged.

The real balance effect is an illusion

Here, we need to mention an "effect" that was much talked about, the real balance effect. Let us briefly present this "theory" that does not deserve long developments.

Wages increase. By definition, this means nominal wages. It is induced – hastily as we shall see – that the beneficiaries of the increased income initially detain a proportionately higher purchasing power. The reason put forward is elementary: monetary income is increased but nothing has yet happened on the side of real magnitudes.

In the first instance, the supplementary income brings therefore an equal supplement of purchasing power. Then the additional purchasing power is progressively cast in the purchases in the markets of goods and financial claims. Due to this increased expenditure, prices increase. Finally, real magnitudes have adjusted to the new nominal magnitudes and the increase in nominal wages does not define any gain in purchasing power any longer.

If those explanations were correct, the introduction of an effect on *future* productions might embellish them. Fed by the income increments, excess demand is divided between the products already available and the products yet to come; as far as production reacts to the new demand, prices are not affected and the gain in purchasing power is net and definitive. In this case, it would be erroneous to exclude the positive impact on employment of the general increase in nominal income.

But, the dynamic effect of real balances has never existed in reality; it is purely *mental*. The sophism according to which real variables are first constant in the face of the increase of the monetary variable (the sum of nominal incomes) is the direct consequence of the "dichotomy" in which money and the product are viewed. As soon as we start to understand that monetary income is the definition of the product, we realize that the increase in the general level of wages immediately determines the new price of the set of goods available on the markets: the real balance effect is therefore instantaneous.

It is true of course that only the sale of the product will "express" the new price of the whole product. But, the translation of the costs of production (given in the emission of wages) into sale prices (observed in the destruction of wages) is a general reality, applicable to the whole of nominal income and not just to its increase. In all rigour, it may be said that the totality of the product is positively demanded at the moment of the formation of income, without having to wait for its expenditure.

If, however, we prefer to establish the integration of money and the product only in the real goods market, we may still maintain the reasoning within the path of logic: for that, it suffices to acknowledge that the total sum of available income is destroyed in the purchase of the totality of the product to clear. It is confirmed therefore that the increase of the general level of wages has no effect on future productions. *Unemployment persists to its full extent.*

The theory of emissions shows the exact impact, which is far from negligible, of the general increase of nominal wages. Current product is instantaneously brought up to the new nominal dimension of income; on this side, the gain is desperately nil. By contrast, we know that financial capital cannot follow the movement; it stays first at its previous nominal level: it is therefore reduced. Does it result that unemployment is affected? Rationality imposes more circumspection. In reality, unemployment, caused by the malignant emissions, is in no way linked to the level of wages. The increase in wages is therefore not an adequate remedy. It is a stopgap.

We have demonstrated that the movement is in a way of a pendular nature: the general increase in wages is fighting the empty emissions that, by the continued effect of the amortization of fixed capital, constantly get the upper hand again. It must always be started all over again. Nobody wins at this game. The constant retake of the increase in the level of wages is an induced damage.

The radical solution will be found in "preventing" empty emissions.

There is a last domain where academics and politicians look for a remedy to the crisis, the domain of economic agents' behaviour.

14 Inflation and unemployment are totally independent from the behaviour of economic agents

Before the analytical discovery of emissions – only emissions of paper money or bonds were ever mentioned – economic magnitudes could only be grasped in continuous time or, at most, through "leap functions". Economic theory only knew of the existence of operations that were conceived of as movements in a pre-determined space and time. But it is undeniable that in each period the domestic product is in fact a new space. Time is itself newly produced, precisely in that production quantises time. With the production of each worker being recognized for what it is, an emission, one can no longer be surprised by the inadequacy of the old theory in its confrontation with the concrete pathologies that have been affecting the economy for a long time.

If domestic production were a simple material transformation, all the economic operations would be reducible to two types: some would transform the (raw) materials and the others would convey the material in state, whether transformed or not. Even in the first case, the operation grasps an object that it gives back, under an identical form or not, without adding anything (where would the increment come from?), nor taking anything from it (except in this wastage that is sometimes called the devil's dust or the angels' share, depending on the nature of the lost object, the "losses" which, obviously, do not diminish the matter treated but withdraw some of it from the enjoyment of individuals).

Before the discovery of the emission-production, known operations were all exchanges belonging to one or the other of the following categories.

1   Exchanges defined as the transformation of the objects; a gross product is changed into a more "refined" and eventually finished product.
2   Exchanges between two distinct objects, which, instead of changing shape, will change hands.

But, how could any disorder get into exchanges of the first or second category? It is inconceivable. Exchanges *1* can only follow the principle of identity: the product is the same when exiting exchange even though it is no longer in the same shape. As for exchanges *2*, they exhaust their effect trivially in the reciprocal motion they impart on their objects.

The predicament in which the theory found itself is summed up in an alternative.

Either the economy is already in trouble before the exchanges take place; or the economy can never experience any disorder. But if the first term is satisfied, where does the disorder come from? Economics cannot explain it, because exchanges are the only operations at its disposal.

Salvation comes from the discovery of an entirely new class of exchanges, absolute exchanges of the product into money. And, with all due respect to Gresham, good conceptions drive out bad ones. As soon as the observer becomes aware of absolute exchanges, he realizes that any quantifiable exchange in the concrete economy is of this type. Exchanges *1* involve human labour, so that, at the end of the operation, an entirely new product is found, not just the simple material transformation of the gross object. And exchanges *2* are in fact only barters usurping the name of exchanges: the carp would only be exchanged if it became a rabbit.[1] The only nominal exchanges that are real exchanges have money and the product as their terms.

Being now the domain of monetary exchanges, political economy is suited to its object. Immediately, the disorder becomes within reach of "formalization". The economist now knows that the economy of production is subjected to a crisis because it is a monetary economy.

Inflation and unemployment have their origin in one single operation, the only movement that exists in the whole field of economics and economic reality: *the emission of wages*. All the income, wage and non-wage, is created, transmitted and destroyed by (monetary and real) emissions of wages. *It is therefore within those emissions that the explanation of the crisis must be found.*

But we know at once where the explanation can in no way be found: in the behaviour of economic agents, households and firms. Who would not make the distinction between the operations and their results? Agents can only act on magnitudes the existence of which is positive, therefore on magnitudes *already created* and not yet destroyed. In other words, behaviour acts on the *results* of operations. But the dysfunction in the economy is created by the *operations*; once the result is there, it is too late, the damage is already done.

It is fortunate, by the way, that people should not be, in their behaviour, whether rational or not, the creators of the crisis, otherwise the disorder could not be cured. Human nature would have to be changed! But the remedy does exist.

Before formulating it, let us give a few examples of wrong prescriptions based on the analysis of the agents' behaviour. Indeed, people have nothing to do with their misfortune.

Inflation? Its cause is just at hand: people prefer to live above their means. It is therefore necessary to impose on them a stricter discipline.

Unemployment? But its origin is quite clear: people prefer hoarding to full employment. Idle income has to be supplemented. Already in the formulation of the diagnoses and of the corresponding remedies, the contradiction, in which dwells the "macroeconomics of behaviour", jumps out at you.

Finally, disorders would also have their source in the incoherence of behaviour because two "antagonistic" groups of agents, firms and households, are decisive. It is the whole problem of dividing production and sales between consumption and investment on one side, and consumption and saving on the other. If firms anticipate imperfectly the allocation of income and its division between purchases of consumption-goods and savings, does it not result in a disparity between production and sale of the goods of the two categories, wage-goods and capital-goods? And, if the answer is positive, does it not shed a certain light on the causes of the crisis? We shall observe that these concerns and these hopes are purely based on an insufficient analysis. The freedom of buyers does not provide the beginning of an explanation; even though domestic production is not subjected to determinism, it is not endangered by the "arbitrary" behaviour of its subjects.

XXXV. People do not live above their means. The reason is in a law of logic. It is therefore useless to appeal to moral precepts

To live on credit is not an inflationary behaviour

Let us carefully posit the problem.

It is perfectly true that any ordinary agent may "live above his means". In doing so, he spends an income that is not his own. More precisely, our man dips into the current product a share that he has earned neither in his wages nor in his non-wage income. If the difference comes from a gift, the means of the donor are reduced by the same amount and the anomaly is dissipated.

But another possibility comes forward: the gap may be filled in by the financial market. One must then speak of two simultaneous disequilibria. The agent expresses an excess demand in the products market and an equal excess supply in the securities market. Thus, the operation follows a tautology. The seller of securities buys more products than he sells; the buyer of securities sells more products than he buys. This is to say that it is impossible for the *set* of agents to live above its means. The expenditure in the products market of an income that would have been earned by no one would be an achievement worthy of Baron Munchausen.

It is remarkable that, if the reasoning rises above the tautology, it similarly moves away from the domain of behaviour. No behaviour can overcome the identity of the sale and purchase of financial claims. But, in spite of that, it is still true that the truism according to which any purchase is a sale does not prevent the formation in the products market of a net excess demand for all to see. Logic allows this only because the operation defining the excess demand is an instant alteration, a reduction of the measurement standard.

We know the most striking (but not the most common) example, *ex nihilo* credit granted by the banking system. Insofar as banks lend money that they have not received, they (faultily) insert an operation of creation into an operation of intermediation. The money thus issued collects a product that has not been saved by anyone. Lent without being borrowed, the supernumerary money alters the money-product relation that had been established in the emission of wages. If z units of money are added on, the same product is instantaneously diluted in the payroll (direct and social wages), increased by the sum z. The induced "shrinking" of the standard, the monetary unit, explains how the tautology is overridden: before and after the emission of the counterfeit money, any operation carried out in the financial market is identically a purchase and a sale of financial claims. But in the emission of the counterfeit money – within this operation – the bank lends an income that it has not borrowed and thereby increases the sum of nominal income available in the global economy. Who is behaving badly in this affair? Neither firms nor households who have to pay back the entirety of their loans. The banking system? But could it be called a wrong behaviour? It is the rule that is imperfect. And if there is a human fault, it is an analytical, intellectual, not practical, one: a "treason of the intellectuals". A great deal of research is necessary to approach, deepen and finally master the distinction of banking operations, between creations and intermediations. Once the criterion is known, we can think of applying it. And banks' behaviour will not be modified. It is the *rule of the game* that will be different.

The conclusion is the same for firms. A petit-bourgeois Marxism has spread this harmful image of the good workers facing exploiters. Capitalism, even in its pejorative sense, is not a (conscious) creation of man. The economy suffers from it in all classes together. It is certain that the historical development of empty emissions has greatly contributed to equipping industries and therefore to general well-being. If it is time now to fight against the production of profit-goods, it is again, after having penetrated them, a matter of modifying the rules of the game currently in place in the production mode such as it has evolved naturally (and not at all lead by human hands). Today, firms are also subjected to Capital.

When every production is a full emission, firms will behave in the same way as today, that is, as profit-seekers. This behaviour will not, and it already does not, create any disorder (apart from in the mind). Quite the contrary, profit is the driving force behind innovation. Whatever the amount of dividend-profits, they do not add one centime to the sum of final demands that find their outlet in the products market.

To set aside part of one's income is not a deflationary behaviour

If it is true that people can only spend the income created by the mode of production and, therefore, that excess demands are not at all their fault, should we not however attribute to them the advent of clearing crises, in so far as they are caused by the hoarding of income? Are not income holders free, indeed, to set aside part of their means, so that they only spend the complement? Subtracted from expenditure in the products market, income condemns the product to invalidation and the economy to experience underemployment. It would be better not to produce the goods that would be left over in the markets. On further examination, *hoarding proves to be an ill-formed concept.* A more advanced reflexion demonstrates that once again the truth of some *or* of the others is not the truth of some *and* of the others, taken together.

XXXVI. Global hoarding is a pure fantasy. Whatever their behaviour, economic agents spend the totality of their income. Logic requires it, while fully respecting free choice

Let us distinguish the two historical states of money.

Before the advent of bank money, money issued in wages was "material". In that state, money does not lend itself to any hoarding, for a very simple reason; if it were to happen, hoarding would not concern wages, but money itself, in its matter. We shall explain this.

As soon as bank money is introduced, monetary wages can no longer be distinguished between wages and money; on the contrary, they form an indivisible unit of the two magnitudes, wages and money being perfectly homogeneous, born in the same operation. Under those new conditions, hoarding cannot "transcend" wages to reach the monetary matter, which no longer exists. It would seem therefore that, this time, hoarding has wages for its object, income itself; the consequence would be an impact of the behaviour of savers on the clearing of domestic output. But this is not so, because the same evolution brings both the redefinition of hoarding and its necessary annulation. In general, economists only see the first aspect and therefore conclude to the "offensive" character of hoarding. As soon as the analysis moves one degree forward, one realizes, however, that due to its very nature, bank money cannot be hoarded.

Hoarding of material money logically has matter as its object and not money

In the development of this work, we have established the immaterial character of money. Money is not and never was a matter. However, it is of course true that before the advent of bank money, the "species" were material in the sense that they were carried by a matter, usually precious by the way.

Even issued under the form of material money, physical product is located in a negative money, until the moment of its clearing in final purchases. However, it must be well understood that the income in material money is twice physical or real: it is so, like any money, in its body, the current product; and it is so a second time, in the monetary matter. Hence, one must choose between the two matters because one cannot add them up without duplication.

The solution is beyond doubt. At the instant of its formation, therefore in the emission of wages, income is defined by the new product and not by the monetary matter that comes from another, previous, production. Similarly, at the instant of its destruction, monetary income is identified to the product cleared. But in between the two operations (formation and destruction of income), money is necessarily identified as its own matter: it is gold or silver. Hoarding cannot therefore ever be positive; unspent income does not exist because in the time interval separating the birth and the spending of income, the money is a matter and not an income.

In the case of bank money, the impossibility of hoarding results from a different law.

The hoarding of bank money is an ill-formed concept because, by nature, bank money is lent right from its birth. A lent hoarding is a contradiction in terms

We shall not start the demonstration again: banks issue their money in an operation of quantum credit and not in an ordinary credit. It is obvious that the operation of issuing wages does not lend an income since it creates it. However, quantum credit is so "unstable" that it is immediately transformed into an ordinary credit.

New income is immediately cast by the producing services market into the financial market where it defines the formation of a net capital-time in the society. It is indeed common sense to declare that the income not (yet) spent is saved. It follows that, right from its formation, income is integrally saved; but at the same instant, it is entirely lent: no fraction of savings is lost.

The conclusion we are reaching should not surprise the reader if s/he has understood that income is, in all cases, a purely instantaneous magnitude. Domestic product is cleared at the very instant it is formed. One might accept that, on this point, the analysis is less "intuitive". However, it speaks more to common sense, once it is approached in a slightly different way: it will be easily admitted that the product not yet cleared in the households is stocked in the firms. But this is enough. Any stock is a capital-time and any capital is formed by the expenditure of an income. Thus, the observer gains access to the stocks through the destruction of income. And the destruction of income means *ipso facto* the clearing of the product.

The difficulty bounces back somehow, because of the ambiguity of the "clearing of the product". Products in stock are already cleared since they have been bought in the operation of the transformation of income into capital-time. However, it is obvious that the products in stock are not yet cleared into households. Not only is the theory not affected by this ambivalence but, quite the contrary, it enforces it: being by definition a future income, capital can only disappear by reproducing the income from which it comes. Stocks are finally bought by the reproduced incomes; more exactly, they are then bought for the second time since their transformation into capital-time (into stocks) is already a fully constituted purchase.

From then on, there would be nothing to say if the analysis could stop at positive proofs. In reality, it must also deal with ill-founded objections that sometimes hide the truth. Let us summarize what the "honnête homme" might tell himself.

Since the theory mentions the two clearings, it is the good one, that is, the final sale to households that must be retained. Is it not obvious that the clearing of the product, under the form of capital-time, does not provide any guarantee of successful completion of production? The proof of the necessary or logical nullity of hoarding will be given only if we establish the certainty of the final clearing of stocks. Any non-zero difference between the two clearings would mean, in spite of "abstract" arguments, the existence and the persistence of a positive hoarding, with all the consequences it carries: being not cleared by households, the product would be invalidated. Has unemployment any other cause? Firms naturally try to produce only the goods they can reasonably expect to sell off to households.

The objection has a certain strength because it is engaged in the right direction; simply, it has stopped on its way. At the beginning, it is perfectly true that the clearing that counts is the final sale of the product to households. However, the clearing in firms must be analysed, not just in itself but in its consequence; otherwise, the objection cannot be conclusive. But what is the consequence of the instantaneous transformation of the new product into a capital-time?

It is univocal: the newly issued income has now become bank loans and borrowings. All the rest is unavoidable.

Let us reason in an alternative.

- Banks do not do their job; they are confronted, on the one hand with a stock of wage-goods, and on the other with equal monetary savings. They leave things the way they are, instead of looking for and finding borrowers who would substitute themselves to firms by buying their stocks. In this highly improbable case, it is correct to say that the goods will stay in stock until the expenditure of income by its holders. Now, let us push things to the point of absurdity and suppose that savings are never spent. In this case, it is tautological to say that entrepreneurs are forever relieved from delivering to savers the object of their claim. This is to say that the goods in stock are *cleared* free of charge by savers in favour of firms.
- It is far more interesting to consider the only realistic case: banks do their job. They transmit savings to the sellers of financial claims, who buy the stocks instead of savers. The only fear that may still be entertained concerns the alleged imperfection of the functioning of banks that, by excess of prudence maybe, might not transmit the totality of available savings. The argument is mistaken because it is based on statics; even if banks accumulate a "buffer" of savings, the savings of the successive periods are relayed within this reserve, so that every individual saving is carried to the product. The only effect of the buffer is to delay the clearing of the product. And even then, this delay is negligible. Let us assume, for example, that half the domestic product of one month is kept as a guarantee of solvability in bank

deposits: this fund of idle money being maintained over a long period, for instance ten years, one sees that the average waiting time of the product is only of a month divided by 240. This completely insignificant delay is, by the way, entirely covered by the corresponding interest.

The hidden reasons for the enduring belief of the damaging effect of "hoarding"

Why does public opinion believe – until the end of time? – in the damaging effect of a net hoarding in the economy?

The reason is daunting, because there are three aspects: it is thought that money is material; it is believed that it circulates; finally, an erroneous interpretation is given that any income holder can freely reserve part of it to bring it neither into the goods market nor into the financial market.

The whole edifice crumbles as soon as the analysis becomes serious. Nobody can retain any bank money at home because bank money is tautologically deposited in bank. The saver who prefers hoarding rather than investment is investing his income despite himself because the bank can lend it to whoever it wants. The money hidden under the bed is only the claim bought by the savers-who-do-not-buy-financial claims. *Volens nolens*, the saver who thinks he holds a stone in his hand is actually providing bread to the clients of the bank.

If hoarding were net for the whole of society, it would indeed be necessary to find a replacement income. But the remedy would be as uncomfortable as the illness itself. Where to take the income of substitution and to whom should it be given? Would an aggravation of inflation be the price to pay to reduce unemployment? It is fortunate that these questions are not even to be asked. They are just expressions of false problems.

Any income created by domestic production is brought to the purchase of domestic output.

It is certain that firms must nevertheless take care of the quality of their products because income holders – whether they have obtained it in the producing services market, in the products market (dividend-profits, interests, rents) or in the securities market – are obviously in their right to ignore certain offers in favour of other purchases. It remains that the "holding back" of income is never and nowhere the cause of a lack of sales. *A general slump in sales of part of the product has a much deeper cause than the alleged hoarding*: we know that *it is the malignant emissions*.

Before arriving at the solution, we only have still to denounce the errors of the "macroeconomics of behaviour".

XXXVII. The behaviour of income holders is free or arbitrary. The domestic economy is therefore not subjected to determinism. In spite of that, behaviour complies scrupulously with the logic of the emissions

Before arriving at the fundamental point of this topic, which however is not really serious, we must mention explanations that are lacking in consistency but that are of positive interest, first because they are taught in universities all over the world, and chiefly because they are entrenched in public opinion. Without even talking about harmonization of the decisions taken by firms and households concerning the division of the product into investment-goods and consumption-goods, the behaviour of economic agents would be able to stimulate or slow down domestic production that would depend on the decisions of consumers and investors as well.

On both sides, the hypothesis is the same. Domestic income would not be *divided* into the two categories of goods; on the contrary, the *addition* of the two primary categories of consumption and investment would constitute the domestic income, up until now indeterminate. In other words, it is supposed that expenditures are independent from each other, and thus that the increase in consumption in one period has no consequences on the sum of investments, which are free to grow at the discretion of firms. The converse is obviously postulated at the same time: the variations of global investment have absolutely no effect on the sum of the consumption of the period.

Right from the beginning, those ideas are all the more suspicious since they are not applied within the two categories. No one claims that the increase in consumption of a fraction of the population has no link, during the same period, with the budget at the disposal of the other consumers. We easily understand on the contrary that the increased expenditures mean correlatively a diminution in the consumption of the agents who up to now were benefiting from some savings or who are providing some now. We are aware of the "solidarity" of consumers who, in each period, share the domestic income, at least the part that is not invested. Similarly, no one misses the fact that firms could not invest in the period an income that they could not have obtained either in the products market or in the financial market. Any individual investment is therefore taken from a predetermined sum.

As soon as the two categories are put face to face, the constraint applied within the categories would disappear as if by magic. Although flagrant, the contradiction that results at once is not perceived. It cannot be claimed both that *within* the categories the sum of expenditures is given or constrained and that *between* the categories, it is free, undetermined.

Any error of logic is the sign of a substantive error. Why are consumptions constrained between themselves but (it is thought) free with regard to investment? This is because expenditures in the products market are supposed to generate income. The illogicality is extending to the other goods: investments undoubtedly share the sum of non-distributed profits (realized or borrowed), but are not investment expenditures generating income? We may attribute a part of truth to the two contradictory ideas: within the categories, the sum of expenditures is pre-constrained because it refers to an income already given; in the interaction of the categories, the sum of expenditures may on the contrary increase because this time income varies accordingly and brings a new supply, an additional product.

Thought finally overcomes the contradiction when, meeting reality, it introduces the perfect separation between expenditures in the producing services market and expenditures in the products market. The first create the income; the second destroy it. Whatever their behaviour in the goods and financial market, agents can only destroy the income available to them. No decision taken in the products market has the slightest repercussion on future productions.

We shall review the main errors concerning the effect of consumption and, separately, of investment, on the evolution of the level of domestic income. We shall observe thus that neither inflation nor unemployment can be attributed, in whatever small measure, to the behaviour of economic agents.

In conclusion we shall deal with the more fundamental problem already mentioned, that of the harmonization of decisions. We shall observe again that the free choice of firms and households applies once the domestic income is already determined. As for future productions, the decision whether to bring them about is totally independent from the division of the previous products between consumption and investment, even if the autonomous decisions of households and firms do not coincide.

Inflation cannot originate from a sudden increase in consumption; for its part, unemployment cannot take root nor worsen due to the abstention of consumers who suddenly give more preference to saving

The correct idea is very simple. Each period brings the totality of the wages issued – and it brings nothing else – to the products market (through the "screen" of the financial market). Within purchases, wage incomes are partially redistributed in dividend-profits, interest and rents. Each income holder is individually free to consume or save. But two types of savings must be distinguished: the sum of individual savings and the savings of the set of income holders. It is clear that the two "sums" are not identical.

Indeed, individual savings are offered to other income holders as well as to firms. Savings finally lent to a consumer are annulled inside the set of income holders. Therefore, firms tautologically borrow the net savings of this set. Two consequences maybe drawn from this.

- If the savings of some income holders finance the increase in consumption of others, the sale of consumption-goods remains stable. But if the increase in consumption is net for the set of income holders, firms taken as a whole borrow less and, therefore, spend less: in total, the increase in consumption is not a net increase of expenditures in the product market. And in both cases, the induced inflation is strictly *nil*.
- Symmetrically, the new abstention of consumers provides increased savings, which are absorbed by income holders or by firms. In the first case, expenditures in consumption are unchanged. In the other case,

firms spend additionally what consumers have saved. And the effect on unemployment is identically *nil*.

The reader may feel that logic is "forcing his hand". Is not saving, after all, a force hostile to production and employment? *But ideas, as credible as these, claim exactly the opposite*: by facilitating investment, saving leads to the increase of domestic production.

It is good to let opposite naïveties fight each other. The truth is simply that saving is *neutral* as regards the emission of wages. Any saved income will be found intact at the disposal of the borrower. Neither net saving nor net dissaving have therefore the least effect on the total sum of expenditures. Whether firms sell their product to one or the other, they clear it for a sum of income that the behaviour of their holders can neither increase nor reduce. Even anticipations are powerless; optimism or pessimism of economic agents leave unchanged the total sum of available income.

All the remedies aimed at encouraging saving or consumption, whatever the case may be, are ineffective; the reason is far-reaching; when production is taking place, the corresponding demand can only be its faithful reflection: it is formally impossible that it should be overabundant or insufficient. The behaviour of economic agents, once they only have at their disposal the income created by production, cannot cause inflation; and if another income is cast into their expenditures, households and firms only spend it because it exists. The trouble comes from the creation of the supernumerary and not from the fact that it is spent; it is necessarily so – therefore whatever the behaviour – once it exists. As regards saving, it is a *positive action* not just an abstention. Saving is by definition an automatic or voluntary purchase of financial claims. Savings are finally recycled. This is to say that hoarding exists for households and the sum of them but *it does not exist for the set of households*. The behaviour of savers would only affect the clearing of the product if all the savings were not – as is necessarily the case – spent by a borrower, a consumer or an investor. Briefly, income holders are totally *innocent*; the crisis is superimposed on them and whatever they do, they cannot fight against it because they are totally disarmed.

The last false trail needs to be examined: that crises are caused by the mutual maladjustment of the two important events, production and demand. Firms decide to allocate the product according to a certain proportion between consumption and investment. For their part, income holders cast their expenditures on the products of their choice. The two free choices exercised face to face would not involve any net risk if the product only belonged to the sole category of consumption-goods. It is true that certain goods are ignored in favour of the "over-sale" of other goods; but the only effect of this "mismatch" of demand in relation to supply is an equal sum of profits and of losses; after compensation, it appears that the two events, production and demand, are perfectly aligned.

The difficulty seems more serious because of the division of the product into consumption-goods and investment-goods. This time, the errors of calculation have, it is claimed, far-reaching consequences. They happen in both directions. Let us suppose first that firms produce too much investment-goods, and income holders are not forming enough savings. In this case, how could capital-goods be all cleared? Conversely, if the production of consumption-goods is too abundant, the savings of the set of households being larger than the level anticipated by firms, will this not partly result in the consumable goods being unable to find buyers?

The correct analysis demonstrates the non-existence of the risks mentioned above: any error in calculation can be repaired. If there is a crisis, *it would remain the same in a world where expectations are perfect.*

The division of the domestic product into consumption-goods and investment-goods does not constitute the "ground" for the crisis, even in the case where firms' expectations are wrong

The real subject of the enquiry to be carried out is the relation between consumption and investment and, more precisely, the comparison of the two definitions of this relation as freely decided by income holders and, on their part, anticipated by firms.

However, before coming to the subject itself, it is useful to examine the "theories" that would have the level of domestic income depend on the division of expenditures between consumption and investment, whether or not this division is perfectly anticipated by firms.

Most of the confusions are located on the side of investment. Let us start from the periphery of the body of errors and then let us move progressively to its most significant part.

The relation between men and machines

According to certain opinions, technological factors would impose the employment of men and machines to respect a certain relation, at least inside the different branches of industry. An addition to the stock of machines would therefore enable more employment to be provided. The conclusion lacks any foundation because the alleged proof is a particularly amusing example of a *petitio principii*. It can be said with the same logic that the number of available workers determines the number of machines to be produced and used.

Machines drive out men

If we think of the London *Times* and the introduction of phototypesetting in the making of newspapers, it is true that new technologies increase the physical productivity of labour and threaten employment. This is the case in a lot of firms. It seems therefore that, everywhere in the world, machines are "evicting" men who, the trend going one way only, cannot find work again. By petition it is posited that, the *Times* being unique, the diversification of products is not increasing with technological progress. Under these conditions, it is inevitable that unemployment should increase; the "theory" – but not the facts – requires it.

Quite the contrary, the new techniques give access to countless new products. If men are prevented from creating them, machines have nothing to do with that. It is on the side of the "economic apparatus" (the mode of production) that the responsibility must be searched for.

The preceding argument is, by the way, countered by the opposite error.

Machines increase the productivity of labour; net investment therefore creates income and the increase in domestic income translates into a proportional increase in employment.

With these propositions we are still far from a serious analysis. To be convinced of this, it suffices to expose the, in truth blatant, contradiction that they carry. As far as the increase in income is due to the productivity of labour, the link:

number of workers and domestic income

or even:

number of actual working hours and domestic income

is broken. It is therefore false, under these circumstances, to speak of a general increase in employment (or of a reduction in unemployment) that would be caused by net investment.

The enquiry approaches the field of science, even though it remains far from its "hard core", when its purpose is to study the relation between investment spending and future income. Does investment expenditure affect future income?

We show that this is not the case. The theory of the multiplier or still of the oscillator (multiplier-accelerator) is a stage of our knowledge that should be quickly forgotten. Current investment has only an effect on current income.

However, and this is where the analysis is starting to become interesting, the decision not to invest may lead to a net diminution of final purchases and therefore to the aggravation of unemployment. This effect is only understandable with the help of the empty emissions.

Net investment has no effect on future income

We know the theoretical scheme according to which the income earned in the production of new investment-goods is spent (at least partially) on the purchase of consumption-goods, the production of which would thus be stimulated. The "wave" goes on, the income newly created in the production of consumption-goods leading to a second instalment of induced income; and so on, from induction to induction, until the final amortization of the shockwave.

Where is the truth in all this? The answer is known today with certainty. It is essential to start precisely from the "shock". Net investment brings an entirely new income, the expenditure of which would have an "inductive" force. But what is the nature of the income derived from net investment? It constitutes a whole bulk with the other income created in the period. The production of new consumption-goods creates an income in the same way as the production of new investment-goods. In total, the induction would be positive only if the sum of new incomes spent were higher than the sum of the new incomes created.

Clearly posited, the question calls for a clear conclusion: in their clearing, the new products (including the new investment-goods) *absorb the totality of the income born from production.*

The paralogism of the multiplier comes from a presupposition: investment-goods would not need to be cleared. This discriminatory judgment is not entirely arbitrary since the goods produced in the "crown" have already been cleared in the producing services market; they therefore do not need to be so in the products market. But we are far from the alleged inductions. In any case, insofar as empty emissions, yet unknown, were absent from the argumentation, new investment-goods would necessarily be sold in the products market like new consumption-goods. Thus, the income of the period, including wages originating from the production of the new investment, is destroyed *in its* entirety to clear current product. And there is no income the expenditure of which may be prolonged into a future production.

We have just established that the increase in investment does not lead to a multiplication of the additional income over time. In all logic, we must even conclude that net investment is not in itself an increase of current income. Like consumption, investment is fed from an income already given: the increase in investment means therefore the equal diminution of consumption. Even the initial income undergoes therefore a zero increase on account of net investment.

The *diminution* of investment also leaves income intact.

Any diminution of current investment is compensated for by the increase in current consumption

Let us assume that firms could buy investment-goods only in the products market. Undoubtedly, this assumption can only seem innocuous. But it comprises a logical consequence that can only seem surprising. Incomes are all born in the producing services market. Now, no product being yet cleared, the available income is carried to the purchase of goods from the two categories. In the exact measure in which income is withdrawn from purchasing investment-goods, it is added on to the purchase of consumption-goods. It would be otherwise only if the new income were not spent entirely on the product of the period. But, in this case, the reduction in investment would no longer be involved. And, anyway, it is established that the domestic product of each period necessarily absorbs (according to a formal law) the totality of the domestic income of the period. This is to say that the increase in consumption resorbs any diminution of investment. Undoubtedly it might be possible to "blame" the agents for preferring current consumption to future consumption. But they cannot be imputed a diminution in the sum of final purchases.

There is only one case where the decision (taken by firms) not to invest a fraction of their available income translates into a diminution of employment.

Captured in the sale of core products, the inflationary income denied to investment defines a contraction of the "crown" and therefore an equal diminution in the volume of domestic employment

Until period p_0, overaccumulation has continued, each additional share of instrumental capital will have found sufficient remuneration in the total sum of profits derived from the sale of the products of the core. But assume that from p_0 the rates of profit were now lower than the rate of current interests. The most elementary calculation then shows firms that it is in their "interest" to divert at least part of the inflationary profits to offer them in the financial market, instead of continuing to spend them in new wages. A contraction of the "crown" follows and, *pari passu*, a reduction in domestic employment.

Let us notice carefully that we are looking at the only case where the reduction in investment is not compensated by an increase in consumption. In the core, it is impossible that the reduction in the sale of investment-goods (an accumulation as opposed to an overaccumulation) or else of dividend goods should not imply the equal increase in the sales of wage-goods. This is necessarily so because, in the core, the purchase of the product is the only way to close the circuit.

In the *core*, any final expenditure in the products market designate an equal expenditure in the producing services market: it is therefore inconceivable that a (final) purchase of product should not release the financing of a productive activity or of a work.

In the "crown", on the contrary, the closing of the circuit is obtained through two distinct paths. The excess demand may translate into a purchase of the product of the "crown"; but it can also come into competition with the expenditure of income holders, to buy the product of the core: in this case, excess demand does not finance any production additional to that of the core.

Let us recall that the inflationary profit gives firms the means to buy labour. If they effectively use this profit to that end, they employ workers in the "crown"; but, if instead of buying labour, firms spend their inflationary profits in the financial market, production is reduced in the "crown" without being increased in the core. We see therefore that the contraction of domestic employment is due to the reduction in investment only insofar as the mode of production allows two anomalies:

- the formation of inflationary profits, and
- the expenditure of those profits in the financial market.

The second anomaly is obviously only the consequence of the first. To eliminate them both or, rather, to prevent them from appearing, *the rule of the game must be modified so that no empty emission could come to life within domestic economies.*

The errors that we have just listed do not exhaust the fertile imagination of the authors searching for explanations; how to stay idle in face of the crisis while public opinion is getting impatient? The last series of errors that we are going to mention concern the problem apparently serious of the two divisions of domestic income. But any error in expectations regarding the division of the domestic product in its two components, consumption-goods and investment-goods *has a zero effect on employment.*

The errors in expectations regarding the division of the domestic product into consumption-goods and investment-goods can only be temporary; all errors of this type reside within the "general exchange"

Finally, one should not speak of the shock of two freedoms, because, notwithstanding empty emissions, only income holders can choose between the expenditures of the two categories. From a strictly logical point of view, firms even produce undifferentiated goods; the product is divided into two categories only by the choice of consumers, between immediate consumption and saving.

It remains true, however, that the goods answering those two choices are not *physically* identical to each other. Savings of the set of income holders can be spent only on buying instrumental capital, and it is rare that the same goods should lend themselves indifferently to capitalisation or consumption.

Suppose thus that firms have produced goods the physical nature of which would be such that they can be bought only with savings or, identically, profits – and not through consumption by the set of income holders. In this case, two disequilibria may happen:

- defined at production, instrumental capital occupies too large a share of the product, the sum of profits and savings captured by firms *being insufficient* to clear it;
- in the production of the same period, instrumental capital occupies an insufficient part, the sum of profits and savings captured by firms *being superabundant.*

Is not the first disequilibrium deflationary? And is not the second one defining an *inflationary* gap?

A somewhat careful reflexion enables to dissolve the disequilibria, which are only apparent.

Dissolution of the deflationary disequilibrium

The problem is interesting because it enables us to revisit our knowledge of capital. We have demonstrated that any capital is both real and financial. But the difficulty mentioned comes precisely from the fact that instrumental (or real) capital is greater than the corresponding financial capital. We know though that any difference between the two capitals, financial and real, is just the difference between two aspects of the same reality, that of *a unique capital*.

Consequently, this difference does not exist, except as evidence of an error in the reasoning. In the present case, the error is easy to detect. It must be one of two things: either the missing savings define an excess in consumption spending; or it is in waiting because by definition it has not reached the firms.

The first term of the alternative is in contradiction with the statement of the problem, because the excess in the consumption expenditures would define an equal additional profit. Therefore, only the second term remains. To say that the savings captured by firms are insufficient means that the set of income holders withdraws part of its resources both from consumption and from voluntary lent savings. The gap designates therefore both an income that is spent neither in the financial market (by the set of consumers or house-holds) nor in the products market; the definition of this income is univocal: it is transformed into pure capital-time. The part of instrumental capital that has not yet been cleared corresponds to the equal part of current income the spending of which is reserved for "later".

Now we only need to conclude.

The instrumental capital yet unsold is nevertheless "saleable" because the corresponding income exists integrally, set into capital-time. Nothing distinguishes stocked capital from a stock of consumption-goods. It is clear that instrumental capital is the property of income holders until the moment when firms are able to acquire it by means of the income earned in realized profits, or by borrowing in the financial market. In the meantime, the capital remains stocked. The (deflationary) disequilibrium would only be confirmed if the unsold capital would no longer find an equivalent future income facing it.

Dissolution of the inflationary gap

When firms capture superabundant profits and savings, it is amusing to notice that the two disequilibria are as plausible as each other. Are not the savings of the set of income holders failing to clear the consumption-goods? Insofar as savings are not allocated to the purchase of investment-goods either, how could firms cover in the final sales the totality of wage costs? However, let us carefully pay attention to the opposite disequilibrium. The purchasing of instrumental capital is excessive to the full extent that the profits and savings captured by firms are superabundant. Any excess demand means inflation. We might therefore conclude that inflation is "eaten up" by the simultaneous deflation. But it is more interesting to dismantle deflation first in this new case; the dissolution will then extend to inflation.

Firms have made too much profit, or they have sold too many securities or still they have committed both excesses at the same time. It seems therefore that income holders have no longer at their disposal the sufficient means to "close the circuit": some of the consumption-goods will not find a buyer. It would be pathetic if, in this way, firms were themselves the source of their misfortune. But it is not so; *only the reasoning is pathetic*. In reality, the excess of income captured by firms does not relate *to the instrumental capital already produced*, the wording of the problem itself forbids it: the instrumental capital "occupies an insufficient part" of the product of the period. Firms have made an error in their estimates: in the final analysis, they have more resources than they counted on. The difference is a *future* instrumental capital and not an already produced capital. But how is income transformed into capital goods? It is very simple. The income collected on current production, and which cannot be used to buy the capital goods already produced insufficient by hypothesis, is cast into a future production: paid for by means of the profits and savings earned as supernumerary, workers bring the instrumental capital the production of which was not initially anticipated. By the same token, any worry about the closure of the circuit appears to be vain. Consumption-goods, not yet cleared, will be so in the expenditure of the wages paid from the overflow of captured income.

Let us now unravel the question of inflation. The gap would be confirmed only if the income derived by firms were entirely brought to the purchase of the *already produced* instrumental capital, even though it were insufficient, because of imperfect expectations. *But reality is different.* Firms' super-abundant income can logically be spent only in a *new* production, in the remuneration of producing services of an ulterior period. Inflation is *nil* because, even in the absence of empty emissions, the non-redistributed profits can only be spent in the producing services market.

The question of the errors in expectations finds its stronger solution in the notion of the *general exchange*.

One may start from the study of expenditures within each category. It is clearly obvious that the equivalence of expenditures in the two markets does not mean the purchase of consumption-goods by their own producers. Similarly, it is unlikely that a firm would convert its profit, or the savings it has attracted, into a product manufactured by itself. The law of the circuit is larger, while still compelling. The production of each firm – it might even be possible to disassemble further the operations – gives birth to a sum of negative money and, correlatively, to an income that can only disappear in this firm, that is to say *at the precise place where it was formed*.

But the identity of the reflux and the flux is defined through a total freedom of exchange, any income holder buying the products of his choice. It remains nevertheless that each worker buys on his own behalf or (partially) on behalf of the holders of non-wage income, his own product through the mediation of the products of the set of workers. General exchange is such that any income spent on another good (other than the one to which its production gave birth) creates a "chain reaction"; the income spent is reproduced until it disappears precisely in the negative money which is its "*alter ego*".

Despite the freedom of buyers, income is therefore finally destroyed by the collision of the same two monies created in the first emission. It is the consequence of the objective unity of the two half-emissions. Any production is an autonomous act, which closes on its two opposite and complementary realities, the creation and the destruction of the product perfectly identified.

If the reader wanted to resort to a simpler but faithful representation of reality, he might think of the convenient clause that we have already used: it is as if the workers of each firm were buying their own product to then exchange it at market prices, against any products of their choice.

General exchange thus in no way thwarts the severe law of the circuit, which could not open on the product of one firm and close on the product of *another* firm.

The same constraint is exercised on firms. Each one produces *inwardly* and nowhere else the instrumental capital or the production goods that result from the conversion of its monetary profits. As for the other category of goods, investment-goods are first bought (or financed) among the products of the firm, to be then transformed, at market prices, into goods produced by any other firms.

Being applied within each of the two categories, general exchange is also verified in their relation.

Any purchase of a consumption-good carried out with the help of a money earned in the production of an investment-good implies the equivalent purchase of an investment-good by the expenditure of an income earned in the production of a consumption-good.

General exchange finds its conclusion in the sequence of emissions of successive periods. This is the reason why the errors in expectations, insofar as they simply concern the synchronism of the supply and demand of the goods of each category, are *automatically rectified*. If the current period produces too many consumption-goods, the excess part logically defines a financial fund of capital-time, which is resorbed in an ulterior period, by producing the opposite discrepancy: new consumption-goods are reduced by the same amount. Production, in the current period, of too many investment-goods does not create any more difficulties. Investment-goods that do not meet a profit or a saving in the current period, are stocked to be sold in another period: income spent for this purpose will then have been earned in the production of consumption-goods.

The crisis is difficult to grasp, to conceive. The errors committed by courageous spirits going out to search for the aetiologies of inflation and unemployment are far more numerous, that is certain. But it is time to propose the true remedy. When the solution is found, it is useless to persist in studying false problems.

Note

1 Bernard Schmitt refers here to the French expression "le mariage de la carpe et du lapin" (the wedding of the carp and the rabbit) about trying to match two mutually incompatible things.

Part IV

The solution is in the division of the activity of banks in three departments. Liberated from empty emissions, the domestic economy follows Say's law: it ensures full employment

In the study of the functioning and dysfunctioning of the domestic economy, we have been able to penetrate the law of bank money that imposes in each period the division of industrial production in two sections, full emissions (wage-goods, amortization-goods and accumulated investment-goods) and empty emissions (over-accumulated capital-goods). Like the laws of nature, the law of money is far stronger than any will; our societies are fighting against inflation and unemployment in vain. The only efficient solution is in the invalidation of the law itself.

Indeed, unlike physical laws, the law exerted by money is accessible to the dominion of man who has all power to repeal it. As soon as the mind grasps the "deep mechanism" of money, it also perceives the means of breaking it in order to replace it by another logic.

The difficulty is first of all analytical. Political economy has been developing for a little more than two centuries to this precise end: to progress in the knowledge of the "mechanisms" that define in a way the *determinism* to which economic magnitudes are subjected, whatever the decisions of agents and the policies (monetary, financial, fiscal, social) of states.

The "mechanics" being well disassembled, academics have from now on the ability to provide politicians both with the exact explanation of the disorder and the fundamental measure that will enable the avoidance of it. Note carefully that the question remains a logical and analytical one even in the normative domain. It is out of the question to ask either morality, political science or law to legislate, because economic laws are as objective as the laws of nature and man has to step back. It is money again, once discovered, that dictates the correct reform, in its principle and in its applications, appropriate to establish the new economic order in the conciliation of the determinism of money with the definitive "prevention" of empty emissions.

The whole history of money will then have unfolded in two phases.

Since its origin through industrial revolutions and until the present day, money has exercised its *secret* power, greatly facilitating the growth of instrumental capital, an evolution from which our societies have obtained their material well-being. *Empty emissions were a blessing.* Since the beginning of our science, the analysis has progressively moved closer to its object and it finally has knowledge of when it becomes urgent to stop over-accumulation as the persistence of empty emissions has now become *harmful*.

It is not quite that the law of money has to be repealed, as we have said. In reality, money is the form of real emissions and it can only stay that way: its nature is constant. But the blind functioning of money is double: full emissions deposit the product into money and in (chronological) time; by contrast, in empty emissions the product instantly passes through money and is therefore not deposited in time: it defines on the contrary an immediate new increment of Capital. It is only empty emissions that have to be eliminated in their principle.

From now on every money issued in a payment must carry a product. Any emission of wages must enrich money with a product that it will keep until the expenditure of wages. After reform, the law of monetary emissions will be complied with – and how would it not be? – but it will no longer happen that a product is withdrawn from money (directly to the benefit of over-accumulation) even before the corresponding wages are spent.

The division of the banking activity in two departments translates into practice the logical distinction between money creation and financial intermediation. It will therefore no longer happen that banks create in a credit operation; in technical terms, seigniorage will be definitively abolished. It is true that seigniorage had already practically disappeared and that it only subsisted in the minds where it has the status of an analytical error. Most economists think that bank money is created in a credit operation. This is entirely false. In reality, if we want to speak of credit, we must add "quantum" credit. The emission of money is a spontaneous operation that does not add anything to the real emission, except a pure form, a "container". In the emission of the nominal form of the product, nothing is lent, neither the form nor the product ("the content"). No creation is an intermediation. The converse is also true: no intermediation is a creation. Indeed, if banks lend a sum of money they have borrowed, they do not create anything.

If the idea of seigniorage does retain nevertheless a little truth, it is that, in the current organization of the banking system, banks lend an income that does not exist. We have offered the explanation. Any income really created *ex nihilo* is finally surreptitiously withdrawn from its legitimate holders. The money created as a supernumerary borrows its "body" from the money created by domestic production. The illicit operation is nevertheless an intermediation since the incomes bitten into define a forced saving.

Good order requires therefore that only the savings deposited beforehand in banks may be lent in bank credits. Any empty emission operated by a bank defines a seigniorage, that may be taken in capital or in interest. Income holders lose savings, capital; banks and firms share the corresponding interests.

As soon as bank accounting is held in two departments, the emission and the intermediation being maintained in perfect separation, seigniorage will have completely ceased to exist and any monetary emission will define an (ordinary) credit operation strictly nil. We shall show this in Chapter 15.

At first sight, bank reform must stop there. There is no doubt, indeed, that banks will function neutrally if they confine themselves to lend deposited incomes. Why then must a third department be added to the other two? The reason is already known. But we shall give it again. Only the advent of bank money has enabled the formation of a net capital in society. Any capital defined in "material" money is annulled within the arithmetical tautology of the identity of loans and borrowings. The lender has (financial) positive capital at his disposal; it follows necessarily that an equal negative capital is formed for the borrower. In the end, financial capital is nil globally, as it is for real capital, which is the other aspect of the same reality.

Even though banks do not create social capital, they enable its existence. The automatic and instantaneous transformation into savings of issued wages define the creation of the net capital-time: the new product is stocked and the claims on stocks are real positive claims, to which no negative claim corresponds. Income holders have become holders of capital: they have a claim on banks; firms are correlatively indebted. However, the sum of claims and debts is not nil, because the debts are annulled, the object (the stocked product) and the debt of the object (the commitment of firms towards banks and, through them, towards the savings holders) being the association of equal assets and liabilities. Savings holders are the true owners of the stocked products, which are deposited in firms.

Without bank money, saving money formed in income would be globally nil, because it would have as an object the *matter* of money, already saved before the payment of wages. Even "primitive" accumulation would be an ill-formed concept, because hoarded gold or silver is not at all implicated in the emission of wages. Adam Smith knew it: new income is the result of new labour and not the result of dipping into pre-existing capital.

Only bank money brings the logical possibility of net claims in society as a whole, the new income being instantaneously transformed into an equal sum of future income. The bridge between present and future, that Keynes spoke about, is only brought about with the emissions of bank money. And, without this bridge, social capital exists neither under its financial form nor, consequently, in its real form. We understand therefore that the reform of banks has a logical scope that goes beyond the regulation of banking activities; the capital of society being "tied up" in banks, it can be "screened" in its formation in banks, even though it immediately comes to life to the benefit of non-bank agents.

Fixed capital is an appropriation by firms; nonetheless, it is formed in the emission of bank money and therefore its birth can be exactly controlled through the regulation of bank accounting. Precisely, empty emissions caused by the amortization of fixed capital are only imputable to the action of banks; but, banks can prevent the very emergence of the disorder: in a sense, they must be equipped with a filter such that only full emissions would be possible.

In Chapter 16, we shall build this filter and we shall show that the third department of banks will only carry the fixed capital born of accumulation, any overaccumulation being impossible from now on.

15 The division of banks in two departments

XXXVIII. The first department of banks

Like today, deposit banks will only carry out payment for clients considered solvent; this is obvious. However, any payment is an emission and, therefore, any payment is carried out by the first department of banks. But would it not be appropriate to restrict access to the department of emission solely to firms and for the creations of income, excluding any other operation? It would seem so because any monetary emission is logically the payment of a wage. But, the payment of wages is positive in the producing services market, negative in the products market and both positive and negative in the financial market (in the transfers). Besides, wages are created n times, in the sum of final purchases and intermediary purchases. Logic allows therefore that any money should be issued by the first department, whatever the identity of the client, firm or individual, and whatever the object of the payment. However, only wages contain the product of the nation; any money created (by the first department) in a payment distinct from the emission of wages must at once be recorded in the *second* department. It would seem, in these conditions, that money creation could never be superabundant.

The problem is the following: can the creation of money, subjected to no restriction, become excessive?

It would indeed insofar as money would come to life "empty of any product". The excess would be a purely nominal magnitude, a form without content, so that the available product would be expanded into a monetary supply uselessly (and even illicitly) enlarged. On reflexion, the risk incurred is nil. It is so because any emission is a "half-emission": at term, the bank destroys the money created. The complete operation is a creation-destruction, a zero creation, the effect of which could not be excessive.

However, the answer seems too good to be true. The proof overshoots the objective. It is not only that the creation of money cannot be in excess but it is not even positive. And if one answers that money is in fact positive during the whole interval of time separating its creation from its destruction, it may as well be in excess in this interval.

The definitive solution is the following.

Solution

Any creation of money defines a "demand without supply", a net or excess demand. Indeed, the client spends in his purchases a money newly born that he therefore does not receive from his sales. Conversely, any destruction of money defines a "supply without demand", as the money destroyed, earned in the sales, cannot be spent in the purchases. If economic events were happening in continuous (or discontinuous) time, the two gaps would be irreparably net from each other, as the excess demand and supply could not appear at the same time. We know that, in reality, production, distribution and consumption all happen in quantum time: any new product is retroactively cleared at the precise instant it appears. Chronologically separated from the creation of money, the destruction is eventually efficient at the same time, so that both gaps are brought to coincide: excess demand and excess supply cancel each other.

The only positive risk is therefore perfectly known: one must avoid bringing money created in the production of one period to the purchase of the product of another period. If the payment of wages is carried out with a periodicity of a month, only one constraint has to be imposed on the first department; it should not take any debt from operations the duration of which exceeds one month. Any shorter period would give a similarly satisfactory result: it may be agreed, for example, that the operations should be compensated at the end of the week and that their balance should be transferred to the second department. Under those conditions, no bank can finance any excess demand.

The distinction between the two departments is necessary because the economy is equipped with a financial market

At this stage of the reasoning, it might seem that the second department would be necessary for a primordial reason, to ensure the limitation in time of the commitments of the first department. It is necessary to disprove this conclusion that reflects an incorrect understanding of the distinction between monetary magnitudes and financial magnitudes.

Imagine an economy where no financial operation would come to life. Despite appearances, this economy might (and should) dispense with the imposition of a term to the operations of the department of emissions (which would be identified with the bank in its entirety). The risk of a bad synchronization between expenditures creating and expenditures destroying income would be nil in that economy, because the only income holders would be the workers (or their beneficiaries) themselves. If they buy the product today with the income of yesterday, it is then just an application of "general exchange", because it logically follows that they buy, for an equivalent sum, the product of yesterday with the income of today.

Excess demands can come to life only through the imperfect separation of money creations from financial intermediations. It must be ensured that income changing hands in the financial market should be brought on the very same product of savers; otherwise, it increases global demand for the goods produced in another period.

Only the existence of the financial market makes it necessary to impose a time constraint on the operations of the first department. Any issued sum of money, the repayment of which does not happen in the week (or the month), is from now on taken from the financial market, the second department "taking over" from the first.

The rule of operating the first department of any deposit bank is now known, but it still might be interpreted incorrectly on one important point: it might seem, indeed, that the money created would become savings only after the end of the time allotted to the completion of the operations of the first department. Any money created during the week, for example, would remain "un-saved" until the end of the week, only the positive balance of the operations defining positive savings. Logic requires a little more discrimination: in fact, any money constitutes positive savings right from its birth.

Everything becomes clear in the distinction between the assets side and the liabilities side of the department of emission.

- In each of its operations, the bank indicates on the assets side the person for whom it has carried out the payment. The delay imposed on every monetary emission concerns the recordings on the assets side and them alone: at term, they are taken over by the second department.
- As for the recordings, born in each emission, on the liabilities side, they feature at once in the second department. In other words, any emission is instantly indebting the first department towards the second. It follows that the final beneficiary of any emission, the "payee", obtains a money that is at once savings.

In its own functioning, the first department involves therefore the second one.

XXXIX. The organic unity of the two departments

Description of the simultaneous functioning of the two departments

To describe the simultaneous functioning of the two departments, it suffices to use again and stylize the explanations already given.

If we have chosen to record firms F and workers Wr, it is only to avoid useless developments. Emissions have a net result only in domestic production; therefore we have represented the example of a basic domestic production .

case of an ordinary emission

department of emissions			department of savings		
assets		liabilities	assets		liabilities
F	x f	II x f	I	x f	Wr x f

Figure 15.1 The case of an ordinary emission

The income created is of x francs. The producing firm appears on the assets side of the department of emissions, where it will "stay" until the end of the delay imposed by logic, a week for instance. But, within this delay and from the instant of the creation of the x francs, workers hold savings. It is the reason why income holders Wr appear on the liabilities side of the department of savings. Two operations belonging to the same category cancel savings (of the second department), withdrawals and loans.

At any instant, *the amount of claims of the second department on the first* precisely defines "loanable" savings. As soon as the department of savings pays x francs on behalf of savers or as soon as it lends y francs to a (final) borrower, its assets and liabilities sides are simultaneously reduced by y francs. Then department II is a creditor of department I only for the amount of $(x - y)$ francs, which remains available in the financial market.

We have just found very naturally the answer to the question that might have appeared serious: the recording on the liabilities side being immediately brought to the account of the second department, what is the use of keeping a separate first department? It is clear that, without this separation, banks would not know the amount of savings they have accumulated in their own money.

Now, what happens when firms are moved automatically, at the prescribed term, from the first to the second department? Let us first notice that they may have settled their debt, partially or totally, before reaching the term. But any subsisting debt is now a financial one whereas it was only a monetary one up to now. That is to say, insofar as firms keep their stocks beyond the prescribed period, they use some savings to that end.

The reading of the results does not present much difficulty. As long as firms are present on the assets side of the first department, the x francs define a social capital-time, i.e. the claim of the second department on the first. As soon as F moves from the assets side of the first department to the assets side of the second, the x francs are only capital both positive and negative, the claim of Wr being annulled by the debt of F. It must be understood therefore that firms appear in the department of savings as sellers of net claims. From then on, the stocks are no longer owned by savers but by firms. Thus, the emission of x francs has effectively reached its logical end: firms buy the

case of an emission
at its logical term

department of emissions				department of savings			
assets		liabilities		assets		liabilities	
F	0 f	II	0 f	F	x f	Wr	x f

Figure 15.2 The case of the emission having reached its logical term

corresponding product, by means of the income earned in the sale of claims. The initial lender of this income is none other than the set of income holders. The interpretation of the recording in the second department is perfectly univocal: the holders of income x have exchanged it against an equivalent claim on the bank; symmetrically, firms have obtained this income, which they have cast in the purchase of the stocks; F owes the bank the x units of income borrowed and spent.

The desired goal has been reached. It was about ruling out the possibility of any positive excess demand. Let us recall the exact nature of this risk. Before the reform of bank accounting, therefore in the contemporary economy, the financial market can convey (to the sellers of claims) an income, the spending of which relates to the product of another period; in this case, demand is in excess because old incomes are spent in competition with the new income. The anomaly can no longer happen in the regime of the two departments. Under the new rule of the game, any new product is necessarily cleared by the expenditure of the corresponding income. If the borrowers of the savings department (or the first depositors, beneficiaries of the income created) do not spend the totality of their resources to purchase the new product F, the automatic transformation of the monetary debt of F into a financial debt completes the destruction of current income on the current product. No part of the new income can therefore be brought to the product of another period.

Let us make it clear that the cancellation of capital-time obtained by the automatic transfer of the assets-side recordings from the first to the second department is just a last resort. The very function of the savings department is to lend the deposited funds. The beneficiaries of those loans spend the borrowed income to buy the product. If, at the end of the period, a part of the product remains stocked in the firm after all, the automatism intervenes: firms themselves buy the remainder by drawing the equivalent part of savings.

In the explanation just given, we see that capital-time can only have a temporary existence. Each new "share" of income makes the department of savings a creditor of the department of emission. However, all the operations of department II tend to reduce its claim on department I. In last resort, the automatic relief of the department of emissions annuls the claim; any subsisting capital-time is therefore destroyed.

However, there is a capital-time that cannot be reduced nor, let alone, annulled: *fixed capital*. The essential reason for the existence of the second department is precisely the necessity to carry the perennial capital-time, the true social capital. To this end, the savings department must be related to a *third department*. Before introducing it and showing how it operates, let us recall that as long as banks are deprived of it, the economy will be subjected to empty emissions, the unique aetiology of inflation and unemployment.

XL. An economy that has introduced the two bank departments would still suffer from the crisis because empty emissions would continue; the introduction of the third department is therefore necessary

We cannot go back to the demonstration of the "dual" production caused by the amortization of fixed capital. But it is probably not wasteful to insist on another, equally fundamental point: no capital, even a material one, could be formed in the domestic economy if the money issued were not bank money.

Only the existence of banks enables capital to be grasped conceptually; it is natural then that only the existence of banks enables capital to be grasped practically and, thanks to the third department, to maintain its neutrality

An economy devoid of banks would also be devoid of capital.

Even though we do not have the ambition here to cover entirely such a large problem, we propose to show quickly its three aspects. Let us designate this society by the letters SWB (society without banks). There, the formation of material capital is necessarily nil. The formation of financial capital is similarly nil. Finally, it is confirmed that no capital comes to life in the SWB because of the absence of any operation able to generate in the same movement material capital and financial capital.

The society without banks could not create any material capital

It is certain that, even in the SWB, human beings can equip themselves with the means of production. But it would be "vulgar" to consider those instruments or those machines as capital. Again, we must fight against a frequent allegation: the use of words is entirely free and to refuse the name capital to the means of production could only be a semantic restriction. Then, would it not be a similar pure linguistic effect to say that Antiquity did not know the bicycle? Even in its common sense, capital has a meaning that it cannot have in the SWB.

This can be rigorously proven by means of the distinction of the two categories of purchases, consumption and investment. There, it is no longer the vocabulary that is at stake but the *reasoning*. If, in a given state of society, no formal criterion can distinguish investment from consumption, capital has only a nominal existence: it is the second name of consumption, in its unchanged reality.

Precisely, in the SWB, any purchase is logically a consumption. Once the proof is given, it will remain true that man can consume goods in different ways, possibly to be "helped in producing": even in that case, it will be a consumption and not at all another operation, of a distinct nature, that might be legitimately called investment.

There is one and only one logical distinction between consumption and investment: it is based on the distinction between consumption and production.

If, in the economy under study, the operations of the two categories respond to each other without being intertwined, any production being net of consumption and any consumption being net of production, consumption is a category co-extensive with production since it is identical to it, but for the sign. However, it is conceivable *a priori* that part of the consumption might be merged with part of the production; this is the case in the "intersection" of the two opposite movements. This phenomenon, known for ages, is generally called "productive consumption" or "producing consumption". The very act of production then consumes part of the previous product, exactly like an automobile only produces movement by consuming energy.

The analysis thus imposes the distinction between consumption-goods in the strict sense, originating from a production net of any consumption, and investment-goods, the production of which is at the same time a consumption.

Now, it suffices to apply the criterion to the society without banks; we realize at once that, in that society, the process of production absorbs in each period an exactly zero sum of previous products. For it to be different, it would be necessary that, in the SWB, firms might be able to receive the consumption-goods saved by income holders, in order to inject those goods into the new process of production. The condition is not satisfied; it cannot be so and for a compelling reason: insofar as their holders save income in "material" money, *they prefer gold or silver to products*, which means, it is consequently certain, that they do not withdraw it.

In the SWB, income saved is a fraction of the product that firms do not sell to households. It would therefore be illogical to anticipate the transfer of the products saved by income holders to firms for their productive consumption,. In the society without banks, capitalization of part of income is eventually just a story *à la* Robinson Crusoe: there, instrumental capital can only be formed within households themselves. As soon as society produces in the wage-employment regime, it is able to provide the means of production to workers only because they are paid in bank money. If wages were paid in a material money, no capital could be present either in households (where production is nil by definition in the wage-employment regime) or in firms (that would have no access to the possible savings of income holders).

Reasoning has enabled us to avoid the purely semantical question. Even if we kept the naïve definition of capital, no capital could be formed in the society without banks, once it functions under the wage-employment regime.

The proof is even more straightforward regarding the second aspect of capital.

The society without banks could not create any financial capital

Any financial capital is a claim on the borrower. Suppose that the only money at the disposal of society is material. We are then in a "two-dimensional" world: any loan is an equal borrowing. It is inconceivable in the SWB that the sum of loans should be smaller than the sum of borrowings. That is to say that any positive financial capital is born at the same time as an equal negative capital.

The sum of loans can be positive in society only if it exceeds the sum of the corresponding borrowings. Not only is the condition not fulfilled in the SWB but it seems that it cannot be so in *any society*. Yet, we recognize the profound nature of bank money in that it enables the escape from the tautological equalities of loans and borrowings. The formation of net claims in the society as a whole was not known in pre-quantum theories. The conditions that must be met are indeed impossible to fulfil, except precisely in the emissions: the creations-destructions of domestic income.

In itself, we know it well, the emission of income is not a financial operation; it generates neither claims nor debts. However, defined in quantum time, the emission deposits its result in continuous time: *it is in this deposit that net capital can be found*. In an economy equipped with a financial market, bank money is, right from its birth, taken charge of. However, any money spent in the financial market defines the net claim of the depositors and, what is more, the net claim of the whole society: no debt corresponds to the savings obtained by the transformation of quantum deposits into ordinary deposits.

Only bank money can lend itself to this mutation that we can explain in a figurative way: firms do not owe the money that is transformed into income – on the contrary, they own it negatively. Then this money is, in the households or income holders, transformed into a claim on banks, without the mutation bringing the least additional debt of any agent towards the bank. It is therefore very true that the operation generates a positive claim and a zero debt.

This is the origin of social capital. Born from labour, income is created without involving the formation of a *debt for anyone*; deposited in time, income is a positive claim; the sum of debts and claims is therefore equal to the sum of claims. The financial capital of society is, by definition, equal to the sum of the income not yet spent in the clearing of goods to the benefit of households.

The emission of bank money adds therefore the "third dimension" that alone enables the avoidance of the tautology of the equality of loans and borrowings. If income were paid in material money, monetary income would be transformed in capital only in the operations voluntarily concluded by its holders (the automatism of the transformation of quantum deposits being absent); then, the tautology would prevail immediately, any purchase of claims being a sale of claims. The financial capital of society would be invariably zero.

Let us turn towards the third, synthetic, aspect. Capital is a two-faced objective reality. The simultaneous formation of financial capital and of real or material capital can only result from an emission that destroys income. As soon as the emission destroys an income in material money, it disappears without leaving any trace. That is to say that only bank money casts an objective bridge between the present and the future.

The society without banks is unable to cast a bridge between the present and the future. In its two aspects indifferently, capital is identified to this "bridge". It is true that in the SWB the product is already measurable because it is created in the monetary form or mould. However, the unity of the two half-emissions does not enable the definition of more than two operations: the first half-emission creates income and the second one destroys it. Once constituted in material money, the destruction of income is "pure and simple"; no income can disappear while leaving the promise of a future income, for the reason that any promise of a future income would be a net claim in the society and that the SWB does not have any.

Once wages are issued in bank money, the second half-emission is subdivided into a definitive destruction of current income and, for the other part, into a destruction of current income and the simultaneous creation of an equivalent future income. Indeed, products are first born within the negative money; given that income is immediately deposited in the financial market, products are at once dislodged from the money: in other words, they are constituted in stocks. Income is destroyed by the same operation; more exactly, it is obliterated as current income, to be replaced by an equal measure of future income.

The first destruction of income is therefore of the first type: it disappears in an instant to be transformed into future income. We must understand the mutation of income into capital, or, identically, the mutation of current income into future income, in the strictest sense: any income born of the destruction of a capital is the reproduction of the very same income, the destruction of which had initially formed the relevant capital. Thus, the sale of stocks creates an income, which is none other that the income previously destroyed at the instant when the products were formed into stocks. It is finally in the purchase of the products by households that income disappears without leaving any trace.

The chain of events is therefore the initial creation of income, its immediate transformation in a future income, the realization of this income and finally its conclusive destruction.

One question of real scientific interest arises regarding income in material money. It cannot be transformed into capital. One may be tempted to deduce that this income does not disappear at the instant of its birth; unlike income constituted in bank money, income in gold or silver would have the ability to travel through time. The well-founded conclusion is completely different: in reality, any income disappears at its birth because any income is the result of an emission. The final sale of the products deposited into a material money is not the reproduction of the initial income but simply the repetition of its unique destruction, retroactively defined right from the creation of wages. The profound nature of capital appears therefore in a brighter light. Being the unique bridge cast between current income and future income, capital is the only entity that is capable of ensuring the simultaneity in chronological time of the creation and destruction of any income; the intercession of capital has the effect of duplicating the emission: current income is created-destroyed in the expenditure of wages. It remains therefore that *the faculty to travel through time is granted to income only by capital.*

Before the introduction of bank money, money was a two-dimensional entity: it was the form of physical products and, in the alliance with these products, it defined social income. Bank money adds the third dimension; social capital is the state of bank money grasped between the instant of the creation of income and the instant of the purchase of the product by households.

The division of deposit banks into two departments enables the "visualization" of capital perfectly, since it identifies with the sum of the claims of the first department on the second. As soon as the product is cleared – and it is so, at the latest, in the transfer from the assets side of the first department to the second (the product being then purchased by households under the form of zero-sum claims of which it has become the object) – the social capital is destroyed. It will only be reconstituted by the effect of a new production-emission.

Once analysts are truly convinced that capital is the third dimension of bank money only, they can no longer doubt the double nature of capital, an entity which in its unity is financial and real altogether. They can no longer be surprised either when they are told that *mastering social capital is entirely confined to the operation of bank recordings,* even regarding fixed capital, the logical evolution of simple capital-time.

The optimism of the proposition is perfectly founded: in its pejorative sense, capitalism will be overcome by reorganizing the way deposit banks operate. The creation of two departments is the first stage; to complete the reform, it suffices to join the department of fixed capital to the pairing formed by the department of emissions and the department of savings. Banks have brought to the domestic economy the dimension and the blessings of capital; the time has come when banks must be subjected to a new rule, the effect of which will be to filter all emissions, in order to "let through" full emissions only.

16 The economy equipped with a network of deposit banks all divided into three departments will be totally free from empty emissions

Basically, the production of capital in profit-goods is caused by a "malady" of money, precisely an adulteration of money defined in its third dimension. It remains perfectly true that banks do not cause the illness, because their behaviour is neutral even to the point of respecting the dysfunctions created by the logic of fixed capital and its amortizations. It is therefore not a case of "bringing banks into line" like David Ricardo had planned to do. The illness is far deeper. It must be reached and eradicated in the only operations where it comes in the open, the locus of monetary emissions, which is the creative activity of banks.

XLI. The adjunction of the department of fixed capital

Let us first summarize the principle of the tripartite division.

- The emissions department sees the birth and death of money, whether it is created in the formation of the product, in its transfers or in its clearing.
- The savings department (or capital-time) receives all the ordinary deposits formed in the banks in order to recycle them in the financial market, to the benefit of depositors or final borrowers.
- The fixed capital department (or of the advanced form of capital-time) takes charge of all the savings initially formed in the second department and that must be withdrawn precisely because they are invested in instrumental capital: if these savings were left at the disposal of the second department, they would feed excess demands and would thereby generate empty emissions.

We know the functioning of the joint organization of the first two departments. The functioning of the third department is a little subtler, but we shall try to describe it briefly while following carefully the stages of the reasoning.

As soon as a firm acquires a net claim on the bank, it is credited in the third department

This initial measure is fundamental, and it is protective. It is obvious that in the process of production firms find countless claims, particularly because of intermediary purchases, without this leading us to conclude that every net claim is a profit. However, it is equally clear that monetary profits are net credits of firms on banks. The problem is therefore the need to put into place the automatism enabling the "treatment" of all claims in order to keep only net profits, and even then, only insofar as they are invested. Meanwhile, it suffices to give the third department the initial control of the totality of the creditor positions of firms.

Let us reason on a firm F_q. In the period under consideration, it acquires a net claim of x fr. on its bank; at once, the claim is transferred to the liabilities side of the third department.

If the profit of F_q was put into the second department, it would be defined as an amount of *savings still available*. But it is illogical that it should be so, because profits result from a final expenditure already *carried out*. Wages spent in the formation of profits must not define monetary savings still available in the financial market: if wages transformed into profits are not withdrawn from the financial market (represented by the second department), they constitute a loanable fund that will feed *a second tier of final expenditures*. Borrowers will spend the incomes already spent by households in the operation of the formation of profits. The second expenditure of the (same) income is an *empty emission*, the root of the disorder, inflation and unemployment.

The immediate withdrawal of monetary profits gives the assurance that they will never be offered in the financial market. It is right that they should not be, because non-distributed profits are invested in instrumental capital: "sunk" into the equipment, they would be *used a second time* if they were still available in the financial market to feed new final purchases.

Monetary profits being, right from their formation, withdrawn from the second department, the "rule of the game" governing their expenditure has to be discovered.

The payment of wages is never imputed on the profits formed

Suppose that at the instant it is going to issue new wages, equal to y fr., the firm has a net claim of x fr. on its bank.

It is important to leave the debt of F_q in the first department and the claim of F_q in the third department.

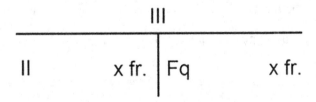

Figure 16.1 The transfer of firms' profits into the third department

Figure 16.2 The payment of wages leaves the third department unaltered

Thus, it can never happen that a profit is spent *in the producing services market*.

And it is essential that it should be impossible, because any net expenditure of profit in the emission of wages defines an *empty emission*.

Even after the emission of new wages (y), the firm still has at its disposal the totality of its profit because the department of fixed capital (III) keeps it entirely at its disposal.

It is still not certain that the profit has already been spent; that is so only if it is (already) invested into fixed capital. How can this be ensured?

In any period, the bank writes off the profit (recorded in the third department) to the exact amount that, in the market of products and claims, the firm's purchases exceed its sales

Assume, in the period, x' to be the amount of *net* purchases of F_q in the markets of products and financial claims. In the third department, the profit of F_q only appears for the amount $(x - x')$ (see Figure 16.3).

Any profit that is *finally* not spent in the net purchases of F_q in the two markets (products and financial claims) is necessarily *invested*.

A double and permanent recording on the assets side of the second department and on the liabilities side of the third discloses invested profits

Assume again x' to be the amount of the net purchases of F_q on the two markets (products and financial claims). Invested profit is $(x - x')$.

The method reveals that it suffices to add up all the invested profits of F_q.

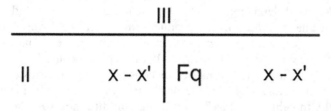

Figure 16.3 Invested profit recorded in the third department

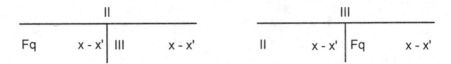

II				III			
Fq	x - x'	III	x - x'	II	x - x'	Fq	x - x'

Figure 16.4 The relation between the second and third departments

In the succession of periods, the net investment of any firm is equal to the cumulated sum of its definitive claims on the third departments of all deposit banks

The same firm can obviously accumulate capital in several banks. But it suffices to apply the same rule everywhere: in each period, the net investment of the firm appears in the sum of double entries that concern it, on the assets and liabilities sides of all the second and third departments of banks.

XLII. To conclude, let us briefly show the perfectly ordered functioning of the economy of the country in the new regime of bank payments

All final purchases now come from income holders or households

Income holders carry out all the purchases within the country; no purchase will come from a "non-person". Firms are not affected, it is well understood, but they are now only physical or legal people, reducible to the set of shareholders. Before the reform, firms were more than that since they constituted the only category of buyers able to pay by means of empty emissions.

Income holders, as a set, choose, at all times, to spend their earnings to consume or to save. It is true that this choice is limited by the formation of profits, which are automatically saved. But if profits do not exceed the interests rewarding accumulated fixed capital, they are a simple redistribution of wages: income holders retrieve them to allocate them, according to their desires, to saving or consumption.

Even surplus profits can be redistributed to households. Only invested profits seem to reduce the choice of income holders since they are necessarily saved.

Through some further reflexion, one discovers though that the levy operated by the third department on the loanable funds of the second is just the effect of a final purchase in the product market, in other words, of a consumption. By consuming *today*, the set of income holders enables the formation of the *current* profit of firms. If the set of income holders were to save (and lend) its earnings instead of consuming them, firms (that would borrow them because they are the only partners of the set of income holders) would thereby "advance" their future profits, not yet realized. It is therefore true, in last analysis, that the holders have the complete freedom to cast their wage and non-wage income into the channel of their choice, consumption or saving.

For their part, firms enjoy an equal freedom: they accept or not the savings on offer. This free negotiation determines the rate of interest.

By stylizing the presentation somewhat, we may consider profits as savings freely released by the set of income holders who choose thereby to exchange part of their current consumption for a larger future consumption. Let us note carefully that it is out of the question to give ourselves the increase in consumable goods through the effect of a productivity in value (wage-units) of fixed capital. Any capital is rigorously unproductive, the product of each period being measured (and measurable) solely in wage-units. However, it is clear that for a constant working population, more physical goods will be found within the sum of wages issued, due to the productivity in volume of invested capital.

Controlled by workers and other income holders, the investment of each period cannot present any drawback. If, in its free decisions, society chooses (through a variation in the rates of money) to reduce from period to period the fraction of current incomes allocated to savings and investment, no one can suffer from this choice as current consumption will be facilitated. The opposite choice is equally neutral: any income saved is, by definition, invested; only confused thinking would fear a clearing deficit that would be induced by increased saving.

As for the amortization of fixed capital, one cannot see what problems it could still create. "Filtered" at the level of net investments, empty emissions are totally eliminated from the domestic economy, so much so that amortization is now only an intermediary purchase. In the history of thought, the third department will therefore bring victory to Smith over Marx (the latter remaining victorious in the "pathological economy"). Whatever the rhythm imposed on the rotation of instrumental capital, by its wear and tear and its obsolescence, any income cast in the purchase of amortization goods will be derived from the production of those same goods.

And then what about the crisis? Theorists have some scruples about saying that it can be overcome by *human intelligence*. Are not inflation and unemployment the product of fate? But then what would be the usefulness of political economy? Would there be any? Why cast doubt on the solution if it is the outcome of a long and profound tradition? The common work, patiently elaborated, of all the generations of thinkers since the great Classics.

In this study of quantum macroeconomics, we have proposed an outline analysis of the crisis and of the solutions which follow. The ideas that we have presented will be tested. If they hold, there is room for hope. Let us show again why neither inflation nor unemployment are incurable evils.

The three departments of deposit banks issue in the economy the exact measure of money that is necessary to produce and clear goods. The first department refuses its services only to agents known to be insolvent. It could not happen that a firm, the goods of which are considered "saleable" might not obtain the money necessary for their production. As for the opposite danger, that of a supernumerary emission, it is avoided by the conjugated action of the second and third departments. Being known for what it is, i.e., a double expenditure (a purchase in the market for products hidden inside an emission of wages), the investment of profit is neutralized in its damaging effect: the "second expenditure" (the definition of excess demand) is cancelled by the withdrawing of equivalent savings, by the third department from the second. In the end, *investment will be financed by savings and no longer by empty emissions.*

As for "involuntary" unemployment, it will truly be reduced to a contradiction in terms. The three departments eradicate the (continuous) functioning of capital. In the new order, only Man can employ Man. It will no longer happen that capital renounces employing people, as it does today when it cannot find enough profits to remunerate the over-accumulations. In pure logic (that is away from any pathology), Jean-Baptiste Say is right (Say 1821): it is inconceivable that the expenditure of income should not provide a work, equivalent to the expenditure, to the producers of the goods purchased. It is equally inconceivable that part of the income created should not be spent in the products market. Clear thinking dissipates the ills conceived by an incomplete science and it shows the essential vulnerability of the illness that it discerns.

One last worry is often expressed, in particular by students in our economic departments. Even if the solution were found, how could it be put into practice, in spite of powerful interests? Is not the world condemned to class struggle?

Everywhere in this book, we are developing an analysis, the objective of which is not to agree with one class over another but, on the contrary, to show that the deepest economic problems arise with a comparable acuteness for *all classes at the same time.* As long as capital is able to employ all the labour force available, one might think that it benefits one social class, even though the invested part of profit-goods is put at the service of the production of wage-goods. But, today, *capital is fighting against itself.* Can it be doubted that firms would then benefit from putting a stop to continuous over-accumulation? In "Wicksellian" terms, the new order will enable a parity between the rate of profit ("real" interests) and the rates determined in the financial markets ("monetary" interest): firms will thus recover a normal remuneration for invested capital. In no way will the increase of the well-being of the working population be obtained "on the back" of capital. The whole country, in political as in economic order, has the greatest interest in getting rid of unemployment. Whoever grasps the functioning of the three bank departments cannot doubt it: the eradication of empty emissions will harm neither workers *nor firms.*

And what about the transition period? It will be painless. The day after the introduction of the new regime, the price of wage-goods will stay unchanged. The "core" will extend to the whole production but the price of the product of the core will still include the price of (old) profit-goods. In this sense, the "crown" will persist somewhat over time. However, unemployment will already be under attack; silently, the "core" will extend day by day until it comprises the totality of the population able to work. Inside the core, the "baskets" will progressively include more goods per given wages. Therefore, the general level of wages will not be subjected to the pendulum effect that we have described in the analysis of empty emissions. *The economy will no longer live under capitalism.* And it is not a utopia to think that the level of nominal wages might be at last maintained constant in face of the slow and continuous increase of real (in physical terms) wages.

New net investments are now the economic property of the set of income holders or of households

Let us conclude this part by a brief examination of the investment-amortization of profits, in the current mode of production and in the future economic order.

Captured in profits, invested wages "return" to workers under the adulterated form of claims to the saved wage-goods. The cause of all the disorders, excess demand is the expenditure by households of the monetary capital received as a remuneration for the production of investment-goods. The remedy is therefore obvious: "false wages" have to be withdrawn, eliminated. Savings taken by the third department from the second one are limited to that; they do not destroy an income that would stay free, the agents being able to bring it to consumption or saving: they only eliminate incomes already definitely transformed into savings and that it is illogical to spend on produced goods.

The withdrawal operated in the second department is only sanctioning a now irreversible fact: invested profits are the indelible savings of households. However, to leave the disposal of the corresponding income, born from the production of instrumental capital, to households is to tolerate disorder; thus fed, excess demand is the exact action that is the unique source of the capitalist mode of production: the expenditure of false wages attracts and fixates instrumental capital in the holdings of firms, households being dispossessed. As soon as the adulterated income is effectively withdrawn and destroyed, it appears that instrumental capital has been formed in the original expenditure of wages, at the moment of the formation of monetary profits, later invested. From then on, households are the only owners of instrumental capital, now fixated in the set of income holders.

It might seem strange that withdrawing part of wages brings an increased well-being to income holders. Actually, this "paradox" helps to understand the essential: the reform of bank accounting is not at all directed against firms. But nor is it detrimental to workers. The measure is neutral regarding people and social classes; it is far more fundamental: without taking one centime from anyone and, therefore, in the strict respect of all the incomes and all the profits earned, the reform liberates the nation from inflation and unemployment. The benefit that will be gained is net for everyone.

Let us consider the instant when the wages captured in profits are cast in the remuneration of workers, employed in producing investment goods. Let us call AW (for adulterated wages) the result of this second payment. The units of AW face two real capitals: the wage-goods "lost" by households when the monetary profits currently invested were formed, and the investment goods, newly produced. This duplication of real capital is the profound definition of capitalism. It is the source of every overaccumulation. Once the third department intervenes, adulterated wages are withdrawn and destroyed.

Immediately, the mode of production is fundamentally corrected: we now only find units of wages first saved (in the formation of monetary profits) and, for the same measure in units of wages, real capital first composed of wage-goods and now transformed into instrumental capital.

Retrospectively, the formation of invested profit appears for what it is, the purchase by households (holders of wage and non-wage income) of fixed capital, initially born under the form of saved wage-goods.

This is the time once again to grasp in its deepest sense the idea of the "dispossession" of workers and, more generally, of income holders. The existence of adulterated wages means the substitution of firms to households, in the appropriation of the means of production. Once the units of AW are destroyed at the source, fixed capital is accessible to the income (of households), which is completely *"genuine"* in the new mode of production. The recent experience (1984) in a country like France, where the political power took the decision to nationalize (that is to establish state control) an important fraction of firms, misses its true objective.

As long as the economy continues to produce adulterated wages, men (all human beings and to the benefit of Capital, that "non-person") will continue, in every period, to be dispossessed of all the part of current goods, the production of which is financed by the expenditure of a "wage fund". Only the reform of the banking system will establish an economy where in each period all the wages will be paid by live labour.

Let us go back to the study of the units of AW facing the two types of real capital. The third department withdraws and eliminates these false wages. We see at once that households no longer have the power to buy saved wage-goods. However, they did have it, precisely through monetary savings. It is the set of undifferentiated households that is the unique holder of the monetary savings fixated in the third department and, thus, is the sole owner of fixed capital.

One might fear that, resolved for investment, the problem might remain unsettled on the side of amortization. A simple reasoning will restore full confidence. "Dual" production is a particular case of net investment: overaccumulations are investments. The presence of the third department gives therefore the desired guarantee: no income will ever be spent in the payment of a (new) income, amortization goods will be bought by the income newly born from their production in each period. Domestic economy will no longer produce amortization goods in two stages: in households and (under the form of over-accumulation) in firms. Dual production will no longer exist and the reader knows that it is (soon it will be possible to say it was) the source of all the disorders pertaining to inflation and unemployment.

Part V

General conclusion: the micro-macro distinction in economic analysis

The theory of emissions brings the exact meaning of the distinction between microeconomics and macroeconomics. It is well known that these "two sciences" have developed side by side, without anyone being able to define the precise boundaries. One wonders thus on the "microeconomic foundations of macroeconomics". Besides, if the distinction is maintained, is it not a purely methodological one? These questions are now clearly settled. Emissions are the heart of macroeconomics. We shall demonstrate that they are "absolute relations", of the agents on themselves, and not relations either between agents or between objects, i.e. "goods". The exact definition of microeconomics will be known at once by contrast and with the same rigour: any transaction between several agents and several goods is an object of inquiry of microeconomics. We shall reach therefore an unexpected conclusion: well understood, macroeconomics obliterates microeconomics, which correspond to an intermediary stage of the development of our science.

In the last chapter we shall show, with the help of the criticism of a recent theory of the crisis, that it is difficult, even for authors who turn away from microeconomics, to be entirely faithful to the spirit of macroeconomics. We shall meet again ideas already mentioned in the body of this work. The "circuit", a macroeconomic concept *par excellence*, excludes any idea of disequilibrium or of inequality between Supply and Demand. The studies that claim to expose the aetiology of glut crises by some insufficiency of global demand are guilty of eclecticism. Macroeconomic thought is only coherent in the absolute respect of the equality, in all periods, and even at all instants, of the two opposite flows of formation and expenditure of income. Unspent income, or income that would not be brought (immediately) by its holders on produced goods, only exists in incomplete macroeconomic explanations. We shall solve again the paradox that, since the great Classics, and particularly Say, is at the heart of macroeconomic reflexion: the identity of Demand and Supply is the only foundation, concrete and logic, on which the theory of crisis can be built. Any autonomy of Demand in relation to Supply is a fiction the origin of which still belongs to microeconomics.

17 Macroeconomics is the domain of absolute exchanges

In its common meaning, exchange is a transaction involving at least two people and two goods. It is true that even in its usual sense, exchange is mostly viewed as a purchase or a sale. However, a purchase and a sale are monetary transactions. Once money intervenes, exchange is no longer conceived as a relation from good to good, because, even in the mind of the man in the street, it is at least doubtful that money should simply be one good among other goods. As soon as income is viewed like a claim to collect domestic output, exchange of the claim against its object is getting closer to an "absolute relation", the exchange of the object with itself: "represented" in the claim, the product is twice present, in itself and in the claim. It would therefore be unfair to attribute to common naïvety the idea that exchanges observed on the markets are moving, between suppliers and demanders, distinct goods that "cross" each other. It is more likely that the uninformed man is reasoning in terms of purchasing power, money being not an "item" in the collection of goods available in the markets but a ticket enabling the withdrawal of them. In the next chapter we shall find a confirmation of this judgment because it will appear that it is the scholar and not the layman who propagates the "sophisticated" and erroneous idea of the identification of monetary exchanges to transactions concluded between one real good and another (distinct) real good.

Let us start with the expression of inductive truth: in all economies, even those purely "real" (like those that existed in remote times), all observed transactions are "absolute relations". One may doubt it at first. Let us carefully indicate the logical importance of the doubt: it is certain – therefore indubitable – that absolute relations have existed since prehistorical times because they are defined by human labour. But could we not imagine the co-presence, during long periods, of exchanges of the two types? This is the only question worthy of interest: have relative exchanges coexisted with absolute exchanges for a long time?

We shall see that one must choose between a lax and imprecise language and a scientific terminology. "Exchange" is not a formless term: it has a precise sense; to exchange is to *change*; it is as difficult to exchange lead with gold as it is to change it into gold. The difficult step is in acknowledging *absolute* exchanges; it is far easier after that to accept that absolute exchanges replace purely and simply relative exchanges, to consign them to the domain of pre-scientific opinions.

It so happens that current economies barely experience barter any more, except in international transactions. As soon as money counts bartered objects, they enter the payments: they are now directly present in the compensation. The only category of exchanges that maintains its originality is that of "non-monetary barter": I lend you my car and you give me products from your garden. It is true to say that these operations have very little significance in national accounts.

This is not the case for production "outside wage employment". However, goods "meet" money in the products market, not only in the producing services market. Any good sold is integrated in the monetary economy.

Only the pure barter that we have mentioned remains as a relative exchange; not only is its place in the network of exchanges numerically negligible, but there is more, pure barter is not an exchange if we want to give a precise meaning to the term. Any exchange *proprio sensu* is an equation, the objects given, one for the other, featuring in the same measurement space.

This is essential; if the "exchanged" objects are not commensurable, science cannot grasp them. The idea according to which exchanges are concluded in the inequality of the terms comes from a grave confusion of the mind: if exchanges were not equations, they would not even enter the field of knowledge. Thanks to the theory of emissions, we shall have no difficulty demonstrating that all transactions in the three markets – producing services, financial claims and products – are absolute exchanges, the only exchanges that introduce effectively exchanged goods into a common measurement space.

From this, we shall induce the exact definition of *macroeconomics*; it is the *science of absolute exchanges*. We shall observe thus that the notion of "aggregation" or "summing up" is totally foreign to the constitution of macroeconomics. If an isolated transaction is not macroeconomic right from the start, it will never be. Summing up microeconomic transactions only gives a similarly microeconomic result.

There is therefore no bridge between microeconomics and macroeconomics: no operation, not even an "aggregation", can transform a relative exchange into an absolute exchange. Macroeconomics is the science of emissions and every emission, as small as it might be, even if it concerns only one agent and for only one centime, is macroeconomic. Macroeconomics is the domain of *sets*: precisely, an exchange defined on an agent is identically defined on the set of agents on the necessary and sufficient condition that it is "absolute on this agent".

XLIII. From the origin of humanity, human labour is an absolute exchange

We have already developed the idea; let us sum it up.

Usually, economists mention labour without seeking its meaning, whereas in physics labour is a well-defined notion. Then one turns to questions as fundamental as that of "labour-value" or "labour factor".

It is obvious though that without knowing exactly the nature of labour one cannot decide its exact definition.

Today, this knowledge has been acquired: labour is an emission; it is even the only emission that ever happens in the economy, monetary emissions being only applications of it. And this emission is perfectly known as well: it is the creation-destruction of the "economic form" of matter. Before labour, matter is entirely "natural"; labour transforms matter into value in use.

It is clear that labour is not the creation-destruction or emission of the value in use but only of the form that matter has to take in order to become a value in use (new or increased). If the form were not created, matter could not be moulded in it and would stay "gross"; on the other hand, if the form were not destroyed, it would remain attached to matter, which is inconceivable, no matter coming from the hands of man is anything other than a matter; it contains no additional matter, even under the appearance of an "envelope".

Thus, the emission is indeed an operation both positive and negative, the simultaneous coexistence of creation and destruction of the utility-form of material objects. The creation of the form is its production; the destruction of the form is its consumption. Nobody will ever be able indeed to confuse economic consumption and biological consumption, for example. The good is consumed at the precise instant it is formed as value in use: it is completed. Consumption of the value in use is therefore foreign to the discussion. The only relevant consumption is identical to production, but for the sign. The emission is a production-consumption.

We immediately find therefore the absolute character of the exchange: the emission is a production that changes or transforms on the spot into a consumption.

In all rigour, we must therefore take back the statement about the absence of money in pre-historical times. As soon as labour appeared, money was present within the emission. What is money, if not the equivalence of production and consumption? It is not necessary for the equivalence to take place through an object that remains present through time. Pebble-money is undoubtedly already an evolved form of money; it remains that money was, at all times, present in human labour, *inside the real emission.*

Once money is perceived in the emission, the thought process avoids the common opinion that views the monetary exchange as an agreement between two "partners". In fact, the worker operates by himself a perfect exchange.

Even the second mistake is avoided; let us express it. Worker A exchanges his product (*a*) against product (*b*) of worker B. It seems therefore that the exchange of products between themselves is relative. This is incorrect. To think right, one must consider the two emissions, those of A and B. Without these emissions, goods *a* and *b* would not exist as products. Once the emissions are given, the exchange between *a* and *b* is included in the two absolute exchanges. Worker A changes the production of *a* into a consumption of *b*; correlatively, worker B changes the production of *b* into a consumption of *a*. Apparently relative, the exchange between *a* and *b* is in reality *the relation of two absolute exchanges.*

To judge otherwise would be to commit a serious error of logic, nothing less. The exchange of *a* and *b* as products means *ipso facto* the exchange of productions, the labour of A and the labour of B. The reflexion has therefore access to a truth of the very primary importance: the exchange of *a* and *b*, as products, is conceivable only if money is interposed. Already present within the emissions, money must be so a second time, "between" products *a* and *b*. That is to say, the exchange of products means necessarily and right from the origin (at the instant of the completion of labour-emissions) the conversion of the products of A and of B into money. To this end, it is indispensable that money should be present in the duration of time, for example under the form of pebbles.

For want of having given this question the attention it deserves, it is generally said that the exchange of *a* and *b* is either real or monetary. The real exchange would be a direct transaction from *a* to *b*, whereas the monetary exchange would involve two half-transactions, the exchange of *a* against a sum of money, then the exchange of this sum against *b*. Reality is far more demanding: if the "exchange" between *a* and *b* were exclusively real, it would not exist as an exchange. One would then be able to detect only two absolute exchanges, the emission of *a* and the emission of *b*, since no subsequent exchange would define the relation of the two absolute exchanges. The absence of money not only undermines the existence of monetary exchange; which is a pure truism; but it also undermines the existence of real exchange, as the product of A cannot be changed into a product of B nor the product of B changed into a product of A.

The exchange of products can only be carried out through the mediation of money. This is so because each emission is already a perfect exchange; the production of *a* is changed into a consumption of *a*, the production of *b* into a consumption of *b*. If now one claims to add the exchange of *a* with *b*, it is logically necessary to embed this additional exchange into the two absolute exchanges, the product of A being right from the origin (by the well-known effect of retroactivity) changed into a product of B, and conversely. If the exchange of products were conceived independently from the two absolute exchanges, it would no longer be "formalized": it would not exist in the eyes of the scholar. In a word, the exchange of *a* and *b* is defined between the two products only if it is grasped in the two emissions; otherwise, it would be an "exchange" between values in use and no one has ever been able to measure values in use or utilities. However, even if these "magnitudes" were measurable, they would not be so *because* of the "exchange", which would be totally unable to introduce them into a common measurement space. Only money is the common form of product *a* and product *b*.

The (logical and not chronological) course of the operations is the following.

- Once we know that products *a* and *b* are exchanged between them, we know that they are so through the intermediary of a money, for example interchangeable pebbles.

- We know thus that right from the production-emission, worker A produces pebbles in his holdings. Instead of changing his production into an immediate consumption, he changes his *real* production into a *monetary* production. Similarly, worker B changes his production (the operation and not just its result); he transforms it: he produces pebbles and not immediately good *b*.
- Given that good *a* is by hypothesis finally exchanged against good *b*, we know that the two products are exchanged against the same number (*x*) of interchangeable pebbles.

Thus, by his labour, A issues *x* pebbles in his holdings; B does the same. Those two emissions are observed within the exchange of good *a* against good *b*.

- The pebbles being interchangeable, products *a* and *b* are so as well. The converse is true and this is crucial; if products *a* and *b* had not, from the beginning, been changed into pebbles, they would not be interchangeable: they could not therefore be the object of an exchange.
- The relation of equivalence between product *a* and product *b* in no way means therefore that the values in use or the utilities of the two goods are equal; not only is the equality of utilities not established but it is devoid of any meaning. If we content ourselves to reason "qualitatively", we may even say that for A the utility of good *b* is far superior to the utility of good *a*; otherwise he would not find any reason to be present at the exchange. In fact, the equivalence of products is the consequence of two absolute equivalences.

$$x \quad \text{units of pebbles} = a$$

$$x \quad \text{units of pebbles} = b$$

- Economic exchange is no more a net creation or destruction than physical, chemical or biological exchanges; changed into *b*, product *a* is still equal to itself, under this new form. Once again, only the confusion of the values, in use and of exchange, gives some credibility to the proposition according to which the terms of the exchange are (or may be) unequal.
- It is totally insufficient to define exchange as the conservation of product *a* in the operation that has seen it change hands. One must move much further on, otherwise the exchange is identified as a simple journey through space: good *a* is conserved in the operation that changes it in good *b*. Tautologically, the exchange means the interchangeability of goods: *a* is conserved in *b* and not simply in *a*, that is in itself.
- If money existed only within the emissions, and not in interchangeable pebbles or any other "concrete numbers", the alleged exchange between good *a* and good *b* could be written with two arrows.

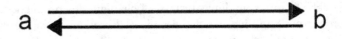

Figure 17.1 The direct exchange between goods

One is not at liberty to transform the opposite arrows into a sign of equality. The equality of *a* and *b* expresses only one thing: their respective equality with number x of interchangeable pebbles.

- We end up therefore with the announced conclusion: relative exchange between *a* and *b* is only the relation between two absolute exchanges, those of *a* and *b* in pebbles. Relative exchanges are therefore disposed of. It is unthinkable that goods *a* and *b* should enter a relation of exchange if they are not first defined, each on its side, in an equivalence in pebbles.

XLIV. All transactions on the three markets are absolute exchanges

Today, it is of course useless to make an effort of the imagination to look for the analytical presence of money in the apparently relative exchanges. Money is effectively present everywhere. However, the idea of relative exchanges is entrenched, and it is difficult to resist the temptation to distinguish two categories of operations in the concrete economies, monetary exchanges and real exchanges. This is because the most common philosophy holds relative exchanges to be the general case, of which monetary exchanges would only be an application. The truth is exactly the opposite: *any exchange is absolute, real exchanges being only an application of monetary exchanges.*

In the body of this work, we have established the reality of absolute exchanges in the context of the strict wage employment regime. Now, we only need to generalize.

Let us first sum up the general argument, which is by the way similar to the one we have briefly developed for pebble-money. If worker A had not changed his product into money, he could not spend money to buy products. Up to this point, the proposition is a truism. It becomes a positive piece of information once we add one or the other of the two following propositions that are both true, therefore conjointly.

1   If A had not changed his product into money right from the act of production, he could not exchange it against any (other) product. This time, it is not monetary exchange that is denied but the possibility of any kind of exchange: product *a* could not be exchanged against any (other) product, even in an exclusively real transaction, from good to good, except if giving exchange the insipid meaning of "transporting" goods between agents.

2   Having, from the start, changed his product into money, A can exchange
it only against his own product: the expenditure of income A is the purchase of product *a*.

The demonstration of proposition 1 is based on the criterion of interchangeability. Good *a* is exchangeable against good *b* if, and only if, *a* and
b are changed, in the act of production, into the same number of monetary units.

As for proposition 2, it is established by the analysis of absolute exchanges,
of *a* and of *b* into money. Money can take the place of the product only
because of the monetary emission: object *a* is lodged in *x* units of negative
money, and so it is for good *b*. Each act of production thus creates its own,
positive and negative, money. Any expenditure of income is the meeting of
those same two monies, born from production. Transactions thus follow the
identity of the product as it is present in the two "half-operations", formation
and expenditure of each worker's income. The fusion of positive money into
negative money defines the "purchasing power of money". It follows that
each worker obtains in the expenditure of his income (in the products market)
the good that he has produced.

Let us take advantage of this opportunity to develop somewhat the principle of the closure of the circuit in the purchase of the exact same good, the
production of which had defined the circuit at its opening.

It suffices to keep the example of workers A and B, producing goods *a* and
b. If money were not interposing, we would nevertheless discern the existence
of two circuits, the productions-emissions of A and B. In the completion of
his work, A creates and destroys product *a*; similarly, B creates and destroys
product *b*: these creations-destructions are circuits. After the intercession of
money, it would seem first that worker A might create product *a* and destroy
(in the final purchase) product *b*; B might thus symmetrically create *b* and
destroy *a*. But the truth is more rigorous: the intervention of money does not
alter the nature of the circuit which is, in all cases, the creation and the
destruction of the same object by the same worker.

It is so because money has only one power (in addition to its function as a
numéraire), that of separating in chronological time the two half-transactions
defining a unique circuit. It is therefore not possible, from a logical point of
view, that the money earned by A should be destroyed in the negative money
created by B. Each worker can only destroy his own product because he can
bring it to life in the unity of the creation-destruction operation. Still, as we
have constantly noticed, any worker is free to buy the product of his choice;
consequently, A may indeed buy the product of B. The substitution must be
pursued to its consequence. As soon as A casts his positive money in the
negative money created by B, the money earned by B (which is identical to
the negative money created by himself) is identified to the money destroyed
by A. It follows that the substitution of money A to money B implies the
reciprocal substitution, of money B to money A: the two substitutions being

completed, it does appear indeed that money A can only be destroyed in the purchase of good *a* and, in general, that money Q can only be destroyed in the purchase of good *q*.

It is important to refrain from allowing ourselves any "degree of freedom" in the definition of the circuit, otherwise its very existence would elude insight. Even after the intervention of money, the circuit is simply the creation-destruction by human labour of the utility-form of matter. In the last analysis, circuits and absolute exchanges are one and the same reality.

We can therefore try now to carry out the generalization announced above: is it really true that all the transactions in the three markets are absolute exchanges or, identically, circuits?

Any exchange in the producing services market is absolute

The law that we have described in this work stands against both classical and neoclassical teachings. According to those schools, workers sell their activity to receive undifferentiated products in exchange, in money, for a "value" equal or, more often, lower than the "value" of their own product. This is completely incorrect. The payment of wages is an emission: this is to say that (in full emissions) workers receive *their own product*, in money. It is not simply an equivalence but an identity: each worker obtains a money that, due to its emission in wages, is identified to the real product of this same worker. In the same transaction, the firm gives and receives the same object: it is indeed an absolute exchange.

The time has come to examine an interesting objection, which does not fail to come to mind. Is it not possible that a firm should give the workers of a given qualification lower wages than the remunerations issued by competing firms? In this case, is one not to conclude with the inequality, in the "Malthusian" firm, of the wages and of the product of these workers? This question has the merit of testing the degree of the reader's insight into the circuit theory.

The "truncated" part of wages is simply a *transfer* to the benefit of the firm. Thus, two events happen simultaneously: workers receive their reward and they give up some of it to the firm, in addition to the profits "honestly" gained. In no case does logic allow another answer: the amount of wages is always rigorously determined by the carrying over, in general exchange (in the goods market), of wages on the good produced by the remunerated worker.

Thus, suppose that the final sale of product *a* "produces" 20 units of money: then, wages of the producer of this good are strictly equal to 20 units of money. The existence of a positive profit, made by the capture of wages issued by other firms, does not hinder this law; this is because the profit thus formed finances the production of dividend-goods or the production of investment-goods: in both cases, wage-goods are strictly sold at their cost of production.

The practical rule is equally simple; wages of any worker being determined by pure convention, wages of all the other workers (and therefore, by consequence, also the agreed wages) are determined by the rule of the equality of the flux and the reflux of wages. Any firm owes the exact wages, the expenditure of which is brought on the product of this particular worker. It is certain that, if analytical accounting does not allow a determination precise enough of all the remunerations that are owed, the discrepancies are a zero-sum.

Exchanges in the products market are just the "reflection in a mirror" of the exchanges in the producing services market; in principle, it would be useless to look for another proof. Nevertheless, let us offer one.

Any exchange in the products market is absolute

To take a superficial view, it seems that the exchange of an income against a product is a purchase on the side of the demander and a sale on the side of the supplier. This is obviously true since it is a truism. But the event is of a further depth; we can perceive it only by becoming aware of an initially strange fact: the purchase defines in the same movement the equal sale by the buyer and, therefore, the equal purchase by the seller. In any expenditure of wages, we detect the presence of two purchases and, therefore, of two sales. The theory of emissions gives a simple explanation of this. Wages are the product in money; thus, the expenditure of wages moves the product *in two opposite directions at the same time*: in money, the product moves from worker to firm; in kind, the same product moves from firm to worker.

A small uncertainty remains: if the expenditure of wages is an absolute exchange, what about the expenditure of the other incomes? The answer has been known for a long time. All non-wage incomes are formed and spent within the circuit of wages.

The only real problem concerns empty emissions: are they absolute exchanges like full emissions?

Even empty emissions are absolute exchanges

The question is interesting because it determines the consistency of the theory. If empty emissions were not absolute exchanges, we would eventually have to make room in the analysis for exchanges as they were conceived before the discovery of the quantum nature of production. However, the answer is already present in the fact that empty emissions are emissions indeed; is not any emission an absolute exchange? Let us give some lift to the argument, all the more so as it will lead us to a little deeper perception of the "osmotic" phenomenon that characterizes empty emissions.

We have seen that empty emissions belong to one of two categories, depending on whether they create a positive difference between the domestic product, in money or in kind, or they simply boil down to an imposition carried out on workers in the wages payment itself. Let us go back to these two cases in order to determine if they answer the definition of absolute exchanges.

Empty emissions of the first category: they add a purely nominal income to the "nominal-real" income created in full emissions

Are those empty emissions absolute exchanges? Let us recall that all the emissions of this category are loans-expenditures of non-existent incomes, as banks lend more income than they have received in deposits. It does seem, on these conditions, that borrowers spend an income that workers have not perceived (in wages); thus, is not the money created as a supernumerary a monetary asset exchanged against a real asset, therefore a relative and not an absolute exchange?

In this first particular case, we would observe the coexistence of two distinct assets, the money created "in excess" and the product on which it is spent. However, the transaction between the two distinct assets is the very definition of a relative exchange.

If we look at it more closely, the opposite conclusion will definitively prevail. As soon as a sum of money is created from scratch, by an abuse of power, banks transmitting more income than they have received, the available product on the market is instantaneously spread, distended, into the increased volume of money. It is formally certain that this dilatation affects each unit of wages with the same "intensity"; if the quantity of available wages increases from 100 to 110, each unit of wages is immediately subjected to a loss of its "body", the product of workers, to the amount of a unit multiplied by 10/110. Why is the "loss of substance" everywhere equi-proportional? The reason comes from the nature of money, a collection of "concrete" interchangeable numbers. After the empty emission, it remains true that, facing the available product of the particular period of production, each unit of money taken in the set of income holders, including borrowers in the financial market (therefore without excepting the beneficiaries of the empty emission) is equivalent to any other monetary unit simultaneously taken in the same set.

It follows that the empty emission merges totally into the sum of full emissions: wages the expenditure of which comes into competition with the expenditure of the "fake money" obey the following circuit.

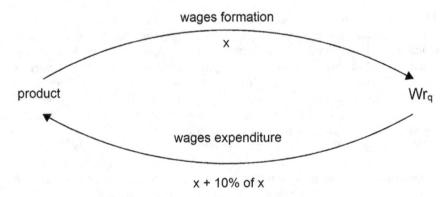

$$x + 10\% \text{ of } x$$

Figure 17.2 The merger of empty emission into full emissions

where x + 10% of x is equivalent to x. Households spend x units of wages and, in addition, the money borrowed as a supernumerary. Everything is going as if, despite empty emissions, households were buying x units of wage-goods in the expenditure of x units of monetary wages. The empty emission is then grasped in the retrocession by households, to the benefit of the borrowers of the money created as a supernumerary, of x (10/110) units of wage-goods.

Empty emissions of the second category: they take away the product of workers in the payment of their wages itself

Are these other empty emissions also absolute exchanges? We know that absolute exchange has only one definition, the purchase of the product of Wr_q by Wr_q himself. If there were purchases of another type, the theory would lose its simplicity. It is therefore particularly important to enquire if the empty emissions of the second category are "ordinary" purchases. It does not seem so, because the payment of wages from the monetary profits made by firms is the only case, in the concrete economy, where human labour is reduced to the status of a commodity. Thus, in dual production, firms pay workers by means of an accumulated monetary capital (wages captured in the production of amortization goods). The exchange is therefore completely unequal, which no other absolute exchange could be: workers employed in producing profits-goods receive an empty or nil remuneration, which they are not aware of, only because they share the full wages of the other workers.

Again, the development of the analysis until its term enables the safe-guarding of the unity of the theory: *all* purchases are absolute exchanges. The essential reflexion is this: workers employed in the production of profit-goods create their own wage, like any other worker. This is so because labour is always an emission, a real emission that no other monetary emission may disrupt: nominal emissions are based on real emissions. The emission of wages in the section of profit-goods therefore initially conform to any emission of wages: workers receive their own product in money. The fact that some profits are cast into the emission of wages is logically secondary: it is "then", and only then, that workers lose the benefit of their wages, in the appropriation of their product by firms. The primary fact is therefore not at all invalidated: even in the section of profit-goods, workers receive their own product in money. This suffices to confirm the absolute character of the exchange in the case that seemed yet to constitute the only exception to the rule.

Before starting the study of the purchases in the third market, it is fitting to take into account the extension of the products market to the goods produced in the past. Is the purchase of products already cleared in previous periods absolute too? The solution can be interesting, because it enables the exact nature of the purchasing power of money to be grasped from another angle.

Suppose t_q a particular instant. What is the definition of a purchasing power the existence of which is observed at instant q? It is identified (by fusion) to the goods produced but *not yet cleared*.

Suppose thus that households clear all the goods produced in the current period and in the past; if that were the case, no real money could exist at instant q. The product not yet cleared is the only "body" of money: it follows that any money present at instant q defines a product waiting to be bought by the set of income holders.

Now, let us cast a money on a product at instant q; if it is a new product, the exchange is absolute, without question; but what if the product is an old one? The conclusion is identical; money would not have the power to purchase the old product if it were not real, therefore if it did not have the power to buy the new product. The purchase of the old product boils down to the purchase of the new product, on behalf of the seller of the old product: the exchange is absolute.

This is also the case for any transaction in the financial market.

Any exchange in the financial market is absolute

The brief analysis that we have just given of the purchase of "second-hand goods" applies immediately to the purchase of financial claims or securities, old or new. Whether the securities are newly issued or just transmitted, the seller does not simply obtain money but a new product, in money. Exchange is therefore absolute: the buyer of the security is in reality the buyer of the (new) product on behalf of the seller of securities. This analysis, which we cannot continue here, is the starting point of a new theory of interest. It is indeed impossible, contrary to what is argued in traditional explanations, for the variations of the price of financial claims or securities to define the inverse variations of interest rates. It could only be so if the transactions in the financial market were relative exchanges. In reality, the price of securities, new or old, is a share of the price of the new products, perfectly known before any determination of the rates of interest. It is correct to say that, at the moment, there is no satisfactory theory of the formation and variation of interest rates. "Quantum analysis" will master this question someday.

As soon as we understand the nature of every purchase, we grasp fully the macroeconomic object.

XLV. Macroeconomics is the science of absolute exchanges

The distinction between microscopic and macroscopic analyses was already known in physics and more precisely in thermodynamics. It seems that this terminology was introduced in economics by Ragnar Frisch, who speaks about "macrodynamic" magnitudes (Frisch 1933). It is undoubtedly to Paul A. Samuelson that we owe the expression in the current use of macroeconomics that is made today everywhere in the world (Samuelson 1966–1977). But, as we shall shortly confirm, even if the term is new, "macro-theory" itself goes back to the origins of our science. Since the Physiocrats and during the whole classical era (from Smith to Ricardo and to Marx), political economy has been entirely a macroscopic theory. If the distinction has taken its relevance only in the middle of the twentieth century, it is in contrast with the microeconomic theory, then dominant. Macro-analysis is only original relative to neo-classical theory.

Scholars approach macroeconomics from their microeconomic preconceptions; consequently, the definition they give of it is gravely flawed. In all handbooks – but also in fundamental texts – we find the idea of aggregation: the object of macroeconomics would be identical to the objects of microeconomics, the only difference being that the magnitudes are taken in isolation or "summed up".

However, another definition is also frequently offered: macroeconomic magnitudes would be global. The ambiguity is striking. A "globality" is a set, a totality, an indivisibility. A magnitude obtained through aggregation, or an aggregate, is, on the contrary, a sum that can be freely divided since it has been obtained by adding up its components.

As soon as we become aware of the real nature of economic exchanges, we understand that the second definition drives out the first one; macroeconomics is the field of absolute exchanges; and each absolute exchange is defined on a *set*, on an *indivisible whole*. Once we conceive the link between macroeconomics and sets, aggregation is not just a lapse in judgement but an error of logic: a set is not the addition of its elements.

If agents A and B are the elements of set P, no event defined on A or B is an event of P, unless A or B is redefined, to become a sub-set and not just an element of P. Let us identify the elements of P by letters A and B; the same agents are A' and B' if they are conceived as sub-sets or parts of P. Any event defined on A' or B' is macroeconomic because it is defined on P. Conversely, no event defined on A or B will concern P: the event is annulled on the set. The question is therefore absolutely clear: what are, among all economic transactions, the events defined on A' or B'?

The answer is equally univocal: all absolute exchanges, and only absolute exchanges, are events defined on A' or B'. Any exchange observed in reality being absolute, macroeconomics extends to the whole field of exchanges taking place on the three markets.

Why is any (absolute) exchange of A' or B' an exchange of P? It is enlightening to approach the question the other way round; suppose we can define a (relative) exchange between A and B: why is it not an exchange of P? This is because any relative exchange implies the opposition of the partners, supplier and demander: thus, the same event (exchange) is both positive (in A) and negative (in B), a magnitude that is objectively nil, as we can see as soon as the analysis embraces the two partners (A and B). It is entirely different with absolute exchanges: any emission of A' or B' is an emission of P. If A' works, the set of workers is working, even if B' does not work; the set P works in its part A'. Human labour is a macroeconomic magnitude; and the three markets incorporate no other magnitude.

The deposit of (for instance, bank) money in time enables another formulation of the macroeconomic character of the emissions to be given. If money were "moving" in relative exchanges, any monetary movement would be both positive and negative in the predetermined space: set P (the country) would therefore not experience any net monetary movement. Money would be strictly immobile on the set. Even more, money would be immobile on each part of the set: in no "global" economy – on any of its parts – would we be able logically to detect the slightest monetary movement.

If the movement of money is an inductive reality, this is because money moves in absolute exchanges: far from moving between points in a space, it is created and at once destroyed on the same agent: any creation-destruction of money "affects" the relevant agent as a part of P; if it is agent A, then we must write A'. In the economies that we can observe nowadays, the emission is depositing money in the holdings of agents who are then income holders.

The nature of macroeconomics is never as obvious as in the payment of incomes. If income B came from an expenditure of A, it would be nil in set P: the domestic economy would be forever devoid of any income. Since the income of B is the result of the labour of this agent, it is the income of B': this time, the income of B' is identically the income of P; any labour paid in money is depositing an income in the set of the nation. The converse is also true; any income of one agent is a wage or comes from a wage: any income is therefore defined, not on one element, but on a sub-set of P. The judgement may seem exaggerated but is profoundly correct: individual (of B') and national (of P) income entirely eludes the "science of aggregates".

Macroeconomics being clearly the science of absolute exchanges or of emissions, microeconomic analysis retrospectively reveals itself in its exact nature; it is the "science" of relative exchanges, *magnitudes that never existed.*

18 Confrontation between the two paradigms: absolute exchanges, relative exchanges

Is an economic exchange an event involving at least two partners (the trade partners) and at least two objects (the goods exchanged)? It is certain that nearly all economists would still agree today. This is always the case for the really fundamental questions: they are not even seen. The existence of relative exchanges is laid neither in an axiomatic proposition nor in the body of hypotheses: it is taken as an obvious truth, a tautology, a truism. How could we establish an economic exchange between an agent and himself? The question seems absurd. And the absurdity is not lessened in the idea of an exchange between good a and good a. This is why it is ironic to find, through careful research, absolute exchanges right into the (neo-classical) theory of relative exchanges. We shall briefly demonstrate that this is indeed the case.

We shall then see that absolute exchanges hidden within relative exchanges, of which they are the "secret" foundation, suffer from a fatal flaw; they are expressed through "dimensionless numbers" although it is logically impossible, in the science of exchanges or relative prices, to transform a "good" into a number.

The transformation of a product into a dimensionless number is the macroeconomic operation *par excellence*, the emission.

Nonetheless, the judgement on neo-classical analysis – which is the same as microeconomic analysis – could never be severe. The discovery of prices expressed by the means of a pure number is a progress of the first order. The Classics undoubtedly knew of the existence of absolute exchanges but they could only elude them, precisely for the reason that there was no way then to build the identity of product and *numéraire*. Without its *numéraire* dimension, the product cannot be grasped.

We shall conclude this quick overview by showing that the theory of emissions solves right from the start the problem on which classical thought has stumbled: the non-coincidence of the events observed in the two "spheres", production and circulation.

XLVI. The presence of an absolute exchange within the system of relative exchanges

The exchange of physical products

Good a is measured in physical units h and good b in units k. Suppose that A has an initial endowment in goods a and B in goods b. The exchange observed at a certain instant is of x units h of good a against y units k of good b (see Figure 18.1).

A thus exchanges 3 kilograms of tomatoes for 10 litres of milk. If the written expression of the exchange were to stop there, it would not be accessible to science, because magnitudes h (kilograms) and k (litres) would remain incommensurable; besides, even if the two physical measures were given in the same dimension, the goods themselves, a and b (tomato juice for example and milk) would have no common economic measure. We can express these difficulties by saying that the exchange in Figure 18.1 cannot be written under the form of an equation. It is true that, if it really is an exchange, the equation is established. But, precisely, it must be explained why it is legitimate to write the equality.

$$(1) \quad x \; units \; h \; of \; good \; a = y \; units \; k \; of \; good \; b$$

Equation (1) assumes that one of the two goods, a or b, is chosen randomly as the "*numéraire*". Let us choose good a. Expressed in terms of good a, the price y of k *units* of good b is equal to x units h, because, in the exchange, we see that A must give x units h of good a to obtain y units k of good b. Calculated in the same way, what is, expressed in good a, the price of x units h of good a? In other words, how many units h of good a do we have to give to obtain x units h of this good? The tautological answer is x. But x "what"? Again, the answer is a tautology: x, and that is all. One must "spend" x times a unit h of good a to "hold" x units of good a. In the expression "x times", it is obvious that x is a pure number. It is (erroneously, as we shall see) deduced that the price of x units h of good a is number x; similarly, and in the same *numéraire*, the price of y units k of good b would be number x. Only the definition of the *numéraire* (even if a defective one) enables to express prices in pure numbers.

$$(2) \quad x \; units \; h \; of \; good \; a = x$$

$$(3) \quad y \; units \; k \; of \; good \; b = x$$

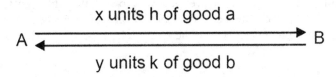

Figure 18.1 The exchange of physical products

It is only by bringing together equations (2) and (3) that equation (1) can be written.

Usually, instead of defining the *numéraire* in x of its units, it is defined in only one of its units. Thus, one unit h of good a is the definition of the *numéraire*. What is then the price of the *numéraire* in *numéraire*? Instead of number x, it is now number x/x, number 1. One must give a unit of the *numéraire* to "buy" one unit of the *numéraire*. And what is, under these conditions, the price of y units k of good b? It is clear that it is always equal to x since one must exchange x times the unit of *numéraire* to acquire y units k of good b: x units of *numéraire* being "equivalent" to x times the unit of *numéraire*.

The exchange of the numéraire *against the* numéraire *is absolute*

We have just detected the existence of an absolute exchange within the system of relative exchanges. Even if the economy comprises only agents A and B, with their initial endowments in goods a and b, the exchange between a and b would not be constituted (as an exchange) if one of the two goods were not acting as the *numéraire*. However, it is the same to say that one of the goods is the *numéraire* and that it is defined in an exchange in relation with itself, an absolute exchange. It is only in the exchange of a (or of b) against a (or b) that the analysis is able to generate a dimensionless number, a number that is the *sine qua non* condition, in practice as well as in theory, of the existence of relative exchanges. Without the *numéraire*, only relation (1) could be written, and it would not define an exchange: no price would be known because no price could be expressed in a number. Without any *numéraire*, the price of good b could only be given in good b, and it would be the same for all the goods that would only be defined in relation with themselves. Do we really obtain information when we learn that the price of y units k of good b is y units k of good b? If we cannot give it in a number, the price of a good remains completely unknown.

We demonstrate that neo-classicism has never succeeded in defining the *numéraire*. In relative exchanges, it is formally impossible to transform a good, whatever it may be, in a dimensionless number.

XLVII. Even in pure theory, no good can, within the system of relative exchanges, be transformed in a dimensionless number

The neo-classical definition of the numéraire *is a* petitio principii

It is out of the question to go back on the necessity of the *numéraire*; it has been established indeed that prices are impossible to grasp in physical quantities: they can only be determined by numbers. Prices of the different goods are commensurable only if they all belong to the set of numbers; otherwise, they only repeat the heterogeneity or the "enumeration" of the physical quantities.

However, the construction of the *numéraire*, as we have proposed, is fundamentally vitiated: it has the zero power of a *petitio principii*. Let us take up the argument again.

What is, we asked, the price of *x* units *h* of good *a*, given that this price is expressed in units of good *a*? We have answered that the price sought is the pure number *x*. This is completely false. The price, in good *a*, of *x* units *h* of good *a*, is not just *x* but *x* units *h* of good *a*. In this context, it is absolutely impossible to separate number *x* from its dimension, units *h* of good *a*.

Let us consider again the question in its other formulation. How many units *h* of good *a* must be given to receive *x* units *h* of this good? The correct answer is indeed *x*, a pure number. But this number is not the price of *x* units *h* of good *a*; it expresses only one "truth", a pure truism: *x* is the number of units included in *x* units *h*. Thus, even if good *a* is chosen as a *numéraire*, it remains that the price of *a*, in any quantity, is not the number expressing this quantity but this quantity itself, that is, a physical dimension.

Any clear-headed economist knows that the neo-classical theory has never – in any of its attempts – succeeded in transforming any good in a dimensionless number. To tell the truth, only two fundamental attempts have been launched, many times each, one through the utility of goods and the other through the method of "input-output" analysis. It suffices here to sum up the principle of the two attempts and to confront them to a true "theorem of impossibility"; whatever the subtlety of the authors, they will never succeed in transforming an economic good, a commodity, in a purely *arithmetical* magnitude: the success would not simply be alchemic (which would leave some hope) but prodigious, magical.

The failure of the two attempts to build the numéraire

First way: attempt through the utility of goods

At the origin of relative prices, we find the "psychic values" of Walras. If the two exchanged goods each contain the same number of units of those values, it is clear that the *numéraire* is the psychic value and not the physical good. But nobody has ever been able to discover those values. The use of indifference curves is not of any great help either. The points of tangency cannot be determined if relative prices are not imposed by the market. The method would enable at best an explanation of the variations of prices; but, before making them vary, it is necessary to know them in their initial determination: and this knowledge is beyond reach. We also know that the more modern works on the measure of utility, cardinal or ordinal, have not (yet) succeeded. No theory based on the analysis of preferences can be tested, unless the demand for goods is measurable, at least in money. This is to say that the "measurability" of demand cannot be founded on preferences. Even if it succeeded, the theory would only have a power of explanation in a world where prices, at least monetary ones, would be already given.

Second way: attempt through the method of "input-output" equations

The second way has not brought any better results. It is true that it is ingenious to try to introduce goods into an "input-output" matrix in order that production and consumption of each good should define each other. If the goods present at the "entrance" are also present at the "exit", and even if this identity is only verified at a factor of proportionality, we might hope to explain one day the transformation, in the real world, of physical goods into each other. In the end, an automobile would be identified with a certain weight of leeks: the heterogeneity of physical goods would be overcome. In fact, we meet again the naïvety of the previous attempt. It is inconceivable that goods might be introduced "without a price"; and if they already are prices (or numbers) at the "entrance", the relation "in-out" *presupposes* prices instead of determining them.

The true proof of the double failure is logical; let us express it in a "theorem of impossibility"

It is impossible to transform a good already produced into a dimensionless number.

Suppose we might be able, in a probably far away future, to build relations of equivalence between goods and numbers. Let us designate the physical quantities of goods (and not just the goods themselves) by the letters a, b, c, ... We find for example the following equivalences.

$$a = 3$$

$$b = 4$$

$$c = 2$$

That would be a triumph. But it would be a failure at the same time. Indeed, the terms a, b, c, ... being *goods* and not numbers, and the terms 3, 4, 2, ... being *numbers* and not goods, the enumerated relations of equivalence are as many contradictions in terms. This is the formal impossibility: as long as goods are goods and numbers are numbers, no science will succeed in establishing relations of equivalence between goods and numbers.

The theory is therefore caught in a real dilemma.

- If prices are not pure numbers, they cannot be determined and economics has no object.
- If prices are pure numbers, they cannot be related to goods.

We know that the solution becomes possible thanks to a change of level: logic does not allow the creation of relations of equivalence between goods and numbers; but logic allows the establishment of the equivalence of two productions, the production of goods and the production of numbers. What is formally forbidden at the level of *product* (the result) is on the contrary allowed in the *action* (production). And how could we be surprised since the problem is heterogeneity? It can only be solved by the proof of the generation, in one and the same movement, *of two magnitudes at the same time, goods and numbers.* This movement does exist in concrete economies and the analysis has brought it forward well enough: it is the *emission of money.*

XLVIII. The transformation of products into dimensionless numbers is the macroeconomic operation par excellence, the emission

We have said it already, as soon as Man works, he issues. We have recognized also that money was present since the first labour-emission. However, in a "society" where workers were not exchanging their products, the emission was only the creation-destruction of the utility-form of goods; it neither created nor destroyed any number. "Primitive" emissions were purely real in their *result*, even though, once again, money was already present in them: they were nominal in themselves.

At the next stage, the economy started to produce numbers. Well before the wage-regime, workers were living in an economy of exchange. Any product exchanged against a "material" money, like pebbles or shells, was changed into a number. Let us make it clear that money enters into the exchange only as a unit of account. If all the pebbles are interchangeable, the product is exchanged against "concrete numbers" set in an arithmetic category, for example the decimal system. And the conversion of products into numbers does not take place at the level of the result of production; even in economies of exchange, the number-money is present in the act of production: finally changed into money, the good becomes so at the instant of its production, *in* its production. Any worker who exchanges his good produces it in money beforehand. At the instant of the exchange of goods, agents exchange in fact their productive activities; the efficiency *goes back* to the real emissions, the labour expended by those taking part in the exchange.

The wage system has not brought anything fundamental to the emissions regime, except for the category of non-wage incomes. As soon as monetary exchange is carried out in the producing services market, firms lend themselves the ability to "capture" part of the wages issued. But it is important to remember the formal conclusion according to which profits formed in a non-bank money cannot be transformed into capital: they are necessarily redistributed (at most to the firm itself that will consume them "productively").

The true revolution came with the emission of bank money. There is a threefold progress.

The threefold progress brought by bank money

1   Bank money is a far better "concrete number" than any "material" money. The advantage does not come only from bank money being nearly free.

Unlike gold money, for example, dematerialized money is rigorously identical to itself in each of its units: it is impossible to "clip". And the content of the tenor can no longer vary since bank money has a strictly zero intrinsic content.

2   Banks are organized in a system where currencies issued by deposit banks are all modelled after central bank money: only one bank money has currency in the whole country, currencies issued by different banks being perfectly interchangeable.

3   As soon as the profit of firms is realized in bank money, it can be capitalized: the distribution of profits is no longer a logical necessity. Neither capital-time nor fixed capital would exist in society if money were "material".

Those three progresses are important, that is obvious. But fundamentally, bank emissions cannot be distinguished from the emissions carried out in material money since any monetary emission equates to a real emission. Thus, the only production of a "monetized" economy is the collection of concrete numbers created by banks.

Let us recall in a few words the exact nature of the relations of equivalence established by production.

Relations of equivalence established by production

We shall never repeat it enough – so much is the need to fight against common misconceptions – the first relation of equivalence between real magnitudes and nominal magnitudes is formed at the stage of the *movements* and not, because it would be too late, at the stage of their results. The real movement (the act of working) and the nominal movement (the monetary emission) merge perfectly. The unique action having thus two aspects, its unique result also has two aspects, real and nominal. This is the profound explanation of the formation of prices as dimensionless numbers. Obtained in the real emission, money defines not just the measure of the product but the product itself. The units of wages issued by the production of the period identify with the real product, which thus emerges as the collection of the concrete numbers issued by the banks of the country.

The *bona fide* scholar cannot but recognize the fact that up to now economics has not had any theory of prices. There are, it is true, many explanatory models of prices in, mainly perfect, competition; but none is adequate to concrete economies. The inadequacy is not superficial. In no way can it be legitimately claimed that microeconomic theories approximate reality. Effective prices are all pure numbers. However, no explanation had yet succeeded in introducing pure numbers in the models. This question does not admit of degrees. One cannot find prices that are more or less concrete numbers: they are perfectly so or not at all. In the economy, pure numbers exist according to two distinct definitions.

First existence of pure numbers. Let us refer to the "zero sphere": the outgrowth of this sphere is a "mass" of concrete numbers, the units of bank money created in the period by human labour.

Second existence of pure numbers. The mass of concrete numbers is countable: we count the units of money or, identically, the units of wages created in the period. Each unit of wages is a number and the number of wage-units counts the domestic product.

In the writer's previous books, the idea of counting-measurements was clearly present. It has not been understood. The reason is twofold. First, this question is difficult in itself. But the aggravating circumstance comes from the fact that all the measurements already known in the other sciences are all dimensional. It is dimensions that are measured, not "objects". If we ignore their dimensions, objects can be counted but not measured. However, it is out of question to change the theory of measurement. Why is it that the same theory, valid in any science, would give so different a result in economics?

The genial inventor of the *numéraire*, Léon Walras, tried to explain it to the great mathematician Henri Poincaré. The theory of emissions is a new "tool" that enables the solution to be grasped at last. Cast into negative money, physical product (even services like transports) is morphed into a pure "mass" of numbers. It is true that counting the elementary units composing this mass is not an operation of measurement. However, by counting the units of wages effectively produced, we also count the physical product. Finally, we count the units of equivalence (between numbers and physical products): that is to say, we count units of measure. The measure is in the relations of equivalence that are the objects of the count.

Microeconomic theory measures in dimensional units; but, in fact, the numéraire *is a dimensionless number*

The microeconomic theory of prices is a failure since the search for utilities is still based on the representation of a dimension that would be specific to economic goods. It is of course true that products are useful. But suppose even that the units of utility are objectively interchangeable: they are "utils". Under those conditions, perfectly utopic, would the theory of prices be established?

It is extremely interesting to note that it would not be so: having climbed that formidable mountain, the scholar would not be more advanced. Let us demonstrate this quickly.

It does not suffice to explain the relations of exchange; one still has to determine the mass of the products that enter those relations. Only the theory of production can answer this second problem, the most fundamental one. However, in any event, even if we grant it this ultimate perfection that is found in the existence of interchangeable utils, the theory of the utility-value of goods can grasp production only in a pure truism: being itself an exchange, production can only give the utils that it has itself absorbed. Thus, it will never be possible to bring about units of utility, any production of utils being, in the action, a consumption of an equal amount of utils. Only the theory of emissions can explain the net formation of a product. It would be pleasant to object that the net product is perhaps a pure imagination of the scholar. But then, we would have to go all the way to the consequence: economics would also be a pure fantasy. If no production exists in the real world, the "science of production" has no object.

In fact, each period brings its new productions and it is time to grasp them by the only type of formalization that embraces them, the analysis of emissions.

Even though it is in the nature of the evolution of thought that microeconomic analysis should leave the place entirely to "quantum macroeconomics", it is fair to recognize that, compared to classical thought, microeconomics marks a progress of the first order. The theory of emissions could not have taken shape if the mind had not first become conscious that economic goods are pure useful matters. The Classics were looking for the philosopher's stone, an "economic matter", distinct from physical matter. The Neo-Classics built on entirely new foundations: the useful goods "do not embody any (objective) value". From then on, absolute exchanges as conceived in the Smith-Ricardo tradition give way. The pivotal progress is not in the substitution of relative exchanges to absolute exchanges but in the preparation of the *new definition of absolute exchanges.*

XLIX. Relative exchanges find their fundamental justification in the rejection of absolute exchanges as conceived by the Classics

One cannot deny that the new macroeconomics relates to the classical thought: the synthesis is closer to the thesis than to the antithesis. It is also certain that the representation of the product as a collection of pure numbers is of a neo-classical spirit. The *numéraire* is asserting its existence and its identity well before the apparition of a money deposited in chronological time. This was not known to the Classics: on the contrary, they thought that the prime fact was the axiological dimension of products.

Let us consider a real emission whose result, the physical product, is never exchanged against money. Before the neo-classical revolution of a micro-economic substance, scholars would attribute to the physical product a specific quality, which, so they thought, was brought by the very act of production. Labour was said to be "embodied" in the objects. One had to wait until the idea of the *numéraire* (prefigured by the last classic works, for example in Marx writings), to witness the disappearance of the concept of a value materialized in the objects. At once production takes on another meaning, free from any meta-physical dimension.

The act of production does not result in the crystallization of labour into the manufactured object: it simply creates a numerical relation of equivalence between itself (the activity) and its result (the product). If, as we have said, money is already present within the real emission, it is so as *numéraire*. Theorists of general equilibrium do not make any mistake about it: money proper, deposited in time under the form of income, comes "after" the *numéraire*, the primal form of money.

The numerical equivalence present within production may be approached naïvely through the "principle of causality": there are as many units of production (the acts) as units of products (the results). Today, the theory of emissions gives its definitive status to the equivalence: it is first asserted between the two aspects of the emission, simultaneous creation and destruction of the same "object", that is the utility-form of matter, a form that defines its quality as an economic good.

As soon as concrete money appears (first under "material species", then under bank entries), it sets in time (the duration) and also in space (due to the interchangeability of monetary units) the relation of numerical equivalence already present within the real emission. The product is "injected" into the negative money: the positive money is therefore its equivalent, its alter ego.

One can appraise the considerable progress accomplished thanks to the idea of the *numéraire*. Confronted with money and the physical product, the Classics were trying to detect two distinct masses, the labour embodied in each of them. The conception of the *numéraire* simplifies the solution so much that it makes it true: the equivalence of the product and money is not the equality of their values (?) but simply the definition of the product changed into the *numéraire*. Numbers and goods have no common value; but in monetary economies, the product is first brought about in *numéraire*. The identity of product and *numéraire* is indeed a "value" relation, a relation of equivalence.

Let us conclude by showing that having driven out false absolute exchanges, the conception of the *numéraire* prepares for the true ones and therefore lifts the fundamental illogicality that was nullifying classical thought: that thought necessarily contradicts itself as soon as it places absolute exchanges in the producing services market and in the products market *separately*.

L. According to their modern conception, absolute exchanges are present simultaneously in the producing services and in the products markets

Thinking in terms of causality instead of emission, the Classics could not avoid the problem of the chronological separation of the cause and its effect. We know that, according to logicians, the cause may precede the effect but that the effect can never precede the cause. This language is certainly somewhat obsolete, because the notion of "cause" is nowadays, even more so than in the past, open to question. However, if it were true that production is the cause, the product would be its effect; it would follow then that no action affecting the product could react on production, the effect being unable to alter the cause. Once again, the idea of causality is not retained by modern analysis; but it was so by the Classics: it is therefore not beside the point to show to what fundamental contradictions it subjects the general theory.

Let us reason like the Classics. The first movement is production. Consumption is a secondary movement because the product is its object. Let us call "circulation" the expenditure of the product under the form of income. Circulation is therefore an operation that *follows* production: it is separated from it by a positive length of time. It follows that production and "circulation" are also distinct: the two "spheres" could not coincide because the operations that they incorporate are chronologically separate. Economics is itself "torn" by this duality. The product is not identical to itself, depending on whether it is grasped in production or in circulation. If the distinction were purely time-based, it would not be troublesome. But it goes far deeper: it is set into the measure of the product, and most of all into the measure of its "distributive shares", wage-goods and profit-goods (in the broad sense). The national product and its distribution do not have the same measure depending on whether they are taken in one or the other sphere.

Let us carefully remark that the theory of emissions initially reproduces the contradiction encountered by the Classics: the measure of products – their expression in units of *numéraire* – is affected by the exchanges carried out in the goods market; this is unavoidable. The problem is therefore a real and current one. But we know that the emissions establish a new conception of time: being not an "effect", the product transmits to its initial measure all the alterations that it undergoes over chronological time. This retroaction is totally foreign to classicism, because it cannot have any status within causal relationships. Let us stay in the theory of emissions and show, on two key points, that it solves the Classics' difficulties.

The formation of income in the sphere of circulation

Classical theory would have been placed in an ideal situation if it had been able to determine all the incomes in the sphere of production alone. But this is impossible. With his clear-sightedness, Ricardo certainly best perceived the obstacle. Even if wages were exhausting national product, another category of income, interest, could not be prevented from coming into the system. Indeed, it is inevitable that time should elapse between the apparition of the product and its final sale. Capital-time must be remunerated. But in what market could interest be formed? How could it appear in the sphere of production? This is inconceivable since interest is due only for the time when the product, already present, is kept waiting, therefore after the formation of "production income". Only households can pay interest, through the expenditure of their incomes. This is to say that interest is an income that comes about in the sphere of *circulation*.

From that point the theory sinks into contradiction: the income created in the sphere of production (wages) must generate additional incomes, in the sphere of circulation. One might as well say that the exact origin of income remains unknown.

Marx succeeded in hiding the problem within the comprehensive category of surplus-value. The sphere of production would not only provide wages, but also surplus-value that includes interest. Far from being solved, the difficulty is now present under another form; surplus-value can come to life in the sphere of production only if it is related to human labour, therefore to the variable part of capital and to it alone. Yet, interest is the remuneration of the total amount of capital, including its constant part; the sphere of circulation has therefore the task of distributing over the whole capital the surplus-value generated by variable capital in the sphere of production. The solution of the problem would create another, far more formidable, problem: defined in production, the measure of products would be "altered" in circulation, which, depending on the goods, would therefore create or destroy value, although it is neutral in principle.

The theory of emission solves the problem definitively. In chronological time, it is inevitable that income must be formed in the goods market. Nevertheless, all the income of the nation is created in the sphere of production, in the producing services market. The production of income solely by human labour has been attested in all periods of time, therefore even before the advent of the wage-regime. However, it is in this regime precisely that some incomes come to life after the emission of wages. The solution would face an irredeemable contradiction if quantum analysis were not able to set aside the principle of the excluded middle.

The formation of income in the sphere of production

All incomes are formed in production; however, some incomes come to life in circulation. We know that the incomes brought about in circulation are profits in the wide sense; but, the explanation of profits has haunted great theorists since Mercantilism; thus, Sir James Steuart (eighteenth century) had profits coming from prices (circulation), that would be higher than values (defined in production) (Steuart 1767). We know today that this is indeed how profits are formed; but the analysis is satisfactory only if it succeeds in overcoming the contradiction that is inherent to it: how could the sum of prices be higher than the sum of values while values – the income created by production – are the only source of prices?

It is remarkable that the opposite explanation is vulnerable to the same difficulty, precisely: thus, Marx, rejecting Steuart's explanation, claims that profits come directly from the sphere of production: surplus-values are first incomes created by labour, like wages. It would seem initially that the difficulty has been solved; prices are not higher than values; production brings the income of the two categories: workers buy "wage-goods" and capitalists buy "profit-goods". On closer examination, one sees however that the criticism addressed to Steuart can also be levelled against Marx. How to deny that profit-goods are part of national income? They are produced like wage-goods. Consequently, real surplus-value is formed in the process of production; it is almost a truism. The real problem is on the side of *monetary* surplus-value, i.e. profit. Even though, in the purchases, monetary profit refers necessarily to a part of national product, it is logically impossible that firms might create profit on themselves. Like Marx often says in his sarcastic criticisms, nobody could enrich himself by transferring his wealth from his right to his left pockets. Capitalists pay workers; but capitalists could not pay themselves.

We have hit the wall met by Steuart: only wages are created in money in the process of production. The formation of profits lies with the expenditure of wages, which supposes again, despite Marx, that the price of wage-goods should be higher than their value. And it does not move things forward to repeat the tautological argument according to which the price of the sum of wage-goods and profit-goods is not higher than the value of the sum of all the goods produced.

Finally, quantum analysis allows the union of the opposites without this union defining a contradiction in terms.

> *First proposition.* Monetary profits come to life in circulation.
> *Opposite proposition.* All incomes, including monetary profits, come to life in production.

In the case of Marx or Steuart, the conciliation of the two propositions remained up in the air. In the works of both writers, indifferently, we find the two "unreconciled" propositions. Even for Steuart, "profit-goods" are part of national income. Even for Marx, monetary profits come to life in the sale of "wage-goods".

The solution is in the perfect union (the simultaneity) of the events observed in the two spheres. The formation and the expenditure of income, of *all* incomes, profits as well as wages, are two movements that constitute only one, in the complementarity of the two "real half-emissions". Thus, in chronological time, prices are higher than values for the whole measure of the formation of non-wage-goods. But, in quantum time, prices are strictly reduced to values, any non-wage income being instantly destroyed in the very operation of the payment of wages.

The emission of wages is the creation of all income, including monetary profits. The reader knows well that the joining into one unique movement of all the creations of income does not mean that profits are (of the nature of) wages. Profits are issued in the payment of wages only in this fundamental sense that the expenditure of wages (will) form(s) monetary profits. It is the part of Steuart's message that is still alive today. The expenditure of wages is the destruction of all income, without excepting monetary profits. Again, the reader is well informed: no more than profits are wages neither wages are profits. Bringing together in one unique movement all the expenditures of income means only that the expenditure of profits forms (has formed) the wages earned in the production of non-wage goods. This is the part of Marx's message that is still alive today.

The theory of emissions unites the two messages finally into one fully coherent explanation.

The simultaneity of the correlative operations, observed in the two processes, production and circulation, and obtained by the retroaction of the second emission (the expenditure of wages) on the first (their formation), is also the profound component that the theory was lacking to explain the determination of wages.

19 The determination of wages

LI. Causality and emission

The Classics were reasoning in terms of causality and not in terms of emission. But, if causality were the road to follow, wages would be known independently from the purchases in the products market.

The pre-determination of wages

The "natural" wage of a worker whose product is systematically difficult to sell cannot be identical, for an equal amount of labour, to the wage of a worker whose product faces a strong demand. In each period, therefore, a fine-tuning mechanism must be put in place, like the little fan of the helicopter, that enables demand to react to supply. This mechanism cannot be added on to the classical theory, its internal logic does not allow for it.

According to current theory, the adaptation is not just possible but necessary, at least before the advent of the wage-regime. Suppose that a worker carries his product to market. According to pure classical theory, the value of the good is already completely determined by the time the labour is expended; the price in the market has to comply with this value and if it deviates from it, the sum of the discrepancies is logically zero. The reality is completely different. Given that the worker has not yet received his wages, his good has no "value" yet: literally, it is not yet measured. One must wait for the transaction in the product market to know the monetary measure – therefore the plain measure – of the product. If the wage-regime starts "tentatively", the company that employs the worker will have to proceed in the same way: it can confirm the wages of its employee only after the sale of its product. And if it has already paid the wages, it will have to adjust them, either up or down, to take into account any discrepancy that would arise in the products market, between effective prices and anticipated prices. (A good understanding of this adjustment mechanism shows that it does not exclude the possible formation of profits.)

In the *generalized wage-regime*, the explanation can no longer be exactly the same. But it is not getting close either to the classical doctrines, even though it remains in conformity with absolute exchanges. For each "socio-professional" group of workers, monetary wages are rigidly fixed for the current new period, even before the product is sold in the markets; even more, the product coming to life only in the payment of wages, the new product does not exist yet, whereas the new wages are already determined in their amount: they will be paid at this, for example monthly, rate, whatever the prices at which future sales are agreed upon. The Classics would have said that wages are pre-determined for the simple reason that, the time of labour being known in advance, the value of the product is so as well. This is completely wrong, because the unique definition of the value of the product is given by the monetary "form" (negative money) into which the physical good is introduced. Using the Classic language, one would say that wages are not the consequence of the (anticipated) value of the product, but its cause; wages paid being of x units of money, the product "is worth" x units of money: if no wages were issued, the product would have a zero value.

Although the Classics had conceived the solution "upside down", they are closer to the truth than the Neo-Classics: this is because the determination of wages is naturally macroeconomic.

The co-determination of wages and prices

In microeconomics, wages are "Walrasian" prices. At general equilibrium, transactions in the product market are extended unchanged in the producing services market: thereby, wages are given by the selling price of the product of each wage-earner. We know now that this explanation is empty because, if all exchanges are relative, no price can be determined.

By the way, the theorists of neo-classicism cannot but introduce a "budget constraint" into their arguments. How, indeed, could the products be cleared on the markets if they were not meeting sums of incomes ("budgets")? Wages (and other possible incomes) must therefore exist even before the sale of products.

It is true that one may hope to maintain the logic of the simultaneous determination of wages and prices, if wages are given "in advance" and if it is anticipated that they will be adjusted to effective prices. But this hope is dashed. The deep problem is not in the synchronization of the two determinations, wages and prices, but in the co-determination of those magnitudes; if they could mutually determine each other, the simultaneity might be obtained through "provisional" decisions; but that is the whole point: can they logically be determined the ones by the others?

We know perfectly well that this is not so; let us not go back to the proof but let us sum it up. If wages and prices were determined by the same movement (the same transactions), wages would be prices; the real problem is then fundamentally adulterated; it is no longer about finding the measure of the new products, but casting against one another goods the origin of which can no longer be known. Under those conditions, it is impossible to find the "conversion keys": heterogeneous by definition (because of their unknown origin), goods could not be prices the ones for the others. The budget constraint takes thereby a completely different prominence. Only new income can buy new products; hence the circle that entraps microeconomic thought; the codetermination becomes a faulty reasoning: the sum of expended income gives the sum of realized prices and the sum of realized prices is the fund from which income is taken.

Labour, the "cause" of the product

The Classics do not live in a closed world: they "open" it by production, even if they conceive it as a cause. Labour is the creation of the product. In each period, the new creations – acts of the "living" labour – bring a new product. The "source" of goods being thus known, they are all homogeneous: the (natural) price is just the expression of the homogeneity. However, wages are not prices but values. What is the exact meaning of this classical definition? We get a glimpse when saying that wages are formed in the sphere of production, whereas prices are determined in the sphere of circulation. But we can go much deeper. Wages are, at least in part, the definition of the new product, as referred to labour, its cause. Prices, on the contrary, are defined at the level of effects: they express the measures of products that already exist and not the measure into which products are formed. Prices are relations between products; value is the relation of each product with its source, labour.

Being a value, wages answer a double definition: they are the equivalence (a "flow"-magnitude) of the product and its "principle", labour; moreover, they are the result of this equivalence (therefore a "stock"-magnitude). Even as a result, wages are not a price, because they are defined in the product taken in relation with its source, and not in the product relatively to other products.

All this analysis, defended from Ricardo to Marx, is correct except on one essential point. Value – relation of product to labour – is conceived of as a "substance" whereas it is just a pure form. Let us recall that the "substance" is postulated in two real distinct ways: in the works of Ricardo, it is a "pool"; in some of Marx's works, the most elaborated ones we might say, the substance-value is only just a form. Having reached this degree of subtlety, why is classical thought still perfectible?

This is because in reality the value-form is not at all attached to the product, any more than the litre-form remains attached to the liquid poured out.

The mistake, in its lightest form, is also to think that human labour forces a form lastingly on matter, a wrapping that would remain attached to manufactured matter through time. At the instant the product is presented in the market to be sold, it would be caught in its form, like a "container", so that products would be exchanged according to their form, values being thus the prefiguration of prices.

It is important to understand well the logical consequence of the mistake: even if value is conceived of as the simple economic form of physical matter, a form that would persist until the clearing of goods, science must, for each product, determine the size of the form where it is cast. Otherwise, value remains unknown and, consequently, so are prices. It would be known that the product "matches" the form but the dimension of this form, its volume so to speak, would remain unknown. Similarly, a fluid would not be measured if we were just saying that it was poured into a form, without indicating the size of the container. However, the problem of the dimension of the value-form is a false problem. And of course, false problems do not have any solution because they only exist in the mind. The "solution" offered by the Classics is known; the measure of the form can only be physical, since economic measures presuppose the existence of the form; labour must therefore be measured in physical terms: the only measure that we can find is chronometric. Thus, the amount of labour would have a double effect; the chronometer gives the measure of the created form and labour introduces matter into this form: matter is thus transformed into a product.

The solution of a false problem can only be a false solution. And false solutions create new problems.

The value-form is immaterial: it is "measure-less"

It is inconceivable that the same worker should produce an equal value in any equal period of time; this is even more obvious for different workers. Chronometry is precise; the chronometry of labour is so as well, if we ignore the necessary "breaks". But the relation of the product of labour to the chronometry of labour is completely artificial. The same physical product can be the result of a very variable labour time (without this variation following any law) depending on the application and the knowledge of the person, in a more or less intense activity, in an environment, especially equipment, that depends itself on qualitative and technological differences that escape any possible measure.

The real problem is far less complex. It is difficult only because it is deep. The fundamental conception of the Classics is correct: human labour produces the form of matter, and the product (or the commodity) is precisely defined by the transformed matter. The mistake is univocal: it lies only in the definition of the value-form. In reality, the value-form is simply the utility-form, wrought matter being more useful to human-beings that raw materials; but, the utility-form is not measurable and it is a good thing that it should be so. The value-form measures the product; it is "measuring"; but for its part it is not at all measured. Economic science has only tried to measure the form in order to measure its content. As soon as it appears that the form is measuring perfectly without being measured, the search for the "measured measure" loses its *raison d'être*.

However, one should not hide that the conception of a form, able to give the measures that it does not have received itself, is not easy. If it were, would not economics have been completed a long time ago? Since the question is difficult, it no doubt deserves renewed attention, until it should be perfectly mastered.

Only the concept of emission enables the immaterial value-form to be grasped

The theory makes the decisive "leap" as soon as it moves from the concept of causality to the concept of emission. As we have shown in this book, human labour is not the cause of the product, but only the creation-destruction, in one single movement (the emission), of the utility-form of matter. As soon as this starting point is accepted, the argument holds a first equivalence, the source of all the relations of equivalence that economics needs in all areas, from production to the sale of goods.

What is the equivalence? It is expressed in a tautology: the product issued is equal to the emission.

Is that really a truism? No, because the tautology just expressed has the status of a logical proposition: it brings a formal piece of information. The emission is an instantaneous creation-destruction; it follows that the product has also a purely instantaneous existence; it is therefore rigorously defined between the two actions that "laminate" it in an instant, its creation and its destruction. Grasped "between" the two opposite actions, the product also receives its measure from the one and the other: it is equal or equivalent to its creation and to its destruction, to its creation-destruction, to its emission.

Again, the question comes back: if the product is equal to the emission, it is not yet measured; it will be so when the emission is itself measured. That sort of reasoning is at risk of falling into the conceptual mistake of the Classics: production is taken as a net creation, the cause of the product. The effect is not measured by the cause but by the measure of the cause. But Hume had expressed a doubt that persists to the current day, maybe with increasing force: are the "causes" present in the world of observable magnitudes? The idea of the emission is far more modest; *homo economicus* is not a creator; his labour is not the cause of any product; human labour does not add even the minutest particle of matter (physical or economical) to natural matter and energy. We must therefore give up the idea that production is an action that must be measured in a dimension; the action of production is strictly nil because in each emission it is both positive and negative.

As soon as it is accepted that production is an action simultaneously defined in the two opposite domains, in positive and negative numbers, a second paralogism lies in waiting: production being nil, is it not the same for the product? Thus, economic magnitudes would be measurable; but they would always be equal to zero. This conclusion is not correct because "concrete" money comes in-between.

Even though it is immaterial, the money-form is measurable

We face again the true nature of economics: it is the science of monetary phenomena. As soon as (bank) money is issued in place of the real product, the emission is a positive action. The positive action is the creation of a positive number of money units; the nil action is the creation of an equal negative money but immediately "filled up" with the physical product. Of course, all the money units grasped at the same instant are interchangeable. From then on, the study is provided with all the data it needs to be perfected.

a   The product is equal to the emission. This equality is not a measure because it is defined from one object (the product) to another (the emission) and not between two dimensions.
b   The emission is measured; but it is not so as the "cause" of the product because its product is both positive and negative.
c   The emission is measured in the money issued. If the emission were purely real, it would not be measurable. Let us remark carefully that the measure of the emission by the monetary product is not a circular operation since the emission does not measure the money issued.
d   The emission being measured, the product is so as well because it is equal to emission (a). Let us repeat that the product is not measured because of point (c) – which would be a circularity – but because of point (a). It is indubitable that the two equal magnitudes have the same measure.
e   The product of human labour accepts therefore only one measure, a "form" that is a pure number, the number of money units

The money-form is a "concavity": negative numbers

If the reader agrees to follow his own imagination, provided it is constantly kept in check by strict logic, he could view concrete numbers the "shape" of which could be altered until they become containers, "moulds". These numbers exist: they are the units of money created in the productions-emissions. Of course, those "hollow" numbers are only numbers: they have *no dimension* of any sort. They are not like the "containers" we are used to and into which we pour liquids. If we want to maintain the accuracy of the representation, its adequacy to facts, we must accept that we have to mentally build a jar, the substance of which or the matter of which is strictly non-existent, like mathematicians who think of a sphere the membrane of which is immaterial, in order to invert its two "sides" without cutting it. In a monetary economy, human labour is the precise operation that casts raw matter (or matter in the process of being "refined") into hollow numbers. We see at once the futility of the grave classical question: what is the measure of the value-form of the product? This means wondering about the measure of numbers. Thus, what is the measure of number 10? In reality, the value-form has no measure because it is a pure number, the *numéraire*.

Let us go back now to the question of the determination of wages in the generalized wage-regime.

LII. The emission of wages in the generalized wage-regime

Is the level of wages fixed by a convention?

By a (social) convention, firms pay out to each socio-professional category a sum of "hollow numbers", ready to receive the product of the period (for example of a month). Hence, if the level in the scale of qualifications corresponds to the sum of 5,000 francs, the monthly physical product of the worker positioned at this level is cast into that sum. We should not be afraid of repeating ourselves. But why is the product of this worker equivalent to 5,000 units of money? In other words, are the wages (direct and indirect) of this worker really equal to the product brought by him? Is it not possible that the real value of his product should be higher or lower than the sum of 5,000 francs? The question is stupid. The product has no value of any sort; if we speak nevertheless of its value, we should not let ourselves be deceived by words: it only means that the product is deposited in 5,000 units of negative money. The 5,000 units of money being the *numéraire*-form of the product, it is obvious that the value of the product is not actually 6,000 francs or 4,000 francs; that would be a blatant and bland contradiction.

The distinction between form and substance, container and content, is adequate to our object. But, in contrast to material objects, the product has no dimension that would be its own; it is cast into a form that is also devoid of any dimension. Thrown into the negative money, the product is a "non-value" cast into a "non-value". The relation of equivalence (or identity) between the "non-values", product and money – the content having matched the form – is, in the whole field of the national economy, the only value that has an actual existence.

If a doubt remains, it is that the question is not yet cleared. We know well that the main mistakes in reasoning are due to identifying economic value and its measure to a physical dimension and its "metrics". It is agreed henceforth that value is a *"numéraire*-form" and that, cast into this form, matter is matter through and through. This knowledge is by far the essential part of the issue and it would even be settled completely if the originality of this field did not make inductions so difficult. There is one point in particular that may bring perplexity: in the generalized wage-regime, is it really true that the amount of wages is determined by conventions?

If the positive answer were definitive and above all if it were comprehensive, it would leave some dissatisfaction and even a fundamental dissatisfaction. The freedom of firms would be too large if the logic of wages allowed them to freely set the wages.

It is true that the first limit imposed on the discretionary power of firms comes precisely from the conventional or contractual nature of wages: they are not set unilaterally but after a debate, in particular with labour unions.

But that is not all. Another limit, of a purely formal origin, is imposed on firms: even in the wage-regime, wages are determined by "economic forces" and not by social-legal conventions. Let us demonstrate this.

As we have implied, the constraint on firms – and on workers – is dictated by logic and precisely by the logic of the *emissions*: it comes from the perfect matching or coinciding of the expenditure and of the formation of wages, in other words, the union, in a double simultaneous movement, of their reflux and flux.

The determination of the levels of wages by the law of emission

As the determination of wages is not the object of this work, let us be brief; nevertheless, we can give the principle that would only need to be developed.

The correct method is doubtless to follow the distinction between "free" labour and waged labour.

Determination of the wages of free labour

Before the beginning of the wage system, men never received their monetary wages in the producing services market that did not exist. But they nevertheless obtained wages for any product that they would sell on the goods market. This operation was simple but it had a double meaning; the amount received was both the price of the product and its value: it was the payment of the product (result of the real emission or of the labour exerted) and the payment of the production (the emission itself). Under those conditions, no difference could arise between price and value since the transaction was unique and simple (instead of being unique and double as in the wage-regime). This is to say that profits did not exist.

Free labour is a regime still active in some parts of our economies, like in some farms, among artisans and in liberal professions; but this regime does not allow the formation of any profit. All the incomes created in an economy lacking a producing services market are wages, rents and interests.

According to what rule are wages of free labour determined? We know this at some level. But it is useful to state it again. It would be insufficient to say that the product follows the "law of supply and demand". That would be repeating the neo-classical mistake. The formation of prices presupposes the existence of the *numéraire*; but the *numéraire* is not only the expression but also the object of wages. Wages are paid in *numéraire*. It would be therefore circular to have them as a given through a *fiat* or *petitio*. Being a collection of pure numbers (the money units), wages are not determined by the relation established between seller and buyer, but by an absolute exchange, a relation defined between the seller and himself. This relation is immediately intelligible: it is the formation and the expenditure of the income of the free worker.

Let us compare the true solution to the analysis offered by microeconomics. In both cases, wages are obtained by the means of two "forces" (this word comes from Alfred Marshall), supply and demand. In neo-classical analysis, supply and demand are applied by the partners in the exchange in the market of products. This is obviously how things appear to be, but it is only an appearance. In reality, the relevant supply and demand are both applied by the free worker; he offers his product on the market, everyone agrees on this first point; but the free worker identifies also to the demander: the product is demanded and supplied *by the same person, the free worker.*

This second point is essential; it is true however that it is difficult to grasp. But the reader should not find the difficulty insurmountable. The best way to "soften up" the problem is to emphasize a fact that goes totally undetected when the analysis remains with relative exchanges: the expenditure of the wages earned by our free worker contributes to the formation of prices in the products market. This, albeit obvious, idea that wages would not be earned in the products market if they were not also spent is totally absent from the "model" based on relative exchanges. Microeconomic analysis only considers one of the two aspects: wages are earned and their expenditure is not of any concern. More precisely, relative prices are all determined without the persons included in the explanation having to be *both supplier and demander;* some agents supply goods, others demand them; it is therefore true that in the analysis claiming to be complete, no agent is identically supplier and demander: the "model" only considers supplier agents and demander agents: it does not have any knowledge, in the same trading session, of the agents who spend their wages, nor of the agents who earn (or have earned) the wages they spend.

Reality, which everyone can check on himself, is different; the formation of prices is an operation implying, on each agent, the expenditure of the income earned and the earning of the income spent.

One can pledge to rectify the situation over time; to determine the equilibria in the markets today, agents are either suppliers or demanders; but the determination of the equilibria in the market that will operate tomorrow will see the permutation of the functions, any agent who was initially a supplier now being a demander, and vice versa.

However, as Marx had already said, there is nothing more dangerous than to cross a precipice in two stages. If a second trading session is needed to transform suppliers into demanders and demanders into suppliers, the theory would only maintain its unity and its explanatory power if it succeeded in embracing the two markets as one single reality. As soon as the two sessions remain effectively separated, in each of them economics only holds a half truth, hence one error. And if the unification of the sessions succeeds, the analysis is henceforth macroeconomic, exactly as we are trying to establish, the same agents being suppliers and demanders in the movements that determine prices of one single delivery of products.

It would seem that, in certain writings, the theorists of equilibrium have succeeded in introducing the idea of the simultaneity of purchases and sales carried out by the same agents.

The first thing to notice is that if some commodity called money indeed must mediate in exchange, this in itself does not yet damage our

conclusions of the previous section if we can take it that sales and purchases are simultaneous. In this case, there is no 'first leg' and 'second leg'
of a transaction and we could continue to postulate that every transaction is of a kind that does not decrease the utility of the transactors. If
this is the case, however, we certainly would be hard put to explain why
any household should hold any money at all (here, of course, we are
abstracting from price uncertainty). On the other hand, if we postulate
that a purchase at any moment of time cannot be financed from the
sales of that moment then every transaction of a household is speculative in the sense that the utility change from any one transaction is
contingent on the completion of all transactions.

(Arrow and Hahn 1971: 338–339)

Concerning that quotation, two remarks are essential.

1   If the analysis does not include quantum time – and no microeconomic
analysis does – logic forbids that it should give to itself at the same
instant the purchase and the sale of agent Q, at least when the sale must
finance the purchase. Simultaneity would require that Q sells (to obtain
money) and buys (in spending money) in *one single movement*, that would
thus confirm the union of the opposites: the movement would be defined
contradictorily. The sale of Q brings him a certain sum of (bank) money;
if Q spends that sum in the same movement that brings it to him, he
becomes simultaneously creditor to his buying-correspondent (B) and
debtor to his selling-correspondent (S): in each case, no money will ever
reach Q (his claim in the bank being annulled at the precise instant it has
been formed: it has therefore never been formed at all).

Defined in the instantaneity, the mediation of money, between the sale
by Q and the purchase by Q, is transformed logically into a mediation of
agent Q, between agents B and S. As it could not be stopped on Q, even
during the fraction of a second, or a time as short as one may want, the
result of the operation is defined only on B and S, Q being only the
transparent intermediary; the operation passes through him instantly.

However, the criticism goes further. If money slips into the transaction
agreed between S and B as assumed, the seller being simultaneously a
buyer and the buyer being simultaneously a seller, the illogicality detected
on Q is also present on S and on B and, by recursion, on any agent:
monetary flows are rigorously nil in the whole economy.

The authors admit that, if it is introduced in the operations of sale-
purchase, the presence of money in households is difficult to explain. But
the analytical benefit is nevertheless clear, because the conclusions of the
(microeconomic) theory are less obviously under attack thanks to the
existence of money, when it is contained within the narrow limits of the
instant. It is surprising that bright minds have not perceived that money

is literally choked if its life expectancy must be so short, money having to disappear on any agent at the very instant it reaches him.

The mistake is explained by the fact that the (microeconomic) theory is caught between two drawbacks, each as grievous as the other. Indeed, if the analysis allows the existence of money, it separates (over time) the sale and the purchase of the agent; but then the transaction (the sale followed by the purchase) can no longer be explained, except in the completion of all the other transactions.

2   The criticism, by far the most fundamental, levelled at the analysis under scrutiny concerns non-monetary exchanges. In the first point (1) we have noticed the difficulty – not to say the impossibility – that microeconomic theory faces when it must integrate money in exchanges. However, and paradoxically, the difficulty is the same for purely real exchanges: their explanation also requires that the "seller" should be a "purchaser" in the same movement. The authors suppose implicitly that money creates a new, specific, problem, except if one succeeds in neutralising it, by assuming that every sale is a simultaneous purchase by the seller. However, the problem is not at all specific to money: even non-monetary transactions are "inexplicable" if the good "sold" is not, in the same movement, "bought" by its seller.

How are authors hiding this fact from themselves? It is very simple: they take the *numéraire* as a given. As soon as the *numéraire* is present, the (mathematical) demonstrations can soar freely.

Gérard Debreu was proceeding in that way; price is introduced in his axiomatic theory of value by an innocuous decision. "With each commodity, say the hth, is associated a real number, its price, ph" (Debreu 1959: 32).

Any theorist from another science would be surprised: can we really *associate numbers to commodities*; and, moreover, can we do it through a pure *convention*? The founder of the theory of economic equilibrium, Walras, associated numbers with commodities only by associating them with psychic magnitudes, homogenous dimensions. The transformation of goods into numbers resulted from a hypothesis and not a convention: the goods are exchanged; therefore they are equal; their equality is not physical: exchanges *reveal* the equivalences that the commodities form with the human-beings "psyche".

It is clear that the Walrasian hypothesis is doubtful; but if it is set aside, another hypothesis or an argument must replace it. Otherwise, the *numeraire* is introduced surreptitiously, by a *fiat*, as if to say, in a discretionary way, that an energy is attributed to every matter: it is clear though that the equivalence of matter and energy is a law and not a convention. Similarly, if we want to associate numbers to physical goods, to marry them in a way, we must establish that their union does not run against logic; however, it does indeed in all appearances.

It is only the theory of emissions that demonstrates the identity through the substitution of numbers and product; the product lodged inside money annuls the negative numbers (money formed in a hollow). It follows that positive money (numbers defining the bulge of the "zero-sphere") has been substituted to physical goods newly produced (issued), to define national income, of which it is the unique object, the unique component.

Let us go on with criticism 2. The authors define goods in purely physical terms.

"A good may be defined by its physical characteristics, its location in space, and the date of its delivery. Goods differing in any of those characteristics will be regarded as different" (Arrow and Hahn 1971: 17). An objection comes at once: so defined, physical goods constitute an enumeration, a catalogue. Therefore, the authors define prices immediately. "All prices are expressed in fictional unit of account-say 'bancors'" (ibid.: 17). As soon as prices are thus agreed upon, goods are placed in the same measuring space.

One can indeed assume the price range by a pure convention since the reasoning aims at revealing general, abstract laws. But the authors do not take prices as given just in their simple numerical value, they assume them in their principle: they postulate units of accounts the existence of which in relation with physical goods has nowhere been explained. It is indeed a fiction. The methodological error would be repairable if, in ulterior developments of their theory, the authors were to succeed in proving the existence of an actual association between numbers and goods. Then prices might be converted in bancors, in exactly that same way that Réaumur degrees are converted into Celsius degrees. *However, the proof is never provided.*

It could not be, it is logically impossible. Let us explain once again the reason why, because this question compromises the neoclassical "paradigm" in its entirety.

The most important thing, right from the start, is to decide if the association of numbers to physical goods must be given only at equilibrium or also before reaching equilibrium. The authors have chosen the only coherent position: goods must be "countable" even before establishing equilibrium; if they were not, economic agents could not act, since, literally, they could not measure their decisions.

> We shall be considering a number of constructions representing economies in which agents take the terms at which they may transact as independently given. This, of course, is a feature of a perfectly competitive economy. A consequence of this is that part of the environment relevant to the decisions of economic agents consists of the prices of various goods that they take as given. Our main concern will be the description of situations in which the desired actions of economic agents are all mutually compatible and can all be carried out simultaneously, and for which we can prove that for the various economies discussed, there exists a set of prices that will cause agents to make mutually compatible decisions.
>
> (Arrow and Hahn 1971: 16)

Let us notice carefully the double convention introduced by the authors; prices are given in a double sense: they are given in a *weak sense* when it is said that the decisions taken by agents cannot modify them (it is the hypothesis of pure and perfect competition); but prices are given in the *strong sense*, because it is agreed that the links between numbers and physical goods – of which it is said that they cannot be modified in the case described – exist already: the economy has carried out the association of numbers and physical goods even before the intervention of the (new) decisions of agents that one aims at studying.

The method would require a two-stage process.

One would have first to establish the links numbers-goods, i.e. the principle of those links, as in physics one establishes the law of equivalence between matter and energy.

Then one might postulate their invariance under certain conditions, the same numbers remaining associated to the same physical goods.

The authors satisfy themselves with postulating the invariance of prices against the behaviour of agents (or, identically, with postulating pure and perfect competition, the only regime where that invariance might exist); the essential law, the link numbers-goods, as it is communicated at every trading session, from the opening, is finally not even postulated: it is "taken for granted".

We are reaching the conclusion on point 2. We can demonstrate today that, far from being obvious, the association of numbers and physical goods *is formally impossible in the neoclassical paradigm* and, in particular in the way of thinking of Arrow and Hahn.

Is it really necessary to prove that microeconomic reasoning takes place within relative exchanges? Anyway, the authors leave no room for doubt.

> Partial equilibrium analysis is to be regarded as a special case of general equilibrium analysis. The existence of one market presupposes that there must be at least one commodity beyond that traded on that market, for a price must be stated as the rate at which an individual gives up something for the commodity in question. If there was really only one commodity in the world, there would be no exchange and no market.
>
> (Arrow and Hahn 1971: 6–7)

We must be thankful to the authors for having so nearly approached truth; they simply stay on the other side of the fence. In so doing, they belong to a "group of scholars" that includes nearly all present-day economists. But the layman is also of the same opinion: for an exchange to happen, *two* goods at least have to be present. The reader knows however that reality is more subtle: the only economic exchanges that exist in the real world are defined within the production of goods. Provided it is cleverly interrogated, intuition offers an answer that is, from the outset, on the right track. It is not true, everybody knows it, that commodities are usually exchanged against each other: they are exchanged against money. Arrow and Hahn wholeheartedly admit it.

> Of course, our model is in no shape to give a satisfactory formal account of the role of money. In particular, it would be hard to 'explain' the holding of money or why it mediates in most acts of exchange.
>
> (ibid.: 338)

But are monetary exchanges agreed between two distinct goods? Nothing is less certain. We even know perfectly today that the "body" of money is the product; the great Ricardo said it: money incorporates the product; according to him, it was so under the form of labour. As soon as modern progress is introduced, one understands that labour casts the product into money. Physical product is deposited into money: it is indeed the physical product exactly as viewed by Neo-classics; the product is purely physical, it does not include any non-material "fabric". But one single act of production, the unique production of *one single worker* is already a complete act of exchange because a production, only one, is enough to "introduce" a product into money.

Not only does the exchange exist in reality *between a good and itself*, between the purely physical good and this good in money, a pure number, but in the world of concrete economies *there are no other types of exchanges*. No one has ever proved the existence of relative exchanges. The question was not even in the mind of scholars. Exchange moves apples and pears. It so happens that real exchanges (unlike imaginary exchanges) are not movements in the space of agents. Exchanges first change physical products into money – this is the explanation of the association of numbers to physical goods – then exchanges change (it is worth repeating the tautology: to exchange is to change) money, monetary income, into products. Production is the unique operation able to change physical goods into numbers.

As soon as two distinct physical goods are confronted, without their production having associated them to pure numbers (it is striking that neoclassical scholars exchange goods against each other, whether they are produced or not) it is formally impossible to give one for the other, unless by means of two reciprocal movements; and one may move goods as many times as one may wish: *the circulation imparted on them will never transform them into pure numbers*. A physical good that is moving remains identical, a good and not a number. Barter *is not an exchange*.

One can find the equivalence within economic transactions only in the metabolism defined by the couple production-consumption; production is the "anabolism", and consumption is the "catabolism". Exchanges that we have before our eyes every day are consumptions (expenditures in the products market) facing productions (expenditures in the producing services markets). Only the non-disjointed study of production and consumption enables the relations of equivalence, prices, to be grasped.

Arrow and Hahn honestly say that they do not know what money is. But they have not offered any explanation of the *numéraire* either. That would still not be very serious if their analyses could receive a sound foundation in a theory of the *numeraire* elaborated elsewhere. However, let us repeat the judgment against which there cannot be any appeal; the theory of the *numéraire* has *the same requirements as the theory of money*; numbers can only be associated to physical goods in absolute exchanges: all goods are equivalent to themselves, and no good is equivalent to another good. Even in the supposedly moneyless economy, only the exchange of good *a* against good *a* enables the association of a number with good *a*.

It is therefore not true that money creates a complication; it is not more "complicated" than the *numéraire*; if monetary exchanges can be understood provided that every seller is a buyer in the same movement, the same condition is necessary to understand apparently purely real exchanges: every supplier must be a demander in the act of supplying.

The authors say it themselves, at the end of Chapter 13 (the fourteenth and last chapter being a draft of the "Keynesian model"), that the economy investigated "is still only a distant relative of the economy we know" (Arrow and Hahn 1971: 346). Indeed, "the absence of production in our analysis so far is significant" (ibid.). It is true to say that the relationship between the theory of equilibrium and the concrete economy is so remote that it is non-existent.

Production and money are part of the economic world in which we live. Relative exchanges are not related to absolute exchanges. As Frédéric Poulon says in the general conclusion of his recent book, *Macroéconomie Approfondie*:

> there is a genuine relation of mutual exclusion between microeconomics and macroeconomics: one excludes money that is integrated by the other; one discards time, and the other is built on time. One and the other are truly within Economics, two disjointed subsets, but, unfortunately, one of them is maybe an empty set.
>
> (Poulon 1982: 373)

Now we can complete in broad terms the analysis of the formation of wages in the generalized wage-regime.

Determination of wages in the generalized wage-regime

We have seen that firms and workers agree to set wages according to socio-professional categories. To look at it superficially, one might believe that the amount of wages is arbitrary. In reality, wages are always – therefore even in the wage-regime – determined by the law of production-consumption, of the flux-reflux of income. The apparent discrepancies are resorbed by the play of the retroaction of the purchase of products on the (initial) payment of wages. Whoever understands well the fact that the second half-emission (the expenditure of income) is "posited" on the first (the emission of wages), will understand that all wages are determined according to a strict economic law, without any exception.

Chronologically, wages are paid before being spent. To avoid falling into a contradiction, let us follow the separation through time of the two operations, identical but for the sign. It is true that firms do not know the amount of wages that, following the free decision of agents, will be spent for the purchase of each group of products. It follows that wages are issued as if the flux of their creation were independent of their reflux-destruction, a differed movement. Undoubtedly, firms can anticipate the amount of reflux, on each group of products. But those anticipations cannot be infallible. Moreover, the agreed rigidity of wages prevents their revision, even if it were becoming necessary due to the new "orientation" of the reflux. If the amount of income spent for the purchase of this good varies while the amount of wages issued in the production of this good remains constant, the new emissions of wages will not be able to take it into account since wages are rigid, by assumption. One is tempted to say definitively that the amount of wages to be perceived by each socio-professional category, by each worker and in each period, is arbitrary, at least partially. In reality, the correct reasoning is far deeper. Let us try to reach it without twisting it.

Even though each issued income is a wage, refluxed incomes are wages, interests, dividends and rents. We know that the redistribution of wages is an operation defined in both markets *at the same time*, the products market and, by retroaction, the producing services market. So, let us suppose that, on a group of goods, firms observe the reflux of x' units of (wage and non-wage) incomes whereas the production of those goods has been carried out by the emission of x units of wages. The discrepancy between x' and x, which, if it is not nil, might be negative as well as positive, cannot lead to a reduction nor a raise in wages (the rigidity being given for a reduction as well as for an increase). It does not at all follow that the non-adjustment of wages brings (or confirms) their conventional character; the difference $x' - x$ is simply the definition of a transfer, negative or positive, of wages to the benefit or at the expense of wage-earners. As soon as these transfers are taken into account, it appears that for any group of goods (even if the accounting system of firms is not analytical enough to make it apparent), the amount of the flux (wages issued in the production of those goods) and the amount of the reflux (the expenditures of all the income brought about by this production) are strictly equal. Finally, the determination of wages is identical for the free worker and for the worker employed within the generalized wage-regime.

That the payment of wages is not the exchange of two goods, as Neo-Classics would have it, is now obvious enough. The payment of wages is the creation of prices – or of the association of numbers with physical goods – and not, even in "pure and perfect competition", an exchange between two goods, money and product, the prices of which would have been pre-determined: they are so neither in their principle nor in their amount. Classical analysis is far more realistic. The payment of wages creates the relation of equivalence between the physical product (at least part of it) and money. Today, the tradition from Ricardo to Marx is enriched with an essential knowledge: cast in the payment of wages, money has no value, neither intrinsic nor extrinsic: it is simply formed as a "mass" of negative numbers that absorb the new physical product.

The absorption of the product by money is the unique true definition of the *numéraire* and identically of money. The law of the formation of wages derives from an immediate induction. For each worker, free or "salaried" (and in that case, the law applies through transfers), *the remuneration of labour is determined by the amount of the income that, on the basis of the money units cast in wages, flows back in the purchase of the (group of) corresponding products.*

The payment of wages is the absolute exchange that is the foundation of all other exchanges, all absolute. The very simple idea of the left-luggage ticket can have a certain heuristic value. If the clerk were to give the depositor of the suitcase a "physical good", we would observe a relative exchange event. Similarly, if the ticket were money, the exchange would be relative, the purchasing power of money (a good) being given for the suitcase (or *another* good). The reality is of course different. The depositor carries out an exchange with himself, the left-luggage office being interposed. The owner of the suitcase is using it in an absolute exchange: he gives the suitcase in kind and he receives it as a note. It is clear that the ticket has no value, neither before nor after the exchange. *Ante factum*, the ticket is a little slip of paper carrying a sign, for example a number. In the hands of the depositor, the ticket has still no proper value: it identifies with the suitcase, of which it is, in a sense, the nominal form. It is true that the ticket does not measure the suitcase; in this the analogy is not accurate: the ticket is not a negative number into which the suitcase would be cast. But, like for the money issued in wages, the ticket issued as a representation of the suitcase is not a good in itself: *post factum*, the ticket is identified with the suitcase-good. At the moment of the withdrawal, the ticket's existence is ended, at least the "real" ticket, since the suitcase is no longer represented. The emission of left-luggage tickets is a first absolute exchange; the withdrawal of the deposited objects is the opposite absolute exchange.

We thus understand more easily the nature of monetary emissions. The emission of wages is a first absolute exchange; the withdrawal or clearing of the product is the opposite absolute exchange. It only remains to add the case of exchanges agreed in the financial market. They are absolute too because the buyer of the financial claims is depositing part of his income with the seller, who issues, to the benefit of the depositor, a claim on the deposit, the right to withdraw it, according to the agreement, at a fixed or indeterminate date.

There is no operation in the economy of production where the existence of an exchange between two distinct goods could be observed. Agents give in kind what they receive in money; it is the first exchange, and it is absolute.

Then agents give in money what they receive in kind; this second exchange is absolute too. The formation and the expenditure of wages are exchanges between workers and themselves, productions-consumptions.

The only obstacle to a direct understanding of absolute exchanges comes from the fact that wages are partially redistributed in profits, rents, interests and dividends. But the transfer of a part of the wages is carried out through exchanges. Therefore, are those transfers absolute exchanges too? They undoubtedly are since wages are transferred in the very operation of their emission: once prices are known in the products market, we know in what exact measure wages issued on workers are deprived of their "substance" (the physical product of the current period) to the benefit of non-wage income holders.

To build economics on relative exchanges is therefore a chimeric enterprise.

Let us remark, in this respect, that microeconomics has never succeeded in breaking the vicious circle that is blindly obvious: if exchanges were relative, wages would be prices "like others". Let pr be the product of the period. The price of this product must be determined twice; $p(pr)$ is the price of the product in the products market and $p'(pr)$ its price in the producing services market. It can easily be shown that $p(pr)$ cannot be determined if $p'(pr)$ is not already known. But it can as easily be shown that $p'(pr)$ cannot be determined unless on the basis of $p(pr)$. The price of the good offered in the market depends on its cost of production; let us suppose that at "equilibrium" (the meeting point of the supply and demand of the good), the profit of the seller should be nil. In this case, the cost of production gives the price $p(pr)$. If the profit is not nil, (classical) theory will doubtless not determine the price of goods; but if it can, it will be equal to $p'(pr)$, except for some minor positive or negative adjustment.

Similarly, wages determined in the producing services market depend on the price at which the good can or will be sold in the products market. Again, the (ideal) solution is in the redistribution, to the producing services, of the entirety of the sales receipt, neither more nor less. If the solution is not perfectly verified, and the theory nevertheless masters the discrepancy, wages $p'(pr)$ will be based on price $p(pr)$, except for some minor positive or negative adjustment.

We see that price $p'(pr)$ gives price $p(pr)$ and conversely. The circle is vicious. We know that microeconomic analysis tries to hide it by the idea of simultaneous determination or co-determination. *However, the introduction of time defeats the attempt.* In the pure theory of relative exchanges, we cannot determine which movement would be the first chronologically: wages are paid before or after the sale of the good in the products market. However, logic commands a chronological order in the sense that both movements, payment and expenditure of wages, must follow each other, in the order that is chosen by the observer. One may decide to start by the sale of the product or by the sale of the producing service; it is indifferent. But, again, whether one sequence or the opposite sequence is chosen, the temporal separation of the two events has to be maintained, otherwise the contradiction is immediate, the producing service being unable to receive a net payment (his wages) if he is credited and debited at the same instant (in the same movement).

Consequently, the vice shines out. If one claims to start by the determination of prices in the products market, one has to suppose that prices in the producing services market are already known; it is so by anticipation, in expectations. For the determination of price $p(pr)$ on the basis of anticipated price $p'(pr)$ to be formally faultless, it has to apply from $p'(pr)$ on $p(pr)$ and not at all from $p(pr)$ on $p'(pr)$. However, the effect of $p(pr)$ on $p'(pr)$ cannot be prevented since the wages paid are carried to the product markets. The contradiction appears clearly in the following formulation: if anticipated price $p'(pr)$ is higher than the price that will effectively be realized, the realized price $p(pr)$ will be higher by the same amount to what it would have been if expectations had not been incorrect.

The opposite order of events leads to the same illogicality. Expected magnitudes determine realized magnitudes; but one cannot prevent realized magnitudes to have an impact on expected magnitudes (not in expectations but in reality).

Microeconomics and the "empty set"

Microeconomics is indeed empty, as Poulon thinks. But let us not forget that it is the necessary stage of the development of our science. The theory of absolute exchanges would not have been reached if relative exchanges had not first replaced, in the antithetic paradigm, the absolute exchanges of the Classics. Today, Economics goes back definitively to absolute exchanges, but they are constituted in *numéraire* or, identically, in *numéraire*-money. The association of dimensionless numbers to physical goods is the great conquest of the Neo-Classics. It is true that the association has not succeeded in microeconomics; logic does not allow it. But it is fully constituted in today's macroeconomics: value is still defined as a pure number and it is associated to the product in the set of absolute exchanges, every worker buying his own product, through any other products.

The strictness of the circuit is such – every exchange being production and consumption, in the same movement, of the same product by the same worker (partially on behalf of non-wage income holders) – that modern theorists of the circuit still have difficulty not to introduce a bit of "flexibility" in their analyses. Logic is really too strict for us not to try to escape from it all the time. Even though we do it in a spirit of friendship and respect, let us conclude this book with a brief critical study of the circuit presented by Professor Poulon, and, in particular, the role attributed to saving. This effort is all the more legitimate that other theorists of the circuit have similar representations, in particular Professor Graziani of Naples University. We shall examine only the work of Frederic Poulon to whom we are grateful for the opportunity given by his important book, which will enable us to review and, so to speak, verify our main propositions.

20 The circuit, the macroeconomic concept *par excellence*, is the identity of income's outflow and inflow

LIII. Money and credit

Money being of a banking kind, money outflows "come out" of banks and inflows "enter" banks. The first big question is to search for the exact nature of banks' contribution: does the operation of money creation belong to the category of credit operations? And if it does, is the credit in money creation given by banks or by other agents? We shall see that, according to Poulon, banks lend the (newly) created money to their clients, especially firms. It seems to us that the correct analysis is different; in reality, money creations are instantly transformed into financial operations, that is, into intermediations in the financial market; banks are only intermediary lenders and borrowers: the initial lenders and the final borrowers are outside banks.

As soon as it is recognized that money creations are reduced to financial intermediations, we understand better the exact meaning that should be given, in spite of the author, to what he calls (after Professor Parguez) the "repayment constraint". If money were initially lent by banks, firms would be indebted to them and not through them. Poulon's worry would then have a basis: are firms always able to meet the repayment constraint? However, the worry has no foundation since the debt of firms (like that of any agent) towards the banking system goes through banks, to reach the initial lender, for example, an income holder.

It is demonstrated that, under those conditions, which are always fulfilled, firms remain indebted only as far as income holders remain creditors (savers): the debt can therefore never lack any "supply", and the repayment constraint could not then have any "deflationary" effect on firms.

We can then turn to the analysis of savings. Even if it is true that they tautologically define a sum of money lent, are they not lacking, and maybe definitively, from the current sales of part of the current product? Are not non-consumed (saved) wages lacking from the revenues of firms, at least to their receipts in the products market? Poulon identifies a saving that, according to him, is effectively formed to the detriment of the sale of (new) products. Correlatively, firms would experience a certain difficulty in fulfilling the repayment constraint. We shall no longer examine this constraint itself but rather the prejudicial question: is it true that a certain type of savings causes a lack of receipts in the products market? We shall see that this is not the case. Any saving, whatever it may be, is a *positive demand* of unsaved real goods: even the purchase of consumption goods is not at all affected by the building up of savings, even if they are speculative.

We shall study finally Poulon's circuit in its time-dimension. It seems to us that the author is effectively still caught in the neo-classical doctrine, according to which money breaks the exchange of products into two half-transactions. The time that elapses between the two partial operations seems positive and irreducible. However, the break from microeconomic thought is only confirmed in an all new definition of the intercession of money: it slips inside production (the action) and not between its results (the products). Consequently, the circuit comes under a far simpler definition and one of absolute precision: every money circuit is completed in an instant.

Having found absolute exchanges again, we shall have also met again the analysis of capitalism. The clearing crisis is not the experimental proof of the imperfection of the circuit. The sum of "inflows" is logically (therefore necessarily) equal to the sum of "outflows": nonetheless (as we have demonstrated in this work) the sum of inflows may be insufficient to "clear up" the full employment product. It is of course of the utmost importance to formulate the exact diagnosis: the dysfunction is entirely due to the existence of empty emissions. Macroeconomics will only achieve its originality by breaking off completely with the study of agents' behaviour. The purpose of political economy is to reform the mode of production. The reader knows that the objective will be reached by restructuring bank accounting. Inflation and unemployment will be seriously and efficiently fought only when money emission follows the logical rules of the creation of real monies, each unit of money "coming into the world" endowed with a positive purchasing power. The whole problem comes from the coming to life in the current mode of production and in each period of a large quantity of purely nominal money units.

No money comes out of the bank without having entered the bank

Macroeconomics describes a hierarchical economy. The second characteristic (the first being that macroeconomics is a monetary analysis) of macroeconomics is linked to the previous one: indeed, insofar as macroeconomics integrates the creation of money, the starting point of the analysis is indicated by the creation of money flows. Financial intermediaries (banks in particular) have therefore a hierarchically higher position in macroeconomic analysis. But credit (the source of money creation) is distributed essentially to firms to allow them to carry out the production process, especially by distributing income to households in exchange for their labour power.

The sense of circulation of money flows indicates therefore the true hierarchy of agents and goes from banks to firms, then from firms to households.

Finally, money creation and the hierarchy of flows and agents are represented synthetically in the instrument *par excellence* of the macroeconomic

method: the economic circuit that is radically opposed to markets' general
equilibrium.

(Poulon 1982: 20)

Our objective is not to show that Professor Poulon may be wrong. It is only
to establish or confirm, through the examination of this writer's theses, the
reality of facts and, first, the exact meaning of the money creations happening
in our concrete economies.

It is beyond doubt that banks are financial intermediaries; this language is,
by the way, accepted even by practitioners. But it is important to respect the
meaning, as long as it is the correct one. The analysis of money creation as a
financial intermediation endangers the hierarchical structure afore mentioned.

If money were simply created by banks, that is if it were "coming out" of a
bank without having "entered" that bank, one may indeed picture economic
activity under the form of a hierarchy, of which banks would be at the
summit. We would start from the "source" of money, the banking system, and
we would follow money flows, through firms to households. It is true that the
money flow is original in the sense that money "flows back to its source": it
comes back finally from households to firms and, higher up, from firms to
banks. But money inflow does not coincide with the idea of hierarchy since
one may well represent the flows as finishing where they started, in banks,
that would thus be both the points where everything begins and everything
ends.

However, banks create in their general function of financial intermediation. Not only does the author use this terminology (which, again, is beyond
reproach), but he takes care to point out that "the distinctions between banking financial intermediaries and non-banking financial intermediaries, between
credits financed through monetary resources and credits financed through
savings resources, or even between commercial banks and Central Bank, are
groundless at our level of abstraction" (ibid.: p.321).

It is certain that non-banking financial intermediaries only carry out
financial intermediations. Since banks are not fundamentally distinct from
non-banking financial intermediaries, it is therefore indubitable that money
creations belong to the logical class of financial intermediations. We do think
that this is the case. But then, one can no longer understand the idea of the
hierarchy of monetary operations. Any bank that creates money acts as a
mediator between a lender and a borrower; otherwise the operation would not
be an intermediation. How, then, could the created money have its source in
the bank?

The banking financial intermediary receives the initial lender's money and
transmits it to the final borrower. Being intermediate, between lender and
borrower, the bank carries out an operation that originates from the lender.
It seems therefore illogical to posit the bank that creates money at the top of
a hierarchy. If there is a hierarchy, its summit is defined by the *initial lender*
and not by the bank. The conclusion is true, whether the bank is defined as an

entity or as a function; in both cases, it is situated at the level of non-banking lenders and borrowers, the agents with whom it is in a financial relation, which is the negation of any hierarchy where banks would be the summit. The criticism is important since it affects the "second characteristic of macroeconomics" (which, again according to Poulon, has only two).

The contradiction detected is due to an imprecise conception of the creation of money.

Reconciling creation and intermediation in one single operation

The author asks correctly "the question of how the intermediary finances the credit it gives" (Poulon 1982: 320). But the answer is dodged. We only learn that banks are firms and that they follow the law of profit. The way bankers finance their credits "corresponds to the function of a capitalist firm, trying to maximize its profit". "If they give too much credit, their refinancing cost may worsen and reduce their profits" (ibid.: 321). We thus understand that, according to Poulon, credit is financed by the bank itself, unless it has to use refinancing. The idea of the hierarchy would therefore be logical – but it would be so at a price; banks create money and they finance the operation until refinancing becomes necessary. However, if the hierarchy is thus maintained, it is the conception of money creation itself that is fundamentally undermined: until the potential refinancing of the operation, the creation of money would not be a financial intermediation.

The fundamental issue is daunting because it is about reconciling the opposites. Creation implies "exiting" without "entering"; intermediation supposes that the money that exits had entered. But why keep only one of the two hypotheses? This is because, taken in isolation, each one of them faces a formal impossibility.

- If money is purely created, or created *ex nihilo* as is said, we do not see where it comes from; it is not much satisfying to say that it comes from "elsewhere", from another world, or from nothing.
- On the other hand, if money is purely transmitted, we would not be able to grasp bank money; financial intermediaries transmit the existing money: but in what operation does bank money comes about?

The only positive way is therefore to admit indeed both opposite truths at the same time; money is created in an operation of intermediation: it is therefore created in an operation that transmits it.

Thus:

- being created in the operation, money "exits" the bank where it did not "enter"; and
- being transmitted in the operation, money "exits" the bank where it "entered".

It is certain that the contradiction cannot be lifted by "ordinary" logic. However, it is so by "quantum analysis".

1   Money is created in the payment of wages. Let us keep the terminology of entries and exits but let us apply it to the operations themselves. At the entry of the payment of wages, we find money that does not yet exist, and that is about to be created. At the exit of the payment of wages, money has come to life in the assets of households.

2   Money wages received are a "form" and a "fund". The (monetary) form of wages is created by banks; the product of workers defines the wage fund, or its body. We see therefore that if the wrapping "comes" from banks, its content has human labour as its sole source. Concerning real money, it is clear that it is only transiting through the bank; though the move is of a quantum nature: the real "content" of the negative money formed in the firm, the product is at once replaced by money in the assets of income holders.

3   At the moment real money (the product in its monetary wrapping) is formed, it defines income. However, income is immediately transformed into capital. It is the transformation of quantum credit into ordinary credit. We see therefore the appearing of the true financial intermediation associated to the emission of wages. Income holders are now savers; savings are lent to or deposited in banks; finally, banks lend the savings to firms. Those movements are also of a quantum nature: they "consume" a zero amount of time. Current income is transformed at once into an equivalent future income, a financial and real capital. Financial capital is formed in the assets of households; the corresponding real capital is deposited in firms, under the form of stocks. The bank that has created the wages is therefore finally a financial intermediary since it transmits the savings of households to firms.

Points 1, 2 and 3 interpret one and the same single operation, the payment or the emission of wages. If the operation were not meaning a creation of money (1), workers could not be paid in bank money; this is a truism. On the other hand, if income was "coming" from banks, workers would not be paid by themselves, by the expenditure of their labour, which would be the negation of the idea (also macroeconomic *par excellence*) of production. Banks create therefore only the form of wages (2). Finally, as soon as income is created, it forms savings; banks collects savings and lend them to firms (3); that last operation is the result of a "quantum mechanism" because it is logically implicit in the operation of money creation (flow *1 stricto sensu*).

The concepts being clearer, we have to examine the hierarchy put forward by Poulon; is it confirmed? The answer is undoubtedly negative. Banks are at the top of a hierarchy only insofar as the creation (of the empty form of production, real money being created by workers) is concerned; they are not "hierarchically higher" as (financial) intermediary. However, the creation of money is only interesting – it has a content – because it constitutes a unit with intermediation: at the moment of its birth, money is also a saving; it is therefore instantaneously lent (by workers to firms). The financing of the operation, which is now known, is an intermediation and not a creation: firms borrow the (stocked) product from banks, that borrow it from households. The claim of households on banks compensates the claim of banks on firms. The content of the operation therefore invalidates the presence of banks at the top of the hierarchy. At first sight, the question is not much important; but we know that the author views it on the contrary as greatly significant (see the "second characteristic"). We are going to observe soon that the hierarchy is effectively at the heart of the *Macroéconomie Approfondie*: therefore, its invalidation has great consequences.

The first effect of the invalidation of the hierarchy is to cancel the impact of the "repayment constraint".

The payment of wages is indebting firms to income holders and not to banks

Let us summarize what we have learned.

We understand well that banks cannot "advance" to firms the (new) product of workers: they are not the source of it. The emission of wages is both positive and negative. In the creation of wages, banks acquire a claim on firms (the "payers") and a debt to workers (the "payees"). It follows that the operation does not bring any net claim on banks. The payment of wages creates the net claims of the whole economy, wage and non-wage incomes. In what sense can we say that income holders are creditors? The answer is known with accuracy. It is based on singling out the payment of wages:

- as a creation, the payment of wages does not deposit any claim in the economy;
- as a bank intermediation, the payment of wages generates the claim of workers facing the debt of firms.

We thus see that the payment of wages does not generate a debt of firms to banks but, through banks, to income holders.

However, it is demonstrated that the "repayment constraint" cannot have the effect alleged by the authors, for the reason precisely that it is not, in factual reality, a relation defined between firms and banks.

The economy would be in crisis when firms are not able to face all the repayment constraints that they would have contracted to banks. Therefore, the "macroeconomics of the circuit, by taking credit into account, is introducing by this mere fact a possibility of crisis in the system: the crisis will appear if the credits cannot be repaid" (ibid.: 21).

In the same sense (and again after Alain Parguez) Frédéric Poulon is talking of a constraint of money cancellation.

To say that any money issued must satisfy, after a certain time, the constraint of cancellation attached to it, is the same as saying that any credit bringing this money to life must be repaid after a certain time. The constraint of money cancellation is fulfilled as soon as the money coming from pole B [banks], goes back to pole B, under the form of the credit repayment.

(Poulon 1982: 342)

It is worth basing the criticism on the observation of facts: in the concrete economy, firms rarely pay wages by means of bank advances; for this, they have at their disposal equity funds, revolving funds. But it would be too easy to deny the validity of the "constraint" analysis by this sole argument. One must, on the contrary, commend the perceptiveness of the authors who have proposed a general rule, applying to both cases, whether wages are paid through bank advances or from revolving funds belonging to firms.

Logic imposes indeed an analysis the validity of which is general, the only difference between the two cases being related to interests: it is obvious that firms do not owe any interest when using their equity funds. But having set aside the consideration of interests, as it should be since this is beside the point, it remains that any payment of wages obeys one same law: it establishes a relation between income holders and firms.

Quantum analysis highlights this relation brightly; as soon as income is created, it is deposited in (continuous or, identically, chronological) time; the deposit of income in time implies the transformation of income into savings; income holders are therefore immediately holders of the new savings. Saved income is *ipso facto* lent to firms through the intermediary of banks (that have issued the money form of the new product); correlatively, firms hold the product, not yet sold, in stock; households savings thus define their claim on firms and, through them, on the stocks.

We have arrived at the exact point where Poulon's thinking crystallizes. The author admits that the saving of income defines the closing of the circuit; at the moment created wages are transformed into savings, the circuit of wages is closing since money wages are transformed into financial wages: they now are a claim on the products in stock. We can induce from this that firms are indebted to households who hold the saved income. This is a tautology. However, Poulon thinks that firms are indebted to banks (and not, let us repeat it, to households through banks):

money is saved by households whereas it is firms that are subjected to the constraint of repaying credits. [...] It remains however that the constitution of money into savings puts an end to the circuit of money and, thereby, raises the problem of its cancellation. It is from the solution given to this problem that the crisis may arise.

(Poulon 1982: 342)

With great clarity, the author exposes himself the predicament in which he has placed himself. He dissociates two operations:

- the constitution or formation of savings from the created income, and
- the loan (by households) of the savings thus formed.

The two operations being disjointed, it appears that the savings formed are not necessarily lent and that the savings lent are not necessary lent to firms. Let us imagine the formation of savings that would not be lent to firms: two consequences would follow:

1   Households who save refrain from withdrawing the new product, which therefore remains waiting in the stocks.
2   Savings that are thus missing for clearing the product are not captured either by firms in the financial market, because they are not lent. As far as they are not lent, savings endanger the solvability of firms.

> The solvability of firms is, in fact, linked to their ability to capture the savings that have been formed. By assumption, the sale of goods that form, well and truly, unsold stocks cannot capture the money constituted into savings. Firms, debtors to banks, can only borrow this money to savings holders, or to sell the property rights on their wealth, that is to say on all the assets they own.
>
> (ibid.: 343)

We intend to analyse the complete logic of saving in the next section. It suffices here to contrast the argument under review with a fact that we have taken great care to bring to light: as long as the savings from households are still present, they are logically (therefore necessarily) lent to firms as a whole. Let us demonstrate it once again. Then we shall dispel one last (false) concern; it is formally impossible that savings should be lent to "other" firms: they are necessarily lent to the firms holding the goods in stock.

No savings may be lost and none might, consequently, threaten the solvability of firms.

Any savings (constituted by households) are lent to firms as a whole. As soon as savings are formed, they define the transformation of an income into a monetary capital. The income thus transformed corresponds to a part (at least) of the new product, the real savings. However, there are only three possibilities once savings are formed: they are lent within the set of households; they are lent to firms as a whole; finally, they are not lent at all.

The last possibility is only considered *a priori*: it is rejected by reasoning. *All savings are lent.* Indeed, if households do not lend to anyone part of their saved income, they do lend it in spite of themselves to firms holding the corresponding stocks. Assume a firm, *Fq*, and the net increase of its stock in the period, Sq. As long as goods Sq are not cleared by households, Fq remains indebted to households (we have established this fact since the monetary debts arising from production always go through banks that are, in all circumstances, financial intermediaries). This is to say that firm q borrows from households (through banks) all the funding of its new stocks: savings "not lent" are therefore lent after all since they are borrowed by firms holding the (new) stocks.

We still have to examine the two other cases. If households voluntarily lend their savings to firms, the repayment constraint is automatically satisfied. However, if households lend their savings to households, the set of households spends the income instead of saving it, the expenditure of the borrower cancels the savings of the lender: in this case, the repayment constraint is again automatically satisfied since the inflow is carried out in the sale of goods, initially stocked, to borrowers.

The "constraint" is therefore devoid of any effect. But does it not nevertheless apply in the case where households' savings are voluntarily lent to "other" firms, at the expense of those where goods are stocked?

Savings are necessarily lent to firms holding the goods in stock.

> The play of capitalist competition, as can now easily be conceived, consists then in this, for every firm: first to dissuade, through advertisement or any other legal means, the consumers from buying the products of other companies; then, to try to capture the savings of those consumers by playing on their speculators motives, with a view to bring to capitulation the competing firms that need this money to repay banks.
>
> (Poulon 1982: 353)

Let us put it a little crudely: the author has a big imagination. Capitalism is a production mode that protects firms before threatening them. Entrepreneurs are "objective allies" facing workers; they only fight each other on a second level. However, let us stay strictly within the subject. Is it conceivable that the in-fights inside the set of firms would bring to some all or part of the savings that are needed by the others, to ensure their solvability?

No, this concern has no foundation. The reasoning is incorrect, not in its assumptions, but in the consequences that are drawn. It is perfectly possible that a firm that has already cleared its goods will find additional receipts in the financial market, where it draws part of savings (of households). But the conclusion that is deduced is incorrect. It is not true that the "misguided" savings might be missing for the clearing of the goods stocked in *other* firms.

The concern and the constraint vanish once we grasp the events in their full reality. Assume Fq' the firm that absorbs the savings that Fq must capture in order to get out of debt. Does that mean that the savings captured by Fq' are destroyed? It will be so only in the expenditures of Fq'. It is certain that firm q' will spend the captured savings; otherwise, it would only be (in this operation) a financial intermediary and savings would not yet be taken away from firm q. But how can Fq' spend the captured savings? Let us follow carefully the purely logical elements of the answer. It is impossible that the expenditure (by Fq') of the captured savings should cancel the debt of Fq; but it is also logically impossible that the debt of Fq (recorded in banks accounts) should be maintained without an equal claim being so in counterpart (in the same accounts of financial intermediaries).

We know therefore with certainty that the expenditure by Fq' of the captured savings maintains an equal financial claim on the banking system since, once again, it maintains the debt of Fq. The maintained claim defines tautologically the monetary means of financing the debt of Fq. We thus discover, by following double-entry accounting, that the expenditure of the captured savings cannot mean the disappearing or the destruction of these savings, which are necessarily formed unchanged into other hands: they are not therefore taken from the solvability of the firm holding the stocks; the new savers, who get their resources from the expenditure by Fq' of the captured savings, have at their disposal the exact purchasing power that is needed to ensure the clearing by Fq of the goods in its stock.

Let us summarize the correct argument

If savings reach Fq spontaneously, the problem is solved. In this case, the expenditure of savings means their destruction, because the debt of Fq disappears: the corresponding claim is therefore cancelled too. But if savings reach Fq' first, they cannot be cancelled in their expenditure (by Fq') since the debt of Fq is maintained. It follows that the captured and spent savings are fully reconstituted: they are always available facing the goods stocked in Fq. Logic requires that savings should only disappear when they reach the firms holding the stocks. It is therefore inconceivable that they should provoke a clearing deficit.

The cause of the crisis is much deeper; up until now it has not even been outlined. It is of course possible that a firm may never succeed in selling the whole stock, which happens for example when goods are not or no longer to the taste of the public; but it is essential to understand that *the constitution and the use of savings are never involved*. The amount of goods unsold defines an equal amount of saved financial claims; this is a consequence of the truism of the equality of credits and debits brought about in bank money. Savings are therefore always available, ready to be used, in order to fund the remaining of the debt taken out by the firm (Fq). If it so happens that no agent is willing to take it to the purchase of the goods in stock, the lack of sales is not caused by savings nor by their insufficiency (which only appear in erroneous deductions).

Further, whatever the true reason for the lack of sales, it is quite remarkable that it always leads – even in the case of the company being declared bankrupt – to the forced sale of unsold goods by some agent, the identity of whom depends on legal regulations, and to whom falls the obligation of capturing the savings left waiting, in order to destroy them in the payment of the goods left over.

The author is not far from the truth when he closes the circuit by means of savings. It is quite true that saving is an action, a flow, and more precisely a reflux. When any new income is created, saving flows it back instantaneously and completely, because the agents who have just received it have had not yet the time to cast it, even partially, into expenditures. The mistake only concerns captured savings that would be diverted from their primary aim; however, no savings may fail, as long as they exist, to be borrowed (continuously) by firms holding the goods in stock. Even the savings captured by other firms are borrowed by Fq; they never cease at any time to be borrowed by firm q, where the stocks are: the logic of the repayment constraint implies this conclusion, because Fq only remains under constraint in the limit of its unsold goods and that those same unsold goods define *ipso facto* the corresponding savings, *wherever they may be*.

Before moving on to the next section, let us notice the close connection of the two mistakes already identified.

Authors usually conceive of money as an asset that would circulate within the economy, facing the real assets, physical goods and services. In that spirit, savings are assets that households decide not to bring to "meet" real goods. At the top of the hierarchy, we observe the creation of monetary assets, that "go down" to firms then to households. If "going back up" is not carried out in good conditions, we may observe the existence of a certain number of money units remaining fixated somewhere "below" firms. The crisis is there, at least its possibility: the "stubborn" monetary assets that, due to the behaviour of agents, refuse to go back, create a gap in the receipts of firms; however, this gap is critical since firms must repay the credits that have created money. There is open crisis once the failure of the reflux cannot be made good.

It is a good thing that positive economy does not work *at all* according to that scheme. Any money created by banks is, during its existence, both a claim on banks (for the saved-income holders) and a debt to banks (for firms holding the goods in stock). Created both as an "active unit" (the claim) and a "negative unit" (the debt), each money unit is formed between firms and workers and not between banks and the rest of the economy. It follows that no positive money "descends" from banks. In addition, no positive money may be saved and remain so if it is not constantly maintained, always available, facing unsold goods.

No savings disappear in a trap. If agents refuse eventually to buy a good or a collection of goods, this is not because they prefer savings to consumption, but simply because they do not want those goods. In a word, saved money is not lacking for the clearing of consumption goods because, due to the double nature of money (a magnitude both positive and negative), savings can never disappear unless, precisely, in the purchase of the goods in stock.

The strict equality, in all circumstances, of money's flux and reflux is the very definition of the circuit. Any approach that claims to detect a non-zero discrepancy between the formation and the expenditure of income is therefore illogical within the theory of the circuit.

Of the fact that, in generating the clearing crisis, savings should be completely innocent, we have another proof; let us sum it up in the next section.

LIV. All savings are finally spent and the expenditure of any savings is a purchase of consumption goods

The savings of the whole set of households

According to Frédéric Poulon, only "speculative" savings are not reducible to consumptions; "the transactional-precautionary savings are only differed consumption" (Poulon 1982: 327). This judgment is interesting because it goes in the right direction, but it stops too early: the logic of the circuit requires that *even speculative savings are entirely reducible to consumption.* Since circuit analysis is just a reading of reality, any savings constituted in our concrete economies are differed consumption. This is not a wish but a *fact.*

Let us reason on two firms, *1* and *2*. In each period, firm *1* issues ten units of wages and firm *2* issues 15. Considered as a whole, households save five units of their income of period *p*: they therefore consume directly 20 units. However, the consumption of the set of households is lower, because a set is not an aggregate. Some households lend indeed part of their savings to other households. Suppose these internal loans amount to two units of wages. In this case, savings of the set of households is equal to three units of wages.

Do we have to wonder to whom households lend their savings? Logic has the answer ready. Given that the circuit is defined on three apexes (taken functionally), banks, firms and households, it is futile to worry about the assignment of the net savings of households: they are *necessarily* lent to the set of firms; let us not forget indeed that, in the circuit, banks are operating only as financial intermediaries. We might call the savings lent within the set of households precautionary-transactional, only net savings of the whole of the household being speculative. Whatever the names, it is vain to search for the destination of the net savings of households; whether they are channelled through all sorts of sellers, of gold, currencies, paintings, lands, buildings, it must always be one of two things: they come back to households or they are lent by their set. Only the second case is interesting since savings left or returned to households are nothing more than a simple differed consumption.

Let us pursue carefully the analysis of the savings of the set of households. The question is difficult, and it is of importance. Savings are captured by firms. It is crucial to note that before this capture, neither *F1* nor *F2* could fear for the clearing of their goods, because the possible deficits are only the effects of the capture (how could it be different, given that savings lent within households are postponed consumptions?).

We see then that firms do not search at all for the savings of households to finance their stocks. The income created and kept within households already fully finances goods in stock: firms would not finance them a second time.

That being said, for what reason do firms participate in the operation of forming households' net savings? It is certain that they do participate, because any savings that would not be captured by firms *would not be the savings of the whole of households*: they would be cancelled within this set. But, let us repeat the haunting question: why have firms an interest in borrowing households' savings?

If this question is imposing itself so forcefully, it is because the incomplete theory of the circuit may obscure it. In this regard, what has been experienced by Professor Poulon may spare researchers a lot of tribulations in the future.

"The agents who seem to have the greatest interest to hold the saved money are the firms competing with the firms indebted to banks" (Poulon 1982: 353). The reasoning is the following. The firm that has succeeded in capturing the savings is holding the others at its mercy; indeed, the captured savings are missing for the clearing of the goods stocked in the other firms that must therefore sell the whole or part of their capital to retrieve the saved sums. We would have here the fundamental reason for the concentration of capital in favour of a smaller and smaller number of firms; "ultimately, firms that will not be able to carry out the necessary recovery will have to sell out their property and will be absorbed by the others, as we have just indicated" (ibid.: 356).

It would not be fair to dispose lightly of this argument because the theory of the circuit raises enormous problems for any researcher. However, let us tirelessly show that the repayment constraint has not at all the meaning that fascinates the author. The fundamental error, but we might also find it in Keynes, consists of the idea, apparently correct and certainly in line with common sense, that savings of the whole of households, that is, savings effectively captured by firms are definitively withdrawn from households' expenditures in the goods market. Nearly all economists think that way. However, a greater allegiance to the stern logic of the circuit leads *to the opposite conclusion: households spend even their net savings in the final purchase of produced goods.*

The savings of the set of households are finally consumed by households

Suppose that *F1* has captured the savings of the set of households, equal to three units of wages. The operation has been concluded in the financial market: *F1* is therefore indebted for this amount. Does it really follow that *F1* is now able to absorb the social capital of *F2* for an amount equal to three units of wages? This is not at all the case because *F1* must first confirm the income that has just been "advanced" by the financial market.

Suppose that *F1* does not obtain, in the sale of its product, the expected amount of profit. In this case, it will need help. For the borrowed or advanced profit to be available on the stock market, it must first be realized in the sale of the firm's future products. We find again a truth that it would be dangerous to leave out of sight for too long: *F1* captures savings in order to invest them. If the investment succeeds, expected profit will be realized; it will be time to think about allocating it to an increase in capital or to the take-over of the capital of a less productive firm. But that is not all.

Even if *F1* succeeds in "parlaying" its investment, the profit that it will get from it must be allocated in the first place to repay households.

Professor Poulon has therefore skipped two stages: advanced profit must be realized, then realized profit must be used to cancel the firm's debt towards households. Those two stages are essential and are also common-sense truths.

All the attention now turns to the investment of captured savings. As soon as *F1* borrows an income equal to three units of wages, it becomes the "owner" of this income; this is so because *F1* has relinquished part of its future income for a part equal to the current income of households (this is indeed an equal part, because interest is not a capital). Acquired at the cost of a future income, current income is a profit advanced on *F1*. We have therefore to examine a new category of expenditures. If households had at their disposition all the created income – and therefore that no income would be transferred to firms – all the expenditures would be pure purchases in the products market (through the intermediation, if need be, of the financial market, as far as inter-household loans are concerned). Advanced profit (or the profit earned during the period on the sale of goods to households, because the two profits are perfectly additive, on condition that neither of them is redistributed to households) is spent in a movement, or an *original* flow, that only quantum analysis enables to grasp.

A simple circuit would be the formation of income in a first movement and the expenditure of income in a second movement, the two opposite flows being never juxtaposed. In reality, one must take profits into account, especially profits advanced by households. The circuit is therefore more complex: the expenditure of wage and non-wage income remains a pure expenditure or a destruction of income; but the expenditure of profit (a captured income) is of a different nature. *F1* invests its profit, which means that it casts it into a new production: it uses profit to feed wages. The simplest way to represent this event is to distinguish the production of the two periods. *F1* captures part of the product (equal to three units of wages) of period *p* under the form of the monetary profit advanced by households. This profit is cast into the production of period *p+*: the expenditure of the profit is included in the payment of wages carried out by *F1* for the production of period *p+*.

The income transferred by households (the dotted arrows) on the product of period *p* is used by the firm in the payment of wages for the product of period *p+*: investment is the utilization of an income of households to pay for a new instalment of wages. The graph above represents two complete circuits, all the wages created by *F1* in the production of the two periods, a sum of 20 units being spent to purchase the product of the two periods.

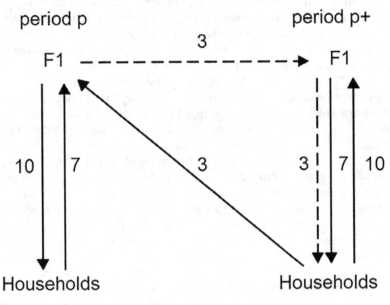

Figure 20.1 The investment of profit by F1

- The product of the two firms for period *p* is first bought for an amount of only 22 units of wages; this is really so since households save the complement, equal to three units of wages.
- However, households get back, in *p+* and in their *new* wages, the savings transferred and spent: they spend those three units of wages to buy the rest of the product of the previous period (*p*).
- It would seem then that the wages created by *F1* in period *p+* are no longer sufficient to clear the product of that period. This is not correct; they are sufficient. Let us not forget that in the product of *p+* we find the investment goods that originated from the expenditure of profit: these goods are not bought by households but by the firm, this is indeed logical.
- One last perplexing thing remains: in what movement exactly are investment goods bought (thus three parts of ten of *FI*'s new product)? In other words, what is the precise movement that completes the closing of the circuit? This is the point on which we must reflect. The answer is quickly given but it is difficult to understand. The dotted arrow that comes down from *F1* (for the production of *p+*) onto households is by definition a final purchase in the product market: the expenditure of profit is the necessary and sufficient condition for the acquisition by *F1* of a product of period *p+*, for an amount of three units of wages.

- Finally, we confirm the perfection of the "complex" circuit: households have bought the total product of *F1* and *F2* for the two periods for an amount of 47 units of wages, and *F1*, that has found (through advances) a profit equal to three units of wages, buys an equivalent product. The sum of final purchases is equal to 50 units of wages, the exact value of total production of the two periods.

We have just established, in a stylized example, that even the definitive savings of households are finally consumed by households. The representation according to which definitive savings are definitively lacking to purchases in the product market is somewhat naïve. The economic circuit is not similar to a hydraulic circuit. The opposite flows intertwine to the extent of the formation-expenditure of undistributed monetary profits (especially profits advanced by households under the form of net and definitive savings of their set). Feeding the payment of wages, invested profit produces new wages, the expenditure of which defines *the final consumption, by households, of the definitive savings of households*.

A more technical problem arises concerning the time-dimension of the circuit. Are not the definitive savings of households consumed in the production of period *p*+ whereas they are formed in the production of period *p*? Would the closing of the circuits then not obey the same law, depending on whether the economy includes or not invested profits? We know already that the truth is more compelling: any circuit, whether it includes or not invested profits, is closed in the instant.

LV. The time of every circuit is the instant

Definition of the time of the circuit

The time dimension of the circuit:

> is the time of the money cycle, that is to say the time that elapses between the instant of its creation and the instant where it is constituted in speculative earnings. This is why it is also defined as the time needed for the constitution of the equality S = I.
>
> (Poulon 1982: 329)

"[W]e take S as the savings of households and I the investment of banks, which is nothing else, as we have indicated, than the money created" (ibid.: 326).

When the question is clearly solved, scholars will know that every circuit of money is completed in the instant. However, some time (of which we might only give a probabilistic assessment) is needed before this fundamental truth is recognized.

The time of the circuit seems positive because the analysis overlooks the nullity of any money motion in society

The author remains attached to the idea, very common of course, that money units move through a space. It is certain however that the notion of a monetary circuit implies a non-material money. If money were material, it would be moving through a space, a movement that might be circular (the space being closed), but that might not necessarily be so. Given that money is immaterial – it has always been, from the beginning of humanity, "material" money being only the physical support of money – it is "moving" by quantum leaps, absolute exchanges: it leaps instantly from the "payer" to the "payee"; more exactly, it is created in that leap: it does not therefore even move instantly; it does not move *at all* (in a pre-determined space).

Once a theorist wonders about the time taken by the journey of a money unit, between the moment it "goes out" of the bank and the moment it "comes back" there, he remains, like it or not, inside the neo-classical paradigm of relative exchanges. All the mistakes step into the breach and we meet again all those futile distinctions between short term and long term, statics and dynamics, and even distributed lags.

Let us quote only one model-text. The time of the circuit is:

> fundamental: it gives an objective definition of the period of analysis for economic dynamics. In parallel, it provides a definition of the short term and of the long term: any analysis within the time of the circuit is a short term analysis; any analysis beyond the time of the circuit is a long term analysis. Entrepreneurs' expectations are assumed to be established at the beginning of each time of the circuit, valid for the whole duration of the time of the circuit, and revised at the end of the time of the circuit"
>
> (Poulon 1982: 329)

This is no longer the analysis of the circuits but Hicks "week"!

No writer will ever succeed in defining the circuit's time-dimension in the *length of time*, because the economy does not comprise even one unit of money that we might track from its creation to its destruction. Poulon betrays himself incidentally by the very words he uses: he thus talks of the first return of a money unit to its source (the time that elapses "until the first return" (ibid.: 329)).

How could money destroyed in a first return ever return again? We see clearly that the thought hesitates between circuit, creation-destruction of money and circulation, like in quantitative theory, a unit of money being able to carry out an indefinite number of "laps" within the economy (by the way, Poulon does not refrain from speaking of a "velocity of money" (ibid.: 336)). In the sketch of the circuit presented by the author, we find however I as a flow of creation and S, the symmetrical flow: if I "opens" the circuit and S "closes" it, it is undeniable that, I being a creation, S is a destruction. It is therefore obvious that each unit of money is used only once.

The circuit of money is distinct from the circuits known (at the present time) to physics, because even an electric circuit, for instance, "consumes" time. Let us start from the emission of wages of period p. If the time of the circuit were of a positive duration, savings resulting from the creation of new income would be firstly zero: a certain time would have to elapse before households might save all or part of their new income. But how could the logic of this argument be maintained? Precisely, is saving not waiting? If income is earned at instant t and spent at a later instant t', is it not saved during the whole interval, therefore since instant t? At the very instant when income is created, it is (entirely) saved: this induction is necessary, because any income that is not consumed is saved and households could not logically spend their income (even partially) in the operation of the creation of income. The instantaneous saving of newly-formed income defines the instantaneous closing of the circuit.

Matters get somewhat complicated in a reflexion that is nevertheless obvious: how could the circuit be closed at the instant of income's creation since households still have it at their disposal and they can cast it at any moment into the goods market? The answer is a tautology: the expenditure of income is a circuit, a completely new circuit. And is that really surprising? The creation of income is a complete circuit; the consumption of income is another. It is evident that the two circuits are linked, but they are so only by their object, the same income being created by one and destroyed by the other. The representation of the circuit of the destruction of income reproduces the representation of the first circuit, in the permutation of the two poles, firms and households.

We can conclude by re-examining the stylised case of two firms, 1 and 2. Production of period p is brought on by a complete circuit, the creation of 25 units of wages by the two firms. The creation of income does not require any explanation; its destruction is first given in the formation of households' savings, which are indubitably equal to 25 units of wages when measured at the precise instant of the formation of income. The formation of savings is logically a destruction of income: current income is destroyed, and it is replaced by a future income. Then households "actualize" their income in the operation of withdrawal of savings. We have assumed that households' consumption is firstly equal to 22 units of wages to purchase the product of p. Those acts of consumptions are circuits, only one circuit if they are simultaneous, and as many distinct circuits as there are distinct acts of consumption. (The "circuits of production" follow incidentally the same rule of division.)

But what about households' definitive savings, that is, the savings of the set of income holders? By assumption, they are taken from the income created in the production of period p. It is certain that these three units of wages are first lacking for clearing the product of p. But the conclusion is not yet reached. Right from the production of $p+$, captured savings are invested; they are cast into the new wage payments: initially taken from income, the new income comprises the savings. Savings of period p are a part of the product of period $p+$. The circuit now closes on the product of p: transformed into new income, invested savings are spent for the purchase of the products of p still available. Let us sum up the total flow of savings: formed on the product of p, they are transformed into a product of $p+$ and are finally carried onto the product of p. However, is not this whole movement taking some time? The answer would be positive if the creation-destruction of savings were defined over two distinct periods. It does seem that this is the case since $p+$ is distinct from p. However, we have not yet taken into account one key fact: the investment of savings, meaning their expenditure in the production of $p+$, is a final purchase in the producing services market: firm 1 that invests borrowed savings, buys the product of $p+$, up to three units of wages. We observe thus that firm 1 transforms the stocked wage-goods, first form of fixed capital, into instrumental capital, the investment-goods produced in $p+$ and that are the definitive form of fixed capital.

The only proposition that is formally adequate to the situation is therefore the following: savings from the product of p, equal to three units of wages, define right from the origin (therefore right from the formation of savings) the constitution of fixed capital, under the form of stocked wage-goods: that is to say, savings are immediately invested.

Formed on the product of period p, savings are destroyed on the product of the same period (p). Consequently, the circuits are closed *instantaneously*. The circuit of p is closed by consumption (equal to 22 units of wages) and by savings (equal to three units of wages); the circuit of $p+$ is closed by investment (equal to three units of wages) and by consumption (equal to 22 units of wages).

It is only on the day when the circuit theory is taken seriously that political economy will at last be able to propose a "regulation" of the economy to politicians. All the "disequilibria" come from empty emissions, false emissions. The reform of bank accounting will enforce the true regulation: the introduction of the three departments.

Crises (in particular clearing crises) are not experimental signs of circuits' imperfection; in any economy, even in "disequilibrium", creations and destructions of income are rigorously equal movements: the pathology resides in the empty emissions, that are also perfect circuits.

Crisis and circuit are compatible

Frédéric Poulon quotes (without adopting it) the common error: "in the circuit theory, the notion of crisis is unthinkable" (Poulon 1982: 340). This is the opposite to the truth: without the notion of circuit, no economic magnitude is thinkable. We have demonstrated it in the critical analysis of the association of pure numbers to physical goods: this association only succeeds in absolute exchanges; and any absolute exchange is a circuit, *a perfect circuit*, completed in the instant.

As long as the opponents to neo-classicism are not thinking rigorously in terms of circuit, they will spend their power in vain because, in the whole history of our science, there are only three stages: the first theory of absolute exchanges, the theory of relative exchanges and, inaugurated by Keynes, the new theory of absolute exchanges (the circuits).

It is therefore a great contradiction and a great weakness to avail oneself of a theory of "ideal" circuits that would never exist in their perfection within concrete economies. Many too conciliatory minds are thus tempering the incidence of Say's law: if it were verified, how could a national economy experience inflation and unemployment?

However, we shall never insist enough: unemployment and inflation are applications and not refutations of the economic circuit, which is an absolute truth, *without any exception*. It would be a beautiful law indeed to which even one exception may be found!

Let us slay the heresy one last time.

> Marx had noted that money, in separating the purchase and the sale of commodities for the same trader, contained already in itself the possibility of a crisis. He meant that the crisis would erupt, in the capitalist system, as soon as the sale, normally consecutive to the purchase of goods by the capitalist, would be lacking. The sale, in bringing back value to its starting point, the money form, cancels, so to speak, the initial purchase and, with it, the threat of a crisis. In the Keynesian circuit, we find again this idea but in a more general form. The absence of crisis is linked to a certain condition of cancellation of money, from which a condition of crisis or of no crisis might be expressed.
>
> (Poulon 1982: 341)

One must admit that here the mind is really showing too much flexibility: the circuit does close, or else it would not exist, but it closes in a condition of crisis or of no crisis; that depends on the circumstances. But if the economy experiences a crisis in order for the circuit to close, it might be better if it were not to close. Marx remarks are not all brilliant. The dissociation over time of the two sides of the sale transaction is proposed as well by Arrow, as we have seen. A rigorous thought requires to accept the strict simultaneity of the two "half-transactions". Thus, the idea of crisis introduced (or made possible) by credit is really a superficial one.

The functioning of the economy would be perfectly in order if every money emission was creating real money. In the mode of production still current, two (perfect) circuits co-exist.

1   The circuit of real money is defined by the creation-destruction of wages and, within this movement, by the destruction-creation (because the order is inverted) of all the other incomes: interests, dividends, rents.
2   The circuit of nominal monies is the creation-destruction of profits in the strict sense, income of non-persons, firms in their state as adulterated by the capitalist regime.

The two circuits answer absolutely the same description: each created income is destroyed in the same movement.

However, the circuit of purely nominal money creates income that belongs or does not belong to national income:

- real profits belong to national income because, like all the other goods, they are created by workers;
- monetary profits do not belong to national income since they immediately lose their "product-substance", in favour of over-accumulation.

When one understands well that the circuits of purely nominal money are the aetiology of the great disequilibria, inflation and unemployment, one can no longer hesitate: the government must be advised to reform the functioning of the banking system so that all empty emissions will be "filtered" and eliminated from the outset.

Full emissions are indeed a norm, but a *logical norm*; the elimination of empty emissions will create an "optimum" as positive as the Pareto optimum. The true obstacle that remains is not the persistence of the neo-classical school but the analytical difficulty that faces any scientist whatever his persuasion. Reform will only be achieved by intellect.

Synopsis

of quantum macroeconomics

21 Production and time

The two definitions are not easy to grasp.

Time

Continuous time or the continuum

In classical or Newtonian physics, time is considered like the continuum, any finite lapse of time being infinitely divisible. As far as it involves time, economic analysis is founded on the continuum, that is, in mathematical language, on a time equated to the set of real numbers.

In economics, there is no reason to question this conception of time. The time of economic events is nothing more than the continuum.

However, the continuum is only the foundation of economic events. Indeed, production is not passively set in continuous time. In order to grasp production and, from it, the other transactions, the continuum has to be "deformed". However, continuous time may be transformed into two other types of time, discontinuous time, already known to science, and quantum time, much more intriguing.

Discontinuous time

We start from the continuum and we divide it in periods called "discrete", in general equal to one another. At first sight, one may wonder where the analytical progress is. It is positive at two levels. First, actions may happen in a well-defined part of the continuum, for example within the calendar month. Repeated actions of the same type happen month after month, within each discrete period. The analysis by discontinuous time is useful at a second level, a much deeper one. It is conceivable that an action, like production, might have to be started at an instant t_n and impossible to complete immediately; even more, one understands easily that the action may only be completed at an instant t which, in the continuum, is at a *finite* distance of t_n. In that case, the operation extends from t_n to t while being constantly nil within that interval: it only becomes suddenly positive at its completion at instant t. We see that the interval of time (t_n, t) is not simply a duration taken from the continuum, because the action defined in that interval is nil at each instant, since t_n till t, the only instant when it becomes suddenly positive. Prepared since t_n but continuously nil, production is all at once positive at instant t; it appears in time as a discontinuity: it is said to be situated in discontinuous time.

We see well that the second transformation of continuous time into discontinuous time is much more profound that the first one. If the continuum is simply cut into "slices", it remains that actions are set into it continuously, in each interval. Everything is different when the action is not first set in the continuum but needs on the contrary a time of preparation before completion: in the preparatory phase, the action is nil, in the continuum, where it appears all at once, instantly, at the moment it is completed.

However, the discontinuity of time may be grasped at a third level, an even more radical one. One has then to talk about quantum time, about finite and indivisible intervals of time.

Quantum time

Let us go back shortly to the preceding case, the action having initially no extent in the continuum: nil from the first instant of its preparation, t_n, it becomes positive only at instant t. The action appears suddenly into continuous time, *then it maintains itself there* for a more or less long time. Before t, the action is still nil; it becomes positive; then it maintains itself until a later date. If the transaction had simply unfolded over time, it would have been positive since t_n; by contrast, it develops over discontinuous time if, started at instant t_n, it becomes positive at instant t, from which instant we can observe its existence over continuous time.

We see easily that a new step has to be taken if the operation, which started at instant t_n and became positive at instant t only, is nil at any instant posterior to t. The transformation of the continuum into discontinuous time enables the actions that become all at once positive at the instant of their completion to be grasped. But the continuum must be submitted to a far more fundamental transformation once the analysis detects the existence of actions that are positive only at the instant of their completion. An action of this type cannot be set into continuous time: not only does it appear there only after its preparatory phase has elapsed, but, more importantly, it disappears at the exact instant when it becomes positive. Simply transformed in discontinuous time, the continuum is therefore unable to "receive" or "track back" any action that, prepared since instant t_n and having become positive at instant t, is again nil at any posterior instant. An action of this type can only be grasped through a more radical transformation; the continuum is transformed into quantum time: it is "quantized".

Production is an action like the one we have just described; the analysis, even quickly carried out, demonstrates it. Any (economic) production becomes positive after a time of preparation and is a positive action at the instant of its achievement; it is nil before *and after*.

Production

Since the beginning of our science, every theory has recognized that human labour (we shall simply call it labour) is productive. The doubt only concerns the existence of other "factors of production"; thus, can land (or natural resources) and capital carry out a productive action? The analysis of the relation time-production may build upon an initial certainty: labour is indubitably productive. We soon discover that labour is set neither in continuous time nor in discontinuous time; *labour quantises the continuum*. We shall induce the exact definition of the product: it is quantised time or, identically, an indivisible lump taken from the continuum. However, only labour is able to quantize time; land and capital are the environment and the instruments of production.

Any labour is a quantum of action

Let us assume that a basket-maker works only with his hands, from the wicker crop to the completion of the basket. He starts his work at instant t_n and completes it at instant t, for example an hour later. Is the preparation of the basket a continuous action from t_n till t? Before answering, we may conceive of "elementary gestures", each movement of the hands, the succession of which leads to the result aimed at. Each gesture is an indivisible whole, the "quantum of action". It is therefore certain that the preparation of the basket is not a continuous action in time. On the contrary, the complete action is divisible into a finite number of indivisible actions, the quanta of actions. However, the analysis may be greatly simplified by considering the addition of the quanta as a unique action, the production of the basket. It is clear then that the production of the whole basket is the quantum of action; this is to say it is an indivisible whole, *in one single movement*, in a "quantum leap".

The action being global, therefore indivisible, or, that which does not change anything, the action being the addition of indivisible gestures, one can induce that if the production of the basket were set into even a very small part of the continuum, it would be divisible (and even indefinitely so) since the continuum is thus in each of its finite parts. A precious teaching is drawn from this: production is an *instantaneous* action. However, production has also a positive extent in time.

Production is both instantaneous and nevertheless extended in the continuum

It is flagrantly obvious that we have just formulated a contradiction. However, reflexion establishes the two opposite propositions: any production is instantaneous, and any positive production is an action that has a positive dimension in time (or in the continuum). Reality imposes the double nature of production; thus, the contradiction is only apparent: production is instantaneous, but it quantises (in an instant) a finite duration.

Production is an instantaneous action. We know it already since any act of production is a quantum of action. Let us repeat the demonstration. Each elementary gesture leading to the finite basket is an indivisible whole; it follows that each elementary gesture is instantaneous; if it were not, it would tautologically have an extent in the continuum, and it would itself be divisible. In the sum of the quanta of actions we find a finite number of elementary actions; since each quantum is instantaneous, the sum of the quanta is also an instantaneous action.

Production is a positive action only if it has a positive extent in the continuum. This is almost obvious. Suppose that our basket-maker devotes only a zero amount of time to each of his gestures: his time is then "free", and the basket remains completely unformed. Appearing at instant t, the product is the result of a labour started at the earlier instant t_n, the duration (t_n, t) being for example one hour. If the amount of time of applied labour were reduced, the basket would remain incomplete; finally, if the amount of labour time were annulled, the basket would not even have been started. All this is pure truism. The difficulty is not understanding that labour is an action extended over time. Even if this is more profound, we understand that labour is a quantum of action. The true difficulty is in the conciliation of the two natures of production: even though it is a quantum of action, production is set in duration. How can *the same action be both instantaneous and extended over time*? There is a solution, only one: production is an action that quantises the continuum.

Production quantises the continuum. Let us represent the time axis. We put there instant t_n and, at a finite (measurable) distance, later instant t. The production of the basket is linked to the duration; what is the nature of the link? It is worth proceeding by elimination. Production is set neither in continuous time nor in discontinuous time.

1   *The production of the basket is not set into continuous time.* Even though the labour of the basket-maker is carried on from t_n to t, it would be illogical to conclude that it extends over the period (t_n, t) of the continuum: if it were, it would not be a quantum of action (nor the sum of quanta of actions). However, to deny that production is a quantum of action leads immediately to a mathematical absurdity. Indeed, if production were continuous in the time interval (t_n, t), it would be infinite in that complete duration, unless infinitely close to zero in its infinitesimal parts; and if production were nil at each instant (or an interval of a zero duration) of (t_n, t), it would be nil in that complete duration. Briefly, if productions were not quanta of actions, they would be either nil or infinitely large in each positive fraction of continuous time: every day, the product of each worker would be nil or infinite. Common sense and reality are, on

the contrary, complied with as soon as production is conceived of as a quantum of action; thus the production of the basket is an indivisible action in the time interval (t_n, t): this is the reason why production is a positive and finite action in that duration.

2   *The production of the basket is not set in discontinuous time.* The argument is already well prepared because we know the exact definition of the discontinuous time of production. Started at instant t_n and becoming suddenly positive at instant t, the production of the basket would then be maintained in the continuum, where it could be observed after t. Production being measured on the vertical axis and the continuous passage of time being on the horizontal axis, production in function of continuous time is represented by a curve, the first point of which would be known at instant t (the production being nil prior to that) and the other points of which would correspond to the instants posterior to t. In reality, the production of the basket does not answer that description. Let us distinguish the instants preceding t (t_i) and the instant posterior to t (t_j); the analysis by discontinuous time states that the production is positively defined at the instants t_j (until such a future date, where the curve would meet the time axis); in fact, however, the production of the basket, positive at instant t, is nil both *at instants t_i and at instants t_j*. We express the nullity of the production at any instant posterior to t by saying that production is an action the inertia of which, through time, or in the continuum, is nil. Production could only be set in the continuum in a discontinuous way if the production carried out at instant t were subsequently maintained through inertia over time. The production of the basket, although completed at instant t, would have to be prolonged for a certain measurable time. Since it is tautological to say that production stops at the instant when the product is completed, production is finally positive neither at instants t_i nor at instants t_j: it is positive only at the sole instant t, strictly. The representative "curve" is therefore limited to one unique point, defined at instant t.

3   *The production of the basket quantises the continuum.* Here it is worth making a very simple mental experiment. Time is again given on the horizontal axis. If the production of the basket were a flow in the continuum, its representative curve would start from instant t_n; on the other hand, if the flow of production were given in a leap or a "discontinuity", it would be represented by a curve starting from t; since production is a quantum of action or a "quantum flow", the curve that represents it is a unique point; *however, it remains that production is a flow in time: it is not simply defined at instant t but at all the instants (combined into one same whole) of the duration (t_n, t).* It suffices then to make an effort of imagination to find the concrete solution; first nil from t_n to t, production becomes positive at instant t: at that instant, *production refers to the whole period, the indivisible duration (t_n, t).* This means that production is not a flow that follows the direction of time (from t_n or t depending on

the analysis, continuous or discontinuous) but, on the contrary, a flow *defined in a loop*, from t to t_n and simultaneously from t_n to t. This is the exact definition of production, as a quantum of action; it quantises the duration (t_n, t) because, instead of being a flow in a single direction (which would imply an absurdity, namely that a given production is infinite in a finite duration), it is a flux-reflux. Production is an action that flows back instantly to instant t_n where it was started, to go back to instant t when it is positively completed.

One last reflexion should be convincing. It is accepted that production is a flow in time: however, if it were simply a flow in continuous time, production would have a positive and finite depth in time; it would therefore be positive and finite at each instant of its flow in time, like the instantaneous velocity of a moving body; we would necessarily deduce that the product is positive at each instant of the flow-production, that is to say at an *infinity* of instants. The production of any finite period would indeed be infinite. Like the product of a finite period is in reality a finite magnitude, production is a flow that is neither continuous nor discontinuous in time; it is a flux-reflux or a *wave*, a "back and forth" movement: *the production of the basket is the wave that travels instantaneously through (continuous) time from t to t_n and from t_n to t.* The reasoning thus obeys the two constraints at the same time: *production is a flow in time; it is nevertheless a perfectly instantaneous action.*

Production is a flow in time precisely because its inertia in the continuum is nil: no production is efficient after the instant of its completion: but every completed action is efficient from the instant it was started. It follows that the product is simply a quantum of time, the "period of production" being, at the end of the quantum of action, instantly covered by the production flow. The wave-like nature of production being thus known, the problem of the duration of the product itself may be solved.

Production is wave-like; the product's duration is thus reduced to an instant

At first sight, it is not certain that the product has only an instantaneous existence; it is indeed true that production is an instantaneous action, but the result of this action might be conceived of as having an existence extending over time. However, on reflexion, it appears that the wave-like nature of production has the logical consequence of strictly limiting the duration of the product's existence: it comes about at the instant of the completion of production and it disappears *at the same instant*. Thus, the basket is a product only at instant t. We must indeed comply with the distinction already known to the Classics: the basket, *value in use*, has a life expectancy that may be of several years, but the basket, *value of exchange* or product in the exact sense, is defined by the time quantum (t, t_n) and simultaneously by the *opposite* quantum (t_n, t). *Production is a wave in that it is defined by the instantaneous creation-destruction of the product.*

It is clear that, being a quantum of time, the product is not a piece of matter. However, the result of production does have a close link with matter. In this regard, one might speak of the corpuscular nature of production and product.

Production is corpuscular.
The product is a matter cast into the utility-form

The wave-production or the flow of production results in a quantum of time. Production on the contrary is corpuscular in that the product is a matter defined at the contact of its "utility-form". Let us briefly explain. Let us first formulate a truism. The basket is material and any matter involved in making the basket is purely and simply preserved; nothing is created and nothing is lost in the process. Suppose the basket is only made of wicker. It is clear that the production of the basket does not create nor destroy even one atom of matter. However, the wicker is more useful to human beings under the form of a basket than if it were still attached to the trunk of the tree. The basket would first exist in the imagination of its producer as the *utility-form* of the wicker. One may thus formulate a law: *to produce means to cast matter (or energy) into a pre-conceived utility-form.*

This new definition of production grasps it in its second aspect, the corpuscular one, and it enables the essential conclusions that we have been able to induce from the wave-like nature of production to be found.

1   Started at instant t_n, production is nil until instant t because the basket is a useful matter (or *more* useful) only at instant t when it is completed.
2   Even though production is only positive at instant t, once it is completed, it does come to life at instant t_n of the first gesture or quantum of elementary action accomplished by the basket-maker.
3   The product exists only at instant t; the following instant, the matter is already out of the utility-form: the wicker takes at last the basket-form at instant t, then it is matter out of this "mould" and offered to the world of use values.

Production and consumption form a unity; the two opposite actions are simultaneous

In the common representation, consumption is an operation posterior to production. However, one must immediately remark that in its loose meaning, production is an action ill-defined and even a mysterious one. It would be, it is said, a costly creation. Thus, economic activity would be creative. Science cannot stop at this judgement. How, outside imagination (thought and art), could man be creative? It is more satisfactory to comply with the law of Lavoisier: production-creation is rigorously nil; similarly, consumption-destruction is rigorously nil. So, is economics caught out when it tries to analyse production and consumption? That would be all the more serious as those concepts are crucial. We know now that in reality production is a positive action, because it is instantaneously coupled with the opposite action, consumption. The logical couple production-consumption is simultaneously given from the two sides at once, by the wave-like aspect and by the corpuscular aspect of the action. Being *wave-like*, production quantises two opposite times, from t to t_n and from t_n to t: it is simultaneously positive and negative. Being *corpuscular*, production that is being completed (the only positive production) casts matter into a utility-form at instant t, *and takes it out at once*: again, it appears clearly that the action is simultaneously negative. Thus, analysis remains confined to the domain of science; it does not venture into theology. Production is constantly nil and so is consumption; those two actions, taken separately, are nevertheless not nil, because they are given in one same whole: any *positive* production defines immediately an equal *positive* consumption. The object of economic analysis is not production followed by consumption, but one single reality with two sides, production-consumption.

The discovery of the logical conjunction of the two opposite actions casts also a bright light on the two great periods of development of our science.

The two aspects of production involve the two fundamental teachings of the Classics and the Neo-Classics

For the Classics, production is identified as human labour; for the Neo-Classics, production is the creation of utility. But the two teachings are true in their synthesis: labour introduces matter into the utility-form. The measure of the product, the law of which was identified neither by the theorists of labour-value nor on the basis of the utility of goods, results from the union of the two "factors". The product is injected by labour into negative money, the utility-form under the appearance of the *numéraire*: the (pure) number of money units constituting the enveloping of goods thus gives the measure of products.

Before examining the integration of the product into money, let us offer the solution to the problem that we had mentioned, that of the identity of the productive actions: only human labour defines production in its two aspects, wave-like and corpuscular. The activity of machines and land could not introduce the least amount of matter into the utility-form; indeed, this form is a *conception*, a *projection*, and it is first *imaginary*. Only man is able to imagine; production-consumption is not an action coming under classical mechanics like the motion of a clock; it is a far nobler activity. If we desperately wanted to assimilate production to a mechanism, we would have to speak about *quantum* mechanics: to produce is to give a new form to matter, so that it lends itself better to satisfying the biological, social, cultural, artistic and even, sometimes, artificial ("gadgets") needs of man.

The unity of money and product results from an operation whose name is known by everyone, expenditure.

22 Production and expenditures

Money is "infiltrated" in the very act of real production and not between products.

Any monetary expenditure is a real half-expenditure

What is an expenditure?

The word expenditure is one of the most common but its meaning is not at all known by "the man in the street". The economic expenditure that founds all the others is *real*: it is human labour. Let us go directly to the conclusion. Expenditure is an operation with two facets: positive and negative. Any labour in activity is a real expenditure, production-consumption of the utility-form of matter. Monetary expenditures obey the same definition. Any monetary expenditure is the creation-destruction of a sum of money. One must then move away from usual representations; to spend 1 franc means neither to destroy nor, of course, to create 1 franc; the operation is complex, because it includes both opposite actions: any expenditure of one franc is simultaneously the creation and destruction of one franc.

But how can we demonstrate it? We must demonstrate that monetary expenditures identify with real expenditures, that is to say, to production-consumption. The proof is given in a very simple experience. We must determine if the worker receives a sum of money in exchange for his product or, on the contrary, for his labour. In other words, in the wage-regime, does the product come to life first in the possessions of workers? It is certain that this is not the case: the product is first formed in firms and it reaches wage-earners (and also other income holders) only by the expenditure of the sums of money earned, that is "income". We thus see that money is present within production: it acts inside the real action (the flow of production) and not on the results of the action, when it is already finished. It is most often believed that money is an intermediary good between the products sold and the products bought. In that sense, it is said that money breaks barter. However, money is already present when products come to life. The creation of money and production of goods are one and the same action. Let us sum up again the two theses.

- If money had the objective and the effect of transforming the exchange between two products into a (separate) sale and purchase, (workers') production would always be strictly real. The world is then represented in a "dichotomy": workers produce real goods and banks create money.
- Money being present in the flow of production and not simply as a good interposed between the results of real flows, it appears that monetary flows are substituted to real flows; in nominal emissions, workers produce the real goods under their monetary form: literally, they first produce money. Money is not created by banks, because it is not just present in the result of the payment; it is already present in the payment itself.

Money does not break barter but production, that is the action: it has the effect of separating the two opposite aspects of the act of production. In the absence of money, production is immediately a consumption; money being introduced in the real flow, it operates the splitting up of production-consumption into a net production and a net consumption.

Net production

It is obtained by the payment of (monetary) wages.

The isolated worker pays himself; he obtains immediately his product in kind. The result is that his product is consumed as soon as it is formed. The product appears in the meeting of matter and of the utility-form; it is consumed when it is withdrawn from this form; however, the two events are simultaneous: at no moment is the utility-form attached to matter.

Everything is different in the wage-regime, in the strict sense. Workers receive their product in money. We induce that, defined in the payment of wages, production is *net*: it is a production and not a production-consumption. Indeed, wages can only be consumed in a second expenditure. It is logically impossible that money should reach the worker in the very action that withdraws it from him. This time, the two opposite acts (formation and consumption of wages) cannot merge in a single flow. The production of wages is net, because the consumption of wages is not given in their formation.

It tautologically follows that the expenditure of wages is net too.

Net consumption

It is defined by the expenditure of wages.

Let us repeat it; if money did not exist, every product would be consumed at the precise instant of its completion; language does not make any mistake about it: a completed product is consumed.

However, being present in real production, in the payment flow of wages, money renders the utility-form "tangible". Matter is cast into monetary wages instead of taking directly the shape of the real utility-form. In other words, the money-form is the first, temporary, state of the utility-form. As long as matter resides into the (monetary) utility-form, consumption is *differed*. Consumption only becomes effective at the instant the matter (goods and services) is withdrawn from the money-form; this withdrawal is operated *in the expenditure or consumption of wages*. The expenditure of wages has two instantaneous (therefore simultaneous) effects. The money-form of matter is destroyed, but the utility-form is so as well (utility is no longer a form but a "substance", a value in use, that is, a psychological magnitude) as it would have been right from production if money had not been interposed to give it a temporary shelter.

The (temporary) substitution of the money-form to the utility-form brings on the principle and the unity of measures to the economy and to economics.

23 Measurement in the economy and in economics

We understand well today why it has not been possible to solve the problem of measurement in classical and neo-classical theories.

The measure of the product according to the classics

By focusing on labour, the Classics had nearly reached the objective. Working time is not incorporated into the product, but labour quantizes time (the wave-like aspect of production) and gives a "body" to the product, by putting matter into contact with the utility-form.

Labour is not incorporated into the product

The two following propositions are close to each other.

a   Production is the operation that introduces working time into matter.
b   To produce is to work and working is the operation that creates the time quanta.

However, the first proposition leads science to a dead end. Deemed present in manufactured matter, working time is not measurable. By measuring the time during which a work is carried out, it is time that is measured and not labour: the measure is physical, not economic. The classical measure supposes the existence of a labour unit, whereas in reality the analysis only has the unit of time at its disposal.

Is not proposition b leading to the same failure? It seems that it is.

Labour quantizes time (the time of production)

The quantum of time is a purely physical measure. Let us suppose for example that two identical baskets are produced one in an hour of work and the other, more skilfully, in only half an hour. The two products are different time quanta. However, nothing enables us to say that the first basket has an economic measure twice as large as the second one.

Thus, analysis has undoubtedly made progress since the Classics; indeed, working time is now a discarded concept: since it quantizes time, labour is not present in the product that is a pure quantized time and not a working time.

However, does not the measure of the product stay physical? It is so even more openly. Quantized time is a *physical* measure only.

In conclusion, matter is not at all measurable as a product of labour even if it remains established that only labour transforms matter into a product.

Even though, in all appearances, it reproduces purely and simply the problem of measurement, proposition *b* brings the fundamental condition of its solution.

In the presence of money, the quantization of time takes the form of the quantization of the numéraire

Being a quantum of time, the product is transformed into a quantum of *numéraire*; this transformation results directly from the introduction of money into the real flow of production. And, as soon as the product is taken as a *numeraire* quantum, it is *ipso facto* measured. We thus find confirmation of Keynes's great intuition: wage-units are the measure of products. As soon as money is introduced through the payment of nominal wages, labour quantizes the *numeraire*-money, the time quantum being only a constant factor of proportionality. If the payment of wages is done monthly, the quantum of elementary time is the month, that is assimilated to the indivisible number 1. Hence, wages of the month are equal to the flow of production multiplied by the time applied, a month, number 1 in the set of integers.

$$Production \cdot time\ applied$$

$$= production\ of\ the\ month$$

$$= product\ of\ the\ month$$

We thus see that the product, equal to the integral of the production of the month, is defined by the "constant" production (it is so since it is unique, a one-off, in the month) and not by this constant multiplied by time assimilated to the set of real numbers. Production is multiplied by time assimilated to the set of integers; a month being the elementary quantum, production is simply multiplied by integer 1.

In the end, the measure of the product is indeed the one that the Classics were looking for; labour quantizes the *numéraire*-money; thus, the product is the result of labour only. Even more, the measure of the product is given by labour, that is, by its result, the quantized *numéraire*-money, in other words wages issued during the period.

But what is the contribution of the Neo-Classics?

The measure of the product according to the Neo-Classics

It is quite remarkable that the new analysis confirms the neo-classical theory as much as the classical theory. It is also true that we initially encounter a failure.

The measure of the product through its utility

The explanation is made up of two links, the measure of the product by utility and the measure of utility itself. The first link does not create any difficulty, even though it has apparently the status of a postulate; but the second link defines a new impasse: utility is not a physical magnitude and psychological magnitudes are not measurable.

Today the problem is solved in full conformity with the intuition of the Neo-Classics. The product is measured by its utility. The solution comes from the fact that the measure of utility is radically transformed: it is no longer psychological by purely *numerical*.

Utility only measures through the utility-envelope; but this envelope has to be in money

The Classics take production in its wave-like aspect, that is, labour. The Neo-Classics conceive of production under its corpuscular aspect. But both aspects are equally "true" and "correct". And the completed analysis reaches the same result on both sides, wave and body. As soon as the flow of wages is substituted to the flow of real production, the money-form is identified by substitution to the utility-form: issued wages are the *utility-form* of the new product. However, nominal wages are "graded" in dimension-less numbers. Unlike the real utility-form of matter, which is not measurable (because if it were, it would be so in, undefinable, psychological units), the money-form of matter, that is to say its nominal utility-form, is a numerical quantum. The measure of the utility-envelop is thus purely numerical: the measure of the product is therefore a number too.

The solution to the mystery of measurement in economics

Léon Walras wrote to the great mathematician Henri Poincaré to explain that measurement is not of the same nature in economics and in physics. A kilogram is the measure of a mass, of a dimension; the franc (identified to the *numéraire*) is the measure of a product and not the relation of a number of francs – francs being concrete numbers like the beads of an abacus – with a matter (a "physical quantity"). The great mistake is to seek into economic measures what defines physical measures, the relation between a number and a dimension; in economics, a measure is the relation between a number and a good or a service; goods and services are doubtless a mass or an energy but they are devoid of any *economic* mass. The economic measure is a number referred to a "non-dimension" or, as we say nowadays, a number without dimension.

Should we conclude that economics deviates from the mathematical definition of measure? That would be very surprising, logic being the same in all sciences. Precisely, it is fully complied with even by non-dimensional measures. Walras could not convince Poincaré because of an essential stage missing in the argument that could not yet be conceived in the days of Walras. *Numéraire* and product belong to two distinct sets: numbers are not goods and goods are not numbers. Relations of equivalence could therefore not be established between *numéraire* and product. Under those conditions, measuring is impossible in economics unless one might succeed, against all odds, in discovering a specific economic mass, in which case the measure would be dimensional in economics like in physics. *A priori*, two directions are open to the researcher: to discover the economic mass (like the philosopher's stone) or to demonstrate the existence of relations of equivalence between *numéraire* and product. The second direction is the right one, because it is demonstrated by induction, the analytical observation of facts. Cast into wages, the *numéraire*-money is introduced into the real flow of production that it splits into two henceforth distinct movements, production and consumption. It follows, let us repeat it, that the result of the real flow is net at first: *the economy produces without consuming.* Later, it will consume without producing in the same act. However, what is then the net result of production? We know it well, it is a quantum of money. Thus, the mathematical definition of the measure is fully satisfied, even though economic measures are relations between numbers and products; the payment of wages is a monetary flow substituted to the real flow; it follows that the product is a sum of money substituted to goods: monetary wages are the *definition* of the *real* product. It is thus exact to say – this is required by logic – that the economy produces firstly a sum of money the body of which is constituted by goods and services, and it does not produce directly goods and services under their material form. The mathematician finds here the satisfaction of his requirement; monetary wages are not the measure (complete or partial) of the product that would be foreign to them: not only wages *are* the product but, moreover, *no product would exist in time, therefore would not exist in the eyes of the scientist, if products came to life directly real, outside money.* As soon as wages are measured, the product is so as well since wages are the definition of the product. Finally, the *number* of units of wages issued is the *measure* of the product of the economy. The substitution of the monetary flow (the emission of wages) to the real flow (production of goods and services) creates the relation of equivalence required for the constitution of the measure. Then, the equivalence being established, it suffices to measure money in order to measure the product: *however the measure of money is a simple enumeration because numbers are counted.* If Poincaré had known that the material product is deposited into money as in its form, he would have accepted Walras thesis: in economics, measures are carried out through *accountancy* since in counting the money issued (in wages), the domestic product, the *body* of the money issued, is counted at the same time.

The problem of measurement in economics cannot be solved if money is set apart from the process of production. Thus, even if the theory tries to integrate money into exchanges on the goods market, it is too late: goods have already been produced and, by assumption, their production has not involved money. Monetary economies function in an entirely different way, money being present within the flow of production, in the very movement that engenders the product: instead of producing real goods directly under their physical form, the economy produces real goods in the monetary form.

It is undoubtedly easier to conceive of mutations or exchanges at the level of results, between products, good *a* being changed or exchanged. However, in reality, dialectics between what is "nominal" and what is "real" is much deeper: it is situated at the very source of goods, at the level of production. The action of production is monetary or nominal precisely in that the interposition of numbers (money of account) splits the operation into two opposite half-transactions: the substitution of net products to numbers follows the substitution of numbers to real goods. The first substitution defines the net product; the real product gives way to *real money*. The product is included in money as in an envelope. The second substitution defines net consumption; real money gives way; it is destroyed and it dislodges the real product: at that instant, the operation is completed, consumption being henceforth welded to production as it would have been immediately if money had not been interposed.

If exchanges were first to occur in the products market, they would be *relative*, every exchange implicating then at least two distinct goods. However, exchanges appear right from the act of production, in the movement of which the product is the result, one induces that exchanges are *absolute* because the same product is firstly monetary (real money) then real (the physical product, instantly denatured into a use value).

Absolute exchanges place the two following relations in their true light: the relation between "nominal" and "real", the relation between product and time.

Nominal magnitudes and real magnitudes

In public opinion, we find two opposite ideas.

a   Nominal magnitude par excellence, money is facing the set of real goods, to which it does not belong: it is exogeneous.

b   Money is one element of the set of real goods: it is endogenous, because it is produced like any other, consumption or investment good.

Apparently, the opposite operations cover the whole field of possibilities: how, in the world of real goods, could money be neither endogenous nor exogenous? In fact, the principle of the excluded middle does not apply to money, which is a good both exogenous and endogenous. If the two doctrines persist in public opinion, without one being able to overcome the other, it is indeed because money has a double nature. The thesis and the antithesis are both equally true. A nominal magnitude, money is exogenous; a real magnitude, money is endogenous; however, the same money taken at the same moment is altogether (therefore in an equivalence) nominal and real. Let us repeat the fundamental information. If the flow of real production were not changed or transformed into a flow of formation of wages, the product would be immediately absorbed into the category of use values. As the real flow is in reality changed into a monetary flow (in the emission of wages), *the net product is absorbed by money.* The exact representation is that of money, a pure form comprising the product, which is the *body of money.* Ricardo intuited it, the product is incorporated ("embodied") into money. Monetary wages are therefore a form, a nominal magnitude, into which is found the domestic product, a real magnitude.

The identity in money of nominal magnitudes and real magnitudes may be expressed in another way, by the concrete consideration of the source of money and of the source of real goods. If money were purely nominal, it would be created by the activity of banks. If money were purely real, it would be the product of specialized firms. Given that money, a nominal-real magnitude is a form created by banks and simultaneously a body (the content of the form) produced by firms, money and product are perfectly *homogenous*; the two magnitudes proceed from the same source because, leaving aside its content, its *tenor*, money is an empty shell.

The perfect proof of the identity of money and product is given by the identity of the operation that generates both. One may imagine that the real product is formed independently from money and that it remains in waiting until the moment it is completed. This is false. The real product comes to life *within money* because if it were to come about before, it would instantaneously be nil, being then only the result of production-consumption. The interposition of money being the only means to separate consumption from production, the product is net only within money. The product comes to life "inside" money and it dies when "exiting" money, at the instant it leaves it.

Thus, the product exists (in time) only within money. But the opposite is true too. If the emission of money were not identically a real emission (a formation or an expenditure of incomes), the created object would be defined contradictorily, the positive money being then only a claim on the negative money. Even more, the operation would be an "implosion", the two monies of opposite signs destroying each other instantaneously. There is therefore in concrete economies no money that has not been issued "with its body", that is to say, in an operation (one of the emissions of the product) bringing together in one same movement the payments of the bank and the payments of the economy.

The money-form of the product is purely temporary. Thus, the product is itself ephemeral.

Product and time

If money were splitting barter, it would be an intermediary good standing between final goods, the object sold and the object purchased. In those conditions, a grave problem emerges: if the terms of the exchange are real and money is simply interposed, it is inconceivable that a sale would not define the simultaneous purchase by the seller; indeed, if a sale is net, even for a very short time, the money obtained is a term and not a means of exchange. The bi-partition of exchange into two half-transactions implies that the money earned in the sale is at once cast into the purchase; otherwise, we observe the succession over time of two *complete* transactions, the sale followed by the purchase. However, it seems logically impossible that the same movement should be a sale and a purchase by the same person. The conclusion would be that money is not an intermediary good and that it does not split transactions in their opposite halves.

In reality, it is true that money splits transactions, into sales and purchases: it is not a final good like consumption and investments goods; this has always been known. It is therefore formally necessary, as we have said, that sale and purchase should be brought together in one single movement of the same person. However, induction confirms the reality of this movement; it is that money does not split barter – it does not intervene "between" products – but the action of production: it infiltrates, in the act of which the product is the result. Thus, the payment of wages is a purchase-sale, an absolute exchange; workers exchange the physical product against the same product, in money: the release of the physical product is a sale and the acquisition of the product in money is a purchase. The act of production is split into two half-transactions, that are brought together in the same movement.

However, the thesis of the splitting of the operation into two half-transactions is confirmed on a second level, already well explored. The payment of wages is the purchase-sale of the physical product: one of the terms of the operation is the product in kind; the other, the product in money. In that operation, income is *formed*; it is not yet *destroyed*. We distinguish therefore two opposite operations, the formation of income and its destruction. Now, let logic speak, in the terms already mentioned. The real operation is the production-consumption; money interposes; however, it is inconceivable that it should have the power to alter the operation, because, on the contrary, it is real production that makes possible the existence of money. Thus, even in the presence of money, production is a consumption. If it were judged otherwise, the conclusion would be that production is suddenly net, consumption being an autonomous operation, posterior and, in some sense, optional. We would then fall into metaphysics because in nature nothing is created and nothing is lost, unless in the unity of the creation-destruction. Let us repeat it; human economic activity is unable to create any matter of any kind. One must keep to the strict principle of production-consumption, the product being only the prior matter taken in the utility-form. Nevertheless, the result is that the formation and the expenditure of income must be given in the same movement: they are logically, therefore necessarily, simultaneous.

We find again here the teaching according to which any production is *at once* annulled by an equal consumption. It is quite obvious that this does not result in the uselessness of the production; precisely, the destroyed product gives way to the value in use, the matter reshaped into the utility-form. Immediate consumption means simply that at the exact instant when the matter finally takes the shape of the "mould", it is withdrawn from it. Being defined by matter at the contact with the "mould", the product has no instantaneous existence; but this suffices for it to be transformed into a *useful* matter, a value in use endowed with a variable longevity depending on the objects. The product in its exact sense (the "use value") will have only existed at the instant of production-consumption.

The rule that we have just found again seems really draconian, too hard not to be tempered by reality. Most think indeed that logic is pure only in an ideal world; in the real world, logic would be "qualified". This is gravely incorrect; the imperfection is not in the factual exercise of logic but in the thoughts, often unable to follow logic in all its rigour. How can we choose between those two propositions? Production is net, at least temporarily; incomes are destroyed at the instant they come to life. The first proposition is metaphysical because man is not God. The second proposition is just unbelievable; the observation of facts does not seem to be confirming the strict instantaneity of income. One must look into it more carefully. Once the scholar is determined not to foray into metaphysics, he knows that production is necessarily an immediate consumption and that reality cannot fail to include income endowed with a non-zero life expectancy. The only obstacle that he meets on his way is "common sense", the pure appearances of things. However, analysis has no difficulty proving the nature of income that exists effectively only in the space of an instant. *The key to the solution is in the fact that the expenditure of income has a retroactive effect: it goes back to the instant of the formation of income.*

The demonstration is rather easy. We know indeed that expenditures are instantaneous operations that have nevertheless a finite dimension in time. This is to say that the expenditure of an income quantizes a certain duration in the continuum. However, what is the duration quantized by the expenditure of income? It is known accurately: it is the same duration already quantized by the *formation* of income. Not only is retroaction the right solution, but it is logically necessary since the expenditure-consumption of income is, except for the sign, identical to the production-formation of income: the dimension of the two events is rigorously *the same quantum of time*.

Ultimately, inductive analysis confirms twice the nature of money, simple intermediary in (absolute) exchanges. In itself, the payment of wages is already a sale-purchase. Then the couple formation-expenditure of income is a second sale-purchase. In both cases, the two opposite movements are given *at the same time*. In the first case, the simultaneity is immediately detected because it happens directly in continuous time. In the second case, the simultaneity results from the fact that the product in money defines the same quantum of time as the product in kind. The common view that income earned today will feed the future, perfectly free expenditures is naïve. As soon as an income is formed, it is *certain* that it will be spent; and at the instant it happens, the expenditure of income will define a "quantum flow", the wave traveling over the time already quantized by the formation of income. If money splits consumption from production, it does not have however the power to disintegrate the couple production-consumption; its only effect is literally to introduce "a time interval temporarily" between the two opposite actions. Finally, *income will have disappeared at the exact moment it was formed*. Why should we be surprised given that income is only the product in money and that any product exists only at the instant of the encounter of matter and its utility-form?

24 The creation of money

Money is created in three operations: formation of income; transfer of income formed; destruction of income.

The three creations of money: the formation of income, the destruction of income and the transmission of savings

Money is created in emissions

For centuries, one has talked about the *emission* of money. It is true technically that the expression is mainly reserved for the creation of central bank money. However, in economics the analytical meaning of the emission is now known: it is a wave-like movement, a creation-destruction. Thus, production is an emission because it is a movement both positive and negative: the product is created and destroyed in the same "quantum leap". The creation of money answers the same definition: the same flow creates and destroys any money, whether it comes from the central bank (the *issuing* institute) or from commercial banks.

Usually, it is true, the operation is represented in two stages: the money created would stay in the economy for a more or less lengthy time and it would be destroyed only at the end of the credit operation that had generated it.

The temporal separation of creation and destruction of monetary units is corroborated by a reflexion that seems decisive: if money disappeared at the instant of its creation, the economy would never have a positive money at its disposal.

Nevertheless, one must have the intellectual courage to go beyond appearances; two conclusive arguments establish that in concrete economies each unit of money is destroyed at the instant of its creation.

The creation would be a metaphysical concept if a positive money were "generated" from a zero money. Suppose that at a given instant money supply was increased by x units; it is stated that banks cast in the economy the sum of x units of money *that have been taken from nowhere*; indeed, if banks had simply transmitted the x units of money, the money supply present in the country would not be increased. One must therefore imagine that banks take the x units of money from "somewhere else", in another world, or still, which is not very positive, from "nowhere". The truth, experimental and logical, is totally different: money comes to life in double entry accounting, simultaneously on the asset and on the liability sides of the accounts, in banks and their clients. The x units of additional money are a sum of money both positive and negative; this is to say that the *algebraic* sum of money creations is always nil. Thus, the mystery is far less dense: it is quite true to say that the x units of money have not been taken from anywhere; however, money has to be grasped in the world of algebraic numbers and not in pure arithmetic. We find therefore number zero, the money created being of $\pm x$ units. Finally, even though number x is arithmetically non-zero, banks cast zero units of money in the economy. It is no longer a question of claiming that banks have the power to cast even one unit of money without having obtained it from the economy. In a word, in spite of the existence of creations of money, banks are only financial intermediaries: any money that comes out of a bank came in, or is coming in, in the act of creation.

The specific action of banks is to create an algebraically nil money; the joint action of banks and firms is to create algebraically positive money. Banks cannot create money by themselves; the creation of money is the joint action of a country's banks and firms. We have already formulated this conjunction; let us now demonstrate it in detail.

The fusion of the two emissions is literal: the emission of money exists only because it is combined with the real emission, the production of goods and services. Let us explain rigorously the merging of the two emissions, the nominal one and the real one, in a unique movement.

Real production is an emission, the product being created-destroyed in the movement.

The creation of money is an emission since the money created is algebraically nil.

However, real production does not precede the creation of money, because workers receive the product initially in money and not in kind.

On the other hand, the creation of money does not precede real production since, without being associated with production, the creation is algebraically nil.

It follows that monetary emission and real emission are one and the same movement; (positive) money is created by domestic production: it is the result of the expended labour. Money earned in the remuneration of labour is positive because it is the form of the product. The law allows for no exception. Any money that comes to life without any product, therefore in an operation separated from real emissions, would be a purely nominal magnitude, an empty form, algebraically annulled, of no reality. Cast in the real emission, money "comes out" as real; monetary wages are not the price of the product, but the product itself. The two merged emissions result in the product in money; banks create the envelope and workers produce simultaneously its content, matter deposited within money-form (that temporarily takes the place of the utility-form).

The creation of money is a financial intermediation of a special type: a quantum financial intermediation

Banks create monetary wages even if the cost of wages is taken from the equity funds of firms; indeed, in this case, banks debit firms and credit workers, exactly as they do when they issue wages through an "overdraft". The law is therefore comprehensive: any emission of wages, whether or not it is based on the equity funds of firms, is a new creation of money. However, the creation of wages is, as we have seen, a double movement: banks create the nominal form of wages; the content of the form, namely transformed matter or energy, is produced by labour. The real emission united to the monetary emission has therefore two simultaneous effects: it generates the product in money, and it transmits the product thus deposited in its nominal form, from firms to remunerated workers. Money is positive insofar as it identifies with the product contained in itself. However, the body of money is not at all transmitted in the operation of money creation: it is, directly in the assets of workers, the result of a real emission. It is only the money-form of the product that is the object of quantum intermediation. In the emission of wages, the monetary form of the product comes to life in the firm and is instantly transmitted (by the bank) to workers. The intermediation is of a quantum nature precisely because it concerns only the form of the product, the product itself being immediately (without any mediation or intermediation) generated at the pole of workers. In the emission of wages, banks give exactly and instantaneously what they receive; they bring to workers the monetary form of the product that they obtain in the same movement from firms (where this form comes from the creation of money).

Money being positive only in (direct and indirect) wages, the emission of wages is the measure of the whole domestic product

Keynes' intuition is thus verified: the whole domestic product is measured in wage-units. The reason is simply that banks issue a pure form, of which only the content is given by the real emission, the creation-destruction by human labour of the utility-form of matter. The emission of wages is the monetary form of the real emission; we conclude thus that the payment of wages is firstly a pure operation of *production*; the reasoning reaches production before being able to tackle distribution. It is quite certain that part of the product of each period does not eventually reach the workers. It remains nevertheless that the emission of wages is the "monetization" of the whole domestic product. We shall understand soon that the two following propositions are not contradictory:

- the product is entirely included in the issued wages;
- part of the product defines non-wage incomes.

Before considering the distribution of the product, let us conclude that the Keynesian theory is more profound than it seems: not only are wages measuring the whole product, the share of other income holders as well as the share of wage-earners, but there is more: *even non-wage incomes are at first issued within monetary wages.*

Wages are at first issued positively; at a later date, they are issued negatively. In retrospect, the two opposite emissions are strictly superposed: they form one single movement

Let us repeat the well-known piece of information. The operation of wage spending is identical, except for the sign, to the operation of the emission of wages: the two emissions are each one of them a "real half-emission". As soon as wages are spent, the real emission is completed; the product is then denatured into a value in use because it has definitively abandoned its monetary form, as well as the utility-form, of which it keeps only the imprint.

We know that in all rigour the destruction of wages is effective at the very instant when wages are formed. However, the two opposite half-emissions are of course separated in continuous time; the simultaneity of the two half-emissions is obtained by the retroaction of the second onto the first one.

Let us briefly review our knowledge. Let us call positive the emission of wages and negative the destruction of wages; the negative emission is of the same nature as the positive emission: it quantizes the same period of time of the continuum. It is precisely because the two half-emissions coincide in quantum time that they are simultaneous. However, it is certain that the event of the second half-emission is posterior to the event of the first one. One has to wait therefore for the instant of the expenditure of wages to observe the coincidence: at that instant, the operation goes through the length (of the continuum) initially covered by the formation of wages.

Finally, and given the retroactive annulation of the lifespan of income, we verify that money has perfectly followed the real emission, the instantaneous creation-destruction of the product.

In addition to positive emissions and negative emissions of wages, there are emissions that are both positive and negative: these are transmissions or ordinary (non-quantum) intermediations

We know that in the emission of wages banks carry out three operations in one: they generate the monetary form of the product; they receive from firms the monetary form of the product; they transmit it to wage-earners. The emission of wages is thus an intermediation, which we have called a quantum intermediation, because it concerns only the form of the product, the product itself being not transmitted since it is formed directly at the pole of workers.

However, issued wages are not necessarily spent in the products market; they may be spent in the financial market. Any wage brought to the purchase of a financial claim is *transmitted* from its initial holder (the saver) to its final holder (the borrower).

The transmission of wages may be direct, but part of wages are transmitted through the mediation of specialized persons or institutions, financial intermediaries in the proper sense.

Quantum intermediation refers to the form of the product, that firms generate at the pole of income holders through banks. The ordinary intermediation refers to the product itself, which it moves from saver to borrower.

In observable reality, banks operate quantum intermediations and ordinary intermediations. If banks were didn't carry out quantum intermediation, no bank money would exist in the economy. However, the economy could function in the absence of any ordinary financial intermediation. *A fortiori*, we easily conceive of a monetary economy functioning perfectly where banks would abstain from any intermediation on financial markets. However, it so happens that in our concrete domestic economies, banks are present in the financial market. There is high need therefore to distinguish the two kinds of bank actions. They are "ordinary" financial intermediations insofar as they take hold of the savings of income holders in order to carry them to individuals or firms, who thereby "advance" part of their future income in the purchase of current product. Any ordinary financial intermediation destroys the income on the saver and creates it on the borrower. Even when it is carried out by a bank, the ordinary financial intermediation is in no way identified with a quantum financial intermediation. The two operations are radically distinct and cannot be confused either in logic or in reality. Quantum intermediation is limited to creating or destroying the nominal form of the product. Ordinary intermediation takes hold of part of a product already formed in money to transfer it to the financial market. Quantum intermediation is a positive operation (the creation of wages) or a negative operation (the destruction of wages in the product clearing); ordinary intermediation is both positive and negative since the same income is "lent-destroyed" on one side and "borrowed-created" on the other side.

We have just verified that national money is created in three operations, namely the formation of income, the expenditure of income in the final purchase of the product and the transmission of savings. However, those three operations encompassing the totality of monetary payments, are all referred to only one category of income, *wages*. Let us call profits in the broad sense non-wage incomes. Are not profits formed, spent (invested) and lent by monetary emissions? It is quite clear that this the case. But then, do monetary emissions create incomes other than wages? We are going to observe that the answer is of the highest interest: even though every monetary emission is a creation (in the producing services market), a destruction (in the new products market) or a creation-destruction of *wages* (in the security or financial market), the economy also issues profits, that are not wages. The emission of profits is subsumed into the emission of wages, that is to say in a set to which it does not belong. Quantum analysis brings the complete solution of this proposition which, in classical or neo-classical analysis, is a flagrant contradiction in terms.

All incomes, wage and non-wage, are issued in the emission of wages alone

It is worth reaffirming first the fundamental principle according to which only wages can be issued in money, especially bank money. Neither in theory nor in fact does it exist emissions that are not a creation, a destruction or a creation-destruction of wages. This point being remembered, we shall have to try to bring to light the very nature of the emission of profit.

In the national economy, any emission is an emission of wages

In the economy, any emission is real or both real and monetary.

In the case where the real emission is not associated with a monetary emission, it has a univocal meaning: it is the creation-destruction of the product, the instantaneous transformation of matter defined in the quantum leap, its "coming in-going out" of the utility-form. Production is thus a movement situated in a natural environment ("land") and the efficiency of which in terms of value in use is multiplied by "instruments" (that are matter previously cast in the utility-form): this is to say that production is the action of human labour alone. Even in a purely real economy, we observe therefore that the product is only a *wage*; it is integrally the product of labour.

In the case where the real emission is associated with a monetary emission, logic teaches a necessary consequence: the only effect of the merging of the two emissions, real and nominal, is to split production in its two opposite aspects. Production is no longer an immediate consumption. "Clad" in money, production remains equal to itself: it is still the projection of matter into the utility-form. Production in a monetary economy is of the same nature as production in the real economy: to produce is to work.

Hence, banks generate money in an operation that is logically unique; they pay wages on behalf of firms. *The domestic economy cannot comprise any other creation of money.* Any payment observed at any instant in the economy is a creation, a destruction or a transmission of wages. To judge otherwise would be to admit in thought what is necessarily denied in facts. Indeed, any money that comes to life outside the payment of wages would be detached from real emissions; we know well enough that under these conditions it would be positive and negative for the same amount: it would be nil (and even non-existent). Only the presence within itself of the domestic product transforms money into a net asset, thereby enabling it to exist. And, we can no longer doubt it, only one operation has the effect of depositing the product in money: the payment of wages. We can therefore imagine all sorts of monetary emissions beyond the emission of wages; we shall never succeed in adding even one single unit of *real* money to issued wages: supplementary emissions are in reality only duplicates; otherwise, they are nil and void because any money without a body is aborted. In the concrete economy, any money that exists at some moment is real money or, identically, a monetary income. And every income is the result of the emissions of wages. Thus, even if it were difficult to convince the public opinion, the domestic economy – whether it is "balanced" or not, therefore even in the presence of inflation and unemployment – experiences no monetary payment that is not a formation, an expenditure or a transfer of wages.

It is true that wages are issued several times because the economy comprises "intermediary purchases"

The distinction between final purchases and intermediary purchases is banal. It is not necessary to insist on this here. Before reaching its final recipient, the product is "monetized" *n times*; from the second time on, the emission of wages is repeated. In fundamental analysis we posit $n = 1$, because only the first emissions (positive, negative or both at once) will retain the attention of theorists.

However, how can we explain the emission of non-wage incomes, i.e. profit in the broad sense?

Quantum analysis offers the rigorous solution to the problem that, let us note it carefully, did not see the light with it. Neither classical analysis nor neo-classical analysis succeed in integrating profit in the explanations. The solution always faces the distinction of the two "spheres", production and "circulation". Monetary profit is precisely the income formed in circulation or in the sale of the product. Since available income all comes from production, one does not conceive how the selling price of the domestic product could be higher than its cost of production. Costs bring incomes that are absorbed by prices: the difference between prices and costs could therefore never be positive over the totality of the product. The theory is thus condemned to stay outside reality: the economy includes profit and the *logic* of the theory does not integrate it.

The analysis of emissions reconciles theory with facts.

The difficulty is initially unchanged: it is tautological to say that production generates only "production income", entirely reducible to costs. The mystery is therefore complete: how could the economy spend more than the totality of issued income?

The solution is in the principle that we know well, that of the retroactive merging of two half-emissions. Flows are at first split according to the two spheres. However, we know that the two half-emissions belong to one unique action, the real emission. The division is therefore temporary and even, as we have remarked, its reality is retrospectively erased. The second half-emission, the purchase of the product, ends up imposing itself on the emission of wages. In all logic, this is to say that *the emission of wages must be reinterpreted by the expenditure of wages since the two opposite movements are finally perfectly merged.*

The retroactive effect of the expenditure of wages on their formation is the very explanation of the formation of non-wage incomes, i.e. profit in the broad sense.

Clearly perceived by Adam Smith, present at the heart of classical tradition and carried over by the marginalist revolution, the difficulty is overcome by quantum analysis: the formation-expenditure of non-wage incomes is comprised into the formation-expenditure of wages

In its most simple expression, the problem concerns the equality of the expenditures observed in the two markets, that of labour (the first market) and that of products (the second market).

In the "rude state of society" (according to Smith), wages are the only income spent in the products market, but they are also the unique category of national income. Even if the analysis complies with the logical equality of the flows on both markets, it is therefore able to explain everything because the totality of income is composed of wages.

The difficulty appears with the appropriation of land and the accumulation of instrumental capital. The economy comprises henceforth three distinct incomes, wages, rent and profit (or interest). The solution would be immediate if the first market could distribute income into three categories; the logical equality of the flows on the two markets would be maintained. However, if the three flows are effectively present on the second market, where we can observe, in addition to the expenditure of wages, the expenditure of rent and of profit, only one flow, that of the payment of wages, is seen on the first market. Indeed, firms cannot pay profits to themselves; the impossibility is the same regarding rent, which is a *yield*: it is earned in the sale of products. One must therefore accept the inequality of the flows on the two markets, something logic cannot accept. How could the flow of expenditures (in the second market) be higher than the flow initially cast (in the first market) since expenditures are fed only by created income? The absurdity is the same on both sides, whether one "imports" the flows of rent and profit on the first market or, on the contrary, whether one restricts the transactions of the second market to wages alone. It is remarkable that the Walrasian economy is as remote from the solution. At equilibrium, flows are, by definition, equal in the two markets; how, then, could equilibrium include profit in its exact sense (surplus) since, by nature, the first market only sees the remunerations of productive services?

The discovery of the classification of expenditures depending on whether they are positive or negative opens a new way. Neither the Classics nor the Neo-Classics see that the flows in the two markets are of opposite signs; if every expenditure were in some way "neutral", income would be continuously preserved, the expenditure of one being the income of others: the opposition of signs would be verified only on the *persons*, buyers and sellers. In reality, expenditures are *objectively* positive or negative; they are so in their nature and not in consideration of the person who casts or receives them. The assimilation of expenditures to positive or negative numbers, depending on the case, is the only way to render income intelligible. If each expenditure were a conservation of income, the theory would never know the movement from where income comes to life. Thus, any income that exists comes from an expenditure that forms income; this is tautological. The truth is therefore not in the neutrality of expenditures. Income comes to life in the first market and is destroyed in the second one. The problem of the equality of the flows takes then a new meaning: in relation to the product of the same period, is the economy creating and destroying necessarily the same sum of income?

The answer is certain; expenditures in the two markets are of opposite signs for only one reason; it is that the two opposite flows are the two half-transactions defining production-consumption. These are really the two halves of the same transaction: the equality is therefore certain. It would be illogical to contend, for example, that a positive difference could be found between the formation and the expenditure of income, the flows being then truncated on the second market by "hoardings". This is impossible because hoarding by income holders is necessarily "paid" by the clearing deficit: firms bridge the gap in the purchases since the costs of production are irreversible. However, it is the opposite inequality that is of interest to us: how could profit come to life in the positive difference between the expenditures of the second market and those of the first? It is absurd to assume that the flows of the second market exceed the flows of the first, because it would be positing the expenditure of non-created, inexistent, income.

We have thereby arrived at the definitive position of the problem. Negative expenditures (the expenditure of income) and positive expenditures (the creation of income) are necessarily equal to each other. The first market, that monopolizes the creation of income, only sees the formation of wages. The second market sees the expenditure of *all* incomes, including *non-wage* incomes. How then does the economy spend wages and profit, while production only creates wages?

The problem would be forever irresolvable if the theory were to choose to contract the two opposite flows again in one neutral set. Only the strict observation of facts enables reasoning to make progress. The first movement is the creation of wages; in this flow, income is created on the whole society and not only on workers: wages are the income or the net product of the domestic economy. Wages are spent in the second movement, subsequent in continuous time. The expenditure of wages is not a neutral flow (as it would be if we were claiming that the income lost by purchasers is to be found in the hand of sellers) but a negative flow: income is destroyed in itself and not simply in the eyes of purchasers. The two opposite flows define the real emission, the unified operation, the unique one, of production-consumption.

The fundamental principle being thus recalled, the problem of profit becomes resolvable.

The first step is to recognize free pricing in relation to the costs of production: the identity of production and consumption in the real emission does not say anything about the selling price of goods. Any good the production of which is given in the emission of 10 units of wages may be offered on the market at a higher price, for example at 20 units of money. Suppose it is effectively bought at this price. In this case, it seems that the reflux of 20 units of wages corresponds to the flux of 10 units of wages; however, this is only an illusion. The identity flux-reflux, which is nothing else than the identity production-consumption, gives a degree of liberty to prices in relation to costs. Logic is complied with in the freedom of prices if the *supplementary* expenditure is acknowledged for what it is, that is to say the payment or the financing of a production that is *supplementary* too. As soon as firms make a profit, they find the financing of the production of "dividend-goods". Production brings wage-goods q in the emission of 10 units of wages. If the sale of goods q brings 20 units of money to firms (by the expenditures of 20 units of wages), the total receipt is constituted of two sums: the reflux of 10 units of wages on goods q and, in addition, the financing of the production of dividend-goods q', the cost of which in wage-units is equal to 10 units of money. *The identity flux-reflux is complied with on the goods of the two categories.* Wage-goods (q) were brought about by the emission of 10 units of wages and cleared by the destruction of 10 units of wages. Dividend-goods (q') are purchased (paid or financed) by the reflux or the destruction of the 10 units of wages earned in the sale of q. This destruction or this reflux is carried out in only one possible way, namely by the payment or the flux of 10 units of wages in favour of workers producing or having produced goods q'.

Analysis gains thereby a certain higher position enabling it to see the evolution of thought on the fundamental problem of profit in perspective. In the rude state of society, expenditures in the two markets (labour and products) do not intertwine at all: no income is destroyed in the first market and no income is created in the second one. In advanced society, we observe the existence of non-wage incomes, profit in the broad sense, as well as rent, interest and pure surpluses. However, under those conditions, of course in conformity to reality, the very explanation is *unchanged*. The national economy produces only wages and any expenditure or destruction of income is an expenditure or a destruction of wages. If logic were to confine itself to the principle of the excluded middle, it would go straight to the conclusion that non-wage incomes do not exist at all, unless they are purely real. In fact, monetary profits are not nil in our society; the observation of accounts show it indubitably. Then "binary" logic has to be revised: non-wage income comes to life by the expenditure of wages. When the price paid exceeds the cost of production, the difference is not a reflux observed directly on the second market but a reflux *effective in the first market*. In other words, profit is formed in the expenditure of wages and profit is destroyed in the formation of wages. The production of the period comprises q' units of dividend-goods because the emission of wages encompasses, *in the producing services market,* the purchase of products equal to q', which means symmetrically that the expenditures in the products market comprise, for a measure of q' units of wages, the *formation* of q' units of non-wage incomes.

Profit flows back (is spent) within the flux of wages; conversely, the flux of profit (its formation) is given within the reflux of wages.

The "rude state of the economy" only experiences fluxes that do not comprise refluxes and refluxes that do not comprise fluxes. In the advanced state of the economy, the flux of wages contains the reflux of profit (dividend-goods being bought by the remuneration of workers producing those goods); logically the reflux of wages contains therefore the flux of formation of profits (insofar as prices paid exceed the costs of production). The "nesting" presence of negative flows inside positive flows and, symmetrically, of positive flows inside negative flows, is the explanation of the formation and of the expenditure of monetary profit.

All incomes, even non-wage ones, are created and destroyed in the creation-destruction of wages. But the destruction of income is a consumption or the formation of capital.

25 Capital

In its first form, capital is simply the bridge between present income and future income: this is then capital-time. The second form of capital is still time but now it is fixed in the capital: this is called fixed capital.

Capital-time

Like consumption, the formation of capital results from the destruction of an income; consumed income is destroyed definitively; capitalized income is saved: it is destroyed today in order to be transported through time. The formation of capital is the transformation of a current income into a future income.

An income is consumed or saved: in both cases, income is destroyed

It is almost inevitable that theorists should at first consider saving as the conservation of income. A life saved is kept alive; similarly, a saved income would be saved from destruction. The truth is a little less simple. It is formally impossible that income should have a positive inertia over time. We have established it well. Being a wave, production is an action the result of which – an income – is given in one movement both positive and negative; it follows that income only occupies one "point" of the continuum or of continuous time. Right from the instant following the formation of an income, its annulment has already taken place. The strict instantaneity of the existence of income is intuitive; indeed, income is matter (or energy) taken at the precise instant of its "moulding" completed in the utility-form. It would therefore be vain to try to follow income in the passing of time; no income flows with time since all incomes meet the continuum only in the space of an instant.

One has to conclude that saving an income is an action in which income disappears as in consumption. But what is the distinction between the cases? Saving is precisely the action enabling income to follow the passing of time, that is to say, to exist again at an instant posterior to the one of its formation, at a future, more or less distant, date. As soon as the existence of today's income leads to its existence tomorrow, income is preserved or saved. It seems therefore that, in the end, saving enables the persistence of income over time, setting it in the continuum. *This is not so.* Saving destroys today's income. If income is preserved nevertheless, this is because saving is a double action, a negative or destructive one today and a positive or creative one tomorrow: the same action that destroys today's income recreates it tomorrow. The two opposite requirements are thus satisfied; the existence of income is nil during the whole period it is saved; nonetheless, born from today's savings, the income of tomorrow is a simple re-creation: saving is the operation enabling income to rise one day from its ashes.

The first explanation of saving: the permutation of the income of two distinct people

If A holds a current income and B the assurance of holding a future income, the two incomes may be given up, one for the other, at the will of the holders. The operation agreed upon means that A's current income becomes B's current income and that B's future income becomes A's future income. We thus see that the lender has succeeded in preserving his income through time, until the day when B hands over his income that has become current. The income of today is preserved because it is changed into *another* income, of tomorrow.

The essential explanation of saving: the conversion of the income of the same holder

It is obvious that the permutation of the incomes, current and future, of two persons is a zero-sum operation in the society as a whole. Positive on A, the operation is negative on B, the borrowing being a negative loan. Global savings are nil since current income is destroyed on B instead of being so on A: income disappears definitively because the lender will be paid with an income *newly* created in the period of settlement of the loan.

Another type of savings is far more interesting because these are net in the whole of the national economy. These are the savings created by income holders on themselves. Another formulation is logically identical: in contrast to the savings formed between lender A and borrower B, the savings created from H (the set of income holders) to H preserves the equivalent part of *national* income.

At first sight, saving from H to H is a contradiction in terms. But the theorist is prudent because he knows that income is formed precisely on an operation from H on H: workers are part of the set of income holders; however, workers create income on themselves. But how can the set H effectively destroy a current income in order to replace it by a future income? If future income is an income to be, the problem remains; to reach the solution, future income has to be a simple reproduction or an "avatar" of current income.

Nevertheless, it is certain that we are heading towards this solution since the destruction of today's income is net on the *lender* (the set H). If the credit operation were observed among the elements of H, the income lent would be destroyed by the borrower. When the operation is on the contrary a relation from H to H, income is destroyed on H, on the *lender. It follows one of two things: lenders lose definitively their income, unless they retrieve it in the re-creation or the "repetition" of their saved income.*

Under what condition is the second term of the alternative established? It is necessary and sufficient that the income lent by H to H should be recovered in the sale of the saved product. Let *pe* be the period of the term of the credit and *p* the period of its opening. The borrower B sacrifices part of his income of a future period; this is the reason why the credit from A to B is a zero-sum. For the operation to be net from H to H, the set of income holders must, at term, sacrifice its incomes saved in period *p*, the income of period *pe* being not at all implicated.

When a credit is opened between A and B, *no product is saved in the whole of society*, because B spends the income saved by A; once the loan is defined from the set unto itself (and not between its elements), *the product is saved for the whole measure of monetary savings.* Saved in period *p*, the product is cleared in period *pe*: the income lent is thereby recovered by the sale in *pe* of the product of *p* and not that of *pe*.

The conclusion at which we arrive is very simple. Any monetary savings are nil in the national economy unless they are brought about in an operation that defines real savings simultaneously.

The co-existence of two savings, monetary and real, defines capital-time

Monetary savings are subjected to the tautology of the equality of the purchase and the sale of financial claims: borrower's negative capital annuls the lender's positive capital. As soon as monetary savings are associated with real savings, capital is net. Indeed, real savings are destined for a future sale; at the instant of its completion, savings are transformed into income: they bring about the income which they had come from.

The capital of the domestic economy proceeds therefore from a unique operation, the nature of which is to generate two savings, monetary and real, at the same time. Net capital is the "waiting" of the whole economy; disappeared into monetary savings, income will only reappear later at the moment of the clearing of the product that had itself disappeared into real savings. Neither the product nor the product-within-money have the ability to follow the passage of time; net capital is in a way the mutant of product and income: transformed into capital, product and income are set in the continuum. At term, the opposite mutation will take place; capital becomes an income, that is to say a magnitude the dimension of which is rigorously nil in continuous time.

Income is defined in quantum time; capital exists in continuous time. Capital is exactly the "transcription" of income, from quantum time into the continuum. We thus see that capital is the dimension of income into the continuum; to acquire that dimension, income has to be subjected to a (current) destruction and to a (future) creation or reconstitution; capital is the (continuous) time separating the two opposite mutations; this is the reason why it can be called *capital-time*.

However, analysis demonstrates that net capital, capital-time, can exist, according to logic, only in the economies endowed with bank money. The discovery of this restriction is strange, and its importance is crucial. Any economy that only experiences material money is a pre-capitalist one: any capital in-there is necessarily a zero-sum. The so-called capitalist regime is identified to the functioning rules of bank money.

No capital-time can be formed in material money. Any net capital is formed in bank money

Before quantum analysis, theory had not mastered the definition of income which was assimilated to a flow in the continuum. The mistake was a fundamental one. Thus, the relation between income and capital could not be conceived of correctly. Income was viewed as a (continuous) flow coming from a stock, namely capital; or again, capital was pictured as the actualised value of the flow of income in the future. The great idea was "hydraulic": capital is the reserve, pre-existing or actualized, of a fluid. This is great naïvety. In reality, income is not at all a fluid belonging to classical mechanics and capital is not the accumulation of a fluid. The received theory claims that, unlike income, capital is not a flow through time: an instantaneous magnitude (the existence of which may be observed at each instant), capital would not be a movement through time. The two conceptions are incorrect; in fact, income is not a flow in the continuum, whereas capital is.

One may think of the speed of a mobile in the Euclidian space; speed is an instantaneous magnitude; however, speed is a movement in time. Thus, a magnitude can be a movement even though it is defined at each instant; similarly, even though capital may be grasped in the instant, it is logically permitted to conceive it as a movement, a flow in (continuous) time.

Capital escapes time only in that it is not multiplied by it; speed is not multiplied by time either. Ultimately, capital is like the speed of the flow in time and not a stock that would be passed through by time. Capital is the income deposited on a "point" of the continuum; since the flowing of this point defines continuous time, capital is itself a continuous movement. If the idea and the name "stock" can be retained, it is important to grasp its exact meaning: it is a *quantum stock* and not an integer. Income is transformed into a stock insofar as it is destroyed today to rise again tomorrow: since income can reappear at any instant, it exists under the form of capital at any instant of the continuum between the two opposite mutations of income.

It is true that the profound reality is little subtler; capital is the "bridge" between the present and the future; neither income nor capital take this bridge; capital cannot be both the bridge and the magnitude that travels over it; as for income; it could not move since it is destroyed; the bridge is therefore made of *nothingness*: the bridge is itself the definition of the travel. At the bridge "entrance", income is destroyed; at the bridge "exit", income is recreated. Capital is therefore the conveying of income in the continuum: as soon as income is recreated, it can be said that it has, from the instant it was transformed into capital, followed, "as a point", the passage of time.

Capital being correctly defined, it is easy to demonstrate that it cannot exist in an economy where all payments are carried out in a material money (like gold or silver). Let us recall, however, that the emission of wages is of the same nature whether it is carried out in bank money or in material money. And savings follow also the same definition in both cases. Since the economy is divided into two subsets, firms (F) and income holders (H), part H saves the income lent to part F. In the financial market, any income holder is in relation with another income holder or with a firm; in the first case, the capital is already annulled in the set H; in the second case, it is positive in the set of income holders but nil in the global economy because it is negative in the set of firms. Capital would be positive only if the loan by H, granted to F, were defining nevertheless a nil loan of the set of firms. This is obviously impossible. The formation of net capital runs into the tautology of the equality of loans and borrowings. The replacement of bank money by material money does not enable, it is true, to break the tautology (no tautology may be overruled); but under the regime of bank money there are loans that transcend the borrower, income being, "through firms", lent to the product itself. When loans are not operations defined from person to person but between the global economy and the product, their result is the only capital that is net in society.

Let us turn to the positive part of the demonstration: the introduction of bank money enables effectively the birth of net capital. Let us proceed in a few stages.

- An income is firstly created as it would be in material money. Note that the fusion of the two half-emissions, by retroaction of the second onto the first, is also observed in both cases. It is therefore not the introduction of bank money that caused the distribution of the product into wages and profits.
- At the instant income is consumed, it is destroyed as it would be in material money; the destruction of income in bank money is even immediately perceivable because money disappears at the same time as income or the product-within-money. The clearing of the product means two simultaneous destructions, the alteration of the product into a use value and the annulment in the bank of the money initially created in the payment of wages.
- A third operation verifies the profound kinship of the two monies, the material and the real one. Any income lent to another holder or to a firm defines a zero-sum capital, the borrowing being equal to the loan. Thus,

even bank money lends itself to exchanges the terms of which are the new incomes of two distinct periods. Whether inter-temporal exchange involves only income holders or whether it is agreed between the two parties of the economy H and F, the capital of society remains zero. It would be vain to try to detect nonetheless a *real* positive capital. Any product that releases itself from money is denatured into a use value unless it is "released" in a very particular operation, the effect of which is to reintegrate it into money, at term; this operation has a name, *monetary* saving. Once monetary (or financial) capital is zero, real capital is too necessarily. The problem is therefore daunting; the economy cannot produce any capital, neither a monetary one nor a real one, if it does not encompass an operation the definition of which seems to amount to a contradiction in terms: one part (or a subset) of the economy must lend without any other part borrowing the sum lent.

- The emission of bank money effectively enables "*absolute* loans", the saving by the set of income holders being precisely the loan by H to H. Before turning to the explanation of absolute loans, let us notice that set H is perfectly capable of lending income to firms: the loans of this type are "relative" and the capital that results from them is zero in society. Having said that, let us go back to absolute loans; Let us observe the facts: banks are present in the financial market. We induce that banking operations have two sides; they are monetary and, in the same movement, financial. If banks did not issue money, the emission of income would be a simple operation, purely monetary. The emission of bank money is a double operation: it is monetary, but it is also financial since the income issued at instant t is retrieved later, at a posterior instant. The inevitable implication of time verifies the financial character of the operation.

- Now, let us analyse the savings resulting directly from the creation of income. The *lender* is known at once; it is the set of income holders, more precisely the beneficiaries of the new emissions. But what is the identity of *borrowers*? They do not belong to income holders because, at the instant of the formation of income, no income holder has had the time to lend even a fraction of his earnings to his "neighbours". The same reasoning prohibits searching for borrowers in the other set: in the operation of the payment of wages no firm has obtained a credit from H, except to the benefit of H.

- If we were trying to base the conclusion on the principle of the excluded middle, it would already be attained; the payment of wages is not a loan either in H nor in F; but H and F are the two parts of the economy. It would be ineffective to refer to a third set, the banking system (S): if a loan were granted from H to S, it would be so to the benefit of F because, in all their operations, banks are financial intermediaries.

- If the emission of wages is constitutive of a positive loan, it is only because the principle of the excluded middle is not valid in quantum analysis, that opens a third possibility, by far the most interesting, namely the loan from H to H, or more exactly, the loan that each holder of a new income is offering to himself. The operations of this type are absolute, and we already know the main example: in the real emission, the worker receives his own product within money; thus, the same product is in the same movement given up and retrieved by H. If the product were not brought about by an absolute exchange, from H to H, it would not be net in the economy since firms would lose the monetary earnings of workers. However, there is an absolute operation of a second type, the creation of the net capital of society. Banks being present, in each of their operations, in the financial market, the payment of wages in bank money is a monetary-financial operation. A financial operation, the emission of wages is a loan and precisely a loan from the income holders to themselves. No one can doubt it: if the loan were not absolute, it would not be net in the economy, because it would create a negative capital in firms. Absolute loans do not get anyone into debt because, lending his income to himself, the holder destroys it in order to find it again intact later, at the term of the loan that will see the reproduction of the, instantly destroyed, income.

- Is the absolute loan an "ordinary" or a "quantum" loan? Let us recall that ordinary loans transmit the object of the credit from lenders to borrowers, while quantum loans keep the object of the credit in the hands of the lenders. Absolute loans have a double nature; the object lent has to be distinguished into a pure money and a product within money, the "form" and the "content". In the absolute loan, income holders lend the money-form to firms (through the intermediary of banks); *in this respect, the absolute loan is ordinary*; indeed, firms are henceforth indebted to income holders, *through banks*, and no longer *to* banks. Nevertheless, in the same absolute loan, income holders lend the money-content (the product within money) to themselves; *under this second aspect, the loan is a quantum loan*. The product does not move; at the start of the operation, income holders hold the product within money and, at the end of the operation, they hold the same product in *claims* that are the definition of financial capital: the property rights on the product.

- We have thereby reached a double observation. If the economy were not endowed with any money, at least material, it would not benefit at any time from a net product. But, if the economy were not endowed with bank money, no capital, either financial or real, would be formed within itself. *Money makes the product; bank money makes the capital.*

- Any emission of wages in bank money is a new formation of capital-time in the global economy. Even though the clearing of the product in households has to take place "later", it happens immediately under the form of claims: monetary income is destroyed at birth because it is at once replaced by financial capital, the claims on the product. Claims and identically the financial capital are, in their turn, destroyed when savings make place for consumption: the product then reaches "in kind" the households that were holding it "in claims":

- During the whole life of financial capital, the product is itself a capital; *real* capital is the logically necessary "double" of the financial capital: the two types of capital are the condition of existence of one for the other. Facing the claims, the product is "*stocked*" or *reserved*. Real saving of the product ceases at the instant when monetary savings are transformed into income; then the product falls again into money of which it is the body once more; in the same movement, the product is definitively dislodged or released from money because it is *consumed*.

- In any economy devoid of bank money, income comes to life and dies without going through the capital stage. This is because absolute loans cannot yet exist. In an insufficiently advanced economy, any possible loan is relative: workers can lend part or the totality of their income, but only *other* workers or firms can be the beneficiaries. Like hoarded income, income lent is therefore a zero-sum capital, borrowings being the exact compensation for loans.

- In any economy endowed with bank money, income is destroyed at birth to be transformed in an instant into a *net* capital; correlatively, products are immediately released from money and stocked. The reason is that the creation of wages is an operation both monetary and financial; the saving of income goes back to the instant of the formation of income: there is no moment when one might witness the existence of a non-saved positive income. Being financial intermediaries, banks are in a way managing time; they count the time that elapses in the accounts from the creation of income; this is to say that income is instantaneously (without any delay) transformed into capital, into capital-time. For the same reason, the product enters immediately the category of stocks.

- Let us conclude with a remark. Even though income is destroyed at the instant of its formation, reality encompasses a *net* production because income is destroyed *for a while* only; the immediate destruction of income is the means to have it rise again later, at the moment of its consumption. As a transitory form of any income transformed into bank money, capital-time is indeed the bridge or the objective relation between current income and its reproduction in the future.

- We have just established that bank emissions bring money instantaneously in its two "successive" transformations (the succession is purely logical and not chronological): money is transformed into income and income is transformed into capital.

We know thus the deep nature of capital; it is a claim on banks. Any capital that is only a claim on borrowers is a zero-sum in the economy as a whole. On the contrary, a claim on banks is net insofar as, "going through" the banking system, it expresses a property right on the product in stock. The "final borrower" is therefore, not a person, but the product itself; figuratively speaking, it can be said that the product has borrowed income in order to be released from negative money. A claim to the released product replaces the lost income in the hands of its holders. The net formation of capital (or of savings) is the appropriation of the product in the form of financial claims, whereas consumption is the appropriation of the product in itself.

The now demonstrated fact that the domestic economy would be devoid of capital if it had no bank money has an equal effect in both fields, that of nominal magnitudes *and that of real magnitudes*. Any monetary capital both positive and negative is tautologically zero-sum *real* or *physical* capital. We have remarked it: in none of its correct meanings is capital either purely technological or instrumental. Any capital is a future product, more rigorously a future product-within-money. An economy only endowed with material money may doubtless have tools and equipment of various sorts at its disposal. However, those instrumental goods have there the status of consumption goods; this is so not for a semantic reason but in virtue of a logically necessary induction; indeed, in the economy lacking bank money, the product is necessarily appropriated in kind (within money or outside of money): *it can never be appropriated in claims.*

The lender of an income in material money obtains at first a claim to his product; however, the borrower acquires the product; it follows that the lender only has a claim to a future income of the borrower: he is no longer the owner of his own current product, *which is not transported through time.*

Only bank money enables the transport of a current product of society, in order to have it rise up in a future period. Material money does not bring any bridge between the present and the future; in those conditions, any claim to a future income has for its object a product to be and not, as required by the definition of net global capital, the product of today transformed into a product of tomorrow.

Consequently, in the absence of bank money, it is inconceivable that income should be destroyed to make place for anything else than the appropriation of the product *in kind*: the borrower consumes or destroys the product. We arrive therefore at the formulation of an alternative. Defined in material money, the product is maintained or is spent; and if it is spent, it is necessarily consumed. The product resides initially within money; this is the time of existence of income; then income is spent; the product is then instantly *consumed*, denatured into a use value, *even if it concerns machines or any other means of production*. In the regime of material money, instrumental goods are consumption goods among others; this is so because consumption has a univocal definition: it is the operation that withdraws matter from the utility-form.

Instrumental goods are a specific category only if they enter the category of capital; and a capital is both a product released from the money-form and nevertheless a product not consumed. The two requirements are reconciled in the fact that the product in stock will, at the term of the absolute loan, be reintroduced within its money-form that it will then leave definitively, in the final consumption of the product.

In its double nature, stock and claim, capital-time only exists in bank money. The conclusion extends to fixed capital.

Fixed capital

It is certain that fixed capital is consumed in production or, more exactly, in the "process" of production. But why do instruments of production belong nevertheless to the category of capital?

The answer can only be satisfactory if the meaning, perfectly known (and that we have just recalled), of capital is complied with: it is the transformation of a current exchange value into a future exchange value. The terms of the mutation are precise: current product disappears because it is withdrawn from money (income is destroyed); coming from a capital, the future product is just the reintroduction into money of the product initially "capitalized". Thus, let us repeat the question: why do the means of production enter the category of capital?

A first answer comes to mind. Are not the means of production (tautologically) productive?

Are not the means of production capital because they have a "physical productivity"?

The progressive improvement of equipment in industries ensures the increase in numbers and in quality of the goods produced. Any income allocated to the production of equipment is transformed into capital since its holder will be entitled to at least part of the productivity gains.

This intuitive "solution" is very weak in reality because the gains in productivity are defined in value in use and not in value of exchange. The means of production would be productive in value only if part of the future products could be attributed to them like "effects" are attributed to their "causes". However, let us remember, the product allows only one scientific definition: it is matter in contact with the utility-form. And only one single "cause" casts matter in its projected form: it is human labour. Thus, even though he is "helped" or "assisted" by the machine, man is the sole author of the product because he is its unique *issuer*. Similarly, the pianist is the only issuer of the sound of his instrument.

It is true doubtless that progress in equipment enables the domestic economy to introduce more and more goods into the utility-form; but the product takes the measure of the form and not the other way round; it follows that technical progress and the accumulation of means of production are incapable of multiplying *the products* in their exact sense: a greater diversity and a greater number of goods are contained into an unchanged product. Since "the choice of units" of measure proposed by Keynes (in his *General Theory*) (Keynes 1936), the question has been solved with clarity: the product is measured in wage units; however, multiplication and improvement of the means of production are neutral actions in reference to the emission of wages. Human beings issue wages; machines do not issue any. This suffices: a machine has a product in value (a product in its rigorous sense) strictly nil.

One may not therefore logically classify equipment in the category of capital unless to explain through another completely different way how the means of production succeed in adding *their own product* to the products of labour.

The correct solution is necessarily contained in the idea already developed in relation with capital-time, according to which positive capital is a bridge between present and future.

Fixed capital reproduces the value that it has initially absorbed (in investment)

In economies endowed with bank money, it is *the injection of saved income into new emissions of wages* that produces fixed capital.

Fixed capital is obtained by the simple mutation of capital-time. Let us turn our attention to the destruction of capital-time. If, at term, the income born from capital is consumed, capital is destroyed; however, it is possible that capital-time should reach its term without the liberated (or released) product being consumed; in this case, the chain represented in Figure 25.1 has for its third term a reproduced income and *not a consumed one*: formed in movement *a*, capital is indeed destroyed in movement *b*, but the recreated income defines *new savings*, a *new capital*. The chain must therefore be completed as follows (see Figure 25.2).

The first mutation, *a*, is well known; the action is a unique one and it has a double result: the product is released from money and it is stocked; monetary income is destroyed to be replaced by a claim to the product in stock.

The two mutations, *b* and *c*, are given in the same movement, the transformation of capital-time into fixed capital.

Let us analyse the two "moments" of the unique movement:

- mutation *b* means that the income saved is spent to purchase an equivalent product;

$$
\underset{(1)}{\text{income}} \overset{(a)}{\longrightarrow} \underset{(2)}{\text{capital}} \overset{(b)}{\longrightarrow} \underset{(3)}{\text{income}}
$$

Figure 25.1 The chain income-capital-income

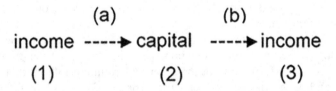

Figure 25.2 From income to fixed capital

• mutation *c* means that the income saved is spent not on the purchase of the stocked product but to acquire new products, the means of production.

The union of the two movements, *b* and *c*, is obtained by the expenditure of saved income in the emission of the (new) wages, earned by the producers of the means of production. We thus verify that the income is destroyed since its expenditure releases the new product, instrumental goods, and that destroyed savings are at once replaced: being unable to go to the purchase of instrumental goods (already purchased in the expenditure of capital-time), the wages created in the production of those goods are *definitively saved*.

Let us call *initial emission* the payment of wages from zero monetary savings; *induced emissions* are on the contrary a payment of wages drawn from pre-existing savings. We may therefore call wage-goods the products of the initial emissions and capital-goods the products of induced emissions. *Capital-goods are all obtained by the transformation of an equivalent quantity of wage-goods.*

The formation of capital-time creates face to face the stock of wage-goods and the claims to this stock, that is to say real capital and financial capital. Part of the capital-time is simply reduced in the clearing of the goods in stock. The complementary part of capital-time *feeds induced emissions* and is thus transformed into fixed capital.

The Classics spoke about "productive consumption". The expression is good even in a modern analysis. The part of capital-time that is formed in fixed capital is consumed like the other part, but it is so in an original way; being caught into the induced emission, the destruction of capital creates a new "stock": the capital-goods are saved by definition. Unlike wages-goods, that form stocks because they are "in waiting", capital-goods are stocks by nature: they are so in themselves (it is therefore redundant to speak of the stock of capital-goods).

An important verification must still be carried out; does capital-time, fixed in instrumental capital, effectively answer the definition of any capital: is it a current income cast to a future period?

Let us consider again the whole chain of movements. Movement *a* is indeed the transformation of an income (1) into a capital-time (2), because movement *b* reproduces (in 3) the initial income. According to the same rule, movement *c* results in a magnitude that is effectively a capital (in 4) if and only if inductive analysis enables to detect in the functioning of the economy an action that defines the *destruction* of fixed capital and, thereby, the reproduction of the initial income. This action does exist, and it has been known since the origins of our science: it is the *amortization of fixed capital*. The word is revealing; fixed capital dies, it is destroyed. And the destruction of fixed capital is, like the destruction of capital-time, the reproduction of the initial income, the very income that had been transformed into capital.

It is true that amortization does not follow the same logic depending on whether its object is capital-time or fixed capital. Let us recall briefly the criterion of the classification. Capital-time comes from the destruction of income *in the product market*: at the instant of their payment, the holders of income (in bank money) consume it and replace it by the claims to the wage-goods correlatively saved or stocked. Fixed capital comes on the contrary from the destruction of income *in the producing services market*: a capital-time previously formed is cast into the emission of new wages, the remuneration of the producers of capital-goods. Capital-time is obtained from the direct transformation of income, whereas fixed-capital is the direct transformation of a capital-time. Workers produce fixed capital insofar as their wages are drawn from a capital-time.

The distinction of the two types of capital comprises the distinction of their amortizations. The amortization of capital-time is a net destruction: capital is denatured into an income and the income thereby recreated is consumed. The amortization of fixed capital is on the contrary a destruction-creation: the income recreated by the amortization is at once reformed into a capital. It is precisely because capital does release income, except to fix it again, that it is legitimate to call it fixed. Caught in capital-time, income is eventually released; but the income absorbed in capital-goods is "trapped" forever; it stays indefinitely fixed into capital. Capital takes its "fixity" from income that it maintains forever. Capital-time is an unstable transformation of income; fixed capital if the *definitive* transformation of *invested* income. The result is that amortization of fixed capital is a double action, a destruction-creation, as we have announced: invested income is indeed liberated but it is instantly caught back and, thereby, it remains in the capital, its "fixed domicile".

It is true that we might fear encountering some difficulty in detecting this movement of creation-destruction of (fixed) capital in the concrete economy. In fact, it is easy. The reason is that capital-goods are all subjected to wear and tear of their matter or of their use value, which disappears all the more quickly that technical progress brings about more sophisticated means of production. We arrive thereby at the formulation of a rule of elementary logic: the replacement of worn out or obsolete instrumental capital employs the expenditure of an income that reduces the formation of net profits.

Let p be one single period of formation-expenditure of monetary income. Let us start from the resolved problem and let us posit the emission of x units of income in the production of wage-goods in the strict sense and of y units of income in the production of amortization-goods (see Figure 25.3).

From the point of view of the domestic economy, the reflux of income is of $(x - y)$ units for the purchase of wage-goods in the strict sense and of y units for the replacement of the fixed capital lost in period p, that is, the amortization of the period. From the point of view of income holders alone, we observe the expenditure of $(x - y) + y$ units of income for the payment of wage-goods in the strict sense. We see thus that the expenditure of x units of income brings to households the product in a measure of only $(x - y)$ units of wages: the difference, $x - (x - y) = y$, is a profit, an income captured by firms. *However, this profit is not a net one*; it is, on the contrary, the part of

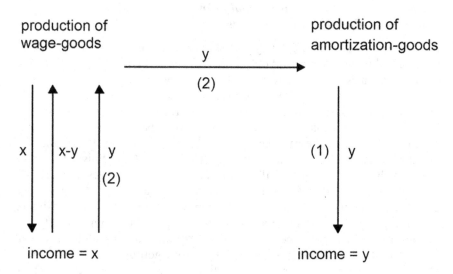

production of
wage-goods

y

(2)

production of
amortization-goods

x   x-y   y

(2)

(1)   y

income = x

income = y

Figure 25.3 From wage-goods to amortization-goods

the gross profit disappearing in the payment of amortization goods. The movement there is consequently both the reproduction (for y units) of the income initially invested in capital – this is flux (1) – and the destruction of this same income, which finds itself at once reintegrated in the capital – this is reflux (2). The unity of the flux-reflux (of (1) and (2)) defines the amortization of fixed capital in its two opposite aspects indissolubly bound.

It remains to define the proportion in which the profit of the period is effectively distributed between wage-goods in the strict sense and amortization-goods. As soon as the rule is known, it is clear that the method followed – not the solved problem – avoids arbitrariness. However, the rule is completely logical: one looks at the gross profit to check whether it is spent in the product market (therefore *between* firms) or in the producing services market (by the firm holding the profit). In the first case, profit is purely gross, and the products purchased are not net investment goods; in the second case, profit is net and the product purchased in its expenditure is an addition to accumulated fixed capital. If y is the part of gross profit made in the period which, according to accounting observation of the concrete flows of payment, is assigned to inter-industrial purchases, the breakdown of the income of p into its two parts x and y is not arbitrary but established. We know then that flow y is the simple maintenance or the conservation of fixed capital, which undergoes in the period a destruction-creation – an amortization – equal to y units of wages.

It is remarkable that fixed capital comprises a part traditionally called "circulating capital". What is the law of amortization of the circulating part of fixed capital?

The amortization of circulating capital follows the same rule as the amortization of fixed capital in general

Let us examine how the circulating part of fixed capital is formed in period p. At first, it is nil because the period only "inherits" the non-circulating part of fixed capital, machines and equipment of all sorts. However, firms are intermediary purchasers; passing from their gross form to their completed form, natural resources also pass (at least in part) from one firm to the other. It is therefore inevitable that the income issued "upstream" should be spent together with the income issued "downstream": the purchase of the suit includes the payment of the cloth and, higher up, of the thread. The seller of the finished product channels therefore the sum of all the income issued at all stages of "vertical" production. Profits thus formed define circulating capital. Those profits are amortised as soon as the firm spends them in its supplies. The amortization of circulating capital is therefore a destruction-creation of income, exactly like the amortization of the other part of fixed capital. The only difference is in the fact that circulating capital is initially zero: rigorously, the amortization of circulating capital is therefore a creation-destruction (from zero to zero), whereas the amortization of instrumental capital is a destruction-creation.

If we dispense – as logic allows – with defining the operation of amortization (which is *neutral*) as positive or negative, we arrive at the formulation of a general law: any fixed capital is the result of the destruction of an income that is henceforth subjected to fluxes-refluxes. Circulating capital, zero at first, stays at zero by the effect of one single flux-reflux, whereas the other part of fixed capital, positive from the beginning of the period, is maintained throughout it and in an indefinite succession of fluxes-refluxes, in all successive periods.

The law of fixed capital is therefore general and in conformity with the theory: a capital is the result of the destruction of an income that it releases at term

Fixed capital is a simple transformation of capital-time and any capital formed in a firm, even the circulating part of fixed capital, is subjected to the law of flux-reflux. The income initially transformed into capital is, at term, released by it, to be consumed (if circulating) or reinvested, independently from human will, the conservation of fixed capital being a law of logic and not the result of human behaviour.

Capital is also a specific magnitude for another well-known reason that it is important not to lose sight of: real or nominal (and it is necessarily both at the same time), it can only exist in bank money.

The knowledge of capital opens the way to the discovery of the deep nature of inflation.

26 Inflation is a "malformation" of capital

According to its received definition, inflation emerges when an excessive mass of money "chases" the mass of available real goods. This formulation is fundamentally flawed because it posits the existence face to face of two distinct masses, one of which is real and the other "nominal". But what is the meaning of a nominal mass?

What is in effect the correct definition of the mass of money? Money has a mass insofar as it has a body and the body of money is nothing else than the real product.

Consequently, economic science encompasses only two fundamental monetary theories, the quantitative one and the quantum one.

The quantitative theory of money

It is entirely based on the dichotomy between money and real goods. Money would have a specific mass, which can be compared to the mass of goods, of produced services, and of financial claims.

Any mass is real; a specific mass of money is specious

The quantitative theory is too rich; reality is simpler. The theory posits or postulates the existence of two separate masses; hence neither of them can be explained.

What is the mass of real goods? Being not material, it can only be psychological. The goods would have a mass because they have a utility. However, utility is not a mass but a relation between matter and man. Even more exactly, utility, or a greater utility, is the form that human labour gives to natural resources. One must abandon the metaphysical concept of the economic mass of goods; the utility-envelop does not add one ounce to the mass of matter present in nature.

Having no *economic* mass, goods cannot be connected to the mass of money.

Even more, the monetary mass is itself a formless concept. In order to grasp the mass of money, the "pure" theory supposes that money was initially taken from the collection of real goods. But how can bank money fit into this explanatory analysis? The observation of facts rules: it is agreed today that fiduciary or scriptural money is created in an emission and therefore that banks are not taking it from a pre-existing mass of real goods. It is necessarily induced that bank money is from the beginning devoid of any mass.

Even if real goods had a mass, "quantitativism", the theory of the two masses, could not be founded.

In an even more naïve explanation, the money mass (M) is given simply by enumerating money units. It is then said that M has increased at a certain date by x units of money. It is posited that the unit of the mass of money corresponds to the unit of money; but the definition of the unit of money mass is omitted. The result is that M is not really a mass but a *pure number*. The quantitative theory claims to establish the network of relations of exchange between the money-number and the undefinable mass of real goods.

One understands in those conditions that it only succeeds in establishing a network of truisms in the numerical equalities of the terms of every purchase effectively observed.

The quantum theory of money

The two masses, monetary and real, are known at last.

The quantum theory of money brings the definition of the mass of real goods and, identically, of the mass of money

We know that, caught in the money-form, natural resources are effectively formed into a mass: within the wages issued, goods produced (by labour) are homogenous because they come to life in money. Thus, real goods are all in the same "basket", the products contained in x units of money having by definition a mass, the "nominal" of which is the number of x units of money, where x is a concrete dimension-less number. The money mass is given in the same movement. The payment of wages transforms the x units of money into a real product of an equal mass of x since the money issued (in wages) is united to the product like an immaterial container is to the material content. The container (money) does not have any mass, unless we mean the mass of its content; in this case, the two masses are one and the same, money conforms to the shape of the product of which it defines the mass in a dimension-less number.

The two masses being now defined, we may turn to the analysis of inflation.

The definition of inflation

Inflation is manifested when the money-form contains a "body" or a product smaller than itself: then the product is "floating" in its monetary cloth.

It is at first remarkable that inflation, at last clearly conceived, is improbable; it even seems impossible.

The (nominal) form and the (real) substance being given in the same movement, inflation seems logically impossible

Money can only come to life with its positive content; any money that would be "born" empty would in reality be aborted. There is therefore no money that should come to life empty of its product even partially. This is to say that in the payment of wages the product occupies the entirety of the money issued: the inflationist margin is therefore necessarily nil.

The inductive method thus leads to a comforting conclusion; the banking system is unable to create an overflow of money: indeed, any "excess" of money is a contradiction in terms; if there is too much of it, this means it is deprived of any body or product, and if it is deprived of any body, this means it does not exist.

Not having its source in bank emissions, inflation is therefore not efficiently fought by restricting or controlling the creation of money.

If the increase in the price level is today (2021) slowed down in several countries, the reason is partially in income policy; the wage increase being contained, it is tautological that the product is deposited in a number of money units growing more slowly. However, prices increase more slowly for yet another, more fundamental, reason. If wages could follow freely the increase in the price of wage-goods, the share of wage-earners in the national income would be constant for a given level of employment. As soon as the increase in nominal wages is slowed down, the share of wage-earners decreases. This would not result in any slowing down of the price increase (of the wage-goods) if the increase in profit were used to produce capital-goods. But, as soon as the increased profit is assigned to the production of wage-goods, the consumable product is itself *increased* inside a money (the nominal wages) maintained at its previous level. In this explanation, of course too concise, we perceive that the observation of facts does not contradict the theory according to which the surveillance of the activity of the banking system, especially of the Central Banks, does not contribute at all to harness inflation.

Logic does not allow the dissociation of money creation from real production; it is therefore impossible, in any circumstances, that emissions should bring a money in excess of the product. Banking activity is excessive or disorderly only in one respect, namely when the financial market is lending more than it borrows. Even in this case, inflation is not declared at the level of the whole economy, the national product being not deposited in an excessive money: in perfect compliance with the identity between nominal and real magnitudes, the excessive activity of banks is not neutral with regards to the distribution of the product between wages and profits.

Inflation is not a purely monetary disorder; it is a pathology affecting money in its relationship with the product: it touches therefore both money and the product.

But, precisely, how could the relation money-product, or container-content, be imperfect since it is an identity and not a condition of equilibrium? The question is important, even crucial. Inflation is indeed the gap between the form and the substance of the same magnitude, the domestic product within money. *In reality, this gap does exist.*

Beyond appearances, one discerns the possibility of positive gaps between the money-form and its substance, the product

In order to grasp the inflationary gap, one has to distinguish the possible double effect of money emissions, depending on whether or not they deposit the product *in* (continuous) *time.* Consequently:

1   There is no money emission that does not bring about both a money and a product within money.
2   However, money emissions observed in reality follow the terms of an alternative.

- They deposit in the continuum the money and the product within money altogether.
- They deposit only money in the continuum, the corresponding product being instantly withdrawn from the money issued, thereby "emptied of its content".

It is clear that logic is complied with even in the second term of the alternative, no money being ever created "without product". And the inflationary gap can therefore manifest itself despite the fact that every money emission is identically a real emission.

The product is present in every nominal emission, but the money-form prevails over the product-form insofar as the emissions deposit money in the continuum, *without depositing the product in-there.*

Inflation appears thus in quantum time and not in continuous time.

Inflation manifests itself in quantum time

The formulation of the two states of the economy, whether it is in "equilibrium" or affected by inflation, is easy now.

No inflationary gap appears in the economy where all money emissions deposit a product in the continuum, until the day the product is (retroactively) destroyed in the final purchases and, thereby, withdrawn from continuous time.

The inflationary gaps being manifested in our economies are all due to *empty emissions* that, by definition, deposit a "money without product" in the continuum.

It only remains to detect the identity of empty emissions.

Empty emissions are all defined by the transformation of income into fixed capital

Let the wages issued in the period for the production of wage-goods be (Ww) and those for the production of capital-goods be (Wc); the corresponding products are Pw and Pc.

Emission Ww deposits product Pw in continuous time. *Emission Wc withdraws instantly product Pc from money because Pc defines immediately an increase in fixed capital.*

The explanation of the two opposite cases is difficult only on the surface. After reflexion, one understands that wage-goods remain within money until the (final) *consumption* of income, in the clearing of Pw. Undoubtedly, investment is more obscure; however, the light comes quickly as soon as the reasoning is based on prior knowledge about *profit*, the unique source (even in case of borrowing) of investment. The operation is univocal: investment is always the expenditure for the production of capital-goods (Pc) of part of the wages already issued in the production of wage-goods (Pw).

- Emissions Ww consume no wages.
- Emissions Wc consume the fraction of wages Ww captured in profit and spent by firms for the accumulation of fixed capital.

Capital-goods are brought about by the destruction of the wages captured in definitive profit

Thus, the essential conclusion has been reached. Wage-goods (Pw) are deposited in continuous time because they are appropriated in nature (by income holders) only in the destruction of the money issued in wages. By contrast, capital-goods (Pc) are *immediately appropriated by firms, that is to say, from the instant of the payment of the workers that have produced them.*

Earned in the production of capital-goods, wages are therefore a *"money without product"*: the inflationary gap is perfectly constituted.

The definition of the phenomenon is "clear and distinct": inflation results from the expenditure, within the emission of wages, of wages emitted previously.

Let us distinguish the entry and the exit of the emission of wages, Ew.

Inflation is nil when the emission of wages (Ew) comprises no income at the entry. In this case, operation Ew creates the new income of society without consuming an income created in previous periods. One may then imagine two possibilities: the income created in the past is already entirely consumed at the moment when the emission of new wages happens; but if an old income remains, it is not at all cast in the new emission of wages. This result is permanent; finding no *nourishment* in the income previously issued, emission Ew brings the same measure of money and product: the inflationary gap is invariably nil.

Inflation is positive insofar as the emission of wages (Ew) consumes wages already emitted previously.

Suppose Ew brings 10 units of new wages and that inside emission Ew we observe the destruction of 2 units of wages coming from a previous emission. Thus, 10 units of income are found at the exit of Ew and 2 units of income are present at the entry of Ew.

Let us note at once an important fact: all units of income present at the exit (the *10* units) are *net or new*, even though the entry of the emission already comprises positive units of income (two in the example). It would be logically incorrect to impute the 2 units on the 10 units to conclude that the net production of the period is only of 8 units of income. In reality, the 10 units of income given at the exit of Ew are new or novel whereas the 2 units of income consumed at the entry of Ew are old; the creation of the new income cannot therefore meet (in a fusion) the destruction of the income injected in the emission: being unable to merge, the two opposite actions do not constitute a contradiction. It results that in all cases the production is net for the *whole* measure of the emission of the wages of the period.

It only remains to understand how 2 units of previous income are consumed within the new emission of wages. The explanation is already known. The consumption of a previous income inside the emission of new incomes is entirely due *to the transformation of profits into fixed capital.*

We know that the transformation of an income into capital always implies the destruction of the income; on the other hand, the destroyed income is replaced by a fixed capital (and not by a simple capital-time) as soon as the destruction of income is obtained by the expenditure of a *profit.* Henceforth the analysis is really simple.

If profit were redistributed, it would be brought to the set of income holders; when, on the contrary, profit is invested, it is spent through one channel only: *the investment of profit means necessarily its expenditure at the entry of the emission of new wages.* Comprising 2 units of profit (or of captured wages) at its entry, emission Ew has two effects: it brings to firms the ownership of the capital-goods newly produced (and equal to 2 units of wages); and it brings to the income holders 10 units of money containing the new product minus the capital-goods, directly appropriated by firms. We thus see that Ew brings to income holders – *and deposits in the continuum* – 10 units of money and only 8 units of product within money. *Capital-goods are not deposited in the continuum; unlike wage-goods, they are at once withdrawn from the money-form.* The inflationary gap ensues at once; emission Ew deposits 10 units of money in the continuum and it integrates only 8 units of product (the wage-goods) into those 10 units of money; the measure of national monetary income exceeds by 2 units the measure of the product contained within money.

Inflation is defined by the difference observed between *nominal* income (equal to 10 units of wages) and *real* income (equal to 8 units of wages).

The cure for inflation is now known.

In the economy we observe the absolute equality of nominal income and of real income if in any period the emission of wages deposits the totality of the product (including capital-goods) in continuous time

Adam Smith knew it: the product is tangible if it exists in duration; a product the existence of which is purely instantaneous is hard to grasp. However, money precisely enables the national product to be set in duration. However, only wage-goods find shelter within money. We have well understood that even capital-goods are "introduced" into money: this is done, as for wage-goods, in the emission of nominal wages. But, in contrast to wage-goods, capital-goods *do not stay within money.*

Before turning to the broad terms of the generalized theory of empty emissions, let us summarize the three essential points that are now well mastered.

- The emission of wages in the production of wage-goods brings to the domestic economy a product which stays within money until the final expenditures cast by income holders.
- By contrast, the emission of wages in the production of capital-goods brings to firms a product which stays in money for a rigorously nil duration, because the new capital-goods are instantly aggregated to the capital already accumulated.
- Nominal income will cease to exceed real income as soon as the emission of wages follows everywhere the same rule, in order to deposit the *integral* product in the continuum until the final expenditures of all incomes earned in any production, of investment goods as well as of consumption goods.

Let us now pursue the analysis further.

27 At the core, inflation is caused by the systematic dysfunction of fixed capital's amortization

The analysis of inflation that we have just given in terms of net investment remains fully valid. However, progress leads to an important discovery: the empty emission characterized by net investment brings to the producers (of the new capital-goods) a monetary *capital* instead of a monetary *income*. We will demonstrate this. Then we will examine the much more severe case of inflation due to the amortization of fixed capital. We shall observe this time the existence of *"dual productions"*, that bring to income holders a strictly zero remuneration, the deprivation of income is then not at all compensated by a gain in capital.

Net investment brings monetary capital to income holders

Let us distinguish two periods of production, p_0 and p_1, for example two successive months, in a society where wages are effectively paid on a "monthly basis".

We shall conduct the analysis in two stages. The monetary profit is formed in period p_0 and spent in period p_1. It is clearly obvious that a profit can be formed also in period p_1, but its expenditure belongs to period p_2 that we shall ignore.

The formation of profit in period p_0: profit is the transformation of captured wages into a monetary capital in the hands of entrepreneurs

The somewhat careful reader no longer doubts it: wages cover the whole of the domestic income. Consequently, the expenditure of wages is, amount for amount, a destruction of income. If the period sees the production of x units of wages, this sum is fully destroyed in the expenditure of the x units, *even for the part of wages that firms succeed in capturing in their sales in the product market*. It would therefore be incorrect to consider profit as a part of income even though it is indubitably taken from issued wages. The correct analysis is the following. Profit is captured wages; in that respect, they are incomes; but at the instant where wages are transferred, by definition, they are spent: it follows that the income-profit is instantly changed into a capital-profit.

It is not surprising that profit should be a capital. Indeed, captured wages define *"forced savings"*. Any wage that a firm finds in its receipts in excess of the income issued by itself in the production of wage-goods has been created by other firms in the production of wage-goods that now evade the "purchasing power" of income holders; how could it be otherwise since the transferred wages are the net gain of firms? However, the wage-goods withdrawn from income holders are thereby *saved*. Monetary profit is therefore the "counterpart" of saved wage-goods: this is to say that it is the monetary (or financial) capital corresponding to the real capital created in the transfer of wages.

How can firms spend the profits they are holding?

A share of profit is distributed to income holders

There is no need to talk at length about this; interest, rent and dividends are eventually wages transferred *inside* the set of income holders. Consequently, distributed profit becomes income again. Capital will therefore have been only a transitory moment in the transformation of wage-earners' income into non-wage income.

Invested profit is far more interesting.

The investment of profits is the expenditure of monetary capital

Any invested profit is preserved capital since it is not reinjected in the set of income holders. It is clear however that income holders also have at their disposal positive capital: it is pure capital-time, of which they are effectively the only holders, until the final expenditure of income. However, profit defines the other capital, fixed capital. As soon as profit is invested, it is definitively fixed into instrumental capital; even more, right from formation, it was the monetary form of fixed capital. As we have said, distributed profit only borrows, temporarily, the form of fixed capital. But invested profit is already fixed capital at the instant of its formation.

How is monetary fixed capital transformed into real fixed capital? The answer is dictated by logic. Monetary fixed capital corresponds to the wage-goods incorporated into the forced savings (formed, as we know, by the transfer of wages into profit). However, the investment of profit means first of all the destruction of profit-capital and its transformation into a new income, namely the remuneration of workers employed in the production of capital-goods. The analysis requires therefore that we pass from period p_0 to period p_1. Drawn from the wages issued in p_0, profit is invested in the production of p_1. The alteration of invested profit into *new* wages (issued in p_1 and not in p_0) has univocal meaning; destroyed as a "wage fund", invested capital is reproduced but with a new identity: it is now an instrumental capital. It would be incorrect to conclude that instrumental capital is purely real, monetary capital having been sacrificed to bring it to life. In reality, instrumental capital is precisely defined by the fact that it has *absorbed* a monetary capital. Of the fact that monetary capital (and through it income) is fixed into the instrumental capital, we have a clear proof, already well investigated: any amortization of fixed capital sees the reproduction of the *monetary* capital, its transformation into an income and, still in the same movement, the reconstitution of monetary capital and its reintegration into instrumental capital. Consequently, pure capital-time is defined by the juxtaposition of monetary capital (the claims of the savings left at the disposal of the set of income holders) and real capital (the wage-goods in stock); a sophisticated form of capital-time, fixed capital is on the contrary defined by the *amalgamation* of monetary capital (the profit) into the instrumental capital (the means of production). We can now go back to the pathology.

The investment of profit duplicates monetary capital

Being absorbed into instrumental capital, monetary capital should be cancelled; this is a requirement of logic. However, in our concrete economies, the investment of profit has the effect of making monetary capital rise again: it is integrally found again in the set of income holders. Indeed, let us examine the emission of wages of period p_1. Part of the emission is fed by the "wage fund", by profit formed in the previous period. However, in the exact measure where wages are drawn from the fund, workers obtain a *monetary capital*, an adulterated income.

This is so for a clear reason; fed by the fund, the emission of (new) wages is an operation of a double nature: on the one hand, it is a purchase by firms of investment goods newly produced (this is the expenditure of profit); on the other hand, it is the formation of the new income (Wc of period p_1) of workers employed in the production of capital-goods. Why does income Wc become at once a capital? There again, the reasoning is binding. Income holders do not obtain capital-goods in money since these goods are immediately the property of firms (because of the expenditure of profit); the result is that the units of money Wc define right from their formation the monetary capital correlative to the stock of wage-goods constituted in period p_0, at the time of the formation of the monetary profit (invested in p_1).

Thus, one does indeed discern a pathology. Already absorbed into instrumental capital, monetary capital is available a *second time*: it is present in the set of firms (within instrumental capital) and *in addition* in the set of income holders (under the form of claims to the wage-goods in stock).

Logic would be complied with in an orderly way – whereas in pathology it is complied with in a disorderly way – if the emission of wages Wc were not drawn from a wage fund. In this case, all wages, Wc as well as Ws, would be created "ex nihilo" in every period because no wage would be paid by tapping into profit.

Before considering the cure, let us pursue the study of the disorder. In itself, the pathology that we have just discovered, the one due to net investment, is not severe, since income holders obtain in capital what is denied to them in monetary income. However, the amortization of fixed capital creates a far more pernicious dysfunction: "dual production".

The production of amortization-goods brings only "emptiness" to income holders: it gives them neither income nor capital

This time the pathology can be detected within one same period. Let *pq* be any month during which wages Wa are earned for the production of amortization-goods. In order to simplify the reasoning, we suppose that period *q* does not see any net investment the funding of which would be ensured by monetary profits made *previously*. Thus, if any disorder were to appear, all the wages issued in the period would be Wa and Ws, for the production of amortization-goods (Wa) and wage-goods (Ws).

However, a rigorous inductive reasoning enforces another conclusion: the production of amortization-goods has the effect of drawing wages Wp from wages Ws, so that in the period the economy produces:

- amortization-goods for a value of Wa,
- wage-goods for a value of Ws - Wp, and
- *profit-goods* for the value Wp (= Wa) units of monetary wages.

Before getting into the argument, let us note carefully that Ws is the symbol of the numerical value of the wage-goods that would be produced if the production of the amortization-goods (Wa) had not the effect of reducing to zero a part (equal to Wa) of the production of the wage-goods and replacing it with the production of a new category of goods: *profit-goods* (Wp).

We shall proceed in two stages. We shall first show how the production of amortization-goods would function in an orderly system; then we shall observe that in our concrete economies this process is not followed.

The amortization of fixed capital in the absence of any pathology

Wages (Ws + Wa) are spent by income holders to purchase *wage-goods* (Ws) *only*. In the sale of wage-goods, firms earn therefore a gross profit equal to Wa units of wages. This profit is spent by firms to purchase amortization-goods. Finally, amortization-goods are therefore a particular form of wage-goods. Indeed, income holders buy the whole product of a value equal to Ws + Wa units of wages: the purchase is direct for the part Ws and indirect (carried out through the intermediary of firms) for the part Wa of the expenditures.

Why is this simple process not observed in reality? In fact, it is not the operation of amortization in itself that is defective. The trouble comes from far earlier. All the dysfunctions come from the initial operation: *net investment* is at the origin of all the great "disequilibria", of unemployment as well as inflation. It is quite certain that it would be imprudent and even absurd to conclude that investments are harmful. The truth is the complete opposite.

It is good and even necessary to invest. The crisis only concerns the "mode" of the operation. No harm would come if investment resulted from an expenditure by income holders who would then be the owners of the means of production deposited in firms. In this case, amortization-goods themselves would arrive directly in the assets of income holders since amortization is the repairing and the maintenance of (instrumental) capital.

Before turning to the second stage and showing the "destabilizing" operation of amortization in our concrete economies, let us review in an intermediary stage the two movements leading to the private appropriation of the means of production by firms.

The private appropriation of the means of production is not "in the order of things", it is on the contrary due to the fact that in each period the payment of the (new) capital-goods is inflationary

It is didactic to break down investment into two movements.

A. Income holders are the "payers". Indeed, investment does result from the expenditure of profit (already made or borrowed) but wages are the "profit fund": firms obtain a profit only if they succeed in drawing it from the resources of income holders.

To say that at the origin income holders are the "payers" has a univocal meaning: they are the true buyers. Movement A results therefore in the appropriation of the means of production by the set of anonymous income holders.

However, movement B upsets everything.

B. The argument according to which wages are the source of the financing of production goods implies the second movement (B); since profits are transferred wages, the means of production are identically transferred goods.

Movement B is the definitive stranglehold of firms on the means of production.

The inflationary gap is entirely defined by movement B. The same goods (the means of production) are therefore paid *twice*: a first time in the expenditure of wages – movement A – and a second time in the transfer of their ownership from income holders to firms – movement B. Due to net investment, inflation is therefore not defined by a difference between the price and the value of capital goods; price and value stay welded, but production goods are bought "one time too many": inflation is thus the disorder the effect of which is the private appropriation of instrumental capital. If inflation were avoided, the means of production would be subjected to movement A only and they would belong definitively to the set of income holders, except in

remaining, of course, at the disposal of firms because it would be naïve to confuse "appropriation" and "location".

Born of an inflationary movement, the appropriation of the means of production by firms is the only cause of the dysfunction of fixed capital amortization.

The pathology of fixed capital's amortization

The first argument is already decisive. By nature, amortization-goods merge with the capital-goods that they "repair" or "maintain"; capital-goods are the property of firms; even though income holders "pay the price" for the amortization of fixed capital, it would be illogical to conclude that this payment that they have to bear makes them (directly) the owners of amortization-goods. It is formally impossible to retain the process proposed in the first stage of the reasoning. Being the property of firms, fixed capital aggregates the (new) amortization-goods by way of a (renewed) appropriation to the benefit of firms. This is tautologically so. Consequently, one cannot explain the purchase of amortization-goods by the expenditure of wages only.

Another argument is quite clear as well. It is certain that firms find the funding of amortization-goods in the "captured" wages: the selling price of wage-goods includes the cost of production of amortization-goods. Insofar as it is due to amortization, the difference between the selling price and the wage cost of wage-goods is a *gross* profit, but it *is* a profit. And the formation of any profit is an expenditure of wages, the effect of which is always the same; let us discover it through an example.

Let F1 be the firm (or the part of the set of firms) that produces wages W1, captured for the funding of amortization-goods (Pa). Wages W1 correspond to product P1; they are spent by income holders together with the other wages. But what are the goods bought in the expenditure of wages W1? it is certain that the goods directly obtained *by income holders* in the expenditure of W1 *are zero* since wages W1 are, by definition, transferred as (gross) profit. The result is that the expenditure of W1 is in fact the indirect purchase (by income holders) *of product P1*. This is to say that product P1 is constituted of wage-goods and that expenditure W1 generates in the set of income holders an equivalent monetary capital, a claim to product P1. The "collection" of W1 by firms implies therefore that, in the whole body of the issued wages, a part of income equal to P1 is (automatically) transformed into a monetary capital.

The two arguments lead to the same result: *the set of income holders is logically unable to buy amortization-goods (Pa) through the simple expenditure of wages.*

Even though it is completed in principle, the argument remains difficult because the scholar is not yet used to "handle" the distinction between an income and a monetary capital. Let us therefore continue the effort.

- If amortization were a perfectly "sound" process, the expenditure of (wage and non-wage) income would immediately comprise the payment and the purchase of amortization-goods. In this case, the operation of amortization of fixed capital would not imply any transformation of income into monetary capital within the set of income holders.
- But it is demonstrated that the simple expenditure of wages – even if we take into account, as required by logic, the wages earned in the production of amortization-goods – cannot ensure the funding of these goods.
- The payment of amortization-goods is effective or positive because, in reality, the amortization of fixed capital is a *double* operation: (i) it transforms the equivalent part of income into a monetary capital; (ii) it matches the monetary capital thus formed with the investment goods constituted into a real capital.

Let us look again separately at the two aspects (i and ii) of the amortization of fixed capital.

- *Aspect (i) of the flow of fixed capital amortization.* The transformation of wages into a monetary capital is observed in period *p*.
- *Aspect (ii) of the flow of fixed capital amortization.* The matching between the monetary capital created in (i) and the amortization-goods thus "capitalized", is also established in period *p*.

Now, let us take the two aspects and let us reason with *rigorous logic*.

Under aspect (i) of the flow, a part of the wages issued during the period is transformed into monetary capital. But this transformation implies necessarily that the relevant part of wages is taken in a "to-and-fro" movement: captured by firms, it feeds an equivalent portion of the emissions of wages.

It is certain that this operation challenges the intellect; but we must hold fast. The difficulty to be overcome is essentially the following: we are used to considering events in a chronological order. But the emissions that clear the product retroactively affect the "initial" emissions, the formation of wages. The "to-and-fro" movement that we have just mentioned must therefore be analysed in spite of the chronology: for the part of income equal to amortization-goods (Pa), wages are issued and taken back and issued *in the same period*, so that income holders obtain in the "wave" a purely nominal remuneration, empty of any real content.

The first aspect (i) of the flow of amortization result in this complex movement: the producers earn wages that are full but that are finally (and therefore right from the start) *emptied of their content to the benefit of firms.*

The content abandoned by wages to the benefit of firms defines the "*profit-goods*" in the exact sense, corresponding to the pathology of amortization.

Let us repeat it. If wages were not emptied of their content to the measure of the value of the amortization-goods produced in the period, those goods could not be "valued" and, consequently, amortization would not be confirmed.

This is to say that in its aspect (i) the amortization of fixed capital implies a "*dual production*": to amortize fixed capital effectively, it is formally necessary that the economy should produce in the same period an equal measure of profit-goods.

But what is the deep meaning of the empty wages? They are formed directly (and after taking account of the retroactions) as a monetary *capital* and not at all as an income. In its aspect (i), the amortization process of instrumental capital brings to income holders *a claim to the profit-goods* (produced in the period).

There is one last question relative to aspect (i) of amortization: since income holders obtain an equivalent monetary capital instead of the income absorbed in the production of profit-goods, are they really wronged? The answer is undoubtedly positive. Net investment also results in giving income holders a monetary capital as a substitute for income; but this capital has the "power to purchase" the wage-goods stocked in the real savings, the "forced" savings. But what is the identity of the real capital facing the monetary capital generated by the amortization of fixed capital? It is defined by the profit-goods, that is the goods that escape, by definition, the "purchasing power" of income holders. Dual production therefore issues wages that are empty both as an income *and as a capital*. And the final perplexity related to the analysis of aspect (i) is solved by the study of aspect (ii); let us formulate it: corresponding to out-of-reach real capital, how can the monetary capital generated by the amortization of fixed capital be used or spent by income holders?

The answer is effectively brought by *aspect (ii) of the flow of amortization*. The real capital facing the monetary capital caused by dual production is constituted *by the amortization-goods* that take the place of profit-goods as the object of income holders' purchasing power.

Thus, the concluding solution is found: the true funding of amortization-goods is provided by the expenditure of the monetary capital generated by dual production.

To sum up, income holders pay amortization-goods *twice*; the first payment is the funding of dual production and the second payment is the expenditure of the monetary capital created by dual production. Let us say it again: logic does not allow income holders to buy amortization-goods, except through the expenditure of a monetary *capital. If the first payment were absent, the second one would be compromised.*

We now know that domestic production is divided into two sectors.

The sector of wage-goods brings a positive income to income holders; the sector of profit-goods only brings to them an annulled income, a purely nominal income, lacking any real content. Identically, the sector of wage-goods deposits a product-within-money in continuous time, whereas the sector of profit-goods deposits only an empty money, a form without content, in the continuum.

For the last time, let us explain dual production or production of the "second sector". We shall reason in those terms: the production of amortization-goods brings "free" wages, that is, an income that is not directly absorbed in the purchase of amortization-goods. The expenditure of the free income creates a net profit in the set of firms.

Another explanation of dual production: the production of amortization-goods generates net profit in the set of firms

Let Pa be the amortization-goods (produced in the period) and Wa the corresponding wages.

Let us go back to the argument according to which amortization-goods cannot be bought directly by income holders; this is really so because amortization-goods are embodied into the instrumental capital already accumulated and that capital is not at all the property of the set of income holders.

The domestic product being P (and W in wages), the sale of part (P - Pa) of the product draws the *whole sum* W since part Wa is not directly flowing back on product Pa. We see that the set of firms makes, in the sale of product (P - Pa), a *net* profit equal to the wages issued in the production of amortization-goods.

From the profit generated by the production of the amortization-goods, the argument follows a straight line.

Firstly, it is formally impossible that this profit should be distributed to income holders. Distributed part (x) of the profit reduces by the same amount the receipts that are finally available for the payment of amortization-goods; it follows that the production of amortization-goods (of the period) is itself reduced by the whole part (x) of distributed profit. As soon as the production of amortization-goods is given, it is therefore logically certain that the *totality* of net profit generated by the expenditure of "free" income (Wa) escapes distribution.

All that remains is to examine the expenditure of profits Wa (we keep symbol Wa for *captured* wages). If wages Wa had not been transferred, they would be spent – like wages (W - Wa) – in the products market. But since wages Wa are transformed into net profits, they are *already* spent in the products market, because they have been spent in the *formation of wages* (W - Wa).

A fundamental conclusion follows: formed in net profit, wages Wa are *necessarily* spent *in the producing services market*.

The path is straight, but the mind is quick to leave it and go astray. The greatest temptation is to "cast" profit Wa into amortization-goods (Pa): thus, everything would be completed to the satisfaction of the general economic order. But logic itself would not be satisfied. This is because the purchase of product Pa by the expenditure of profit Wa contradicts the heart of the problem: the profit would not be a *net* one, wages Wa would no longer be captured, and income holders would have a direct access (through firms and no longer through dual production) to amortization-goods.

The correct analysis concludes therefore necessarily that profit Wa is spent in the producing services markets, that is *in a production and not on a product*.

At this stage of the study, we already know what is essential, namely that wages earned in the production of amortization-goods are present within a *second emission of wages*; The firms that capture Wa spend this profit in an emission of wages; this fact is proven. This is to say that profit Wa is – at least fleetingly – a "wage fund": *it feeds, for an amount Wa, emission W of the period.*

However, the rule is without exception: as soon as firms feed the emission of wages by dipping into the "fund", they produce goods that are immediately withdrawn from the issued wages (and that are not deposited in the continuum); goods produced in the *second emission of Wa* – the dual production – immediately become the property of firms (and, possibly, of their beneficiaries): no part of the product generated by the expenditure of profit Wa is deposited by the production of the period in the assets of the set of income holders.

It is true that the theorist has still to overcome a difficulty, unless he has fully assimilated quantum analysis and, thus, retroactions through time. Profit Wa is made from emissions W. However, W is the sum of all the emissions of wages in the period. Since it is established that profit Wa feeds wage emissions, it seems therefore necessary to consider the production of *another period*: profit Wa would be cast into the production of a period p_x posterior to period p of the formation of profit Wa. *But this is not at all the case.* In reality, the expenditure of profit Wa is comprised within *the circuit of the flows of period p.* This is so for a clear reason: in the expenditure of their "free" wages (Wa), income holders do not create any real capital, because they cannot save the amortization-goods that escape them right from the beginning. Forced savings can only concern wage-goods, those goods issued in the assets of income holders. Since amortization-goods are not issued in the assets of income holders, they cannot come into forced savings. Real savings being zero, the monetary savings are symmetrically so, since all savings are both monetary and real. We induce that profit Wa is indeed a *dual category* of wages Wa and not a monetary capital. It follows that wages Wa, captured in profits, *are already present in the initial emission of wages W.*

The flows of period p are therefore the following.

"At first", wages W are issued in such a way that they comprise the totality of the product of the period. Then, in a "second stage", the "free" part of wages, Wa, is captured by firms. In a "third stage", firms cast Wa into wage emissions. *However, the third stage coincides with the first one.* It is therefore necessary to conclude that right from the emission of wages W, income holders obtain within W one part that is full (W - Wa) and the other part that is *empty* (Wa). The product corresponding to Wa is, from the start (that is through "post-synchronization"), appropriated by the set of firms.

Everything is now completed. Included in the initial emission (W), the second emission of Wa brings to income holders the monetary capital corresponding to the real capital constituted by the amortization-goods. Indeed, these goods are now a capital since they take the place of the product generated by dual production. Finally, monetary capital Wa is spent to buy real capital Pa, instantly transformed into an income and consumed. Amortization-goods are now consumption goods or wage-goods among others, but they have become so at the cost of a dual production.

The path that we have just followed is straight but "steep". However, it leads to a "plateau" on which it is much easier to move forward. Everything is summed up in the distinction between the two sectors of the economy. On this question, economics benefits from in-depth research, especially that of Karl Marx and John Maynard Keynes.

The division of domestic production into two sectors goes back to the great theories of Marx and Keynes

Let us start from the result.

The global economy would not be divided into two sectors if the amortization of fixed capital were not following a "pathological" way. We might however imagine that the distinction of wage-goods and profit-goods is natural, physical. Reflexion dictates a greater circumspection. Investment goods are not naturally distinct from consumption goods; on the contrary, investment is nothing else than productive consumption: it is "a consumption that produces" instead of being "a consumption that destroys". Any good produced would belong therefore to the category of consumption goods or of wage-goods, if it were not for *dual production*.

We know the principle of the first logical distinction of goods: instrumental capital is accumulated by the effect of a pathology. This is because in "capitalist" economies (in the East as well as in the West), the production of capital-goods issues a zero income, replaced in the set of income holders by an equivalent monetary capital. One might therefore base the distinction of goods by saying that the production of consumption goods or wage-goods brings an income, whereas the production of investment goods brings only a monetary capital to holders of wage and non-wage income.

Limited to this criterion, the distinction of the goods still remains fragile, because in the end everything goes on as if the economy were emitting income in *both* productions, of investment goods as well as consumption goods; to strengthen this result, it suffices to add that, as far as the production of investment goods is concerned, income holders carry out a free transfer to the benefit of firms. The distinction between goods fades away until it disappears, because the set of income holders does not suffer from any net loss of remuneration: the formation of profit constitutes (forced) savings that the production of investment goods reaffirms. Deprived of income in the production of investment goods, wage, interest and dividend holders receive in compensation an equal monetary capital that is finally destroyed in the purchase of forced, real savings.

The logical distinction reappears thanks to the amortization of fixed capital. And this time, it is definitive, indelible.

Let Pp and identically Wp be the sum of profit-goods (in kind and in money) produced in the period. Under those conditions, the sum Ws – wages earned in the production of wage-goods – includes the production of amortization-goods (Pa or Wa). Indeed, amortization-goods are wage-goods once dual production is already taken into account.

The two sectors are henceforth clearly outlined. The *whole* production brings *nominal* incomes Ws + Wp but it brings on only *real* income Ws.

The difference between nominal income and real income is the definition of the inflationary gap. However, this difference – and therefore inflation itself – is here observed for the first time as a *price increase*: wage-goods have a value equal to Ws; however, the same goods have a price of Ws + Wp units of wages. In the case of net investment, the price of wage-goods is not increased. The flow of investment is duplicated, it is true, but in two distinct "moves": capital-goods are bought (first flow) and they are transferred to firms (second flow). In the case of dual production, inflation happens in the single flow of the "valuation" of the wage-goods; this is the reason why it results in a positive difference between the price and the value of wage-goods. Income holders receive Ws + Wp units of wages, the real content of which is the measure of Ws units of wages only; the difference is the "inflation profit", the sum of profit-goods directly acquired by firms in the operation where they issue zero income (and therefore also a zero monetary capital) on workers.

Everything can be expressed in terms of "forms". The domestic economy is divided into two sectors because firms issue on the one hand "filled forms" and on the other hand "empty forms". The second sector is constituted as a pure parasite of the first: the income earned in the second sector is in reality derived from the first. Without this conclusion being in any way linked to an ideology, it is logically certain that the people employed in the second sector work "for nothing", entirely for free. It is quite obvious that they don't realize it since they share the income issued in the other sector. It remains however that the whole workforce in industrial activities receives in wages only the value of the wage-goods produced in each period, the units of wages earned in the production of profit-goods being as many "empty shells".

Is science thus rediscovering Marx's great thesis? It would be certainly unfair to set aside the "reproduction schemes". They do contain a brilliant intuition. However, Marx was wrong on two key points.

A. Surplus-value is not produced in both sectors.
B. Surplus-value is not "really" additive to wages.

Let us examine those two points.

Surplus-value is not produced in both sectors

Workers who produce wage-goods receive the whole of their product and even the whole domestic product in this sector.

Why did Marx think that each worker is "exploited" by the firm? The deep reason of the doctrine is neither ideological nor philosophical but analytical and logical.

Suppose that the theorist defends the following thesis: surplus-value is formed in the sphere of circulation, in other words in the sale of goods. A major difficulty comes at once. It is that the measure of the domestic product (and of its parts) is then defined through two distinct channels, prices (the magnitudes determined in the product market) and values (the magnitudes determined in the producing services market, according to the terminology introduced by Walras) being two different measures of the same product. The difficulty is not just a severe one, but it is without any solution. As soon as surplus-value is given by the difference between prices and values, the theory loses control on prices as well as on values. If the price is higher than the value, what is the "substance" of the difference? Being by definition measured by value, the product cannot exceed it to be "extended" in prices. The price is therefore an inexplicable magnitude. But the value is equally so, because one cannot conceive that the price of the domestic product should not be its measure; and even if the price exceeded the measure of the product, the difference would be "outside" of the product: it would not be a product and, consequently, surplus-value would not be a part of income.

This explains why Marx rejected the definition, though apparently tautological, according to which surplus-value is the difference between the receipts earned in the sales and the measure or value of the goods sold.

Surplus-value is not "really" additive to wages

However, as soon as the researcher decides, following logic, to consider surplus-value as a portion of (produced) value, he faces the principle of the excluded middle. The value determined by production is distributed in wages and in surplus-values; it follows that if the share of wages extends to the whole of the product, the surplus-value is zero; conversely, a positive surplus-value is the share of the product that is lost right from the start – that is, right from the production – to workers: it is the dispossession of wage-earners.

Marx realized that he had only shifted the difficulty; he was never able to solve "realization" nor "transformation". However, these two problems are fundamentally identical: they are both generated by the imperfection of the theoretical matching of prices and values.

It is without doubt that Marx's doctrine is as illogical – in some symmetrical way – as the mercantilist thesis of Sir James Steuart. To shift the creation of surplus-value from the sphere of circulation to the sphere of production results in maintaining the *unilateral* character of the explanation, whereas *both* markets contribute organically to the solution. If surplus-value were born only from production, the product would be generated by expenditures $v + pl$, wages (v) being only a part of the product measured. Let it be clear that expenditures ($v + pl$) are *real*; they can be monetary too but not necessarily. Hence the difficulty is so to speak *mathematical*. Expenditures *v* are "bi-polar"; they imply the opposition between firms (or capitalists) and workers. It is therefore not contradictory to define the formation of the product in expenditures *v* because they are not both positive and negative on the same set: wages come to life in an operation that is positive on workers and negative on firms. As for expenditures *pl*, their definition is vicious because it is circular. On the one hand, expenditures *pl* come from firms; on the other hand, they end up with firms; any expenditure *pl* is therefore defined from F to F: it is an expenditure of the set (of firms) on itself. This time we observe that the same expenditure is positive and negative for the same person (F): it is therefore caught in a *contradictio in adjecto*, as Marx would put it. If *pl* is formed in the set of firms, it is logically forbidden to *add* that *pl* is an expenditure cast by F; and if we choose the opposite method, to decide that *pl* is spent by the set of firms, it is illogical to add that pl is "received" by F.

We now know that Marx could not conceive the solution since it depends on a progress that even "dialectics" could not bring: to overcome the principle of the excluded middle.

1   Wages are the whole of the product (we thus avoid any addition and, hence, the contradiction *in adjecto*).
2   Surplus-value, that is not a wage, is nevertheless a positive part of the product.

Proposition 2 is based on the rejection of the excluded middle. Prices are firstly higher than values; but the expenditures in the product market quantize the duration of chronological (or continuous) time already quantized by the emission of wages: we induce from it the fusion of the two spheres, "circulation" coming to match "production". Finally, surplus-value is the purchase of part of the product in the payment or emission of wages. Prices and values are thus constantly identical, even though surplus-value is formed in the positive difference between prices and values. Entirely resorbed by the retroaction of the second emission (expenditure of income) on the first one (formation of income), the difference between prices and values remains nevertheless positive, because surplus-value is formed *in the payment of wages by means of (captured) wages*: value is therefore exceeded in the exact measure where the price paid by income holders exceeds the cost of production of the wage-goods, *to include the cost of production of profit-goods, measure of the real surplus-value.*

The distinction between labour and labour power that, at the end of his life, Marx claimed was one of his rare scientific discoveries, takes on a completely different meaning: it becomes positive whereas it was metaphysical. In the sector of wage-goods, workers receive an income that is not at all taken back in its very emission. But in the sector of profit-goods, income is entirely taken back within the emission itself. We thus see that in the first sector the purchase of labour (in the emission of wages) is a purchase of a zero product:

there, labour is not a commodity. By contrast, in the second sector the emission of wages is both the payment of labour and *the purchase of its product*: in this regard, labour is a commodity. By the same token, the fundamental contradiction is therefore lifted: the creator of *income*, labour is a non-commodity in *both sectors*; but the labour active in the sector of profit-goods, immediate creator of an overaccumulation of capital, *is a commodity*: it is therefore not illogical to say that labour power is a part of labour and that it is a commodity, whereas in its entirety labour is a non-commodity. Again, the principle of the excluded middle is overcome. And it is no longer necessary to explain the measure of labour power by the vague, and alien to economics, principle of the minimum level of subsistence (the "iron law").

The solution thus found, the division of the economy into two sectors appears far more clearly. Let us go back to the "rude state of society"; according to Adam Smith, it is characterized by the fact that goods are bought strictly at their cost of production. However, the deep meaning of the hypothetical reality is now known; it is that the emissions of wages do not include *any positive expenditure in the product market*. On what condition does society move away from its "rude state"? In first analysis, it is sufficient that the economic activity should extend to net investments. This is perfectly true. However, in itself net investment is insufficient since the production of capital-goods is financed by the forced and preceding saving of wages and not, properly speaking, by the wages created in this emission. Net investment does not experience the presence, in the emission of income, of *newly* issued wages; we thus conclude that the production of capital-goods, like the production of wage-goods, is the creation of a sum of income of which no portion is destroyed in the movement of the emission itself. In other words, the emission of wages for the production of capital goods is a zero operation in the product market. The rude state of society is therefore carried over but for one fact, which is of key importance: the means of production are appropriated by firms whereas the other wage-goods, the true ones, are the property of the set of wage and non-wage income holders. Surplus-value is not yet formed. Society effectively becomes a "capitalist" one only by the effect of the amortization of fixed capital. Dual production is the necessary and sufficient condition that is sought after: it is defined by the emission that, in its movement, *takes back and destroys the created real wages*.

The cost of profit-goods is positive; it is measured in the wages earned by their producers. It is also true that the cost of profit-goods is *issued* like the cost of wage-goods. However, workers who bear the cost of production of profit-goods receive in exchange only purely nominal wages; numerically equal to the cost of production and therefore to the measure or the value of profit-goods, those wages are right from the start emptied of their *content* since profit-goods are directly produced in the firms' holdings. Surplus-value is formed to the exact extent that the emission of wages destroys the wages issued, in the purchase of the profit-goods to the benefit of firms.

Point A is thus demonstrated. The production of wage-goods in the broad sense (including investment-goods or capital-goods, amortization-goods, "rent-goods", "interest-goods" and "dividend-goods") issues *full* wages, whereas the production of profit-goods is the emission of *empty* wages. In the sector of wage-goods (1) production is therefore equal to $v1$ (and not to $v1 + p11$); in the sector of profit-goods (2), production is $p12$ (and not $p12 + v2$). The domestic product of each period is measured by $v1 + p12$ (and not by $(v1 + p11) + (v2 + p12)$).

Proof of point B follows immediately. Surplus-value is an "inflation income". If nominal income were everywhere equal to real income (as assumed by Marx), surplus-value would be strictly zero.

The analysis thus comes very close to the "Keynesian revolution". In his *Treatise on Money*, Keynes (1930) distinguished *normal* profit from "*inflation profit*". Normal profit is the share of dividends, interests and rents. Only the non-distributed part of captured wages generates inflation. But the true inflationary profit is generated by dual production that verifies the famous "widow's cruse": the formation of profit is given in the very act of its expenditure. Surplus-value is formed in payment (Wp) of the workers employed in producing profit-goods and emission Wp is in the same movement the capture of Wp and its expenditure by firms to appropriate profit-goods.

Perfectly followed by Keynes, the method requires therefore that analysis should discern the sectors of the global economy. The first sector issues wages in an operation free from any claw-back. The second sector claws back instantly the entirety of the wages issued therein: it only leaves in the set of income holders (and in time) the "empty shell", the nominal wages deprived of the product, of their content.

Keynesian analysis is far-reaching and it would have succeeded if it had known of the logical link between the two profits, normal profit and inflation profit. Rigorously followed, analysis establishes that normal non-distributed profit defines fixed capital (a magnitude that is both nominal and real). And the amortization of fixed capital generates dual production, that is the production of the second sector. If Keynes had been able to conclude his analysis of the "user cost", he might have arrived at this result.

Empty wages are the deep explanation of the disorders of the global economy, inflation and unemployment.

28 Production of the second sector, inflation is defined in quantum time; its measure in continuous time does not let the magnitude of the disorder become apparent

In a sense, the second sector produces only "fake money". However, it is obvious that if this production is a constant proportion of domestic income, its effect on the general price level is no longer apparent. Prices have undergone a shock during the first production of profit-goods; from the following period on and in the succession of times, prices are stable in spite of the constantly renewed presence of false emissions. Monitored by the usual methods of statistics, inflation is therefore detected in its acceleration rather than in itself.

As perceived by David Ricardo, inflation is a malady of money: instead of only covering the available product, nominal income exceeds the product to the whole extent of the production of the second sector. It would however be inaccurate to say that inflation is a purely monetary phenomenon. In monetary economies, all the magnitudes belong simultaneously to the two worlds, nominal and real. Inflation is also not monetary in the sense that banks do not create too much money. Inflation is entirely due to a real "mechanism", the amortization of fixed capital. And banks are entirely "innocent": *firms* issue the wages of the second sector.

A malady of money, inflation hits the product as well; if the product of each period were deposited in money, until the final expenditures of income, inflation would always be strictly nil. Profit-goods define an "aborted" product or income since they are withdrawn from money at the instant they come to life. If all the goods produced were similarly (from the beginning) taken out of money, the domestic economy would be deprived of income and the domestic product would be annulled. Profit-goods belong to the product only by "osmosis". Empty wages share instantly the substance or the body of full wages. The total "purchasing power" of the wages issued by the two sectors is thus uniformly distributed between *all* units of wages even though it is equivalent to the goods produced in the first sector only.

In each period, the inflationary gap is defined by the production of the second sector

Let us use again the terminology introduced in the main part of this book. The "*core*" is the production of the first sector; the production of the second sector defines the "*crown*".

The "core" produces wage-goods in the broad sense.
The "crown" defines profit-goods in the exact sense.

Any money issued in the "crown" is spent in the core. But any money issued in the core is also spent in the core. The purely nominal nature of the income of the second sector is thus confirmed. Without the income of the second sector, the income of the first would already have a sufficient "purchasing power" to clear all wage-goods. The addition of the income of the second sector on the wage-goods market is pure inflation since the sum of the two incomes is equivalent to the measure of wage-goods only. Wage-goods having a value equal to x units of wages and profit-goods a value of y units of wages, the expenditure of all the income, $x + y$ units, is observed on the wage-goods market. The global inflationary gap is therefore equal to y units of wages, the measure of all the production of the second sector.

The *price* of wage-goods is finally equal to $x + y$ units of money; the *value* of the wage-goods is by definition equal to x units of money; the price and the value of wage-goods are nevertheless perfectly equal because price $x + y$ is in fact both the price of wage-goods (x) and the price of profit-goods (y). The *real* price of wage-goods is x, their *nominal* price is $x + y$; if the same distinction is applied to value, we find $x + y$ for the *nominal* value and x for the *real* value of wages-goods.

We can observe effortlessly an important fact: inflation originates from the second sector and it affects only the first sector.

Common theories talk indifferently of the price increase of wage-goods and of profit-goods (insofar as they conceive of the existence of these goods). But, in the reality of concrete economies, inflation is defined *only on wage-goods*. The two measures, nominal and real, of profit-goods coincide necessarily. This is so because profit-goods are bought in the producing services market: they are therefore bought exactly at their cost of production, rigorously at their value. The price can be (nominally) superior to the value only for wage-goods, the only goods that are bought *in the products market*. It would be illogical to claim that profit-goods suffer from inflation like wage-goods since profit-goods are entirely financed by the inflation that affects wage-goods.

In addition to distributed profits and ("normal") profits formed by capture on the wages issued in the core, the sale of wage-goods brings to the set of firms the "inflation profit", equal to all the current production of the second sector. Inflation profit is necessarily spent financing the production of profit-goods; more precisely, it is *already* spent for this purpose at the instant it is formed. The formation-expenditure of inflation profit is indeed a unique movement: inflationary income would not be of y units of wages if firms were not injecting this income into the emission of the wages of the second sector.

The analysis thus ends up with a theorem. Labour spent in the second sector is provided freely for the only reason that the wages issued in this sector are purely nominal. The labour spent brings no remuneration on the necessary and sufficient condition that the remunerating wages should be purely nominal. *If the domestic economy were not affected by any inflation, workers would receive in any period the whole product in the emission of wages.* The "crown" defines inflation; it defines also the exact measure of free labour. In the core, wages are filled with the whole product (that of all the wages). If the workers employed in the core, and more generally the holders of wage and non-wage income, finally receive only part of the product of the core, it is only because they are forced to share the wage-goods with the workers employed in the "crown".

Caused in each period by the production of the "crown", inflation has no inertia through time. If inflation persists over the periods, it is because in each of them it is renewed *ab initio*.

Inflation is a false emission specific to the period where it manifests itself; inflation persists in n (successive) periods if it is spontaneously created n times

Inflation (or identically the production of the second sector) is equal to y units of wages in period 1. What is then the amount of the inflationary gap present in period 2? The logical meaning of the question can only be the following: in what measure is the inflation of period 1 prolonged into period 2? The answer is categorical: the inflation of period 1 does not generate any inflation in period 2. We formulate this result in saying that inflation is not cumulative in time. It follows that it is not cumulative in space either. It would be so if inflation of period 1 were experiencing a non-zero increase in period 2. However, inflation cannot increase from period 1 to period 2, because it is specific to each period: not persisting in period 2, the inflation of period 1 cannot, a fortiori, either increase or decrease in that period. Being not cumulative in time, inflation is not cumulative in space. This is to say that the determination of the inflationary gap cannot be identified by a "variations calculation". Even in the second sector, the emission of wages of period 2 is totally independent of the emission of wages of period 1.

However, is it legitimate to conclude from the non-inertia of inflation to its complete indeterminacy in period 2 in reference to its (numerical) value in period 1? *Not at all.*

This is because the amortization of fixed capital is a mechanism that operates in continuous time. Let us not forget that capital is a magnitude, a "point", following the passing of time. Fixed capital is preserved, especially from period 1 to period 2. And the preservation of capital implies its amortization. As the amortization of fixed capital implies for its part a dual production or inflation, the false emissions of period 2 are "announced" by the false emissions of period 1.

The conclusion is simple; the amortization of fixed capital is renewed in period 2; the necessity of the false emissions is therefore present again in period 2. Therefore, although (wage) emissions are all independent from each other, the emissions of the second sector follow in period 2 the same determination as the emissions of this sector in period 1.

We can give a stylized example in order to show how inflation is newly created in each period even though its numerical value is predetermined in a way. Suppose that the accumulated fixed capital loses its "value" in each period for a measure of 30 units of wages. The amortization of capital is a movement both negative (the loss of value of fixed capital) and positive (the making up in fixed capital of the lost value). Therefore, in the period under consideration, dual production or inflation is an emission newly cast, without any link with the previous emissions; however, the numerical value of inflation is dictated by the "pace" of the amortization of fixed capital; since accumulated fixed capital loses in each period 30 units of value, the new inflation is in each period equal to 30 units of value: this is to say that 30 units of wages are periodically issued in the second sector.

Fixed capital being thus placed in the continuum, we can determine the maximum amount of dual production and therefore of inflation in proportion to the domestic product in each period.

In no period can inflation (or the production of the second sector) exceed a third of total industrial production

The reasoning is based on a tautology: *net* investment in each period increases accumulated fixed capital. However, over time, the accumulation is not constrained in any limit: one cannot conceive of any period of production that would not bring a new income available for saving or consumption and able to finance new increments in fixed capital. Since the value of the accumulated means of production can increase indefinitely, it follows that the absolute value of amortization goods necessary in each period to maintain the accumulated capital-goods is, in principle, itself following an indefinite increase over time. Let us note that this conclusion does not depend on the "rotational velocity" of fixed capital (the velocity at which it "loses" and "recuperates" its value). If rotational velocity is lower, amortization increases more slowly: however, the principle stated above does not concern the velocity of the growth of the share of amortization goods in the domestic product per period but the theoretically unlimited nature of this growth over time. We must therefore maintain the following judgement: because of the indefinite increase in fixed capital over time, the share of the production of amortization goods in the global production of the economy in each period itself increases indefinitely over time. However, is it permitted to induce that the relative share of the production of the second sector is also an increasing function of the flow of time? If a positive answer were to be confirmed, one would have to formulate the principle according to which the "capitalist" economy is condemned to favour more and more the second sector compared to the first one and, thus, the relative share of inflationary emissions. Yet, there is a *formal* limit to the growth of the share of dual production in the global production.

Dual production is determined in a "tryptic". Any production of profit-goods undergoes *two substitutions*: profit-goods are substituted to amortization goods which are substituted to an equivalent amount of saved wage-goods. Let us recall briefly the rule of those two substitutions. The production of amortization goods generates a *net* profit; there we see the first substitution; profit-goods take the place of amortization goods. But the income earned in the production of profit-goods is spent to purchase amortization goods; it is the second substitution: first constituted of wage-goods (*stricto sensu*), forced savings are now defined on amortization goods.

Let us calculate the incompressible share of wage-goods in the industrial domestic product. Since the production of wage-goods also finances the two other productions, amortization-goods and profit-goods, the share of wage-goods in the total industrial product cannot be lower than a third. It follows that the share of profits-goods cannot be higher than a third, since wage-goods and amortization-goods represent at least two thirds of the industrial product.

We know thus that despite the indefinite growth of the accumulation of fixed capital, its amortization cannot in any period generate a dual production higher than a third of the domestic product in the industry.

One wonders then how the amortization of the additional parts of fixed capital will operate once the share of dual production can no longer grow. The answer is found at the end of the same reasoning, provided it is supplemented with the new piece of information. Production of the additional amortization-goods also generates a *net* profit; however, the additional profit-goods will necessarily undergo an "avatar": they cannot be financed by the production of wage-goods, which cannot increase since the two other productions absorb two-thirds of the industrial activity. *It follows that the additional profit-goods can only be financed by the wages issued in the production of amortization-goods*: this is to say that amortization-goods are identified as profit-goods. It results that the production of the additional profit-goods is in reality a production of wage-goods.

Let us continue the analysis by supposing that in the economy under scrutiny dual production has already reached its limit. Let us first recall a key lesson: inflation cannot be detected in relation to a period of reference.

As the share of dual production no longer increases (it cannot increase once it reaches a third of the production in the industries of the country), it is impossible that the general level of prices of wage-goods should increase: it is therefore clearly established that the measure of inflation by the method of price indices is severely misleading

The only scientifically accurate measure of the general price level is to count the units of wages issued. In the first sector, this amount is equal to x. Let us suppose that x is constant in the periods under consideration. In each period, the inflationary gap is defined by the production of the second sector. During the time when, in the industry, dual production remains equal to a third of global production, inflation is maintained at a level strictly constant; but *it cannot be observed in a variation of the general price level.* The price of the "whole" of the goods of the first sector is invariably equal to x units of wages, even though in each period a *new* inflation occurs, at a high rate since it is equal to 50% of x.

The method of indices and the calculation of their variations are used for an obvious reason: statisticians follow the received, quantitativist, theories. But another explanation is more interesting; income holders are not sensitive to the "absolute" variations of prices: if inflation takes away today their income in the same proportion as yesterday, the loss is "silent"; it is not at all perceived. Only quantum analysis will enlighten consumers: in the *current* period they leave a third of their income to inflation: under those conditions, if they are told that "inflation is under control" (this is indeed the usual terminology) since the global price of consumption goods has not increased, they now see the truth; constant prices only mean that the loss of today is not higher than previous losses: the sum withdrawn by inflation is not annulled; it is simply stabilised at the level of a third of the income that the domestic economy is producing in each period in all its industries.

However, the *relative* increase in the price of wage-goods is a meaningful index even in quantum analysis.

When inflation results, "dynamically", in the continuous increase of the price of wage-goods over time, the theorist is made aware of an important truth: the share of wage-earners is decreasing

Since the share taken by inflation never exceeds one third of industrial production, one may easily think that wage-earners always keep at least two thirds of the industrial product. But this is gravely false. In reality, we have to take into account the transfers of wages and especially the formation of *net* profit.

Wages issued in the "crown" (the second sector) are the measure of "inflation profits"; but additional profits are formed in each period in the core (first sector). Moreover, a law may be formulated: the capital accumulated in the second sector – that is the "over-accumulated" capital in contrast with the capital created in the first sector (just accumulated) – can find its profit only in the income created in the core. It is indeed formally impossible that the "crown" should issue by itself the profit corresponding to the units of capital that come to life there. *All the profit allocated to capital is produced in the first sector*, for accumulation as well as for *over-accumulation*. This is so because the income created in the second sector is by definition issued in an operation of the set of F (firms) on the set of F. The expenditure of inflation profit can therefore only take two possible forms, an overaccumulation or a "consumption of luxury goods". In both cases, the remuneration of the accumulated capital has to be found; it can therefore only come from the first sector.

Caused by the activity of the "crown", overaccumulation therefore triggers a "dynamic" increase of the profit formed in the core. However, the increase of (normal) profit is obtained in only one possible way, namely *by an increase in the selling price of wage-goods*. Again, we observe that the method of price indices is an awkward detection tool: the increase in prices is meaningful if it is related to the costs of production, item by item. Indices are good only if we suppose that the increase in prices compared to costs is uniform in the whole sector of wage-goods (or of consumption goods). But the principle may be formulated independently from statistical methods: the *global* price of wage-goods increases "absolutely" as soon as the number of units of wages transferred in profit increases.

Another difficulty appears; the increase in prices is not observed in the "action" but in its result; however, an action in the opposite direction is concomitant: the productivity of instrumental capital. Prices are stimulated to increase (in order to increase profit) but they are also driven down (by productivity gains). As soon as the increase in prices is *net*, we know that the effect of accumulation and overaccumulation of fixed capital has become negative for the set of workers.

The observation of facts demonstrates that we have been living for a long time under the regime of inflation. And the disorder appears in its true measure if we go back to its source, present in each monthly production; inflation has a unique definition: it is identified permanently to the global production of the second sector of the economy.

But the presence within the domestic economy of the second sector also creates the conditions for unemployment.

Let us first check that no unemployment would be *"involuntary"* if the economy did not include any dual production.

29 Involuntary unemployment would necessarily be nil if the domestic economy did not include any dual production

Regarding Say's law, three attitudes can be discerned. Taken at face value, it means that global demand always absorbs the goods in supply so that domestic production is only limited by the preference for leisure time. At a higher degree of intellectual subtlety, the "law" is purely and simply rejected on the ground that it would only be valid in an imaginary world, conforming to a naively ideal view. Finally, the law is accepted and promoted to the level of perfectly exact laws, to which only the principles of logic can aspire: Say's law is the formulation of an identity.

We shall stand at the third level: Say's law is exact. We shall demonstrate first that, in the absence of production in the second sector, the law means the formal impossibility of any involuntary unemployment. Then we shall establish that the production of profit-goods (or inflation) is not at all an exception to the law, which being logical or necessary, can admit of none. Finally, we shall show that in the presence of production in the second sector, Say's law, in spite of being perfectly exact, is not opposed to the existence of true unemployment, *involuntary unemployment*.

Without production in the second sector, Say's law implies the nullity of any involuntary unemployment

We are reasoning only in the "core" since the "crown" is absent. However, the product of the core is deposited both into money and in (continuous) time. We verify therefore that any good supplied is *necessarily* demanded. At no level of domestic employment could it happen that the set of income holders is not demanding the *totality* of the goods produced. Any unemployment that would happen under those circumstances would necessarily be voluntary or intentional.

Any good in supply is necessarily demanded

The strongest demonstration of the identity between global supply and demand considers the product *in* money. Supply is the action that introduces the product within the units of wages; demand is the *state* resulting from this action. But how could demand be a *state*? In reality, the product is maintained within money by a positive *action*: saving is the action that transforms an income into capital. To say that the product is maintained within money means therefore that the saver will find again the product in the money later, when he decides to consume his income. Any product is therefore consumed or saved; if it is consumed, it is demanded; but if it is saved, it is also demanded; it is true that we might easily make a formal mistake: is not saved income intended for a *future* consumption? It would therefore not be demanded *now*; this is not correct, it is demanded now; an income is introduced into the category of capital only if it is *destroyed*; any income saved is therefore ipso facto a product that its holder has taken, *demanded*, in order to cast it into the future.

Another proof of the equivalence between Supply and Demand is based on the analysis of "absolute exchanges". Public opinion and most economists think that the payment of wages is an operation of the same nature and of the same sign as the purchases in the product market. One thinks therefore that firms are supplying workers with a "counterpart" or a "counter value" in exchange for the product. We know that this prejudice leads to certain failure. Money and product can unite in the same whole only in a very particular exchange: to have money and product as a given *before* being united is a pure *petitio principii*. We know now that the integration of the product-content into the money-form results from the emission of wages, which is an *absolute exchange*. If workers did not obtain their own product in nominal wages, money could not be cast into the payment of wages because it would remain heterogenous to the product. The union of number-money and matter-product cannot be carried out in a simple relative exchange; an exchange that is an objective mutation is needed, the same object being *changed* into a new identity; the payment of wages transforms money, a pure form, into a product, because nominal wages contain the new product. It would therefore be illogical to measure the product before it enters money. This means that the *entirety* of the real product is formed into money. And the absolute exchange satisfies the equivalence of Supply and Demand, because the same operation, the emission of wages, is for the same observer, a worker, the supply of the purely physical product and identically the demand of the same product into money.

Involuntary unemployment is usually conceived of as a loss of interest of the public towards products. By definition, the unemployed are ready to work; but if they were effectively employed, their product would not be demanded by anyone, or, at least, it would not be demanded at its value: part of the additional product would be "ignored", thus creating a clearing deficit. To avoid a deficit, firms limit the domestic activity to a level lower than that of full employment. All this "reasoning" is fundamentally wrong. Any unemployed newly hired person receives an income, the expenditure of which is *certain*; and the expenditure of the additional income defines an additional demand. It is inconceivable that a created income should be lacking to Demand.

Any created income is necessarily spent

The law of flux-reflux is not normative but logical; we know it well; let us sum it up briefly. The domestic product is in a way taken into the "circle" of money; the to-and-fro of wage units, their creation-destruction, grasps the product and liberates it: in the space of an instant, matter is thus embraced by money and receives its imprint. If the theorist were to give himself only one of the two movements of opposite direction, he would not succeed to "lodge" matter into money and his science would be founded on a product that would be *formless* in the proper sense, which would be neither measured nor, even, defined. All the theses according to which the income received may or may not be spent, depending on their holders, claim to derive economic laws from the behaviour of economic agents. However, psychological factors do not have the ability to bring together those two distinct objects: the number-money and the matter-product. Only an "objective" law can obtain this result. The transformation into a product of the matter extracted from natural resources is identically the transformation of the material product into a sum of (dimensionless) numbers. The effect is obtained by the emission of wages, that is, once again, by an operation both positive and negative: the thought process therefore stops half-way when it gives itself the formation of income without its expenditure. The truth incorporates both opposite aspects at the same time; otherwise, it would let both slip away. No income is formed unless in its formation-*expenditure*. If its expenditure is not present in the very act of its formation, income is not formed. It is therefore *contradictory* to speak of a formed income that would not be spent: if it is truly formed, it is *necessarily* spent.

Economists are not always used to "abstractions". Is it not true that in real life the behaviour of agents invalidates the really too strict, "inhuman", law of the instant flux-reflux of income? But at once there is a need to renounce "qualifying" the thought; science cannot gain anything from a bundle of contradictions. If production is a creation-destruction, no income can exist without being destroyed at the instant of its coming to life; the agents can only put up with it: no ballerina has ever abolished the law of gravity.

Minds are somewhat soothed by the fact that income has a positive life expectation in chronological (or continuous) time; the instantaneity of the destruction is therefore only obtained by retroaction. But then, we face a temptation: is not the behaviour of agents fully operating in continuous time? Common sense would finally prevail. It is true, doubtless, that the expenditure of income coincides retrospectively with its creation. It is also certain that the agents are free to differ the expenditure and even to postpone it indefinitely. And is not a constantly postponed expenditure finally no expenditure at all? This is true but the reflexion has to go deeper. The choice between consumption and saving would not exist if money were material; we have demonstrated that savings and capital are of a zero sum in any economy devoid of bank money. To appreciate the true meaning of the alternative, it is therefore necessary to keep in mind its *concrete* enabling condition: only bank money gives to the *set* of income holders the choice between consuming and saving. Henceforth, logic takes its course. Any saving in bank money is a loan. It is formally impossible that savings should be "hoarded"; let us try to understand why; this is crucial. Any holder of a wage or non-wage income holds a claim on the bank that has issued this income; this is tautological. However, the claims on the bank are loans or, identically, *deposits* right from the beginning – from the emission of income: the financial side of the operation of emission has the immediate and automatic effect of transforming the income into a deposit. This is to say that holders lend income to the banking system. The contradiction would be blatant if we were positing the existence of a saved but not lent income. In fact, consumption is drawn from savings; as soon as a creditor draws on his deposit, he transforms it: savings become an income again and the income is spent. It can therefore never happen, whatever the rational or irrational behaviour of the agents, that an income should evade both an expenditure in the product market *and an expenditure in the financial market*. As long as the deposited income is not withdrawn (to be consumed), it is saved *through a loan* since the saver holds a claim on the bank.

Only the conclusion is left to be drawn. Being a loan, saving implies the existence of a borrower. However, the borrower belongs to one of the two parts of the domestic economy, either the set of firms (F) or the set of income holders (H). If the borrower is in the set of income holders, savings are consumed. There would be therefore a "problem" only in the case where the borrower is a firm. The income that firms are attracting in the financial market would be lacking for the clearing of the goods already produced and the damaging result would be confirmed: a part of created income would not be spent. The reader knows perfectly the fault in this reasoning: any income borrowed by firms is necessarily reinjected into the set of income holders where it is again available to complete the clearing that was faultily believed to be threatened.

Suppose then that the economy resorbs part of its unemployment; the additional income finances, in a perfect equivalence, the additional purchases: it is certain consequently that the persistence of unemployment does not at all come from the behaviour of agents. Whatever the purpose we assign it, income is cast into the purchases in the products market by its initial holders or by the borrowers. And one can hardly imagine how a borrowed income might stay "idle" for long; if behaviour were irrational to that point, logic would still prevail because it always does: the strange borrower would in fact be a borrower-lender because his take from the financial market would remain deposited at the disposition of another seller of financial claims; in the end, the absurdity of this behaviour would simply translate into a "meaningless" indebtedness of the first borrower who would pay an interest on funds kept idle by him (and by him alone).

Any hired worker brings a "cost" and a "yield" that are strictly equivalent

The demonstration has already been given. Since not a single "atom" of income issued on the newly employed worker may be lost within the economy, firms will invariably retrieve the entirety of the sum that enters additionally in the wages. The net cost of getting an employed person back to work is therefore always strictly nil. If the unemployed person wishes to work, his job gives him an income that fully "sanctions" his productive activity: he becomes the owner of the added product, except if part of it is given away in the formation of transfer incomes: in no case would part of the increased product be left over.

It is true though that some produced goods may not find buyers. But this obvious truth does not become valid starting from a "threshold" that would be the frontier between employment and unemployment. Even the fraction of the population already employed produces goods that are certain, at the stage of production, to be purchased. The criterion is not the *spontaneous* return on each product of the income generated by its manufacturing but only the equality of the *sum* of the expenditures and of the *sum* of the created income. In this respect, the intuition of Jean-Baptiste Say is brilliant: a clearing crisis cannot be global. As soon as a lack of purchases affects a particular product, the sale of the *other* products is boosted in the same proportion. The sum of the losses caused by the free "direction" of the expenditures in the products market is formally nil for firms taken as a *whole.*

A *general* crisis would be defined by a lack of expenditures; particular crises only mean that the refluxes do not all "flow" spontaneously into the precise channels of the corresponding fluxes. However, the distinction between the two crises, the general and the particular ones, does not coincide at all with the distinction between employment and unemployment: any active worker, whether he is maintained in his job or on the contrary newly hired, receives an income that *flows back integrally* in the products market, through any "channel", that is to say on any goods. It is the reflux that is essential; since it necessarily happens and at any level of domestic employment, the theorist is perfectly aware: he does not know anything yet on the origin of unemployment.

As soon as the domestic economy includes the second sector, Say's law remains perfectly valid but it is henceforth compatible with the existence of a positive unemployment

We shall first recall the demonstration according to which the production of the second sector also obeys Say's law or identity. Then we shall offer the essential proof: in full compliance with Say's law, it effectively so happens that the product of the second sector does not find any purchaser, *because of the insufficiency of income available in the economy.*

Thus, even though any production brings sufficient income to clear its result, "unemployment equilibrium" means that the income created by production does not "cover" the whole product. This seems contradictory and therefore impossible; but we have become cautious: quantum analysis has many hidden surprises. It might be brave to welcome them; but it is especially

368 Synopsis 9: Involuntary unemployment

imperative because no other explanation gets at the core of the mystery of unemployment.

Say's law is valid in the second sector as well as in the first

We can proceed quickly because this has already been covered (and more than once).

In the first sector, the "monetization" of the product is the effect of two half-emissions, of which the second is *posterior* to the first. Wage-goods stay in the money; the income thus defined (transformed into capital-time) is destroyed only by the final expenditures of wage and non-wage income. The ultimate union of the two half-emissions completes the flux-reflux, creation-destruction of the income of this sector.

In the second sector, we observe on the contrary that the created income is instantly destroyed. Profit-goods only pass through the money-form; they are introduced into it, but not to be finally withdrawn *later*: they are liberated from money at the instant of the remuneration of their producers and they never go back into it. We see that, far from being invalidated, the circuit of creation-destruction of income is completed perfectly; the income born from the production of profit-goods is immediately destroyed in the clearing of profit-goods that are appropriated without delay by the set of firms.

Under those conditions, it is hard to imagine that the income created in the second sector should be lacking for the clearing of profit-goods.

In order to get "closer" to the solution, attention must be payed to the fundamental rule requiring that the remunerations (or the sum of dividends) received for the accumulated profit-goods should have the production of the *first* sector as their unique source.

The capital accumulated in the second sector finds its remuneration in the first sector

It is well known that this is so since the monetary profits made in the second sector are, by definition, absorbed in the wages issued to remunerate the producers of profit-goods. In order to ensure a return for the accumulated fixed capital, firms are left to find in the sale of wage-goods a profit in an increasing proportion of the income available in the economy.

However, in advanced capitalism, the growth of profits cannot sustain the required pace.

The law of the tendency of profits to fall

One must be aware of the fact that transferred income (of which dividends are a part) cannot extend to more than half of the income earned in the production of wage-goods. This is so because the transfer of income requires the payment of workers from the "fund of captured wages". This fund must therefore be supplied. Hence, the share of wage-earners cannot be reduced further once it only represents half of the wage-goods produced. A further reduction of their "distributed share" would take away from workers the means of supplying the income of transfer. Any worker paid from the fund of captured wages receives *definitively*, under the form of a monetary capital, the power to purchase the wage-goods corresponding to the fund spent. And no transfer can be fed by a monetary *capital* (instead of an income). The increase in the share of dividends in national income reaches therefore a stopper imposed by logic: whatever their good will, workers cannot give back more than half of their earnings, born in each period from the production of wage-goods.

We have thus arrived at the demonstration of the "law of the tendency of profits to fall". Referred to an ever-growing capital, profit cannot increase indefinitely, nor can it ensure the remuneration of (accumulated and over-accumulated) capital at a sufficient rate, not even, when capitalism is even more advanced, at a rate still positive.

We have thus progressed in the explanation of unemployment; but the goal is far from being reached. This is because it is not yet apparent why Say's law, the validity of which is confirmed, does not keep preventing the possibility of an unemployment equilibrium. Even though profits are henceforth formed at a rate insufficient to enable the remuneration of the already over-accumulated capital, the production of the second sector keeps going in parallel to the production (that is itself kept going) of amortization-goods. However, whether remunerative or not, any production of the second sector is instantly a creation-destruction of income: it could not be conceived therefore that the income born from the production of profit-goods could be insufficient to absorb in any period the integral part of this product.

However, it suffices to put together all the information available to us to see the fundamental reason for the existence of clearing deficits.

Let us be clear that the deficit at issue is *general* in the sense that it defines *the global insufficiency of the created income* and not just an imperfect distribution of income in the channels of final expenditure in the products market. Is not the "law of markets" invalidated since the sum of available income, even completely spent, is not equal to the task and cannot withdraw from the market the total volume of the goods on supply?

In reality, Say's law is unbreakable; if we were to abandon it, it would be at the cost of the coherence of our research and then the goal would be unattainable.

But, if it is a constraint under all circumstances, the law of the markets has a precise definition that must obviously be complied with: any created income is spent *once*. Thus, an income of x units of money is spent for an amount of x units of money, neither more nor less. We start to see the "fault" through which unemployment may set in. The insufficiency of income is a positive fact once certain goods are condemned, by their very nature, to be cleared *twice*.

The careful examination of the identity of profit-goods leads to the solution: it is confirmed that it is logically necessary to clear part of them twice instead of once.

The logical necessity of clearing some profit-goods twice instead of once

The classification of wage-goods and profit-goods is not *physical* but purely *economic*. It is not permitted either to assimilate overaccumulation (constituted in profit-goods) to accumulation (in capital-goods). Let us recall the definition.

Wage-goods. These are all the goods produced in the first sector: consumption-goods, investment-goods and amortization-goods.
Capital-goods. They include investment-goods and they are part of the wage-goods when they result from "productive consumption". Net investment is said to be an accumulation of capital. Overaccumulation produces (in the second sector) additional capital-goods.
Profit-goods. These are all the goods produced in the second sector. They are distinguished from the wage-goods according to an absolutely clear-cut criterion: in the first sector, the emission of wages is depositing the product within money; in the second sector, the emission of wages withdraws at once the product from money. We induce from this that wage-goods are appropriated in nature only by the effect of an operation posterior to the payment of wages. As for profit-goods, they are on the contrary immediately appropriated in nature. The beneficiaries of profit-goods are included in the set of firms, whereas wage-goods belong in money to the set of wage and non-wage income holders.

However, the category of profit-goods has to be "broken up".

Internal divisions of the profit-goods category

We first discern the goods intended to "luxury consumption". It is not at all necessary, either logically or in fact, that firms should employ *free* labour to produce goods that they plan to use in order to obtain new, future earnings. Firms that own profit-goods may decide to assign them to a definitive consumption by persons designated as the beneficiaries of these donations. The complementary part of profit-goods is, by definition, kept in the process of production or in the process of circulation. The profit-goods kept in the process of production are *fixed capital* added on to the net investments produced in the first sector: it is invested profit-goods that create *over-accumulation*. We still have to consider the profit-goods that, without being kept in the production process, are kept in the circulation process: they are clearly defined by saying that these profit-goods are produced and acquired *to be sold*. But to whom can profit-goods be sold? It is obvious that they are offered to the holders of wage and non-wage incomes; this is to say that the profit-goods of the third division *constitute a mass with wage-goods*: we shall call them therefore "wage-goods of the second sector".

We thus arrive at the conclusion mentioned before. The wage-goods of the second sector are profit-goods that cannot be cleared definitively unless they are cleared twice. They are cleared first in the emission of wages (of the second sector) and they are sold again in the product market. The crucial question is raised at once: is the income issued in the domestic economy sufficient to clear twice the wage-goods produced in the second sector? The adverse proof is easily given.

*National income is coextensive to wage-goods (*proprio sensu*) and to the profit-goods consumed or invested; it does not cover the wage-goods of the second sector*

The clearing or final sale of goods is the second half-emission of the product; produced goods are cleared precisely because they are withdrawn from money: monetary income (in other words the product-in-the-money) is therefore destroyed in the clearing operation.

Wages issued in the first sector are equivalent to wage-goods (*proprio sensu*).
Wages issued in the second sector are equivalent to profit-goods.

Let us notice now that no part of the income created in the first sector (Y1) can be assigned to the clearing of profit-goods. Indeed, wage and non-wage income is needed in its *entirety* for the sole clearing of the products of the first sector.

It follows that only the income issued in the second sector (Y2) is able to clear profit-goods.

However, the *total sum* of the income created in the second sector is immediately destroyed in the payment of the wages earned in the production of profit-goods.

A second alternative follows: (a) being cleared in the emission of wages of the second sector, profit-goods are not offered in the products market; (b) even though *all* the profit-goods are cleared in the producing services market, it happens however that part of them are cast in the products market.

As far as the profit-goods of the third division are concerned, term (b) of the alternative is completed.

Let P1 be the product of the first sector and P2 the product of the second sector; the profit-goods of the third division (the wage-goods produced in the second sector) are P3.

Income Y1 is absorbed by the clearing of P1; for its part, income Y2 is destroyed by the clearing of P2. Even though P3 is a part of P2, P3 must be cleared once again: *however, there is no income still available for this.* In the whole measure of product P3, the domestic economy experiences therefore a clearing deficit: Say's law guarantees *one* clearing for the *whole* of the product (P1 + P2) but it does not provide any clearing for product P3, *for the reason that it has already been cleared within P2.*

Domestic production is in equilibrium at a level of industrial activity lower than that of full employment because the tendency of the rates of profit to fall leads firms to produce profit-goods under the form of wage-goods

The flows of amortization of (accumulated and over-accumulated) fixed capital generate dual production, which no one can prevent, except through reforming the "deep mechanisms" of the economy. However, apart from luxury consumption, the "dual" product (or product of the second sector) is immediately – right from its coming to life – aggregated to the mass of the already existing fixed capital. If profit-goods are not consumed, they are saved or capitalized and any capital, the holders of which are firms, is a fixed capital. It would therefore be "natural" that the non-consumed profit-goods should be composed of *instrumental capital*. The tendency of the rate of profit to fall introduces a severe disorder: not finding enough return for their fixed capital under an instrumental form (machines and all kinds of equipment), firms can only accumulate (or "over-accumulate") the profit-goods under the form of wage-goods produced in the second sector. Firms then do not produce in order to produce even more (through increasing the means of production), but in order to *resell*. Under those conditions, the domestic economy no longer creates enough income to ensure the clearing of the whole product.

The sum of the leftovers gives the exact measure of the product that it is in the interest of firms to "cut": they lay off the workers who, kept in employment, would have produced goods P3.

The dysfunction in the formation of capital may be grasped through another channel: the determination of interest.

30 Neither inflation nor unemployment would exist in an economy where all monetary capital transits through financial markets

We are not going to treat this subject, we shall only touch upon it.

In the core, the determination of interest corresponds perfectly to the theory of "loanable funds". Capital is productive because it brings an interest and not vice versa.

Interest is a transfer income. However positive interest brings about positive returns to invested capital

Income holders obtain the entirety of the product deposited into money; this product is first saved under the simple form of capital-time. But, if firms wish to fix savings into instrumental capital, they have to reach an agreement with income holders. The contract is signed at a certain "price"; it is decided that the saver will receive an "interest" for the consigned capital.

But why is interest positive? We know that this question has been raised by the oldest and more profound philosophies. Today the answer is available. Any savings fixated into instrumental capital is *lost forever to income holders taken as a whole.*

Traditionally and even usually nowadays, interest is thought of as being *additive* to capital; in those conditions, it is not at all obvious that interest should be positive: why, indeed, should the lender get both his capital and an interest? It is true that the lender must "wait": would not then the interest be the price of time? This is even less plausible since capital is an income cast through time. Logically, it is not therefore the "lending" operation that introduces time; because, let us repeat it, time is already present in the *object* of the loan, the (lent) capital.

The reality is both simpler and more profound. Income is a magnitude belonging to quantum time. Capital is defined in chronological or continuous time. Capital is therefore literally the *transposition* of a magnitude, from one "space" into another. However, by definition, any capitalised income is saved: it is "rescued" and will reappear. But there is a category of capital that will render income *indefinitely fixed*: each passing day defines, *for the future*, another day of waiting. This is to say that the "liberation" of income is differed from one day to the other: it will therefore never happen. The definition of capital is not affected because the income from which it results is an equivalent future income: that the date of the reproduction of the income should be indefinitely postponed does not change anything to the nature of capital. But it is important nevertheless to draw the correct conclusion: any capital that fix income for an unlimited amount of time is in fact the *definitive* transformation of the initial income.

We now perceive that interest is not additive to capital; it is, on the contrary, the compensation obtained by the lender who definitively loses the income fixed into capital. The compensation necessarily takes the form of a periodic income: indeed, if it were offered at one unique date, only once, it would mean the "restitution" of the capital or, identically, repayment to the lender, a possibility that is precisely ruled out by the logic of fixed capital. We thus see that if capital in general is the transformation of an income in the continuum, fixed capital is itself transformed: this time, the magnitude is caught in the continuum and it is placed, repetitively, in quantum time. Being unable to liberate the income from which it originated, fixed capital results in a theoretically unlimited series of incomes *newly produced in each period*, the amount and frequency of which are decided by the contracting parties.

The explanation of interest implies therefore both an *objective* factor (the loss of the "differed" income and the compensation it calls for) and a *subjective* factor (the evaluation of the compensation that is due and the conditions of its payment). But since the loss is positive, it is certain that the compensation must be so as well; a positive interest is not the extension or the "surpassing" of capital but its transposition into another space: it shifts from continuous time (where it is annulled due to the definitive loss of the fixated income) to quantum time, where it appears under the form of "annuities" or, again, of "monthly instalments", indefinitely repeated.

However, can it really be proven that interest is not additive to capital? In reality, any saver will recover his capital at the term of the loan or even before, at the date of his choice, if he sells his claim. And, at completion of the operation, it will not be said to the lender that he has necessarily renounced the interest since he has taken back his capital. Since what is true for any particular saver is also true for the "sum" of savers, interest is due in addition of capital: in the end, it would therefore not be a simple transposition of the capital from one space to another.

However, the argument that we have just sketched is vicious. It confuses "a sum" with "a set".

Interest is not additive to capital because fixed capital is definitively lost by the set of income holders

The correct reasoning is based on the *set of savers* and not on the *sum* of savers considered one after the other. The set of savers and even, more generally, the set of income holders loses definitively any income fixated into a capital. The theory of interest is one perfect example: macro-economic analysis can logically be carried out only on sets. It is true that any element of the set of income holders may retrieve (and most of the time, does retrieve) the income invested into capital; but the global truth is exactly the opposite: not a single "atom" of invested income is given back by fixed capital. It will never be observed therefore on the set of holders of wage and non-wage income (H) both the retrieval of the capital and the earning of interest. In fact, we rediscover the teaching according to which interest earned by set H is the compensation that it receives for the income lent, definitively lost in the capital. Finally, the chain of the successive lenders is sketching the different points of impact of the payment of interest to the set of income holders: capital is never given back since any refunding implies necessarily the consolidation or the *amortization* of the initial loan, in the hands of a new creditor.

Two important consequences follow directly from the fact that interest is not additive to capital but that it is just its "transposed repetition".

Pure capital-time carries interest only because it belongs to the same category as fixed capital

If no savings could be lent to the productive system (in the financing of the means of production), all savings would be lent from one agent to the other; in this sense, saving would be necessarily subjective. How can the formation of positive interest be explained then? That would be formally impossible for the reason already mentioned; savings do not exist before the loan; the saver does not have the choice to lend his capital or to keep it to himself: since his income is transformed into capital, he has become a lender in the operation. Interest can only come to life in the loan of savings, which is inconceivable, because saving is already lending.

The difficulty is lifted in the preceding case when saving means a loan to production: this is because here savings are *net*, the loan being carried out between a "subject" (the saver) and an "object" (the productive system).

If capital-time may nevertheless produce an interest, the reason is obvious; savers have the choice whether or not to transform capital-time into a fixed capital: since they receive an interest on one side, if they were not receiving any on the other side, no savings would ever be available in the financial market for consumption loans. (We have just mentioned the loan of savings; this is not forbidden as long as the loan is only the renewal of an *income* on a new beneficiary; in all rigour, we should speak of the loan of income. To lend savings is a redundant expression, just like financial capital which is in fact monetary.)

We can now turn to the second consequence mentioned above.

The industrial production of any period is divided into wages and interest only because the capital lent to the industry is given up by the set of savers

Let us recall the principle. Being unable to get back the invested income, the set of savers receive interest in compensation. It is the profound explanation of the production of interest-income besides wage-income.

Should it be concluded then, as Ricardo did, that interest is an income additive to wages? Certainly not; the Ricardian analysis "ended" there because it lacked quantum logic. Unless we reject the rule of the excluded middle, we cannot conceive interests as being part of wages. Thus, Ricardo did not deny the inevitable failure of his brilliant theory: if products come from labour, the analysis accounts for wages but misses out interest. Modern analysis grasps interest *within wages*, like a "telescopic category". The domestic product is entirely measured in wage-units; even "interest-goods" are not an exception.

- If interest were nil, no emission of wages would comprise a positive expenditure in the product market.
- Given that interest is positive, the emission of x units of wages includes the purchase, equal to y, of interest-goods, on behalf of their holders, the savers.

One single remark remains to be formulated. Interest being measured in "prices" and not in "values", "interest-goods" also are sold at a price higher than their cost of production: but it is quite clear that this difference is neutral with regard to the formation of interest that it neither reduces nor increases.

Any idea of a "productivity" or "efficiency" of fixed capital is therefore rejected

No theory has ever been able to *establish* the productivity of capital. It is posited; and it is easy to introduce in equations or in functions. But it is completely illogical and no "axiomatic" can accept inconsistencies.

Production is a wave-like action, both positive (creation) and negative (destruction). Interest therefore cannot be produced in addition to wages because only human labour introduces (creation) and withdraws (destruction) the matter extracted from natural resources, in and of the utility-form (or in and of the *numéraire*-money, the temporary form of the utility-form).

Capital does not produce anything, any more than natural resources, which are just transformed. Capital is purely instrumental. Few modern productions could come directly from the hands of man. Everywhere capital is indispensable. It is therefore not even meaningful to wonder what the specific contribution of the instrument used is: thus, the production of a *complete* computer would be compromised if human beings only had their hands to build it. Machines and technology are necessary everywhere. But what is the fraction of the computer that can be attributed to human labour, the complementary part being the work of technological and instrumental capital? In fact, the relations humans-machines are ancillary. Labour would not produce anything without machines; it produces everything *by means* of the machines. The correct analysis is therefore the following: with the help of capital, man *alone* introduces matter into the utility-form. Capital is not reducible to labour, not for the reason that it itself comes from it but because its role in production is strictly to give "wings", "arms" and even "data" to working people. The formal mistake consisting in putting labour and capital on the same rank in the "production function" comes fundamentally from the fact that labour is conceived of as a commodity: making labour (more) efficient, capital is therefore a "co-producer". Once the thought process succeeds in grasping the essential fact, namely that the product (or commodity) only exists as a projection of man – in matter at the contact with the utility-form – the naïvety is at last revealed: labour never casts itself in the utility-form; consequently, labour is never a commodity. To use the convenient words that economists are used to, one may say that no labour ever *enters* the process of production. Labour *defines* this process and the product only exists at the *exit*. As for capital, it is altogether an "input" and an "output": in a way, it goes through the process. Thus, net product (the output that is not an input) is only the effect of human labour (that is neither an output nor an input).

The fact remains however that interest pertaining to invested capital is a cost of production

Interest is indeed an income of transfer; we have just demonstrated it again. Nonetheless interest is a cost of production, not just for the set of firms but even in the eyes of the whole nation.

The definitive absorption of income into fixed capital is a cost of production for the nation. Interest is but the transposition of a capitalized income, which changes space, shifting from continuous to quantum time. We induce from this that interest is a macro-economic cost, borne by society as a whole.

Finally, the correct analysis observes man facing nature or its "environment"; fixed capital modifies the natural environment to make it easier to "penetrate". If interest were nil, the environment would not take anything back from man: it would allow him on the contrary to collect all the result of his work. But given that the improvement of the environment is costly, it is appropriate to introduce the Ricardian distinction between "producing" and "procuring". Man produces everything but as a producer he can procure for himself only the whole *diminished of the interest* that comes back in a way to the natural environment, therefore to its representative, the saver who is responsible for improving the environment. If, ultimately, interest is a "telescopic category" of wages, the reason lies in the fact that labour is an emission the effect of which is necessarily to inject *all* the product (including the share of interest) in the utility-form. It is therefore as if the saver were, in proportion to invested income, the co-issuer of the product, in the exact measure of the interest received.

Interest being clearly conceived of, we realize that the profits formed in the production of wage-goods are, for the most part, absorbed by interest. Only the "Schumpeterian innovation" can *temporarily* introduce a discrepancy between profit and interest.

Non-inflationary profit is, for the most part, reducible to the interest "issued" by the set of savers

We would not understand the formation of profit if it were not obeying a *determinism*; it would be anarchic, so to speak. However, the determinism of prices exists for two reasons. We have mentioned the first one: profit is identified to interest. The second reason is more hidden: any "clawing" back by firms of invested savings logically means the transformation of interest into a capital.

Interest forms the core of profit

In principle, selling prices cannot exceed costs of production; any apparent gap is based on a partial definition of costs. Since interest – as we have demonstrated – is a cost of production, its formation does not indicate, in the final instance, an excess of prices over values.

If the structure of the markets allows it, given monopolies and oligopolies, the gains in physical productivity due to technical and technological progress (the "innovations") are not immediately passed on to prices: in this case, interest is still, despite everything, the centre of gravity of profit.

We thus understand the fundamental principle; profits are not wages captured "for no reason", freely. If a firm succeeds in making a net profit, it owes it to the creative imagination of the "captains of industry" and to the intellectual and manual competences of the personnel.

But the impeccable functioning of the "profit economy" is confirmed mainly by the fact that firms cannot appropriate both the invested savings and the corresponding interest.

The transformation into profit of invested savings means ipso facto the transformation of interest into capital

It is often thought that profit is the logical source of investments. This representation comes about naturally within our economies, dominated as they are by the *pathology* of capital. For the moment, let us move on with the examination of the orderly functioning of capital.

- If firms are not "compensating" savers, interest is a cost of production that they pay to their beneficiaries.

- Once firms buy back savings, interest is no longer a cost of production; thus, instead of being emitted periodically under the form of interests, profit is at once "an actualisation of this (quantum) flow": it is a capital. And since the monetary capital is no longer lost (or given up), interest is no longer collected by *anyone*. We verify therefore the absolute law according to which interest is never additive to capital.
- However, interest comes to life again, both cost of production and income, when firms transmit the increase in capital to their shareholders. Dividends and interest form therefore eventually a unique category.

We are approaching the moment when we will have to open again the door of the pathology of "capitalism". But let us show again, before leaving the "anatomical" functioning of capital, that, contrary to the so common teaching of handbook truths, interest and national income are not at all co-determined.

In any event, national income is fully determined regardless of the rates of interest

The official doctrine is still these days the too famous "Hicks-Hansen" theory, although now regarded as highly suspicious by one of its authors. The rates of interest and the level of national income would be determined in one movement, like the simultaneous solution of a series of equations. Fundamentally, two equalizations are represented: between the demand (L) and the supply of money (M), and between the flows of investment (I) and of saving (S).

Suppose that L and M are adequate magnitudes; then they stand for the emission of money (M) and the demand for the issued money (L).

Once the analysis succeeds in introducing time into consideration, it suddenly becomes aware of a "devastating" truth: magnitudes L and M are defined in quantum time; by contrast, variables I and S belong to continuous time. The intersection of the two representative curves, on which professors have ruthlessly and relentlessly drawn the attention of generations of students, is therefore a pure fantasy.

The LM curve is set in quantum time

Any emission (or supply) of money has a zero-dimension in continuous time. To retrieve a positive time-dimension – and could the supply of money be devoid of any? – quantum time must be called for. Any emission of money is the creation of an income and any income is a "quantized" piece of the continuum.

Even if we suppose that L may be distinguished from M, the money demand is an action or the result of an action. As an action, L is the "other face" of M; as a result, L is the sum of the "desired cash-balances". However, any (monetary) balance is an income and, therefore, a quantum of time.

Finally, the LM "curve" does not exist because it is composed of only a succession of separated (by finite distances) points, one point and only one per period.

But even if it did exist, the LM curve would be unable to meet the IS curve, the space of which is continuous time.

The IS curve is set in continuous time

As soon as income (in bank money) comes to life, it is destroyed because it is transformed into capital: and capital is a magnitude belonging to the continuum. In this regard, the supply and demand of "loanable funds" effectively matches an analysis of a micro-economic type. Continuous adjustments can therefore be imagined between I and S. Theorists make then the formal mistake consisting in placing the adjusted magnitudes (and not simply their adjustments) in the continuum. It is unfortunate that the mistake does not bring any reward to its authors. Even if the IS curve were set in the continuum, it would never meet the LM curve which belongs to a completely different space.

In truth, domestic income is entirely determined by the emission of wages and the flux of wages is entirely founded on their (expected) reflux

All wages are *absolute* magnitudes. Workers are paid by themselves. Thus, voluntary unemployment is an ill-formed concept. The economy would experience a constantly nil unemployment *if it were not for the dysfunction of capital*.

All the disorder (inflation and unemployment) is generated by the financial flows that do not transit through the market

In dual production, profit does not replace savings that would be formed by the set of income holders. Inflationary profit is formed in its very expenditure and therefore completely evades the rules of the financial market.

A great hope – more than a hope, the certainty of overcoming the pathology – is offered by quantum macro-economics. The presence of the second sector is not a fatality. Man is free; he can liberate himself from it. Louis de Broglie said that science is the conscience that, through man, nature is taking of itself. Pure economic theory is a "re-creation", the *conception* of the formal laws of how money, income and capital are functioning. Then, having, thanks to human intelligence, recreated its pathology, profoundly present in the facts, nature needs man a second time to be *cured*.

One must be wary of a conception of the "norms" that would be too normative. Once the intellect penetrates the pathology (which is, as indicated by its name, a branch of logic and not a field on the fringe of the laws), it arrives at the formulation of the remedy. The same intellectual movement, the conception of the object, reveals – one should say creates – the malformation. Then the mind collects itself: he conceives better and finally delivers the purified object to nature. Normative science is then the perfection of positive science.

From the day monetary flows will run into the three bank departments, inflation and unemployment will be abolished. During the transition period, the global economy will endure a benign imperfection. All production will be contained right from the start in the *core*, the "crown" being immediately destroyed. This is the key point. All the financial flows related to the new increases in fixed capital will be transported by the financial market. Appropriated by firms, capital will only subsist through its "shadow", under the form of circulatory equity funds. Later, these funds will be "consolidated". But this event may be postponed for several years (or even several decades). Nevertheless, inflation and unemployment will be *without delay* cut from their source and will start at once their erosion in continuous time. The effect of the equity funds will simply be the persistence of collecting owed interest.

Glossary of the main concepts

CAPITAL. Quantum analysis breaks the circle that entraps the neo-classical theory where income derives from capital like a flow from a stock whereas capital is defined as the accumulated result of past flows or the actualised value of future flows. Under these conditions, both magnitudes, income and capital, are only reciprocally determined. The new analysis breaks off from the chicken and egg pattern: income is the initial magnitude because its definition is given independently from any conception of capital. Thus, income formed in each period does not originate from any capital whether financial or instrumental; it comes from a human emission, the expense of labour. The income formed is at once transformed into capital-time. Capital is therefore generated by income which is not generated by capital. CAPITAL-TIME is the transformation of a current income into a future income. Only income in the form of bank money is able to constitute a bridge between the present and the future. Any kind of capital starts initially as capital-time. FIXED CAPITAL is the capital-time that has been incorporated into instrumental goods, means of production of all sorts. Genuine capital-time is reversible: it will be eventually destroyed while liberating the income of which it constituted the temporary savings. Fixed capital is irreversible; as indicated by its name, it is fixed into instrumental capital, the saved income will stay there forever.

CREDIT. It has either a real or a monetary object depending on the circumstances. When the object of the credit is monetary, money and credit are still perfectly distinct because credit is one thing, its object another thing. Theorists and practitioners alike often confuse money with credit; the origin of this confusion is to be found in a mistaken conception of money creation by banks. Whether scriptural or fiduciary, money is never issued in a credit operation; it always results from the productive activity in the economy and, more precisely, from the expense of human labour. Credits that have money as their object may be either quantic or ordinary. QUANTUM CREDITS are identified with the creation of incomes in bank money; workers as a whole are the initial lenders and firms as a whole are the final borrowers. Quantum credit is therefore not issued by banks. As for ORDINARY CREDIT, it is defined as the transfer of available incomes from lenders to borrowers; there again, banks, when they intervene, are only pure intermediaries. Ordinary credits concern money and real goods because their object is real money, defined as the product inside money. There are ordinary credits that do not involve money: the object, whether fungible or not is lent and taken back in nature.

CREDIT MONEY. It is bank money. It was believed that banks create money through credit operations. By granting a credit to its client, the bank would create money on him. In reality, only quantum credits are associated with the creation of monetary incomes. And even quantum credits are not created by banks; they start from income earners and end up with firms, banks being only in-between. Money is said to be credit money because it is fiduciary; even the money created by commercial banks is fiduciary in that it is intangible. Monetary incomes come to life in production, which is not a (ordinary) credit operation.

EMISSION. It is the creation and destruction of the same object within one same movement. The expense of labour is an emission because the real product is instantaneously produced and consumed. Money (in particular bank money) is emitted. The emission of money is a nominal operation merged with the operation of real production. Created money is instantaneously destroyed, because it is transformed in savings, that is in capital-time.

INFLATION. It is positive when monetary income is numerically higher than the corresponding real income. Any inflation originates from empty emissions. Inflation will be definitively defeated when all bank money emissions are full emissions. Under those conditions, involuntary unemployment will also be eradicated.

INVOLUNTARY UNEMPLOYMENT. It is defined as an insufficient amount of monetary income relatively to the real income created by full employment. The monetary income is insufficient in so far as firms produce wage goods in empty emissions.

MONEY. It is either material or bank money. Nowadays, money everywhere is bank money; even coins are issued through banks, representing in part their commitments. The VALUE OF MONEY is the relation of equivalence between the monetary form and the product that it contains. PRODUCTION is the act that introduces the physical product into the monetary form.

NUMERAIRE. It is a pure number, without any dimension. In actual economies, money operates as the *numéraire*; in that regard, it can be called nominal money. Real money is the association of the *numéraire*-money with the product. Real money defines income.

PROFIT GOODS. They are the product of the empty emissions and can be identified to over-accumulation.

TIME. Production is defined neither inside continuous time (or dense) nor inside discontinuous time; it is both an instantaneous act and a movement through time; consequently, production "quantifies" time. The product is QUANTUM TIME.

WAGE-GOODS. They are the product of full emissions and they comprise consumption goods, amortization goods and investment goods (accumulation).

Afterword

In the foreword, we announced that the emission or the payment of wages is the unique operation that exists concretely. We have even observed, in the body of this book, that the real emission is, in all countries and at all times, the operation that explains the complete functioning of the economy, from production to distribution of the goods. The action of working defines a production-consumption, a flux-reflux, the only movement that inductive research can detect within the economies, even non-monetary ones.

Money's flow is immediately present within real production. If its presence were to stop there, the product would be real from its birth. But, ever since the first exchanges, money has been substituted by real products. In this respect, quantum analysis brings a surprising piece of information: any exchange between a good and money is an operation concluded between productions and not simply between a real good and a monetary good. Production (the action) is changed: instead of producing a good, the worker produces money.

Absolute exchange is difficult to conceive because money seems to pass through the experiment: it existed before and it will exist after. But this is only an appearance. In reality, money is only constituted in its union with the product; thus, a shell that has just been found is only a money by destination; it becomes an effective money at the exact moment it is given in exchange for a product. In the set of isolated workers, everyone consumes part of his own product; the remainder can be bartered or exchanged; barters are not exchanges except by a misuse of language; the product exchanged is changed into money: worker A deposits his product in the money to exchange it against a product deposited in the money by worker B.

Another difficulty blocks the thought process. It concerns the timing of the operations. Everything would be more obvious if the operations happened chronologically. Workers would give a "body" to money which would be the envelop of the product; then, they would bring the product-in-the-money to "markets", in order to exchange them against each other; finally, the money-envelop would be detached from real products, definitively transformed into values in use. Reality is subtler. It all happens in two instants that eventually constitute only one. In a first "stage", worker A hands over his product against a sum of money. In a second "stage", the same worker hands over the money against the product of someone else. However, quantum analysis teaches us the identity or the confusion of those two "stages". The worker does not carry out two distinct operations, in order to sell and purchase in two movements; he carries out one operation, a "sale-purchase". This is so because the intervention of money is situated at the level of the actions and not directly at that of their results.

Thus, worker A only succeeds in changing his product into money in the very operation where he changes it into the product of someone else: the monetary income (the money-form of the product) only comes to life in the operation of its creation-destruction: it would not exist if it were not destroyed at once. The expenditure of money by A is retroactively present at the instant when A "earns" it. In its deeper sense, the wage regime has therefore always existed, since the first exchanges. Apparently concluded only in the products market, the transactions were (retroactively) present in the producing services market. Any worker that exchanges (eventually) his product, is paying himself a wage, equal to the money earned.

In a narrower sense, the wage regime was born in the division of the economy into firms and workers. The theory of emissions receives then a first, illuminating, confirmation: we now see that the worker changes his product into money, because he does not first obtain it in kind. By separating workers from their product in kind, the wage regime enables the apparition of profits. As soon as workers obtain only a fraction of their own product in the full expenditure of their wages, they issue profits. The analysis shows then that, in the very payment of wages, workers have initially obtained only a fraction of their own product, all the non-wage incomes being immediately spent in the financing of the production of non-wage goods.

The substitution of bank money to "material" money brings the last evolution. The theory of emissions receives then its second, perfectly conclusive, confirmation. Bank money is formed in emissions, the definition of which is precise: they create and they destroy the same object in the same flow. Any other solution is profoundly illogical.

If money were not created, it could not be bank money. But if money were created in a movement that would not destroy it, it would literally be created *ex nihilo*: a positive magnitude would be extracted from a zero magnitude, like a rabbit out of a hat. Any (clearing) bank creates and destroys in the same movement. A critical question is then raised: if money always disappears at the instant it appears, how can the economy have positive money at its disposal? The embarrassment is the greater since this time the destruction of money happens at the instant of its creation in chronological time. If money were destroyed only retroactively, we would understand easily its "temporary" existence, maintained before retroaction comes into play. However, how could the rabbit come out of the hat, even temporarily? Money is indeed destroyed at the instant it comes to life. But even though it is immediately destroyed, bank money leaves a trace in the economy: a trace that is nothing else than monetary capital, a bridge between current incomes, destroyed at once, and future incomes, to be born at the clearing of the goods in stock. It suffices that an income exists at the instant of its creation; its disappearance generates an equivalent capital; and any capital is a future income, again equivalent.

Bank money therefore brings financial and real capital. Any economy devoid of banks would also be devoid of any net capital. But the substitution of bank money to "material" money has not just enabled the accumulation of capital: it defines capitalism, the regime of dual production or overaccumulation. Since the industrial revolutions, over-accumulated instrumental capital has created the material well-being of our societies. Now the time has come for simple accumulation, because over-accumulation now involves more costs than advantages. Entirely caused by over-accumulation, inflation and unemployment have become unbearable. After the reform of banks, investments will be financed by households' savings that will thus convert all non-distributed profits.

The economy will then comprise only two categories of incomes, wages and non-wage incomes. All the incomes that, in the current regime, are automatically and instantly denatured into capital (the over-accumulation) will have disappeared. But how can we explain the persistence of distributed profits? Let us recall that they existed well before the advent of bank money, therefore well before capital-time and, *a fortiori*, fixed capital, were born. This is because the profound explanation of distributed profits is Ricardian: they are closely related to interests. Is it to say that interest precedes capital? Not at all. Capital was a concrete reality well before the introduction of bank money: the borrower owes an income to the lender. In this relation, the capital is both positive and negative; it is not net in society. Nevertheless, it carries an interest. The first form of interest refers to zero-sum capital: the original interest ("Urzins") is a pure transfer, an income owed by the borrower to the lender ("Leihzins"). After the introduction of bank money, capital-time is net in society. But the interest owed on net capital is still a "Leihzins", a transfer income. The only difference is the following: firms must be able to clear their stocks at a price that covers the interest owed.

The fundamental *raison d'être* of non-wage incomes has just been formulated; dividends are the interests of shares, interests in the strict sense being paid to bondholders: in both cases, firms must find in the sale of wage-goods the financing of the production of both wage-goods and "interest-goods". At all times, profits tend to identify to the interests owed by firms on the accumulated capital-time. (Firms do not owe any interest for the invested capital, because the savings collected in the third department have their primary source in the wages formed into profits.)

"Endeavour" alone, creative imagination and innovation by entrepreneurs, give profits a lead on interests, the gap is constantly subjected to the hard law of competition the effect of which is to continuously diminish profits to reduce them to the level of interests.

The day over-accumulation ceases to exist, profits will be like the leaven of production, any net profit (in excess of interest) being the sign of the success of a firm. As Keynes had wished, society will then live under the regime of perfectly liberal socialism. It is true that a great task will then present itself: the reform of the international monetary system.

Appendix

Foreword by Henri Guitton, Member of the Institut de France

I have known Bernard Schmitt for a long time. He was the disciple of the late Robert Goetz. When the latter died on a slippery road one Easter Monday, I tried to replace him. It was through the CNRS (the French institute for scientific research) that we met when he was presenting his works and future publications to the Economics Commission. Later he became himself a member of this commission and I listened carefully when he reported on the works of others. I was struck by the rigour of his thought. I had read his PhD thesis and I followed over the years his numerous, difficult to read, successive books, which puzzled the oldest colleagues. As for myself, even if I did not always understand his wording and developments, I was intuitively caught by the insightfulness of his mind. There is an element of mystery in every intellectual meeting. I have respected this mystery and today the veil is lifted. What was difficult to express at the beginning of our relations comes now under a new light. The first uneasiness has dissipated. I discover in his demonstrations the intuitions that I found difficult to formulate. We are united in a singular way. We are not of the same age. I could be his father and I feel rejuvenated by his contact, even though I no longer have any academic activity and he has not yet reached his peak. One great research theme has more precisely united us: it is the theme of time, which can renew economics entirely. Having myself tried to investigate time in economics and having only outlined its analysis, I was glad to team up with a younger colleague, himself troubled by the same problem. We had the project of writing a book together: one bringing his long pedagogical experience, perhaps too much attracted to the philosophical side of things, always searching for the simplest or clearer formulation – the other far more competent on technical matters, on demonstrations, on the logical links but not always finding spontaneously the best way to present it to others. But we realized that it is very difficult to co-write. Each one of us has his style, his language, his preferences. We therefore gave up this too ambitious project. And now I will confine myself to a general presentation. Thus, through different paths, we have converged. The point where we find ourselves in agreement is for him an ascending path in a long research process that is still going on, and for me the end of a long journey, some sort of landing.

God knows for how long, forever perhaps, men have been talking about time! One may tell us: how could you contribute anything new on this old question? You are probably starting in a different way what so many others have repeated. The reader will judge for himself. But right from the beginning we must justify ourselves. For me it is the distinction between continuity and discontinuity which was the starting point of my reflexions. I was helped in that task by the writings of philosophers. Since Zeno of Elea, they have never ceased to ask the question: is the world continuous or discontinuous? The Greeks thought that physics is the science of discontinuity; the atom, literally what cannot be split up, was its symbol. But since Galileo, movement seemed to imply continuity: speed and acceleration being the expression of continuity. The famous axiom *Natura non facit saltus* stands constantly before our mind. Is it true that nature never leaps? Louis de Broglie made us understand well how two schools of thought dominated contemporary physics, which seems like divided into two parts with opposite sources of inspiration: the physics of matter where triumphed the idea of discontinuity, the physics of radiations where ruled the idea of continuity. But it was rather quickly realized that they could not just be related by a simple parallelism. The two physics cannot but have a common boundary, they cannot but exchange energy between radiance and matter. It is on that boundary that around 1900 came about, and soon dominated, the notion of quantum. Thanks to the research works of Planck, Bohr and Einstein, this notion was generalized – progressively, quantum of matter, quantum of energy, quantum of light, quantum of action were being talked of. The idea of a thick or granular structure of things took root. And with the mathematical and experimental research of L. de Broglie and of Schrodinger, the conflict between the corpuscular and undulatory theoretical approaches, that seemed impossible to resolve, took a new turn. The deepening of the theory of radio waves enabled it to explain the quanta phenomena. A sort of synthesis between the two rival theories was established; classical mechanics was renewed. A mechanics of waves was created. Given that we talk of quantum physics, the appearance of quantum economics should not be so surprising. To tell the truth, behind this name, it is not an imitation of physics that is going to be at issue. The economic quantum is of a different nature from the existing physics quantum. I am referring here to a reflexion by Edouard Le Roy, back in 1929, the very year Bernard Schmitt was born. Let me quote. "the energetic exchanges are operated by small packets, by grains of energy, not in indifferent proportions, that could be as small as we wish: this is the founding idea of the now well-established quantum theory. But then who would doubt it? The emission as well as the absorption of the quantum itself must take a certain time, therefore imply a certain process, which in its turn determines a certain composition of the quantum itself; unless we admit of 'atoms of time', an assumption very hard to accept, a costly supposition, because it would disorganise numerous parts of science." (Le Roy 1929). This hypothesis of the atom of time is at the basis of what appears to us to be a renewal of economics. What physics did not dare to embark on for fear of disorganizing numerous parts of science, is being done in economics, this time taking the lead over the science of matter. If it succeeds, it is going to endanger most of our hitherto well-established teachings. As I have suggested, it is no longer the opposition between continuity and discontinuity that is going to be adopted. It is the idea of a finite, indivisible, unbreakable time. It is truly that of an atom of economic time. It is also that of a metamorphosis of science, to borrow the expression from Prigogine's beautiful book (Prigogine and Sengers 1980). Let us note the meaning used here; Prigogine's quantum time is that of the irreversible time called quantum time because it is imposed by the quantum phenomenon in general, but not specifically by the quantum of time, which is not mentioned by Prigogine.

I was one of those who helped to introduce our students of the old Faculties of Law to differential and integral calculus. I certainly do not repent that. This intellectual exercise was very formative. Without it, it was impossible to understand much of the analyses on growth and of marginal calculus on cost and receipts, in particular. But I must confess that deep inside, I felt some worry. Unlike Samuelson, I was not fascinated by mathematics. By dividing time into smaller and smaller parts, by pushing the division into the infinitely small, are we not at risk of losing sight of the phenomenon that we want to explain? Does not scientific honesty compel us to understand fully what is this economic quantum of time? As for myself, I am quite taken by the criticism of statics and dynamics: those two concepts that have been at the foundation of our education. As suspected by d'Alembert, there is no fundamental difference between statics and dynamics, one can be reduced to the other whatever the direction followed, whether we go from statics to dynamics or from dynamics to statics; this results from the fact that we are dealing with magnitudes that are not posited in a time constituting an environment: that was believed initially, and this is the reason why classical mechanics was applied to them, why infinitesimal calculus or finite-difference equations were used. If statics and dynamics are of the same nature it is because the magnitudes are the same, whether at rest or in movement. But, if we go at the deepest, we realize that the magnitudes do not move through time, staying identical, like an object along a trajectory. Bernard Schmitt will say that income does not age: it disappears before aging. Economic magnitudes are therefore neither static nor dynamic; they are quantic. I would like to pause to examine patiently the graphs where the measure of the variable, in the case of a divisible interval of time, is compared with that of an indivisible interval. In the indivisible interval, there is only one value of the variable; the latter exists in only one sample, it is unique, not constant, for any "lump" of time. In the divisible interval, there are as many values as divisions of time imagined by the mind, as small as they can be. It is the idea of the function that is applied. In reality, an expenditure is not a function of something else, it is a creation, each creation being a quantum of time. Contrary to Leibniz's aphorism: *natura non facit saltus*, one might think that nature does look like leaping by moving from one lump of time to another. In truth, it is not a leap like one made by a flea, which is the same after the leap. It is another flea that has appeared. If we had the audacity to imitate Leibnitz, we would have to write, perhaps in uncertain Latin: *natura facit saltus creatores*. From one time to another, nature carries out a creation. We have lived up till now on the sole distinction between continuous and discontinuous time. The first one is what Bernard Schmitt calls the continuum. In each portion of the continuum, as small as it is, the phenomenon exists. It is, to borrow from the mathematical language, time likened to the set of real numbers. The second one appears when we divide the continuum into discrete intervals: nothing happens in the first intervals, then suddenly the phenomenon occurs and remains in the following intervals. It seems that in continuous time the phenomenon follows a seamless course. In discontinuous time, the course takes the shape of a staircase, moving from one step to another. A third time has to be considered. This is the one that we are dealing with, the quantum time, which we are obviously not used to and which at first is going to surprise us. Before a certain time *t* nothing has happened, and after this time, the product disappears. The image of the wheel, as imperfect as it is, helps us to understand what is going on. As long as the making of the wheel is not completed, it does not exist. One may be tempted to think of half a wheel, a wheel divided by the number two. In reality, it is certain that the half of a wheel is only a half-wheel within the completed wheel. Otherwise the expression has no meaning. The integer cannot be divided as long as it does not exist. Quantum time may then be equated to the set of natural numbers. Therefore, it is very true to say that the phenomenon is not posited in time with as many values as there are times. It is itself embodied time, quantized time. The leap has indeed been creative once production has been completed. But, after the creation, the image of the wheel no longer holds, because it is a physical item not an economic one. There is no longer any production . During the following times, there is no conservation of what has been created, as there would be in continuous time. The logical mind compels us to conceive of a simultaneous destruction. It is the concept of creation-destruction. The serious difficulty that we have to overcome is the relationship that exists between quantum time and continuous time. The analysis of production will help us. We must always distinguish very carefully physical transformation from economic production. What is certain is that we live in the continuum, whereas production quantizes time. At the moment labour completes its action, production is achieved at once. But if it is instantaneous, its useful effects are nevertheless extended in the continuum. This seems contradictory or at least mysterious. Let us employ the usual notations. Let us call t_0 the first time, and t_n the time when production is completed, t_i the instants preceding t_n and t_j the following instants. Production only exists in t_n. It is not maintained through inertia in continuous time. The interval (t_0, t_n) is indivisible, we have understood why. If it were not, applying calculation to smaller and smaller slices until infinitely small, would lead us to an absurd situation. Because it can only be one of two things: either in each *t* production is zero and the infinite sum of zero data would be zero, or it is not zero and the infinite sum of non-zero data would be infinite. Logic therefore must convince us that production is not a flow in the usual sense of the word as appearances would make us believe, whether the analysis is continuous or discontinuous. If we want to keep the word flow, we might say that it is not a flow in just one direction but a looped flow, a circular flow. It is a flux-reflux. Indeed, since nothing happens after t_n, there must be a destruction, in this case an instantaneous move back from the time of the finalization to the time of the beginning. Because the entry was instantaneous, the equivalence, necessary in all economic events, requires an exit that is also instantaneous. A flux-reflux, a to-and-fro, is the expression of a wave. Production is an undulatory phenomenon in that it changes continuous time into one indivisible whole. The mutation is carried out in both directions, forwards and backwards. It is pro-active and retro-active. But, at the same time production is a corpuscular phenomenon. If production is a quantum phenomenon, being a creation, the object that is being made is indeed physical. Matter is transformed as labour is shaping it; this transformation, being not a creation, takes place in the world of our senses, that is in continuous time, at every instant composing the interval (t_0, t_n). We are beginning therefore to perceive the combination of the opposites, which keeps haunting us, as it was accomplished by physics. Since the product is a quantum of time, it is clear that it is not a matter. However, the result of production does have a close relationship with matter. We can say that to produce means to cast matter or energy into a pre-conceived utility-form, a sort of mould, imagined by man; this means that the economic activity does not belong to the realm of classical mechanics. Quantum mechanics enables this requirement to be accounted for. It is in continuous time that is situated the matter to be transformed, then the matter is actually transformed. Another example of the combination of the opposites is the association of value in use and exchange value. Up to now, we were tempted to say: we must choose between the conception of a material value linked to the matter transformed by labour and the conception of a subjective type of value in use expressed by utility. Fundamentally, one does not exclude the other. The principle of the excluded middle does not apply. The exchange value is the quantum form of the same unique reality that has for its content a useful matter and even a matter the utility of which has been increased by the labour spent on it. To this first view, we have to add another inseparable analysis, that which concerns the dichotomy of nominal and real magnitudes. In the quantum approach, the dichotomy no longer exists. This might appear surprising, even unbearable, given how this opposition is rooted deep in our mind. It is of course money that comes into the picture. We have all been trained by studying the sequence of economic events, abstracting them from money, this is the real approach, the point of view of things. Afterwards, we introduce money and this is the nominal approach. Under this perspective, we cannot be surprised that there could be a disparity between the real assessment and the monetary assessment, because we have made them independent from each other and they can have their own destiny. In truth, there is no autonomous money emission. It is the concept and the nature of money that are at stake. One can first say: money is a nominal magnitude, facing the collection of all the goods to which it does not belong, it can be called exogenous. But then how not to recognize also that money is an element in the collection of the real goods? Because it too is produced. Again, as with material value and use value, we are facing a contradiction. And once again, in the same way, we see that the principle of the excluded middle does not apply. We cannot say: if money is exogenous it cannot be endogenous, if it is endogenous it cannot be exogenous. Again, we must be able to combine the opposites. Money is both a real, endogenous magnitude and a nominal, exogenous magnitude. As we have already said, in order to declare that production is a wave-like phenomenon: we cannot dissociate production and consumption, the simultaneous creation and destruction of value.

I cannot deny that some of us will have difficulty joining production and consumption in an instantaneous operation. The two words are associated, by our primary training, to purchasing and selling products. In a sense, this is indeed what happens at any moment in continuous time where the product has been deposited, even if it is distant from t_n. But that is not the key point to understanding the role of money. When it is said and repeated that money is an intermediary good between the products sold and bought, and therefore that it splits barter, one overlooks that it has already appeared in a first operation not yet revealed. It was already present when the product came about. We have acknowledged that production is a projection from the initial time, a projection conceived in the mind of the man who casts it through time, an emission, the result of the imagination that leads to the completion-creation. However, we have to understand that money has to be present when this emission takes place. If the word emission is accepted to describe the formation of money, we shall not be surprised to see the union of the real emission of the subject who carries out the projection and the emission from the banking system. Money, in truth, does not split barter, the exchange of products, it actually splits production itself. It has the effect of separating the two opposite aspects of production, the wave-like nature of which we have discovered. If there were no money, a production would immediately be a consumption. Money operates a division of the production-consumption, or the creation-destruction of value. Production is already an exchange and, undoubtedly, we could say that any exchange is a production. But it is necessary to distinguish the absolute monetary exchange constituted at the level of production and that cannot be separated from it, and the relative exchange that takes place between an already-formed product and another product. In the latter, money and real goods move in opposite directions: there are two objects. In absolute exchange, neither money nor the product move: there is only one object because the content of money is defined by the real product, a new way of expressing the end of the real-monetary distinction. Had Ricardo not had a premonition when he wrote that the product is "embodied" into money?

If money and production are intimately associated, the association concerns also wages, money and production. Wages are paid in money. Undoubtedly, the isolated worker will pay himself and obtains his product immediately in kind. The product is consumed as soon as it is formed. By contrast, under the wage system, the same does not apply: a wage cannot be instantly consumed. That will require another expenditure. As long as the matter stays in the monetary mould, which is its utility-form, like in a temporary shelter, consumption is differed.

However, we also have to understand how the problem of measurement in economics is added on to that. If labour quantizes the time of production, it is an exclusively physical measure. What is physical cannot measure what is economical. Neither labour nor time are able to measure the product. To measure, it is necessary to be able to "number", to introduce numbers that have no dimension. We understand therefore that only money enables the "number". If science requires measures and calculations, one understands that, right from the beginning, if there were no money, economics would not exist. The word *numéraire* takes all its meaning: the *numéraire* is not the nth commodity, as has been claimed, etymology gives it its true meaning.

Quantum time enables to show in a new light the notion of profit, on which the Classics and Neo-Classics had stumbled. Indeed, how can we explain that production is the result of the sole action of labour, that the product can only be a wage, but that there can exist an emission of non-wage income, profit in the broad sense? We should not be surprised: it is quantum analysis that will lift the paradox. A first flow creates the wages that form the income of society as a whole and not only those of the workers. A second flow, subsequent in continuous time, but whose effect is retroactive, is constituted by the expenditure of wages, a flow that might be called negative if the first one is called positive. The two opposite flows define the unified operation of production-consumption. The wages spent in that way give birth to non-wage incomes: interests, rents, profits. The old logic made profit, seen as a surplus, or as unable to exist, cumbersome and inexplicable. Our predecessors were embarrassed with it. It is no longer the case with quantum analysis that proves its existence as part of the product. Is not the mind relieved? It no longer risks having to admit defeat. The spending of wages brings to workers only part of the domestic product. The analysis shows that the part of the non-wage incomes, apparently collected during chronological time after the emission of wages, is, in reality, through the effect of the contraction of the flux and reflux (formation and destruction of income) into one operation, formed in the emission of wages.

Capital itself has always been difficult to understand and to define. From the beginning, it had been clearly perceived that it was both an instrument, a matter, and a fund, a claim. It is not so much that we have to choose between those two conceptions. Yet, here again, quantum analysis opens up a path. Money cast into wages is both of a material and of a banking nature. Wages, between the moment of their creation and the moment, chronologically subsequent, of their expenditure are, so to speak, in waiting, and therefore define a capital. Basically, real capital and financial capital are one same reality. We find again the same thinking process. Capital was previously thought of as the actualized value of the flows of future incomes. The hydraulic comparison was convenient. Capital was the accumulation of a fluid: a stock and not a flow. But here comes a turnaround. We have already understood it. It is the income that comes to life and disappears at the same point in time and is therefore not a flow. On the contrary, as surprising as it might be, it is capital that is situated in continuous time and takes the appearance of a flow. It is the transcription of a value defined in quantum time into continuous time, endorsing the destruction of a current income and its reproduction in the future. This is why it will be called capital-time.

The thought process goes on. We become persuaded that capital, and especially capital-time cannot exist in a society that would not be endowed with bank money. If money were material, no capital-time could be formed. This is so because, if wages are paid in bank money, the creation of wages is both a monetary and a financial operation. What is financial implies the management of time. A material money cannot enable this kind of management; it does not bring on any bridge between the present and the future. Only bank money can do it. Material money that, in the old days, seemed to be the only one possible, fulfilled this function not because of its matter, but because of its link with real production. To put it differently, scriptural money that was viewed as an ersatz, a substitute, must on the contrary be considered as the genuine money. In more modern terms, any economy that only experiences material money is "pre-capitalistic". Any capital is here a zero-sum. What is called the capitalist regime is identified with the functioning rules of bank money.

It is agreed that, in conformist interpretations, inflation arises when a mass of money exceeds the mass of available goods. But one would have to make sure of the existence of two distinct masses, one real and the other nominal. This is the basis of the quantitative theory of money. But, since the mass of goods is not material, it can only be psychological. The goods would have a mass because they have a utility. However, utility is not a mass but a relation between man and matter. The concept of economical mass cannot be thought out. But the notion of a monetary mass is not plausible either. Genuine money, scriptural or fiduciary, is created in the emission. By nature, it is devoid of any mass. It is not a mass, but a number. The quantitative theory of money cannot establish the correspondence between the number-money and the non-existing mass of real goods. However, it still rules. From now on, we set the quantum theory against the quantitative theory. And we repeat that, if we nevertheless keep the terminology of masses, the mass of real goods and the mass of money numbers are given in the same movement. The two masses are united, like an immaterial container and its material content. The two masses are merged, money conforming to the shape of the product, of which it defines the mass by a non-dimensional number. Inflation can now be defined. It is described in that telling phrase: "inflation is characterized when the money-form contains a body or a product smaller than it is; then the product is loose in its monetary cloth". However, if the monetary form and the real content are given in the same movement, inflation seems logically impossible. Money that comes to life empty would in reality be aborted. Money in excess would be a contradiction in terms. If deprived of any body, it does not exist. Since it does not have its origin in bank emissions and since the creation of money cannot be dissociated from real production, inflation cannot be fought by a restriction or control of the creation of money. It is not a purely monetary disorder; it is a pathology defined on money in its relation to the product. The money-product relation, or container-content, cannot be imperfect since it is an identity and not a condition of equilibrium. Yes, without doubt, inflation is impossible, but it does exist! What can we say then? That, if there are inflationary gaps, this is due to empty emissions that deposit a product-less money in the continuum. And it is the analysis of empty emissions that is conducted, and that requires a sustained attention. It is the distinction between the two sectors: those of wage-goods and of profit-goods. Labour is a non-commodity in both sectors because labour is not produced with labour, and labour has no cost. On the other hand, active labour in the sector of profit-goods that creates an over-accumulation of capital is indeed a commodity and has a cost. Finally, the inflationary gap is defined by the production of the second sector. A new terminology is offered: that of the core and the "crown". The core is the production of the first sector; the production of the second sector defines the "crown", that causes inflation and unemployment. The development of the book has to be followed carefully. It is therefore on the second sector that the mind must concentrate. Banks will be divided into two departments: that of the emission and that of savings, of capital-time. Those two departments guarantee the separation of money creations and of financial intermediations. But more importantly it is the creation of a third department that will be able to eradicate empty emissions, the cause of all current disorders. It is the department of fixed capital, the evolved form of capital-time, that will take charge of the savings of the second department that were, up to now, the cause of inflation and unemployment. These savings will from now on be withdrawn and it will not be possible to invest them into instrumental capital. If the overaccumulation of capital is indeed the actual deep cause of our troubles, then we can guess what result to expect.

*

As was written by Paul Coulbois (1974): "the distinction, even the opposition between micro-economic theory and macro-economic theory, has been dominating economic thought for nearly forty years". I have used it in my teaching at third year level. This book brings an entirely new point of view. Bernard Schmitt reminds us that economics has used the terminology of physics. The distinction was known in thermodynamics. It seems that this terminology was introduced in economics by Ragnar Frisch in 1933. I have had the privilege of hearing him at that time at the *Institut Henri Poincaré*. I was struck by the depth of his analyses and at the same time by his simplicity and humility. But it was precisely Paul Samuelson, so often quoted in this book as the master of our generation, who made these expressions familiar. However, Bernard Schmitt adds at once: even if the term macroeconomics "is new, 'macro-theory' goes back to the origins of our science. Since the Physiocrats and during the whole Classics era, from Smith to Ricardo and Marx, political economy has been entirely a macroscopic theory. If the distinction has taken its relevance only in the middle of the twentieth century, it is in contrast with the micro-economic theory then dominant" (Schmitt 1984/2021: 228–29). Our author's thought parts with most of those of our contemporaries. For them, and I admit having been one of them, it is on the basis of micro-economic preconceptions that they gave it a biased definition. The very title of J.P. Fitoussi's book, like the similar one by G.C. Harcourt (*The Microeconomic Foundations of Macro-economics*, Macmillan, 1977) is revealing. I have myself believed for a long time that it is at the level of individual subjects that one had to start from to lay the foundations of truly scientific economics. I still think by the way that the econometrical models, giving and explaining the results for an economy as a whole, could not reach the true driving force of existence. They describe these results but cannot unveil their causes. And now I find myself upturned, if not upset, by Schmitt's ideas. It must be said that this prefix "macro", that I still find inelegant, is in itself misleading. For the physicists, one has to know whether the level of observation does not condition the nature of the phenomenon under study. What can be seen through a microscope is so different from what can be observed by the naked eye. By the way, I have often noticed that micro-economics is, unlike physics, what we see at our level. Macro-economics is not within reach of our senses. We have to build it or think it out without seeing it. The most common way of carrying out this construction has been to add up or aggregate from the visible elements. However, we are learning that it is an incorrect definition. Indeed, aggregation gives another expression to identical data: there can be no difference between those two expressions. In actual fact, macro-economics works on different data. One may wonder if a bridge is possible from one to the other. Whatever the case, one should not talk, like Fitoussi and Harcourt, of the micro foundations of macro-economics. It would be more correct to say, at the risk of a tautology: the foundations of macro-economics are macro-economic. We have already understood that macro-economics is the theory of absolute exchanges, in contradistinction to the relative exchanges of micro-economics. Any absolute exchange is defined over a set, an indivisible whole, and not on a sum. One has to be guarded against confusing a sum and a set. Of a macro-economic character is also the theory of circuits which, by nature, must always be closed. If they were not closing, they would not be circuits. When we go to the bottom of things, at the global level, the conception of a global demand distinct from a global supply is a torment for the mind. Even before the formation of the idea of the quantum, I was impressed by the idea that there cannot be any adjustment between two variables that are not independent from each other, especially if, from their definition and from their inner logic, they are necessarily equal to each other. The measure of a gap cannot therefore have any meaning, neither has the reduction of this gap to reach an equilibrium. In the same way that there is an identity between real and nominal magnitudes, there is an identity between global supply and demand. One sentence deserves emphasizing: "academics got lost in running after two fantasies, a Supply independent from Demand and a Demand independent from Supply, as if the relation between the protons and the electrons could be modified at the whim of the experimenter, in compliance with the nature of a given chemical body. Even in economics, alchemical manipulations are bound to fail" (Schmitt 1984/2021: 163). It is a myth to want to discover those two independent curves. The transposition of the supply and demand curves from the micro level to the macro level is not just dangerous. It should be forbidden. This is why the interpretation of the crisis, either as an excess of global demand (inflation) or as an excess of global supply (unemployment) is completely inadequate. The malady, as we said, comes from the empty emissions. And the remedy has been offered.

While reading and rereading constantly Bernard Schmitt, I cannot but see in him a new Jean-Baptiste Say, but one enriched with quantum time. If the definition of macro-economics according to aggregation is difficult to accept, there is another more satisfactory definition. It is the one obtained through global magnitudes, when globality is viewed as an indivisible whole. The word totality is inadequate. A set cannot be obtained through addition. We cannot either "disaggregate" it, as one sometimes hears, to find again its components. However, this globality must not be considered in relation to space, as in the prevailing fashion, but in relation to time and, in an even better expression, in relation to duration. We have to start from the indivisibility in time. Micro-economics would be linked to continuous time, infinitely divisible, and measurable in terms of spaces. Macro-economics is formed through duration, that is in quantum time. And this is how the idea of globality is legitimized by the conception of the length of time. Global time is indeed the expression of duration, understood also as a whole that cannot be sliced up. What a pity that we cannot give a different name to those two ways of analysing these phenomena! The current names have been sanctioned by usage. It would be imprudent to disregard common usage. By the way, if we still had to change the names, we would be embarrassed and I would not dare to try. To replace macro, a term symbolizing duration would have to be found: "dura-economics" would not really be suitable. Measurable time in relation to continuity would more easily lead to the new euphemism of "tempo-economics". But I feel a little ashamed to be so clumsy.

I cannot resist a last temptation: that is to look straight at the famous IS-LM curves. I am curious to know how an astute reader will react to the idea that the two curves IS and LM can never meet, the LM curve being established in quantum time and the IS curve in continuous time – "this *pons asinorum* for students all over the world being the geometrical place of the confusion of the two kinds of time." The LM curve does not exist because it is a succession of points separated by infinite distances, one point and only one per period. Already the no less famous 45° graph had us worried. The time has perhaps come where simple strokes of the pen and curves deemed perfect will no longer suffice to found a robust knowledge as a sort of definitive orthodoxy.

*

One would have noticed it: in every page of this book, it is supreme logic that rules all the developments. Things cannot be different from what they are. If they were different, they would be stupid, absurd, unthinkable. I allowed myself initially to reply: are men of flesh and blood who do not know of this logic, and who are the unconscious authors of the movements that we conceive of, able to obey this logic? Is it not because they don't follow it that disorders unravel and keep on, in contradiction with the order that we have built? In a few lines of the book, Bernard Schmitt answers this objection. The behaviour of the actors, their moral or amoral attitude, their opposite wills, their mistakes, cannot go against what is unavoidable. These behaviours obviously exist, they may last for a more or less long period of time but, in the end, they cannot overcome the identities that macroeconomics and the theory of circuits have revealed.

Although he innovates deeply, Bernard Schmitt has a sense of tradition. It will be noticed that, at every stage of his progression, he constantly refers to the founders of our scientific field, to the Classics and the Neo-Classics. He is in their lineage. He extends it but he also goes beyond them. When we saw these founders as opposing each other, our writer enables us to see that, in a sense, they were right in their own way. The distinction between quantum time and continuous time is the key to the profound understanding of events. It is not all or nothing. We have kept repeating it tirelessly, it is the famous principle of the non-excluded middle that enlightens each of these pages and that allows to translate differently what was only underlaid by our great predecessors. It is comforting to discover that we are rejecting nothing of what they brought us, all that without which we would not be what we are.

The way is open to go on with the research. I do not remember who wrote: "a philosopher is one who does not understand at once, but who, by intuition, mysteriously senses that we must persevere in the effort to approach truth."

We are not philosophers, but I wonder if, within our field, we should not take an inspiration from the way they deal with temporary incomprehension. This is why I wish that all those who are going to read those pages would not stop at the first hurdle. They too will have to persevere and motivate our author to find even better expressions of his own thought. We shall be rewarded all together.

Bibliography

Arrow, K.J., and Hahn, F.H. (1971) *General Competitive Analysis*, San Francisco: Holden-Day, Inc., and Edinburgh: Oliver & Boyd.

Baron, M.E. (1969) *The origins of the infinitesimal calculus*, Oxford: Pergamon Press.

Coulbois, Paul (1974) "Préface" in J.P. Fitoussi, *Les fondements micro-économiques de la théorie keynésiennel*, Paris: Cujas.

Debreu, G. (1959), *Theory of Value, An Axiomatic analysis of Economic Equilibrium*, New York: John Wiley & Sons, Inc., and London: Chapman & Hall, Ltd.

Hicks, J. (1977) "Capital controversies ancient and modern" in J. Hicks, *Economic Perspectives, Further Essays on Money and Growth*, Oxford: Clarendon Press.

Le Roy, E. (1929) "Continu et discontinu dans la matière – Le problème du morcelage" in *Cahiers de la Nouvelle Journée* 15, Paris: Bloud et Gay.

Poulon, F. (1982), *Macroéconomie Approfondie*, Paris: Editions Cujas.

Prigogine, I. and Stengers, I. (1980) *La nouvelle alliance*, Bibliothèque des Sciences humaines, Paris: NRF, Editions Gallimard.

Samuelson, P.A. (1966–1977) *The Collected Scientific Papers of P.A. Samuelson*, Volumes I, II, III, Cambridge, MA: M.I.T. Press.

Say, J.B. (1821) *A Treatise on Political Economy*, London: Longman, Hurst, Rees, Orme and Brown.

Index

404 *Index*

Printed in the United States
by Baker & Taylor Publisher Services